The Digital Humanist: A Critical Inquiry
Copyright © 2015 by punctum books, authors & translators.

http://creativecommons.org/licenses/by-nc-sa/4.0/

This work carries a Creative Commons BY-NC-SA 4.0 International license, which means that you are free to copy and redistribute the material in any medium or format, and you may also remix, transform and build upon the material, as long as you clearly attribute the work to the authors (but not in a way that suggests the authors or punctum endorses you and your work), you do not use this work for commercial gain in any form whatsoever, and that for any remixing and transformation, you distribute your rebuild under the same license.

First published in 2015 by
punctum books
Brooklyn, New York
http://punctumbooks.com
ISBN-13: 978-0692580448
ISBN-10: 0692580441

Library of Congress Cataloging-in-Publication Data are available from the Library of Congress.

Cover image: Masaccio, *Young Man* (~1420), National Gallery, Washington DC
Cover design: Chris Piuma
Typographic design by Vincent W.J. van Gerven Oei

Domenico Fiormonte, Teresa Numerico & Francesca Tomasi

THE DIGITAL HUMANIST

A CRITICAL INQUIRY

*Translated from the Italian by
Desmond Schmidt with
Christopher Ferguson*

MMXV
punctum books
Brooklyn

Table of Contents

Preface: Digital Humanities at a political turn? ix

Introduction 15
    1. Digital Humanities, and beyond 15
    2. Do we still need humanists, and why? 18
    3. How this book is organized 19

PART I: THE SOCIO-HISTORICAL ROOTS 23

Chapter 1 – Technology and the humanities: A history of interaction 25
    1.1 From Alan Turing to the modern computer 26
    1.2 What computers cannot do: from analog to digital 29
    1.3 Bush's visionary dream 32
    1.4 A mathematician with a Ph.D. in philosophy 35
    1.5 Wiener's ethics and politics of the computer 37
    1.6 Licklider and the man-machine symbiosis 40
    1.7 Libraries and information processing 43
    1.8 Conclusion 46

Chapter 2 – Internet, or the humanistic machine 49
    2.1 The design of the intergalactic network 49
    2.2 The computer as a communication device 51
        2.2.1 The birth of the ARPANET 53
        2.2.2 The WWW: an authoring system in the heart of Europe 55
    2.3 Web 2.0 and beyond 59
    2.4 Leibniz's *Lingua Characteristica* and the Semantic Web 62
    2.5 Social and cultural inequalities on the Web 67
        2.5.1 The digital divide 67
        2.5.2 Geopolitics of the network 71
        2.5.3 The value of cultural and linguistic diversity 73
    2.6 The challenge of open knowledge 79
        2.6.1 Big Data 81
        2.6.2 Open data and the humanities 83
        2.6.3 Open access 84

Summary of Part I 90

PART II – THEORETICAL AND PRACTICAL DIMENSIONS *95*

Chapter 3 – Writing and content production. *97*
   3.1 Writing, technology and culture 97
   3.2 Writing from the margins. 99
   3.3 Modes of production: layers, forms and genres 101
   3.4 Rhetoric and the Internet 107
   3.5 Time in writing 108
      3.5.1 Technology and textuality 109
      3.5.2 Paratexts, microtexts, metatexts 112
   3.6 Content usability and accessibility 114
      3.6.1. Elements of "interaction design" for the Web 116
   3.7 Digital ethnographies. 118
      3.7.1 Cultural interfaces and the ethnoscience of writing 118
      3.7.2. The Machine is Us. 120
      3.7.3 Goodbye Windows?. 120
      3.7.4 Behind the screens: the languages of the Web 121
      3.7.5 The seduction of discretion 122
   3.8 Identity on the Web. 123
      3.8.1 My Website, outsourced 123
      3.8.2 Digital literacy 124
   3.9 Transitions. The edited human 126

Chapter 4 – Representing and archiving. *129*
   4.1 The longevity of digital information 131
      4.1.1 Degradation and obsolescence. 132
   4.2 Balancing tradition and innovation 133
      4.2.1 Proposals for preservation 134
      4.2.2 The role of languages and metadata 135
   4.3 Markup standards and languages 136
      4.3.1 Marking-up a document 137
      4.3.2 XML and the OHCO theory. 138
      4.3.3 XML Schemas and the "document type" approach. 140
      4.3.4 TEI: A standard for the humanistic domain 141
      4.3.5 Schemas and namespaces: why we need formal vocabularies 142
      4.3.6 Beyond text: using annotations. 143
   4.4 Metadata and the description of the document 144
      4.4.1 The unambiguous identification of resources 144
      4.4.2 Metadata and modeling 144
      4.4.3 A Model for understanding metadata: FRBR. 147
      4.4.4 Tools for metadata: the role of Dublin Core 149
      4.4.5 Expressing metadata formally: RDF 151
      4.4.6 Taxonomies, thesauri, ontologies: towards semantics 154
      4.4.7 Metadata and folksonomy: the user experience 155

4.5 Open archives 156
    4.5.1 The open archives initiative 156
4.6 Digital libraries 157
4.7 Semantic repositories and networking. 159
4.8 Text analysis and text mining 161
    4.8.1 Performance or character string? 162
    4.8.2 From text retrieval to text analysis 163
    4.8.3 Towards text mining 164
4.9 New applied technologies in the digital humanities 166

Chapter 5 – Searching and organizing *169*
5.1 The paradox of search according to Plato 169
5.2 Web topology and the (in)equality of nodes 171
5.3 The role of search engines on the Web 172
5.4 How search engines work 175
5.5 The trouble with search engines .180
5.6 Ethical and social implications 184
    5.6.1 Copyright 185
    5.6.2 Privacy 187
    5.6.3 Politics and censorship 189
5.7 Cloud computing and the search for truth 191
5.8 Google, AI and Turing's social definition of intelligence 195
5.9 Communication and freedom. 198
    5.9.1 Corporate knowledge or the end of science? 199
    5.9.2 The power of the archive 201

Summary of Part II 204

Conclusions – DH in a global perspective *207*
1. The periphery-center effect 207
2. Research and teaching experiences. 208
3. Associations, journals and centers 215

Notes *219*

References. *235*

Preface
Digital Humanities at a political turn?

Geoffrey Rockwell

So what exactly is that new insurgency? What rough beast has slouched into the neighborhood threatening to upset everyone's applecart? The [MLA] program's statistics deliver a clear answer. Upward of 40 sessions are devoted to what is called the "digital humanities," an umbrella term for new and fast-moving developments across a range of topics: the organization and administration of libraries, the rethinking of peer review, the study of social networks, the expansion of digital archives, the refining of search engines, the production of scholarly editions, the restructuring of undergraduate instruction, the transformation of scholarly publishing, the re-conception of the doctoral dissertation, the teaching of foreign languages, the proliferation of online journals, the redefinition of what it means to be a text, the changing face of tenure — in short, everything.[1]

THERE HAS BEEN a surge of interest in the digital humanities and its place in the liberal arts in the English-speaking world as represented by the Modern Language Association Annual Convention.[2] Much of the interest is coming from engaged new scholars in North America who are comfortable with new media as they grew up with it. Interest is also coming from outside the Anglo-American world as humanists in Europe and Asia reflect on this field and its opportunities in their academic traditions. I think of the Manifesto for the Digital Humanities that came out of THATCamp Paris in 2011,[3] Patrick Svensson's articles in *DHQ*,[4] or Wang and Inaba's article analyzing the language of the digital humanities.[5] Of particular interest are books not written in English or for an English audience because they introduce the field in subtly different ways. One such work is *The Digital Humanist: A Critical Inquiry* by Teresa Numerico, Domenico Fiormonte and Francesca Tomasi, translated from the Italian by Desmond Schmidt and Christopher Ferguson. This is by no means the first work in Italian about computing in the humanities. The "informatica umanistica" (humanities informatics) school is rooted in the pioneering work of Father Busa, and all three authors have been active in the field since the mid-nineties at well-established research centres in Rome and Bologna.[6] The new version of this book[7] is current, accessible, and argues that humanists need to engage in not only the development of online content but also with ethical issues around computing, especially issues around language, search engines, open access and censorship. The authors call on humanists to acquire the skills to become digital humanists:

> [H]umanists must complete a *paso doble*, a double step: to rediscover the roots of their own discipline and to consider the changes necessary for its renewal. The start of this process is the realization that humanists have indeed played a role in the history of informatics. (Introduction: Do we still need humanists, and why?)

The Digital Humanist is a work of five chapters, introduction, and a conclusion that is designed to introduce humanists to the digital, its human history and the cultural challenges that concern us. The first chapter, "Technology and the humanities: a history of interaction" is a deft tour through the history of computing that emphasizes the importance of human issues while still covering many of the important moments from Turing to social media. The authors start with the computer as a symbol manipulator as opposed to a mere calculator. They introduce Vannevar Bush and the importance of human association in the organization of human knowledge. They write about cybernetics and Wiener's ethical concerns that computers might control us. They focus on Licklider and man-machine symbiosis as an alternative model to our relationship to computers – an alternative to the AI model where computers replace human work. This is linked to Licklider's work on information processing and libraries. They then turn to the development of the ARPANET in the second chapter and its evolution. This leads to a discussion of the Web and Web 2.0 ideas. The second chapter ends with two paragraphs discussing how humanists can contribute to cultural diversity on the Web and make the Web more socially inclusive.

Chapter 5, "Searching and organizing" looks closely at the role of search engines, especially Google, in the organization of our knowledge. The first two chapters and chapter 5 frame the two internal chapters that are about digital philology and textual representation, which is why I will deal with them separately. The chapter titled, "Searching and organizing" starts with the old philosophical question of how you can ask about that which you don't know and connects it to a discussion of how search engines work. The authors argue in the end that a) search engines are important to how knowledge is being organized, even more so now that Google is digitizing scholarship on a large scale, and b) that they are not neutral – that their algorithms are biased against information that isn't popular or in the dominant language of the Web, English. They return to the access issues of the first couple of chapters and ask if we are comfortable with commercial organizations organizing the human knowledge we in the humanities care about. Without preaching a solution they try to show the humanities reader how high the digital stakes are. This ethical-political turn is perhaps one of the features of *The Digital Humanist* that differentiates it from the more enthusiastic discourse around the digital humanities in the English-speaking world which tends to concentrate on modeling knowledge outside the political.[8] *The Digital Humanist* addresses an audience concerned with cultural issues that still believes in political action and still believes the humanities are caretakers of a body of knowledge with political value.

The humanities heart of the book is the third chapter on "Writing and content production." This chapter tackles the digital text through a number of theoretical questions starting from reflections on orality/literacy to questions about how we define our identity through online writing in blogs and other social media. Three moves that the authors make in this dense chapter are interesting.

Layers of Digital Textuality. The authors present a typology of digital texts that illustrates just how difficult it is to talk about digital textuality. The typology starts from what we typically call the Text In Itself (email, blog entries, wiki pages). They then shift to the Coded Text (ASCII, HTML, XML) that underlies the text itself, but, of course, is also a text we write. Then they move to the Processed Text like that text generated by Google when you query it or texts mashed up through social media. Finally they move to the Text Which Writes Us (credit cards, debit cards, text games) and draw our attention to the ways in which we are defined by texts from our credit rating to the interactive games we play. The authors are aware of the limits to this layered typology, but it serves well to break open our idea of exactly what a text is on the computer. One could add other layers like the Inscribed Text, which would be the material ways a text is written on a hard drive or CD-ROM.

Time and Space of Writing. Starting with section 3.5 there is a very interesting discussion of the shift from the temporality of modern narrative writing to the ways in which the Web (which is, after all, mostly writing) is seen spatially. For the authors this shift in metaphor is important to understanding online textuality. They follow this up by describing how in web-writing it is the paratext, microtexts, and metatexts that are important — more important, and stand in for the text itself. It is the metadata keywords you provide for a page that Google uses, it is the headings that people read, and it is all the navigating text that people use to understand what your site is about. The point is that if you look at web-writing advice it isn't really any more the old rhetorical advice about how to write your paragraphs – it is about how to contextualize your text and make it easy to navigate.

Usability and Ethnography. The reflections on the importance of the paratext lead to an argument that the interface is the new face of text and therefore usability is the new metric for studying the interface/text. This leads to a discussion of the place of ethnography as a method for digital humanists who are studying digital textuality as they write it. There is a future in the digital humanities for the way of doing philology which operates as an interface to our cultural identity.

At the end of the chapter the authors return again to identity and the ways the digital writes us as we write it. The importance of the digital humanities is that with the digital text it is not enough to simply study the text as linguistic meaning (layer 1), humanists need to understand the technologies of computing and culture of computing in order to get at the text in all its layers. We need to deconstruct the system that manages the social text from Google to Facebook. We need to ask who owns our text (which writes our identity), who manages it, and who provides access. The good old days when the technology was just a tool are over and *The Digital Humanist* calls for a new hermeneutic for the humanities that can study culture in the digital.

The fourth chapter is the practical sequel to the chapter about writing. "Representing and archiving," as the chapter is entitled, focuses on the pragmatics of scholarly electronic editions and digital libraries. It provides a tour that starts by describing the problems around preserving electronic texts and moves up to big data. The chapter takes us through the uses of metadata, markup and digital libraries. It is a concise review of the key technologies we use to represent and preserve information. It is the sort of practical overview humanists need to have to understand digital humanities electronic text projects.

It is worth noting that the title is not about the "digital humanities," but the "digital humanist." It is about the formation of a new and engaged humanist. This is a work calling for and about the formation of a new persona in the tradition of the humanities. It tries to convince humanities students that they need to engage the digital and then provides a tour through what they need to know from the history of computing and the human to the importance of search engines. It calls them to question the digital infrastructure being built — infrastructure which, to someone outside the English-speaking world, is biased. We need digital humanists who don't just use what is at hand, but inquire critically into what is in their hands. We need humanists that ask about how it might bias the representation, conservation and interpretation of the cultural record.

> Beyond Big Data, mega-platforms and the mass archivation of data, the true innovation of the next decade of DH appears to be its geographic expansion and the consequent enlargement (and deepening) of these questions. (Conclusions: The periphery-center effect)

Above all, we need forms of innovation which are not of the bigger and even bigger kind. The authors call for innovation from the periphery and for the periphery rather than the dominant centralized variety characterized by large centers and mega-projects. *The Digital Humanist* itself comes from outside the loop of English-speaking centres, though I'm not sure I would call Italy a periphery. It imagines a way of doing digital work which doesn't necessarily involve grants. What could we do with the resources at hand? How could we imagine philological projects that could be adapted by others, whatever their resources and wherever they are?

Introduction

1. Digital Humanities, and beyond

As the title says, this book is an attempt to describe and examine critically the main concepts and practices of Digital Humanities. Indeed, such a critical examination, taken from a certain distance, seems to be needed more than ever. The project "Around DH in 80 days,"[1] which gathers links and resources from around the world, reveals some surprises in the relationship between the center and peripheries of DH, and raises many doubts about the ability of DH to document itself. Europe and North America, where the fortunate term was born, has already lost one claim to fame: the sum of projects in Asia and the Middle East (China, India, Japan, Korea, Arabia, etc.) now exceeds that of the West. So, in addition to the increasing loss of economic power to the East, is the West now also beginning to lose supremacy in the digitization of our cultural heritage? The picture is too patchy and incomplete to draw any firm conclusions,[2] but it is clear that the phenomenon demonstrates that it is becoming ever more complicated, if not useless, to define what the Digital Humanities are today.[3] The usual definitions: "the application of information science to the humanities," "an interdisciplinary field" or "an independent discipline?" (Pons 2013, 38–46) appear to conflict with the cultural, linguistic and social diversity of the various geographical areas over which it is being applied. The Conclusion will examine the interdisciplinary and global aspects of DH, but for the moment it may be noted that this movement of DH is part of a vaster phenomenon, a cataclysm that is changing not only the sciences and their transmission of knowledge, but, as is well known, also the worlds of finance, the media, politics, law, commerce and human relations. Digitization already goes beyond changing only what is external to us, to changing what defines our "digital presence": the control of our identity, the representation of our minds (through the technique of neural imaging), even the food we eat, as is demonstrated by the increasingly close relationship between biotechnology and the reduction of biodiversity (Shiva 1993 and 2013).

Although this book is primarily a critical assessment of what the authors regard as the most relevant theoretical, historical, social and practical issues in the field of DH, they also believe that Digital Humanities is a fluid and critical discipline, which, by tracing the history of the communication technologies that underpin it, should try to answer some basic questions such as: what kind of science do we need today to benefit our society? And how is digital knowledge constructed: what do we want to know and why? It is clear that it is not always possible to draw a line between what interests a humanist and the work of a lawyer, biologist or a neuroscientist. As a result, our work is naturally open to contributions from the social sciences, which should be regarded as an integral part of DH (Liu 2012; Quinnell 2012; Fiormonte 2013; Presner 2012[4]). Among all the reflections on the subject of DH the following seems one of the more convincing:

> ... the proper object of Digital Humanities is what one might call "media consciousness" in a digital age, a particular kind of critical attitude analogous to, and indeed continuous with, a more general media consciousness as applied to cultural production in any nation or period. Such an awareness will begin in a study of linguistic and rhetorical forms, but it does not stop there. Yet even this is only half of it. Inasmuch as critique may imply refiguration and reinvention, Digital Humanities has also a reciprocal and complementary project. Not only do we study digital media and the cultures and cultural impacts of digital media; also we are concerned with designing and making them. (Piez 2008)

Piez's definition includes at least four or five different disciplines, which today can be found scattered in as many faculties. These include certainly languages and literature, but also the sociology of communication, anthropological and ethnographic studies of new media, archival and library science, cultural heritage and, of course, informatics. This already poses a problem for the organization of our institutions, which cannot simply be solved by the creation of ad hoc departments, or by the creation of groups within or between disciplines, acting autonomously, as the pioneers of DH imagined in the 1990s (McCarty 1999; Orlandi 2002). One of the undesired side-effects of the tumultuous development of DH has in fact been its own unpredictability. Its success can no longer be delimited by a great boundary wall such as "culture" — and hence Crane's proposal of the term "cultural informatics" likewise seems too restrictive (Crane, Bamman and Jones 2008). If the future is E-Science and the hyper-inclusive digital research infrastructures (see the Conclusion) the proposal by the science philosopher Mario Biagioli, who hopes for the strategic abandonment of the "dogma of the discipline," would seem more flexible:

> The sciences are moving toward organizing their practitioners around problems, not disciplines, in clusters that may be too short-lived to be institutionalized into departments or programs or to be given lasting disciplinary labels. (Biagioli 2009, 820)[5]

Apart from practical considerations (as for example, the Social Sciences and Humanities being grouped together in the "SH" section of the European Research Council), the real reasons why it is useless and perhaps damaging to limit the Digital Humanities to the historical-literary-linguistic domain are primarily epistemological and methodological in nature.[6]

From the epistemological point of view the central theme is the redefinition of the objects of knowledge, or rather of their forms and means of communication. Such objects have today become *perenni mutanti,* which can no longer be studied and analyzed from a single point of view, or in an isolated unit of space-time. One example, which concerns one of the principal themes of this book, should suffice: the concept of the document. Digital encoding of a document of any kind (written, oral, filmed, etc.) is today one of the more important areas in the redefinition of knowledge. First, because every encoding is a hermeneutic act. It is not simply a problem to discover the change in information content when one goes from the original analog document to the digital medium (whether it is the case of a single character in the Hangul alphabet or the manuscript of a canonical author), but to select what and how to preserve and transmit. Nor is it simply a matter of denouncing either the limitations and geopolitical implications of Google's search algorithm (cf. Chapter 5) or the massive control of our personal data by governments and multinationals. The problem runs deeper. For example, is it possible to speak nowadays of human rights without mentioning procedures and values mediated by colloquial practices, documents and information streams that are heavily dependent on the processes engendered by information technologies? And is it possible to speak of politics and society in countries like Egypt, Tunisia, Iran, or even the United States or Cuba, without first understanding how their network infrastructure is constructed or how it works? But the presence of humanists and social scientists cannot simply be inserted into a finished product, because each stage in the process of digitization (or original production) up to the finished product of communication has, among other things, semiotic, social, cultural and political implications.

The question of methodology is connected to all of the above, even if it demands an additional self-reflection (and probably self-criticism). Everyone has to deal with standards, instruments and resources, which influence and inform research and teaching. But the engagement of digital humanists with the instruments they use is more or less passive. To seek to have influence over the process of constructing such instruments and resources is vital to guarantee not only their efficacy but also to avoid the application of those same resources against the interests of democracy and social equality. This is not just a reference to the digital divide, but also to the related problem of information literacy, and the need for teaching digital literacy in all countries, including the affluent ones (cf. § 2.5). But for the moment, pending the arrival of adequate instruments, the relationship between research and teaching (based on the model of "progressive accumulation" and "controlled release") has collapsed. This has had a destabilizing effect on the teacher-pupil relationship because the expertise of the teacher can be immediately verified. And this phenomenon concerns as much the individual as entire nations. As "certified agencies" of knowledge (inhabited by prestigious intellectuals, who write in respected journals) are gradually disappearing, the search is on for new methods of combining research and teaching, which in their present forms have suddenly become uninteresting or unacceptable to society.

In conclusion, how can these immense challenges be tackled without forging an alliance between the social sciences, information science and the humanities? The problem of representation, of production, of access and transmission of knowledge in the digital dimension must be tackled by all the voices and points of view that make up the socio-humanistic-informational galaxy. The reader may be surprised, but the path that this "marriage" must follow, from the intellectual point of view, is already well-trodden. It has been pointed out, from the fifties and sixties, by pioneers and leaders like Pierre Bourdieu, Padre Busa, Régis Debray, Jack Goody, Eric Havelock, Harold Innis, André Leroi-Gourhan, Bruno Latour, Marshall McLuhan, Edgar Morin, Walter Ong, Raymond Williams and many others.

2. Do we still need humanists, and why?

If these are the challenges, what is the current situation? And doesn't what has just been said make the crisis in the humanities into a perfect obstacle course? The answer, at first, does not seem very encouraging. Humanists, with few exceptions, do not appear to be so much at the center of the process of diffusion of culture, neither as managers, nor as producers or designers. Certainly the crisis in the *studia humanitatis* has other more distant causes, and it cannot be summarized here in a few lines. However, this crisis is also an opportunity.

The objective of this book is to show that the profound changes already underway require the skills of humanists and social scientists, their innovation, their historical-critical reflection, and their ability to think outside the square. Technology in fact does not advance with the shrewdness of reason in Hegelian memory, but assumes casual forms, in response to the momentary demands of its own history. In short, technology is the result of choices, or as Alexander Galloway puts it, *technical is always political* (Galloway 2004, 245). The choice for the digital representation of information can also be ascribed to these occasional aspects.

To gain the benefits of their abilities, however, humanists must complete a *paso doble,* a double step: to rediscover the roots of their own discipline and to consider the changes necessary for its renewal. The start of this process is the realization that humanists have indeed played a role in the history of informatics. This book proposes to investigate the bonds between the two disciplines, through an epistemological vision of technology, focusing on the interdisciplinary aspects of informatics and telecommunications. Computer science is a recent discipline, without a clear epistemological statute, born out of a number of open interdisciplinary fields throughout and immediately after the Second World War. Bletchley Park, where the machines for decoding the messages of the German Army, and the Macy's Lectures (1946–1953), where the idea of cybernetics was born, are cases where the transdisciplinary nature of informatics is most strongly evident. The centers of research, throughout the Second World War, and in the years immediately after, created a space between the disciplines, belonging to no one, where, as Norbert Wiener said, innovation became possible. The impression of the authors is that the ethical, social, philosophical and epistemological problems have been discussed since the birth of informatics, and have also been present in the subsequent period of innovation: when the computer was represented as an instrument of communication. This communicative perspective, which one should not hesitate to call revolutionary, has been the basis both for the idea of the human-machine interface and also for idea of connecting all machines into a network. Personalities like Vannevar Bush, J.C.R. Licklider, Robert Taylor, Douglas Engelbart, Ted Nelson, Donald Norman and others have contributed to it (cf. §§ 1.3–1.6). These people either came from a background in the social sciences or humanities, such as Licklider, Taylor, Norman and Nelson, or had a profound sensitivity that stimulated them to be visionary when confronted by the prospect of developing a rapport between the machine and humanity. The humanistic approach has thus had a central role in the history of computer science, and especially of the Internet and the World Wide Web.

Jerome McGann, one of the scholars most dedicated to defining the unstable boundaries between tradition and innovation, wrote: "A hundred years from now, which of the following two names is likely to remain pertinent to traditions of critical thinking and which will seem merely quaint, if it is recalled at all outside pedantic circles: Vannevar Bush or Harold Bloom?" (McGann 2001, 18). Part of the challenge of this book is to try to answer this question. Complex historical reasons are driving the disciplines of information processing and the analysis, production and preservation of cultural output towards convergence. It is up to digital humanists themselves to determine whether Vannevar Bush will be regarded as the first of the new humanists or the builder of a kind of Trojan Horse, which, by the middle of the century, will have deprived the humanistic disciplines of meaning. One thing is certain: we won't have to wait a hundred years because the new house of the digital humanist is already taking shape.

3. How this book is organized

The book is divided into two parts: the first part (Chapters 1–2) serves as a historical, social and critical introduction, while the second part (Chapters 3–5) reflects a kind of ideal (and essential) digital trivium: Writing and Content Production — Representing and Archiving — Searching and Organizing. Parts I and II conclude with summaries to help the reader grasp the main points raised in the preceding chapters.

The term "trivium" is understood here in the sense given to it by Marshall McLuhan, either as a "blueprint for education" (McLuhan 2006: x), or as a project for reforming the instruments of our work. For even the medieval trivium (grammar, rhetoric, dialectics) did not only reflect abstract interests:

> Grammatica, or grammar ... is not to be understood in the sense of parts of speech, sentence structure or any other narrow sense belonging to either prescriptive grammar or modern linguistics. In the widest meaning of the term, and particularly in its relation to dialectics and rhetoric, with which it constitutes the three dimensions of the classical ideal of learning, grammar is the art of interpreting not only literary texts but all phenomena. Above all, grammar entails a fully articulated science of exegesis, or interpretation. Dialectics is, variously, a way of testing evidence or the study of kinds of proofs for an argument, a method of dialogue, or simply logic. Rhetoric, of course, includes the rhetorical devices such as alliteration that are most commonly associated with it in general use today, but ... it proves to be a very complex feature of discourse, involving five divisions ... (McLuhan 2006: xi)

Although all this still sounds very familiar, the digital trivium explored in this book does not necessarily overlap with the medieval one. But it is perhaps in a form remixed and re-mediated in those three tasks (Writing and content production — Representing and archiving — Searching and organizing) that constitute in the view of the authors the main areas in the work of the digital humanist, and at the same time form the principal sources of change, challenge and risk.

The initial chapters aim to retrace the role of humanistic knowledge through its epistemological structure and the history of digitization. The course followed leads backwards from the new media to the idea of the computer as an instrument of communication, by showing how this vision has produced profound changes in the perception of technology itself and in its practical organization. Chapter two takes a critical look at the Internet, its hidden stories and its founding fathers. The history of the Net is assigned the greatest space because it is from the time of the diffusion of the Internet, and the advent of the World Wide Web that humanists began to reflect in depth on the social, cultural and philosophical aspects of informatics. This chapter is called "The humanistic machine" because it is humanists who should, in the view of the authors, take a more active role in reshaping and innovating the network, and in addressing the social imbalances and cultural divides of the Internet.

Chapter three reflects on writing as an instrument for transmitting a culture and constructing its identity, on its material nature, and on the cognitive aspects of changes already under way. In the real world, this chapter describes and analyzes the forms, kinds and modes of production of digital textuality, from Web usability to the ethnographic writing of Web 2.0, from microcontent to collaborative writing.

Chapter four deals with the conservation of digital objects in the form of texts, images, audio and video files, to ensure their accessibility over time. A digital object may be understood as a complex entity, a union of data and metadata. Considered in this way, it is crucial to understand which systems are designed to conserve this entity over time, starting on the level of the document's creation in digital form. Every representation produces a re-reading of an object, and every transformation (required for its conservation) is never neutral. This chapter investigates the role of central repositories in permitting access in the form of ordered collections, and the present challenge of open knowledge — a strategic issue not only for humanists, but also for science as a whole. Digital libraries, open archives and open data are currently among the most researched subjects in DH, which suggests that the role of humanists in the redefinition of the instruments of research should be central. The authors are convinced that these movements, together with the technologies of Web 2.0, will play a crucial role in the future of the Net, through the active presence of users in social networking and the availability of shared spaces for work and research.

The final chapter focuses on access to online information. Humanistic expertise has long held the keys of access to knowledge: from the tradition of manuscript copying to the modern archive, the transmission of culture has always been directed by intellectuals. The cataloging of texts to facilitate their retrieval has been the task of librarians, who devised the mechanisms and conditions necessary to verify the availability (or unavailability) of texts. The new phenomenon of search engines, which control our access to digital information, has yet to be thoroughly analyzed, recognized or sanctioned by culture or politics. The Web has transformed itself into a kind of huge monastery, where access to texts in the library is controlled by a series of technical instruments, among them the powerful search-ranking algorithm, whose operation is mostly secret, but upon which the retrieval of the contents entirely depends. Such a situation cannot fail to have ethical, political and social consequences, which must be confronted by the digital humanist.

The Conclusion explores the reflections of the authors on the "global turn" of DH, indicating its principal evolutionary lines, its national paradigms, the international conglomerates and the various geopolitical tensions that exist in our community.

Finally, a note for the reader. Although in the course of reading this book the fundamental contribution of Anglo-American scholars will become evident, it is probable that the vision of DH presented here does not correspond with that disseminated in the anglophone world. The book reflects in the background of its authors (a sociologist trained as a philologist, an engineer trained as a literary historian, and a philosopher trained as a logician) the irreducibly composite nature of the field. Even in a strong and united effort this work represents interacting points of view, from which to observe digital phenomena.[7] This may inevitably lead to alternative interpretations and visions of certain key factors of DH. But as Virginia Woolf remarked, when speaking of women writers: "That is all as it should be, for in a question like this truth is only to be had by laying together many varieties of error" (Woolf 2005, 105).

PART I

THE SOCIO-HISTORICAL ROOTS

Chapter 1
Technology and the humanities: A history of interaction

THE HISTORY OF modern computing is not simply the history of one particular technology, but is part of a larger history of culture and knowledge, which itself implies changes of perspective, epistemic loops and the emergence, at the end of a complex process, of certain devices at the expense of others.

There are several ways to look at the development of technology, and at least two possible ways to look at the history of computing. One is to focus on the hardware, on the engineering development of the machine, and the other is to study the evolution of machine languages and their logic, and hence the history of software development. Each approach has a limited perspective, and each interprets events of the past in the light of the present. Rather than simply describe the history of these unique and extraordinary machines, this chapter will instead try to pursue a metaphoric, epistemic and perhaps even socio-political path: a way of looking at machines that were meant to simplify, represent, and control the production of information in ways never before imagined. It will try to look at the development of the electronic programmable machine (what we normally call a *computer*) as a project for the production of meaning destined to deeply influence other disciplines and our culture as a whole.

The objective of all this is to investigate if and how the humanistic paradigm — in its broadest sense seen as a relation between philosophical anthropology and the development of human–machine interaction — may have influenced the emergence of information science. A strong case can be made that it did, in several ways. The emergence of a certain humanistic perspective can be traced from the end of the Second World War: the idea that machines should not only be able to solve equations, but could also provide a simple and unequivocal answer to any problem of representation, organization, or enhancement of knowledge.

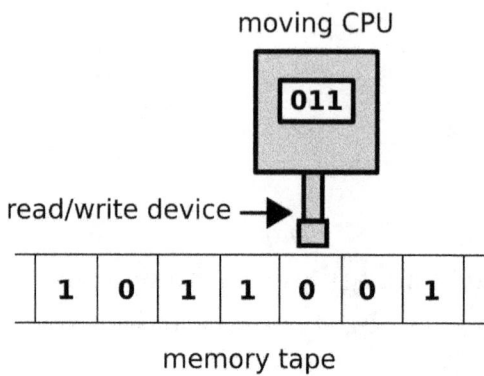

Figure 1.1. Turing Machine

1.1 From Alan Turing to the modern computer

This section discusses the origins of the theoretical model behind the computer, and how it influenced the design of the first programmable electronic machines. The aim is to show the profound historic relevance of certain events, which turned out to have a massive impact on the future development of technology. While the influence of Turing's theoretical machine is widely accepted (especially in historical accounts that focus on software), the historical contingency underlying his model is generally overlooked. This work of reconstruction aims to highlight the happenstance of the story, and to strip away from the computer the fate-like aura of inevitability that often surrounds it.

Information science has not always existed in its current form. According to tradition, it emerged during the Second World War, when the need to carry out large numbers of calculations prompted researchers from various countries to devise machines that could do exactly that. However, these early computers relied heavily on the logical-theoretical model devised by Turing in his studies on logic back in the 1930s. Turing had invented a theoretical machine that was able to solve any task whose execution could be automated (Turing 1937). Initially, the idea of the computer was not born as a theoretical model. In fact, it stemmed from the need to demonstrate the undecidability of logic (Petzold 2008). Turing designed the most powerful theoretical device ever imagined by man, but this almost omnipotent device came with an original sin: it was unable to solve one class of problems, which included the "decision problem" or *Entscheidungsproblem*. The Turing Machine (TM) was extremely simple: it had a two-dimensional tape, divided into squares and as long as needed (although not infinite). It also had a head for reading, writing, erasing and moving along the tape, and a table of instructions representing the task at hand in a precise and unambiguous way (Figure 1.1).

Turing later described his model in the context of his work on the ACE (automatic computing engine):

> Some years ago I was researching on what might now be described as an investigation of the theoretical possibilities and limitations of digital computing machines. ... This type of machine appeared to be sufficiently general. One of my conclusions was that the idea of a "rule of thumb" process and a "machine process" were synonymous. .... Machines such as the ACE may be regarded as practical versions of this same type of machine. There is at least a very close analogy. (Turing 1947/2004, 378–379)

In this passage, written around ten years after his earlier work on the *Entscheidungsproblem*, Turing sought to define the relationship between his theoretical machine and practical computers: the Turing Machine was the study of the "theoretical possibilities and limitations of digital computing machines." John von Neumann certainly became aware of Turing's work during the latter's two-year stay at Princeton (Numerico 2005, 45–48), and he also relied on Turing's constraints and specifications in 1945, when he wrote what is known as the *First Draft*, the document marking the beginning of the history of informatics.

Taken on its own, Turing's 1937 article does not seem particularly promising as the (still unwitting) beginnings of a theoretical computer structure. But computing theory had established the limits within which the discipline could develop (Mahoney 2000, 22), and described the class of problems that cannot be solved by a TM, i.e. those equivalent to the famous *halting problem*.

The TM also produced the awareness that performing calculations was a simple manipulation of symbols, and that there was really no qualitative difference in principle between numbers and formulae.[1] In fact, computer science would develop from the notion of computers as manipulators of symbols and not as "simple" calculators, so laying the foundations for the informatics revolution that came about after the Second World War. The identity of each Turing Machine was represented by a precise table of instructions specific to that machine, and identified by a serial number. In this context, Turing also developed another interesting concept: the concept of the universal machine. This device could emulate any other TM, and later in part inspired the development of the computer. The universal machine was able to replace the others, provided it was supplied with their "programme." Turing's thesis, which equated the TM and effective computability (i.e. the informal notion of definable calculability), was extremely credible. However, it could not be genuinely demonstrated, since there was no demonstration that could connect a formal notion to a semi-formal one such as computability through a TM. One of the arguments Turing used to back his thesis was the identification of the ability of both humans and machines to calculate. In some sense, it was at least a partial realization of a project of the XVII century German philosopher Gottfried Wilhelm Leibniz (1646–1716). The aim of his *Characteristica Universalis* was to find a system that could allow researchers to sit around a table and "calculate" the solution to any proposition.[2] The method, also suggested by McCarthy (2005, 165–169), was a mix of theory and experiment, using a unique technology that could represent propositions as well as calculate their "value." Up until at least the early 1960s, a large section of computer science could relate to Leibniz's project of representation, organization and the production of knowledge. Later in this section Leibniz's influence on artificial intelligence and Semantic Web projects will be discussed in more detail (cf. § 2.4).

The development of the computer resulted from many different requirements and pure coincidences. History did not bear any categorical imperative that necessitated its development or identified it in the digital form it later acquired. In the 1930s the most powerful computing machine was the Differential Analyzer, designed and built by Vannevar Bush (cf. § 1.3), based on an analog computing model. However, due to the interdisciplinary nature of the research and the contact between its various research groups, work on the development of the digital computer certainly contributed to its realization.

Among the fields that most contributed to the development of the digital electronic device, cryptography deserves especial mention for its role in the difficult task of decoding the secret messages of the German military. The protagonists active in this field of research, which had primarily developed in Europe, were mathematicians, engineers, physicists, and logicians, but also experts in linguistics and enigmatography, chess masters, statisticians, etc. The most important research group working on the problem was based in the sleepy London suburb of Bletchley Park. Turing actively participated in the group's mission, marrying his great talents with the diverse and hybrid skills of the colleagues he met there, since this was the best way to ensure success in such a critical situation. In this context what was perhaps the first fully electronic machine was constructed: the Colossus, designed and built in record time between January and December 1943 at Bletchley Park. The realization of that early computer was undoubtedly a complex, collective, and interdisciplinary endeavor, which saw its creators changing their original vision along the way, under the influence of practice.[3]

In this context, it is interesting to note that in the 1940s, when Turing focused on building a device capable of emulating some of the skills of the human brain, he modified the model he had himself created, and had inspired the development of the computer:

> So far we have been considering only discipline. To convert a brain or machine into a universal machine is the extremest form of discipline. Without something of this kind one cannot set up proper communication. But discipline is certainly not enough in itself to produce intelligence. That which is required in addition we call initiative. ... Our task is to discover the nature

of this residue as it occurs in man, and to try and copy it in machines. (Turing 1948/2004, 429)

In other words, Turing realized that, in order to achieve more interesting outputs in terms of machine intelligence, a method was needed that not only fully obeyed rules, but was also capable of exercising initiative. That was because a machine, however universal, might not be enough on its own to carry out intelligent tasks.

Turing's contemporaries understood his prediction that including components other than "discipline" was only needed to obtain intelligent responses from the machine at a later stage in its development. Once they had built devices that were powerful enough, they could reflect more deeply on the possibility of endowing those same machines with abilities comparable to, or even exceeding, human skills.

The next section examines the common history of the analog and digital models, and analyzes the reasons behind the ultimate success of the latter, while keeping in mind the continuing relevance of rhetoric to the orientation of the technological project under investigation.

1.2 What computers cannot do: from analog to digital

Why did the Turing Machine seem so convincing that it became synonymous with Twentieth Century machines, when Turing himself questioned its ability to perform "intelligent" human tasks? According to some technology historians (Eduards 1997), the success of the digital paradigm was due not only to a specific technological development, but also to the power of a metaphor: a machine that could tirelessly control and execute computations and always provide precise and repeatable results. The idea behind this external approach to the history of technology arises from the compatibility of the values represented by the digital machine with the social and political model of a closed society, typical of the Cold War years (Eduards 1997, 66–73). Others have seen the rise of "cyber-science" as a response to the need to re-organize the complexity of science in ways more suited to the current power regime (Keller 1995). This would in turn allow the reformulation of a knowledge-model to guarantee the control — albeit in new ways — of the emerging dynamics of information. And yet, even if it is accepted that the cultural dimension and its "discourse" do not play a central role in the choice of technology, the question remains: how could a machine with a very precise set of constraints and limitations, even before it was built, become the solution to all problems of calculus and "artificial" intelligence? One of the possible sources of innovation in technological development is the exploitation of already available tools. Following this pattern, the development of the computer was based on theoretical studies in computability theory carried out at least a decade earlier, in the mid 1930s. As described above, the theoretical machine developed in that context had a set of specific limitations relating to its ability in solving decision problems. Some problems cannot be solved by a Turing Machine, and they are rather relevant problems too: such as deciding whether or not a formula belongs to the set of theorems of a certain formal system, or again (and this really amounts to the same thing) determining if a certain program will come to an end or get stuck in an infinite loop.

Nevertheless, when moving from the functionality of theoretical to that of real machines, one must also consider other kinds of problems, as von Neumann began to realize by the late 1940s. In his contribution to the famous *Hixon Symposium* (an interdisciplinary meeting held in 1948 to discuss "Cerebral Mechanisms in Behavior") von Neumann introduced a new series of constraints specific to practical machines, as opposed to those valid for purely abstract ones. As a matter of fact, in logic "any finite sequence of correct steps is, as a matter of principle, as good as any other." In the case of automata "this statement must be significantly modified" because "automata are constructed in order to reach certain results in certain pre-assigned durations, or at least in pre-assigned orders of magnitude of duration" (von Neumann 1948/1963, 303). In other words, the recognized father of the computer was introducing the issue of tractability as distinct from the issue of decidability. But what does that mean? For a computer to be unable to solve a certain problem it is not necessary for that problem to be undecidable; it is sufficient for it to be intractable, i.e. the number of steps needed for its solution can be finite, but superior to the physical capabilities of the machine in actually performing the task within a reasonable time. Such intractable problems are in fact rather common: the so-called "traveling salesman problem" (finding the shortest route between a number of cities), school timetables or filling spaces according to certain characteristics. All these problems are known as NP-complete and it is unclear if they can be solved with polynomial (i.e. tractable) algorithms (see Harel 2000 for more details). It is also worth noting that not only are computers unable to solve all these problems for practical purposes, they are also unable to simulate the behaviors of deterministic problems described by precise equations, when the problems are particularly sensitive to the initial conditions. In such cases even a minute variation in those conditions leads to unpredictable results, and hence their behavior cannot be simulated by devices designed to provide unequivocal answers to a certain input (Longo 2009a).

But if things are so complicated, why was the computer so successful as a problem-solving tool in calculation, control, and communication? The answer may lie in the ideology behind the logic that dominated the first half of the twentieth century. In order to provide a foundation to mathematics, logicians set out to model an imaginary agent. This agent would only manage symbols. It operated in complete isolation, and was only able to preserve the truth of its premises in the truth of its result by manipulating other symbols, and by following a set of precise inference rules. In short, formal systems like those used until the 1930s by the Hilbert school always modeled their agent as omniscient and isolated — a vision that aptly represented the perspective of logic in contrast to that of mathematics or other analogous symbolic systems. When forced to defend the validity of his hypothesis, Turing worked on the concept of a machine capable of emulating the absolute computing agent, i.e.

a human being in the isolated and pure act of calculation. Turing even imagined it would be possible to parcel out its operations as a list of basic and accurately describable steps. It would then be possible to represent these steps by means of instruction tables so precise and exhaustive that even a machine could execute them. Obviously, if mathematics is seen purely as the manipulation of symbols according to detailed, strict schemes, whose sole function is to be applied without any ingenuity or intuition (i.e. without any form of individual or collective creativity) then the digital machine becomes the perfect device for representing this kind of behavior, and electronic technology can be used to realize it. However, the reduction of mathematics to the elementary and transcribable steps of calculation takes into account neither the practice of the mathematician nor the limitations of real machines, which, contrary to abstract ones, simply cannot keep the process going for long enough.

Nevertheless, this model provides some very simple, powerful, and convincing answers to the issues of process unification and simplification: the reduction of all operations to elementary ones, a precise and unambiguous instruction list for the computing agent to execute, and the notion that everything that is calculable can be performed by a single machine simply by changing its instructions.

Analog devices were more flexible than digital ones in representing phenomena, but created greater problems in terms of interpretation and repeatability of results. Moreover, with analog devices it was not possible to create a precise and unequivocal instruction table for use with each instance of the same problem. For all these reasons, the analog model did not seem very appealing as a way of simplifying procedures, and digital devices later took over even the control tasks for which analog machines were well suited.

The pioneers of digital technology were well aware that it would be difficult to use their devices without giving them the ability to emulate human self-organization skills. Nevertheless, this was not enough to change the widespread public belief that digital computers could function as real electronic brains. David Golumbia (2009, 10) has labeled this misconception "computerism": the belief that computers can solve any problem, even those that cannot be formulated in mathematical terms (Golumbia 2009, 14–19). Turing's cautious stand on this point has already been noted. Von Neumann also declared himself unsatisfied with the use of traditional mathematical logic by machines, but his objection remained virtually unanswered.

In a posthumous document published in 1958, von Neumann agreed with those who saw language in all its forms as a historical fact. In his view:

> ... it is only reasonable to assume that logics and mathematics
> are similarly historical, accidental forms of expression. They may
> have essential variants, i.e. they may exist in other forms than
> the ones to which we are accustomed. (von Neumann 1958, 81)

Von Neumann went on to argue that, since the brain uses logical systems at a lower depth than we are used to, it is only reasonable to assume that, in order to recreate the decision-making and problem-solving mechanisms of the brain, we must change the traditional language and rules of logic.

These critical voices, however authoritative, could not challenge the power of the digital machine: a device that could apparently solve any problem and emulate any behavior (even intelligent behavior) so long as it was furnished with adequate instructions.

1.3 Bush's visionary dream

The complex relationship between logic and language as forms of communication is not an isolated issue: it lies at the heart of information science, and of software development. For how can we communicate with machines, and how can we interact with them? And how can we formulate our tasks for the machine in a way it can understand? Far from being simple, these questions lie at the core of another inspiring force of computer science. Although this force emerged at the same time as the early computers, it began to wield its influence only some twenty years later. The next section will introduce the analog component into the history of computer development, championed by the father of analogical machines: Vannevar Bush (1890–1974). He was one of the most inspiring figures of contemporary technology. His contribution was significant not only for its scientific results in the field of electrical engineering, but also for his influence on American research policy before and during the Second World War. He was the inventor of the Differential Analyzer, an analog machine, built in 1936, that, during the years of World War II, was still the most powerful calculating device. This was a large mechanical device weighing about 100 tons, which used wheels and disk mechanisms to solve differential equations (Bush 1931).

In 1939 he was appointed Chairman of the Carnegie Institute in Washington and left his career at MIT, where he had been vice president and dean of the Faculty of Engineering. He became one of the most trusted advisers of President Roosevelt, and in 1940 was placed in charge of the institution he himself invented to support the war effort from the scientific point of view, the Office for Scientific Research and Development (OSRD). From this position he organized all the efforts of scientists in favor of the war, and found himself at the center of the largest scientific network ever built for military support, which was one of the key elements of the American victory. After the war, his role became less significant, although he continued to influence the scientific policy of the United States, being one of the founders of National Science Foundation (NSF), the body that still seeks to drive and fund part of the scientific research in the United States.

It was probably this experience, as a scientist and administrator in charge of funding, at a very delicate moment in the history of his country, that prompted him to investigate the role of technology in scientific development and beyond, and the management of information in particular. Starting in the 1930s, his thinking led him to formulate a visionary project made public in 1945, fortuitously the same year in which von Neumann and his group formulated the first project for a calculating machine. Among the articles he published to describe the project, "As We May Think," which appeared in the July 1945 issue of *The Atlantic Monthly*, remains a major source of inspiration for successive generations. Bush's point of departure was the need to redirect the efforts of scientists towards activities more appropriate to a period of peace, without losing opportunities for collaboration, particularly between disciplines.

Two problems facing the world of science were *information overload* and the increasing specialization of scientists, which meant that "the effort to bridge between disciplines is, correspondingly, superficial" (Bush 1945, 6). Bush's solution included the construction of a machine, called the Memex, which was to support the human effort by managing information dynamically and efficiently. He also understood that soon most information would not be produced in text format, but would use other types of media. The dynamic aspect of information included the need to continually update data and to store it adequately, but also to make it easily accessible. The idea of information as an uninterruptible process, which must be shared by people, would also be espoused by Wiener (cf. § 1.5), although, in common with most of his contemporaries, he did not understand completely Bush's position. Indeed, the problem of information overload is still as critical for us today (Yeo 2007).[4] Although digital technology may have made things worse, the use of analog devices, as proposed by Bush, might even today stimulate alternative approaches. Apart from the technology used, the design of the Memex was based on alternative techniques to those traditionally used in a library. Bush's proposal represented a genuine paradigm shift in relation to the access, retrieval, creation and representation of information, and to the management of knowledge itself.

This was Bush's crucial insight: it was reworked in several subsequent revisions of the project he worked on until the 1960s, a witness to how important it was in the construction of this new machine:

> Our ineptitude in getting at the record is largely caused by the artificiality of systems of indexing. When data of any sort are placed in storage, they are filed alphabetically or numerically, and information is found (when it is) by tracing it down from subclass to subclass ....
>
> The human mind does not work that way. It operates by association. With one item in its grasp, it snaps instantly to the next that is suggested by the association of thoughts, in accordance with some intricate web of trails carried by the cells of the brain. (Bush 1945, 32–33)

This idea of simulating the associative strategy adopted by the mind when selecting a set of ideas gave a new perspective to the field of information management and, in a sense, implicitly connected with an empirical tradition in the construction and connection of ideas. Although he may not have been aware of it, Bush's idea was part of a tradition that ran from Locke to Hume, but in opposition to Leibniz (whom Bush cited as a prophet of the machine). This tradition argued that the empiricist construction of associations is the primary and most efficient method for the creation of ideas. In contrast to connection, association may make sense only for the individual who created it, but it is still a powerful tool for finding information and organizing raw data. Bush did not believe that the machine could actually emulate human memory, at least not in the short term, but he was convinced that the machine could "improve" the natural power of the human brain in constructing useful and effective associations. Using analog devices, the Memex would allow the user to select associative blocks and store them in its extensive memory. Bush's machine had nothing to do with the huge, powerful electronic stored-program machines that were beginning to come into service. It was a desktop device, designed not only for scientists but for all categories of workers and professionals. Bush specifically mentioned lawyers, doctors, chemists and historians, who could input useful data for their work, and find it again quickly when needed. He did not recognize the birth of digital technology as such a huge transformation in modeling information; rather, from the very beginning his analog vision recognized that integrated interactive devices would need to retain the analog characteristics of users' cognitive habits. The interface must therefore contain analog elements in order to interact in a friendly manner with the mechanisms of communication and control used by human beings. This is perhaps why he is often regarded as one of the fathers of the development of the Web (cf. § 2.2.2). For digital humanists one of the most inspiring characteristics of the project was Bush's firm belief that "Progress ... depends upon the advent of new technical instrumentalities, and still more upon greater understanding of how to use them" (Bush 1959/1991, 183). The main legacy of Bush, then, can be identified in the centrality of the interaction and integration between humans and machines. Technology is revolutionary only if it is perceived and defined by the relationship between people and their needs. So while Wiener (as will be seen in the next section) was looking for ways to build "the human use of human beings," Bush was creating the social and intellectual space for the "human use of technology" (cf. § 3.6). This aspect can be traced back to the origins of the research tradition that focuses on increasing human intelligence via technical means, instead of trying to simulate and replace it by simple use of the machine.

Bush referred to all those technologists who had contributed to the development of the computer as a tool of friendly interaction between man and machine, and developed the idea that the computer should augment human intelligence, not replace it. Among these can be mentioned important figures who did not regard the computer simply as a tool for performing calculations, but for managing and exchanging information between machines and humans. A special mention should be made of Douglas Engelbart, who repeatedly acknowledged his debt to Bush, and can rightly be considered as the father of some of the most successful projects that transformed computer interfaces, and increased their friendliness for humans. These included the invention of icons, group work and groundbreaking devices like the mouse.[5]

To conclude, it can be seen that Bush's project, even though he was an engineer who became a policy-maker, undoubtedly had a strong humanistic component, because he put the improvement of the conditions of mankind at the center of technological development. The focus of his Copernican revolution was not just on the management and organization of information — typically work that would be directed in any case to the humanities — but on humanity over technology.

1.4 A mathematician with a Ph.D. in philosophy

As explained above, the theoretical paradigm of computer science that arose in the second half of the 1930s was later associated with the economic, social and cultural life at the time. The process of elaboration was long and complex, and at times involved opposing conceptions of knowledge, intelligence, and the ways in which these could be represented. One of the most important steps in this debate, which took place at the same time as the transition from the electronic machine of Turing and von Neumann and the launch of Bush's Memex project, was taken during the *Macy Lectures* (1946–1953). These were inspired by Norbert Wiener (1894–1964), among others, and around them was born cybernetics, "the science of control and of communication in both the animal and the machine" (Wiener 1948/1961).

Participants in the Macy Foundation conferences in New York, in addition to those scientists who have made it into the history of information technology, such as John Von Neumann, Norbert Wiener, Walter Pitts, Warren McCulloch and Claude Shannon, included figures from the social sciences such as Lawrence K. Frank and Gregory Bateson, anthropologists like Margaret Mead (all founding members of the group), linguists like Roman Jakobson, the psychologists Hams Lukas Teuber, Donald G. Marquis, and Molly Harrower, but also philosophers, physicists, physicians, biologists, chemists and psychiatrists. Although the meetings mostly focused on technical and scientific issues (Heims 1991, 22), one of the common concerns was to understand how the cyber-technologies emerging at that time could illuminate the workings of the mind and human behavior (and provide application models), while also asking what the consequences of such applications on society might be. Thus a wide range of technical, theoretical and ethical issues, including social development, as well as the diffusion of information technology, were raised during these meetings. Despite the collective effort in the cybernetics revolution, if there was any one man at the center of the intense cultural exchanges that characterized the birth and growth of this new scientific discipline, that man was Norbert Wiener. As a privileged witness and visionary of what he himself called "the second industrial revolution," he had the ability to recognize in advance some of the toughest challenges of the society of information, a society in which not just culture, but also a large part of the economy, would become highly dependent on information technology and communication.

From a strong multi-disciplinary background — at age 17 he received his doctorate in philosophy at Harvard (Conway and Siegelman 2004, 34–40) — Wiener considered himself a mathematician, but his research fields ranged from control engineering, to physics and physiology. He was among the first to recognize the necessity of a theoretical and ethical dimension that went beyond the boundaries of technology. His most significant work in this regard is *The Human Use of Human Beings*. Among its many interesting pages (worth noting is his warning that the protection of technological inventions will be impractical, almost an anticipation of the movement for free software), there is a passage in which he reports a sentence from a review of his first book:

> Perhaps it would not be a bad idea for the teams at present creating cybernetics to add to their cadre of technicians, who have come from all horizons of science, some serious anthropologists and perhaps a philosopher who has some curiosity as to world matters. (Wiener 1950/1954, 180)

Wiener had, in fact, a genuine interest in further research in the "no man's land" on the border between disciplines, and believed that only in this free space could real innovation flourish. Communication between scientists from different backgrounds was therefore at the heart of cybernetics, not only as a scientific objective, but also as a key tool to promote the opening of new fields of research with implications for cybernetic projects. According to Wiener's vision, *communication* and *control* were two interrelated concepts, because control was a special case of communication: "When I control the actions of another person, I communicate a message to him, and although this message is in the mandatory mode, the technique of communication does not differ from that of a message of fact" (Wiener 1950/1954, 16). Communication was an interaction with other people or machines in an attempt to get feedback. The concept of feedback lies at the center of cybernetics research as the mechanism of reaction and re-balancing of agents in response to messages from outside. Although, by its very nature, this remains inaccessible to the producer of the message, it nevertheless ensures the effectiveness of the interaction. Wiener therefore focuses his attention on the very concept of communication beyond its human dimension. In his text *The Human Use of Human Beings* he clarifies his position on this issue:

> ... society can only be understood through a study of the messages and the communication facilities which belong to it; and that in the future development of these messages and communication facilities, messages between man and machines, between machines and man, and between machine and machine, are destined to play an ever increasing part. (ibid.)

One of the primary purposes of Cybernetics, as a transdisciplinary field, was the study of "a language and techniques that will enable us indeed to attack the problem of control and communication in general" (Wiener 1950/1954, 17). The importance of the role of communication and subsequent research on the languages and technologies that have made this interaction between machines and humans possible was at the center of the line of research that we can call cybernetics. Although the discipline did not have a long or easy life, the seeds it sowed were longer-lasting and more influential than is generally recognized in the subsequent history of science and technology. For Wiener, future efforts would be directed towards constructing the most profitable and efficient interactions between humans and machines. Although, by the time the *Macy Conferences* eventually came to a close, the momentum of cybernetics had been partially depleted, still Wiener's tireless cultural and organizational activities never stopped. He continued to promote meetings, such as the *cybernetics dinners* held in Cambridge, which were attended by many of the scientists who later became part of the technological revolution of the 1960s, and among them certainly Licklider, whose contributions will be examined in the following sections. The problem of language and the integration of communication into the most varied of applications, from prostheses to the education of machines capable of learning, always lay at the center of these interdisciplinary exchanges that interested Wiener so much. In particular, his cultural leadership at Princeton, and more generally throughout the world, from Russia to China, from France to Mexico, meant that his name became associated with cybernetics and a prophecy of the near future, which expanded his influence beyond his immediate field of influence. This can be seen in the interest in man-machine interactions, in the search for "high-level" programming languages (those more oriented to users than machines) and finally to the growth of computer networks to facilitate communication between humans and machines.

1.5 Wiener's ethics and politics of the computer

Before delving into the influence of cybernetics on the development of information and computer technology, it is crucial to recall Wiener's vital contribution to the understanding of the historical, ethical and social implications of the diffusion of information technology in society. He realized very soon that

> Those of us who have contributed to the new science of cybernetics thus stand in a moral position which is, to say the least, not very comfortable. We have contributed to the initiation of a new science which ... embraces technical developments with great possibilities for good and evil. (Wiener 1948/1961, 28)

The moral dilemma to which he refers echoes the loss of innocence among scientists, which took place as a result of the dropping of the atomic bomb during World War II. As Michel Foucault suggests (1970, 21–23), in that context scientists realized their work could not be neutral with respect to good and evil. It was necessary to take a stand and to take responsibility for activities in the gleaming, sterilized and lonely research laboratory. The position taken by Wiener was publicly clear, and he personally paid for his choice in terms of isolation. After the War he refused to be involved in any research project funded, even if only indirectly, by the Department of Defense, or in research involving private enterprise as privileged partners of an academic institution.

It is worth investigating what, according to Wiener, were the risks society would run when the "second industrial revolution" was complete, i.e. when the promises of cybernetics had come true. Once built, machines designed for control and communication would be able to replace not only manual work but also the minds of many workers, and this would cause first of all intellectual unemployment:

> ... This new development has unbounded possibilities for good and for evil. .... It gives the human race a new and most effective collection of mechanical slaves to perform its labor. Such mechanical labor has most of the economic properties of slave labor, although, unlike slave labor, it does not involve the direct demoralizing effect of human cruelty. However, any labor that accepts the condition of competition with slave labor accepts the conditions of slave labor, and is essentially slave labor.
> (Wiener 1948/1961, 27)

The consequences of this situation would have been that "the average human being of mediocre attainment or less has nothing to sell that it is worth anyone's money to buy" (ibid.). This would mean either that the mechanisms by which the working classes were treated would have to be changed, or it would be necessary to rethink the value-structures of society so as not to leave out relevant layers of citizenship. In an effort to create a civil consciousness with respect to the progress of science and its effects on the world of work, Wiener became involved in raising awareness among trade unions, but was disappointed with their inability to understand the situation.

The second area of risk that he saw, and in which he was engaged, was the analysis of the evolutionary processes of science. Wiener opposed the idea that the findings should be shrouded in ever-greater secrecy. The argument he used against secrecy is interesting and topical. His idea was that information could not be regarded as a commodity as any "information is more a matter of process than of storage" (Wiener 1950/1954, 121). Considering the dynamic and procedural characteristics of knowledge transmitted through information, Wiener believed that imposing secrecy on research simply meant slowing it down, without hiding it from the enemy, who could simply maintain strategies that allowed him or her to find out the important details. He also likened military top-secrets to the patent systems followed by private enterprise, and increasingly also by universities, noting the negative consequences of a slowing down in the process of innovation, and the way in which knowledge produced by several people ends up benefiting only a few. His position is expressed as usual with great courage:

> The fate of information ... is to become something which can be bought or sold ... It is my business to show that it leads to the misunderstanding and the mistreatment of information and its associated concepts ... beginning with that of patent law. (Wiener 1950/1954: 113)

His personal crusade against intellectual property, already mentioned, brings him even closer to modern research, the battle for free code and shared knowledge (Hess and Ostrom 2007, Lessig 2004, Berry 2008). The situation nowadays is, however, quite complicated. Although "knowledge is more a matter of process than of storage" it is now easier to store the process and to manage it. This is exactly what happens with social network services that host the process on their servers and then claim ownership of the information produced. Wiener could not expect that storage and communication tools would have evolved so quickly. However, he clearly had in mind one of the characteristics of the knowledge society, the centrality of information access and distribution.

This centrality becomes a strategic asset in the future imagined by Wiener, and, he had foreseen very precisely that if the means of communication did not adequately satisfy this need, we would risk the construction of anti-democratic mechanisms, supported by the misuse of machines (of which the computer would be just an example), favoring the centralization of power:

> ... such machines ... may be used by a human being or a block of human beings to increase their control over the rest of the human race or that political leaders may attempt to control their populations by means not of machines themselves but through political techniques as narrow and indifferent to human possibilities as if they had been conceived mechanically. (Wiener 1950/1954, 181)

This risk and others related to the automation of war (the so-called *push-button war*) could only be averted by producing a generation of scientists, informed and free from all ties with society and politics, who could make decisions by assessing the situation solely in their capacity as experts. This solution may seem a bit technocratic and very utopian, but its echo has certainly informed some of the more extreme positions adopted by the pioneers of ARPANET, the computer network that was the forerunner of the Internet. His idea of the machine as a potential concentrator of power is echoed in some of the most critical literature about the Web, which underlines the risks related to the controversial relation between control and freedom of the digital network (cf. § 5.9 for more details and a discussion of Chun 2006).

The second method identified by Wiener to oppose the worst consequences of the first machines programmed to control society could be categorized as resistance. It was to provide the maximum possible information on what was happening in science and technology to foster the growth of awareness in the general population and to allow the implementation of appropriate corrective measures. The decision to write his two key texts on cybernetics — that of 1948 and another, more accessible work that appeared two years later — was precisely directed at providing remedies to these risks by making them as public as possible. Its purpose was to help build a more just society whose values were more than purely commercial. Such a society would have taken on the contradictions born of an unconscious use of technology, and would choose to rule in the light of sharing and collaboration. Society so reorganized would allow "the human use of human beings" that the spread of cybernetic machines was putting in danger.

In conclusion, the positions taken by Wiener constitute an important lesson for the digital humanist today because they may represent a critical vision *ante litteram* that proposes solutions oriented to humans concerning the kinds of machines that were being built, or had recently become available. His insight into the barriers that patents and copyright posed to the development of knowledge, and his anticipation of current disputes over digital protection methods (whether in art or science) raises the question of whether knowledge can only renew itself through free and open transmission (cf. § 5.9.1). His transdisciplinary education meant that he was continually examining the development of science from a social and ethical point of view. And perhaps it is no coincidence that, despite having proposed perhaps the first project for an electronic machine with stored programming in 1941 (although it was ignored due to a lack of understanding on the part of Bush), he was never again interested in the construction of real machines. Perhaps he feared that without guidelines they would only become mechanisms of automation, instead of improving human communication.

1.6 Licklider and the man-machine symbiosis

Joseph Carl Robnett Licklider (1915–1990) was the right man at the right place at the beginning of the 1960s. "Lick," as friends and acquaintances called him, was a person capable of making everything that he worked on seem simple (Mitchell Waldrop 2002, 7–8). His training was in experimental psychology and his main research field was psychoacoustics — a discipline that currently falls within the domain of neuroscience. His doctorate in 1942 was the first to identify the areas of cat brains that were activated in hearing sound waves of varying intensity. In his field, sophisticated equipment was beginning to be used to study neurons and he was among the first scientists to come into contact with a mini-computer, the PDP1, which allowed direct interaction with its operator (Hauben 2007, 110). But Licklider was also part of a group of people who were influenced by Wiener's ideas of cybernetics: he participated in the cybernetics circle that met in Cambridge, MA every Tuesday evening, and attended their dinner seminars. He recalled those years after World War II in an interview in 1988, and admits that those meetings and dinners had a powerful influence on his career, because his training in psychology became enriched with information about computer science and the theory of communication, which were of great importance for his future as a scientist. Licklider took part in the Macy Seventh Conference, held in March 1950, giving a paper on the distortion of language and its ability to remain intelligible. Licklider's name can thus be added to the list of scientists who were stimulated by the transdisciplinary nature of the new field of cybernetics. Although unknown to the general public, a number of important functions in the development of information technology and telecommunications are due to Licklider, for he was at the head of one of the offices of ARPA (Advanced Research Project Agency), called IPTO (Information Processing Technologies Office), which was a major supporter of man-machine interface research, and which funded the construction of the ARPANET, a network that linked universities and research centers — the forerunner of the Internet.

He held this position from 1962 to 1964, and was also central in the launch of the ARPANET, although that project was only realized under the guidance of his colleague Robert Taylor in 1969. According to Jack Ruina, the director of ARPA who appointed Licklider to his new office, his job was to address such issues as *command and control* and the *behavioral sciences* — two typical areas of research for the military — but the flow of research supported by Licklider helped to interpret them for the realization of human–machine symbiosis. In fact, all projects funded by IPTO were in this area.

What drove him to pursue this line of inquiry? He shared Bush's conviction, from his own experience, that most of the work in research was taken up by putting oneself into a position where one could be creative. So he made every effort to ensure that the machine might not just be an instrument to help scientists save time on mechanical work, but also to share that part of the work devoted to thought, the part he formally called "creative." The device Licklider was thinking about from the early 1960s was influenced by his participation in the Whirlwind project. Whirlwind was to produce the SAGE (semi automatic ground environment) system, able to assist in the discovery of enemy forces through the use of radar, if war broke out. It was a simulation project in which the monitoring instruments and their signals were analyzed by operators with the help of machines. Even though the project, which ended in the 1950s, was already old in technological terms and never became operational, it was extremely important in enriching the scientific imagination: the idea of a machine capable of interacting directly with its operator, without the intermediary of the technician and long delays waiting for program output. In short, the paradigm of human–machine symbiosis was being born, based on theoretical studies on communication that lay the center of all processes in cybernetics, and from the model of a desktop machine like the Memex that would act as a supplement to human memory (cf. § 1.3).

The idea of symbiosis is explicitly opposed to what Licklider called — along with Wiener — "automation," identified with the idea of "mechanically extended man." This was about replacing parts of humans with mechanical devices that would perform the intended task instead of the operator. Symbiosis was not in competition with the first artificial intelligence projects active at that time; it opted for a lower profile, considering that an intelligent machine would probably be realistic in the medium to long term, while in the short term (5–15 years), it would be desirable to develop more sophisticated and real-time interaction with machines.

Licklider explained specifically what he meant by his idea of a symbiosis between man and machine:

> ... the other main aim ... is to bring computing machines effectively into processes of thinking that must go on in "real time," time that moves too fast to permit using computers in conventional ways ...
> To think in interaction with a computer in the same way that you think with a colleague whose competence supplements your own will require much tighter coupling between man and machine than ... is possible today. (Licklider 1960, 4)

His appointment as director of IPTO suddenly placed this project at the center of national science policy. And it translated into an action plan that granted substantial funding to those scholars who were moving in the same direction.

Symbiosis meant the humanization of the computer, and for this reason in his 1960 article the characteristics of dissimilarity between humans and machines were identified, along with the efforts of integration that would be needed. This list of open problems immediately became the agenda of IPTO and the research centers it funded. It also affected the birth of personal computing and the creation of a network of interconnected computers, two essential conditions for the development of digital humanities. Symbiosis, in fact, presented a vision of computers in which their different tasks of calculation and data management were fused with those of storage and information retrieval (Licklider 1960, 6). Once this relationship between such diverse tasks was built, and having integrated the component of communication into all levels (between operator and machine, between machines, and between people via machines, as Wiener foresaw) one is faced with a machine comparable to that designed in 1945 by von Neumann (cf. § 1.1), although still governed by a processor, a memory and a set of programming instructions. To give just a few examples: it incorporates mechanisms for the collective management of machine time, or introduces input–output devices, unimaginable to the inventors of the calculator. In addition, from the point of view of programming languages, it will be seen that Licklider sought to support different techniques to those adopted previously, more suited to human than to machine language. But the newest element integrated into the new machine, designed by cybernetics and related fields, is the role the user has in the development of mechanical processes. This idea was the opposite of that proposed by the Turing Machine, where the operator was replaced by an appropriate set of instructions. Following the model that may be called cybernetic, the machine was, in fact, a participant and complicit in all its activities, replacing the human operator only in the purely automatic components of the task, and supporting but never replacing him or her. From this perspective it may be said that, in the generation of projects funded by Licklider, the human being became integrated with the computer and, to achieve this, it was necessary to construct input–output tools that would facilitate its implementation. It was in this context that some devices were invented that are still useful for the so-called *human–machine interaction,* such as the mouse, the use of icons in the interface, workgroups, screens suitable for graphic applications, and so on.

1.7 Libraries and information processing

Before describing the obstacles to the implementation of the kind of symbiosis that Licklider hoped for, it will be instructive to see first how the agenda drawn up by the research group he financed and built had consequences for both computer science and eventually digital humanities. It was, in fact, a new way to manage and represent data, build information and thus create knowledge — all activities central to the research process.

Licklider was invited to a series of evening seminars on "Management and the computer of the future," organized in 1961 to celebrate the centenary of MIT. At one of these seminars, dedicated to the computer in the university, he openly declared his opinion that the computer has affected "the whole domain of creative intellectual processes" and, in particular, he supported the argument that "information processing" would one day become an important scientific field:

> Planning management communication, mathematics and logic and perhaps even psychology and philosophy will draw heavily from and contribute heavily to that science (the information processing). (Licklider 1962, 207)

Licklider recognized decisively that all disciplines concerned with creative processes of any kind were related to computing, and that every one of them, even the humanities, would contribute to its development. This message has not always been adequately understood in the context of computer science and perhaps not even in the humanities, but evidently it was clear from the beginning to all who had a significant influence on the organization of this discipline.

However, Licklider identified many obstacles to the implementation of symbiosis. The first was the difference in speed between the two entities: the human and the mechanical. His solution favored the development of *time-sharing,* a technology that would allow different *consoles* to make use of the same machine at the same time, taking advantage of the speed of execution of the big machines that were then available. To show the positive effects of this technology, which was the first sub-goal of its leadership to IPTO, he pointed to libraries as places where most could be made of the technology:

> It seems reasonable to envision, for a time 10 or 15 years hence, a "thinking center" that will incorporate the functions of present-day libraries together with anticipated advances in information storage and retrieval and the symbiotic functions suggested earlier in this paper. The picture readily enlarges itself into a network of such centers, connected to one another by wide-band communication lines and to individual users by leased-wire services. In such a system, the speed of the computers would be balanced, and the cost of the gigantic memories and the sophisticated programs would be divided by the number of users. (Licklider 1960, 8)

In the years before his assignment to IPTO, Licklider was appointed by the Council of Library Resources to explore the role technology would play in the libraries of the future. The work by his research group was carried out between 1961 and 1963, and reached fruition with the publication of the book *Libraries of the Future* (Licklider 1965). According to Licklider, the mass digitization of knowledge would become an essential new tool for the consultation of materials; also the availability of these large machines that were accessible by many users would allow everyone to get digital content, thus permitting fast, direct and complete access to all human knowledge. Seen from this perspective, computing would have an immediate impact on content organization, access and searching: some of the key fields of the humanities. Licklider did not pose the question of who should hold the expertise necessary to reorganize the libraries in his research, because he knew that in the cybernetic tradition certain objectives were either worked out within an inter-disciplinary framework or they were abandoned.

The model of time-sharing, necessary to overcome the difference in operating speed between humans and machines, had at least two consequences, one positive and the other negative. From a social point of view, the collective use of a single machine, perhaps at a distance, led to the birth of a sort of cooperative team spirit among the programmers, who laid the groundwork for a culture of sharing and respect for each other's work that became the basis for the development of the Internet, which itself began as one of many related community projects aimed at the distribution of information as an essential characteristic of these new technologies. From a technological point of view the Internet is still based in part on this time-sharing model through its client-server design, an architecture structured on the limited availability of processors and memory, that allocated the burden of work on the server while the "clients" (our computers) use only the results of that work, like the terminals connected to the mainframes of Licklider's era. In the modern world the widespread availability and evolution of technology should have rendered the hierarchical network obsolete some time ago, but once some infrastructures have been built, it is difficult to revise them. The story of the Internet is about the biases of technology and their roots in its complex and cumbersome evolution.

According to Licklider, another factor that hindered the realization of human–machine symbiosis was language. Machines and human beings were using very different languages because they were based on very different principles. The computer had to be precisely guided through a series of detailed steps, whereas humans could content themselves with simply knowing the desired goal and, being bound by the result, putting into place the technical means for obtaining it. Licklider noted that in order to achieve the symbiosis it would be necessary to make use of new principles of communication and control than those then in use. In addition to techniques being tested in the field of artificial intelligence, which consisted in the development of heuristic strategies to get results, and the consequent construction of declarative rather than procedural languages, he called for the strengthening of a second line of research that would move towards creating separate sub-routines which could be called upon by the operator directly as needed. The idea was to build real-time pathways to encourage interaction with the machine, depending on the needs of the moment. This would not be a ready-made program but an agreed set of constraints that would be manipulated by the skill of the operator and the requirements of the situation — a more flexible modular system that would allow integration with the machine.

The relationship with the language of the machine is another "humanistic" issue from the development of information technology.[6] The languages and their structure, although they may be strategies of digital technology, belong to the realm of language-related research. How should a language be built so that it can be used mechanically? Do natural languages have a formal structure? Is it possible to represent — in a procedural way — problems to be solved through the machine? These were the kinds of questions posed by the linguist Noam Chomsky (1957), whose work in developing formal descriptions of natural language formed the basis of all modern computer languages, including markup languages. Such questions cannot be answered directly because they deal with the complex general issue of what a language is and how it works. However, it is still possible to define the challenge of finding methods of communication to facilitate the interaction between humans and machines — an issue which lies at the core of computer science — as related to the philosophy of language and/or to the linguistic turn of the science and humanities of the last century.[7]

Licklider recognized the centrality of the problem and felt that the solution was not to be found in a human adaptation to the mechanical system, but rather a continuous communication between humans and machines, in the definition of a set of programs each of which could be useful in a specific context. The interactive nature of the symbiosis required the implementation of routines written in a language understandable by the machine, but at the same time capable of conforming to the communication patterns of human beings.

The last problem identified by Licklider as an obstacle to enabling a more fertile interaction between humans and machines was the state of current input–output devices that were at that time unsuited to the role of the computer as a communication tool. To overcome this limitation the IPTO concretely funded many projects in the field of graphic interfaces and input–output solutions that would allow a faster and more immediate interaction with the machine. Licklider's idea consisted of the construction of three types of input–output device, the visionary aspect of which is still impressive, given that he was working back in 1960, when machines were very different from today's desktop computers. He supported the creation of desktop displays, able to show results and to control the activity of the machine. Screens like those available only recently, were conceived by his creative imagination. He also foresaw wall displays that could serve to facilitate harmony in the case of group work, and small screens that, although separated from each other, could still display the same information. All these ideas have been realized only recently, such as the use of communal virtual screens to enable real time collaboration (as used when writing this book). And finally, Licklider imagined that systems for the recognition and production of language would eventually become available. In this area as well, very important steps have been taken, although his original vision is far from being realized.

1.8 Conclusion

This chapter has tried to argue that the contribution of the humanities to the early development of the computer is far greater than is generally believed. Many of the leading theorists who shaped the design of the modern digital computer: people like Turing, von Neumann, Leibnitz, Wiener, Bush and Licklider came from very varied educational backgrounds. They were often trained either directly in the humanities or social sciences (Leibniz, Wiener, Licklider) or they consulted with a wide range of academics, including those from humanistic disciplines. The contribution of linguists to the development of computable formal languages is especially significant. Likewise the development of human–computer interaction design can be traced back to the Licklider, and his background in psychology; and Bush's Memex was based on his neurological idea of associative rather than hierarchical links between items of information, which led eventually to the creation of the modern Web.

Another important lesson that can be learned from the development of the early computer is the reluctance of pioneers, like Turing and von Neumann, to concede that the digital computer could ever possess the ability to think like a human — a misconception that persists today. Others, like Bush and Wiener, foresaw how information would become a valuable commodity in a digital world, and that the changes set in motion by the development of cybernetics had the potential to do as much evil as good.

One final point worth making is that the success of the digital computer also owed something to chance: the development of alternative analog computers was cut short by the Second World War and not resumed, and criticism of the path taken in the development of the digital computer by leading theorists was ignored.

For the modern digital humanist the message that this historical analysis provides is one of caution: not to assume that a computer can solve any problem, or that the continued development of digital computing in all its aspects is necessarily in the best interests of society. It should rather be regarded as one particular path which has been followed thus far to the exclusion of all others, and which may still be retraced at some future time. And in this retracing humanists will doubtless play, as before, an important role.

The next chapter will follow the development of the Internet and the World Wide Web, starting from Licklider's involvement in the ARPANET project. It will also investigate the social inequalities and cultural biases that the new global system of information, as envisaged by the pioneers of the computer, created.

Chapter 2
Internet, or the humanistic machine

2.1 The design of the intergalactic network

In April of 1963, as manager of IPTO, Licklider wrote a famous letter addressed to a group of staff scientists, whose names read like a veritable who's who of the leaders of computer science at the time. The letter was sent to postpone a meeting, and Licklider was the point of contact for the projects and their points of intersection, and also managed joint projects relating to longer-term goals. The members of this "intergalactic network" were striving to combine forces to overcome various barriers to communication, with the ultimate goal of creating an interactive and cooperative system. The project involved the construction of a network of connected computers, which would allow different operators to use a program on different machines, and to store the data in memory, even if it came from other parts of the system. To realize this dream, which was the material realization of his project of symbiosis, based on the concept of time-sharing, a number of issues that would have hindered cooperation would have to be resolved.

As seen in the previous chapter, one of the key problems was the question of which languages were to be used. This became even more crucial in the context of the network. For what should the language of the intergalactic network be? The language of time-sharing? Or was there a need for new *koinē*? The use of programs originating on other computers implied that they would have to communicate using different languages, so it seemed a good idea to at least try to standardize best practice for storing data and information. There was also the problem of who should manage the communication protocols and traffic on the machines. Licklider's prophetic suggestion was to allow the network to autonomously manage traffic, data storage and priority of access. It would then be able to modify shared files without recourse either to the users themselves, or to a higher level. For the first time, the user was put at the center of the design:

> It seems easiest to approach this matter from the individual User's point of view — to see what he would like to have, what

> he might like to do, and then to try to figure out how to make a system within which his requirements can be met. (Licklider 1963, 2)

The birth of user-centered design that has played such a leading role in the design of computer systems from the 1980s onwards[1] can be traced to this letter, and other communications from those years. The centrality of the user means computing at the measure of man (or woman), and especially the idea that using a computer does not rely on making things simpler for the machine, but using the machine to support human activities.

In this letter, the relationship between machines and communication devices is expressly constructed through the implementation of standards, interpreted languages or tools to facilitate access and retrieval of previously acquired resources. The computer is no longer limited to a relationship with an individual user, but is seen as one element in a complex system of communication, just as Wiener had predicted in 1948. While Wiener saw at once the risks regarding control and the concentration of power that these new models of communication would bring about (see § 1.4 and 1.5), Licklider saw them as an opportunity to join together his various interests as a scientist and to expand opportunities for collaboration between scientists and the objectives of the military.

> ... the military greatly needs solutions to many or most of the problems that will arise if we tried to make good use of the facilities that are coming into existence. I am hoping that there will be, in our individual efforts, enough evident advantage in cooperative programming and operation to lead us to solve the problems and, thus, to bring into being the technology that the military needs. (Licklider 1963, 3)

Licklider, who in any case was working for an agency funded by the Department of Defense (unlike Wiener), saw in his work an opportunity to steer the computer in a desirable direction for scientists, while at the same time supporting the national war effort. So the technology of network communication was born, between Wiener's warnings of the "human use of human beings" on the one hand, and Licklider's engaging and somewhat naive enthusiasm on the other. Licklider, though, was well aware that this developing technology would enhance the ability of the army, or other similar institutions, in their control and exercise of power. Nevertheless, he did not renege: he portrayed the marriage between computers and communication as a victory for science, rather than as a tool for power. It was this step that transformed the activities of command and control that he had to develop at ARPA, into projects of human–machine interaction, realized through collaborative programming effort.

Although he resigned as manager of IPTO in 1964, Licklider's influence continued to be felt in the Research department. The real network project was led by Robert Taylor, an experimental psychologist who called himself a "professional student," having followed — for pleasure's sake alone — courses in mathematics, philosophy, English and religion. He also obtained a master's degree in psychology, but declined an invitation to complete a PhD, refusing any kind of specialism in favor of a highly transdisciplinary path. Taylor came to be considered as one of the top technology executives of the time: after setting in motion the ARPANET project, the nucleus of the first network that later became known as the Internet, he directed the Computer Systems Laboratory (CSL) at Xerox PARC, from which came the most important innovations in personal computers. It was Taylor who first realized the importance of the screen as a medium of communication between human and machine:

> Which organ provides the greatest bandwidth in terms of its access to the human brain? Obviously the eyeball. If one then contemplated how the computer could best communicate with its human operator, the answer suggested itself: "I thought the machine should concentrate its resources on the display."
> (Hiltzik 1999, 9)

In 1966 Taylor became director of IPTO and realized that if he wanted to communicate with MIT or Berkeley he had to move his chair and turn on different terminals in his room. So, by making use of Licklider's insights, he envisioned connecting the different laboratories with each other through a network that spoke a common language, where everyone could interact with each other's machines. In 1968, he wrote with Licklider a famous article entitled "The Computer as a Communication Device," now considered a classic in the field, in which he prophesied that communication through machines would outperform direct verbal communication.

2.2 The computer as a communication device

This article, which anticipates the birth of the ARPANET by a year, is a sort of manifesto for a new type of informatics with a unique role in society, in contrast to the agendas, concepts and reference models of communication engineering. Licklider and Taylor's idea was very simple, though revolutionary, considering the practicalities of the machines of the time: it was for a device that could be used not just for the transfer of information but for interaction. Some elements, such as communication itself and its agents, would have to be rethought if the benefits of these next-generation devices were to be realized.

Taylor had repeatedly claimed to have been influenced by Bush and Wiener (Aspray 1989, 5), and of course by Licklider, in reformulating the relationship between humans and machines. Already Bush, but more especially Wiener, introduced the idea of communication as something more complex than a mere stream of bits encoded to reach their destination, where they would be symmetrically decrypted. It also included the idea of a response function to the data stream, which took the form of feedback; it was, so to speak, a naturally interactive and interconnected mechanism that included a relationship between the two parties involved in the exchange. If the feedback was at a high level this meant that interaction was no longer confined to the mere passage of information, but produced a real change in the scenario, involving new rules and even a new model in which to frame the various elements of communication.

The position of Licklider and Taylor pushed beyond the simple transmission of data. They expressly stated that "their emphasis on people is deliberate" while denying the centrality of the machinery responsible for the transmission of the data: "to communicate is more than to send and to receive." They were convinced that

> ... we are entering a technological age in which we will be able to interact with the richness of living information — not merely in the passive way that we have become accustomed to using books and libraries, but as active participants in an ongoing process, bringing something to it through our interaction with it, and not simply receiving something from it by our connection to it. (Licklider and Taylor 1968, 21)

The central object of the interests of these two experimental psychologists was the support and help machines could give to the most creative aspects of human communication. To accomplish this end, they needed a medium that could be tailored to the circumstances, a plastic and dynamic medium which everyone could contribute to, and experiment in. They believed that the computer was just such a medium: "a well-programmed computer can provide direct access both to informational resources and to the processes for making use of the resources" (Licklider and Taylor 1968, 22).

If the computer could handle both information and the processes that allow it to be used, it is clear that users of this tool should not only be advanced technical and communication engineers or programmers, but also "creative people in other fields and disciplines who recognize the usefulness and who sense the impact of interactive multiaccess computing upon their work" (Licklider and Taylor 1968, 30–31). The supercommunity of the ARPANET, then, would include, alongside the technicians and engineers, creative people from other areas who were able to exploit the new communication tools for their areas of interest. Part of this community can certainly be identified with as digital humanists, together with engineers and programmers, and groups from other disciplines. All these members of the community had equal priority in the interactive information process as they followed their own research agendas.

The only group excluded from the community interaction, other than those who did not work in a creative or informational context, were those who interpreted the computer as a simple connector and data transmitter, without valuing its potential as a tool to encourage interaction and the building of tools for the externalization of cognitive models.

Starting from these considerations, Licklider and Taylor made it clear that, although computer programs were important because they allowed the raw data to be structured and manipulated at a higher level, they were only a part "of the whole that we can learn to concentrate and share. The whole includes raw data, digested data, data about the location of data — and documents — and most especially models" (Licklider and Taylor 1968, 29).[2]

Finally, they also focused on the future of these online interactive communities and imagined how they would look. This exercise could be seen as a self-fulfilling prophecy, rather than as a vision about the future, because that future was literally "invented" in their 1968 article. That paper imagines a reality of online communities composed of single individuals or organized groups separated geographically but united by interest, along with the use of computers for every information-based transaction, contributing to lower connection costs, and the replacement of letters and telegrams with electronic messages.

Finally, Licklider and Taylor made a prediction that is staggering in its precision and its evocative character:

> When people do their informational work "at the console" and "through the network," telecommunication will be as natural an extension of individual work as face-to-face communication is now. The impact of that fact, and of the marked facilitation of the communicative process, will be very great — both on the individual and on society. (Licklider and Taylor 1968, 40)

This could not be a more precise and detailed description of what happens today in our daily experience of the Internet. Licklider and Taylor, however, recognized a risk that constituted a crack in their enthusiasm for the network-to-come: the *digital divide* (cf. § 2.1). They wondered if "being online" might become a privilege or a right, and this raised the question of whether the network would become a benefit or a risk to society. Subsequent events appear to bear this out, and the communication technology they gave birth to in an excess of optimism has also revealed other problematic areas.

2.2.1 *The birth of the* ARPANET

The rest of the story of the ARPANET is well known and often recounted.[3] In 1966, Taylor won from Charles Herzfeld, the director of ARPA at the time, an initial funding of one million dollars for the construction of the ARPANET infrastructure. In December 1966 Taylor was finally able to convince Larry Roberts, the communications engineer who set up the project, to collaborate with ARPA. From the technological point of view, there were a few innovations and important choices made in terms of function. The first of these was the use of packet-switching — not a new idea, but one rediscovered at the time — of routing the packets of information one at a time, and allowing each to follow its own path independently of the others. Second, the choice of a network architecture that provided machines at each node dedicated to the management of traffic, which did not keep track of the packets in transit. The original plan, however, involved the creation of a single network to control all the data that passed through it. If this original solution had been chosen, the Internet would surely not have been able to grow. The choice to distribute control over all the nodes not only had an impact on the architectural design of the network, but also on its social and political conception. No one could organize the network at their own behest, but anyone could contribute to its shape, at least in principle.

In 1967, the first nodes to be connected were identified. None of these nodes was military; they were all university research centers. The first node to be connected was the University of California, Los Angeles (UCLA) under the guidance of Leonard Kleinrock. The second was the Stanford Research Institute (SRI), controlled by Douglas Engelbart. The first message was sent on October 29, 1969. Later were added the nodes of the University of California, Santa Barbara and the University of Utah, to where Ivan Sutherland, who had directed the IPTO before Taylor, had moved. By December 5 of that year, the network consisted of these four nodes, and could be considered to be in operation. Since then, the network has not stopped growing and increasing its services with the cooperation of all those connected, without any limitation. Innovations came about through the precepts of learning and producing by using. The intergalactic community, as Licklider called it, met and worked collectively for the improvement of common tools, driven by a sense of belonging to a shared project. Each member contributed without any personal gain, apart from the reputation that he or she was building among their peers through the success of their contributions. No scientist among those who collaborated in the development of the ARPANET would ever file a patent to protect the innovations that spread throughout the network; the diffusion of their solutions was the prize that this group of pioneers most desired: the commercial aspect was totally absent.

A special mention is due to Douglas Engelbart, who was one of the designers not only of the network but also of a set of tools, which came together in the construction of personal computers. It was SRI, the center that he directed, which studied the techniques needed to build a friendlier interface for the computer. It was he who invented the idea of technology as human augmentation, experimenting with a way of interacting with the computer that did not conform to the idea of "simulation," the idea so dear to the promoters of artificial intelligence. For this reason, his research was funded both by Licklider, with whom he had a deep common understanding, and by Bob Taylor, first at NASA and then at IPTO. It was at the SRI that some of the features of graphical operating systems that are still our interface with the machine were invented. Engelbart invented the mouse, windows, icons and the idea of groupware. However, many of his colleagues grew tired of his management style, and followed Bob Taylor to CSL at PARC. It was here that proper graphical user interfaces were created and the *object oriented* programming that made them possible. In this legendary laboratory Taylor, with the expertise of part of a group from SRI, and its undisputed capacity for managing technology, in 1973 built the first prototype of the personal computer, the Alto. Although the Alto was not a commercial success, it was later an inspiration for both Apple and Microsoft.[4]

It is interesting to note that the idea of a computer suitable for personal use and the ARPANET grew out of the development of user-oriented technology and the idea of human augmentation, rather than from a desire to replace humans with self-sufficient machines. This concept that underlay both the personal computer and the ARPANET can be traced in the line of technological thinking from Bush and cybernetics to Licklider, Taylor and Engelbart, and is based on an interpretation of communication as interaction with the machine and with other human beings via properly programmed and organized mechanical devices. It was this common strategy in management and funding that produced the most remarkable achievements in terms of changing the role of technology in all sectors of society. As long as machines were shut up in a few computer science centers, they would never have the social impact that comes from the concept of the terminal or a personal computer accessible from the desk. Only the process, originally symbolic, of concentrating on the needs of the user, had the power to transcend von Neumann's model, in the design of more interactive devices that were symbiotic with the common user: a machine designed for humans. Thus even before the digital humanities, it was realized that the computer should be a humanistic machine.

2.2.2 The WWW: an authoring system in the heart of Europe
When Tim Berners-Lee presented the project for the World Wide Web (WWW) at CERN in Geneva, an institution that dealt in nuclear physics, he could not imagine how great an impact his creation would have not only on the Internet but on the whole world. In the first instance, his work was merely intended to facilitate the passage of information between researchers at CERN, to avoid duplication of efforts within the research center. It was supposed to rationalize resources and organize information to make it easily accessible. The first proposal, a memo submitted in March 1989, made no mention of the Web: it was called simply *Information Management: A Proposal*.[5] In an interview[6] granted on the 20 year anniversary of the proposal, Tim Berners-Lee, recalling the origin of his proposal, stated that CERN was the natural place to invent the Web, because of the need to connect professionals and scientists from all parts of the world, who were using the most diverse systems of hardware and software. The need for integration of all that wealth of information required some means of sharing — at this point, only via an "imaginary" tool — that would allow the information to be held in one place, while making it accessible on alternative platforms. This imaginary system had, however, very realistic features: it would have to combine the function of an authoring system with a mechanism for viewing the pages, as well as a strategy for connecting independently produced documents or their components through the use of links. Tim Berners-Lee said that the invention was easy because each instrument was already there, ready for use. The Internet was already there, an infrastructure designed without assumptions having been made about how it ought to be used. Its protocols already existed: TCP/IP (Transfer Control Protocol/Internet Protocol), a group of rules that regulated

the transmission and routing of data, DNS (Domain Name System) that worked to uniformly define the various resources of the Internet by associating each connected server with a unique number. The concept of hypertext was also already present. It had been invented by Vannevar Bush, then independently by Ted Nelson. Douglas Engelbart had also worked on something similar to the Web, limited only by the fact that at the start of the 1960s, the Internet was not yet invented.[7] The idea of the hypertext was simply adapted to the protocols of the Internet.

But a closer examination of the process of invention reveals a situation slightly different from that told by Berners-Lee. As often happens, the main players in the invention of a new technology do not have the clearest idea about what they have done. Above all, the idea that Bush had contributed to the idea of hypertext as an authoring system is problematic. Bush's proposed machine consisted of a personal workstation in which each user could connect to knowledge represented analogically in his Memex (cf. § 1.3).

It was instead Ted Nelson who invented hypertextuality both as a term and as a comment.[8] He had a BA in philosophy and a MA in sociology, and he realized "that, in order to write the essay that he wanted, a hypertextual authoring system that would connect the various parts of his work was needed." It was this that inspired him to launch project Xanadu, historically the first hypertext authoring system (cf. Ch. 3 for more information). It was also to Nelson that Tim Berners-Lee paid homage in the summer of 1992 when, while traveling in California, he made a trip to Sausalito, where Nelson was living on a house-boat. The meeting, as recounted in his book (Berners-Lee and Fischetti 1999, 70–72), was both cordial and a little strained. The fact that it happened at all shows the debt Berners-Lee felt he owed to that volcanic intellect who had given him the idea of hypertextual content. Recognizing this debt in his book, the inventor of the Web also acknowledged how his project depended on Nelson's humanistic background. From this perspective, the meeting between the two pioneers is witness to a constant osmosis between technology and the humanities, necessary to fertilize the fields of interdisciplinary study and make innovation possible. Landow likewise regards hypertext as a humanistic invention, as an embodiment of Barthes' ideal nonlinear text, or as a realization of the digital scholarly edition, where the reader follows from the main text to its variant readings and annotations (Landow 2006, 53–55).

At this point, rather than recount the subsequent history of the Web, which has already been the subject of dozens of books (Gillies and Cailliau 2000), it will suffice here to mention some key ideas that were crucial for its development.

Firstly, the original idea of the Web was that of an authoring system, in which the ability to edit as well as view pages was equally important. The design of this universal Web, in which everyone participated, has only come into being with the proliferation of systems such as wikis, blogs and social software that allow the user to browse pages and, at the same time interact with them editorially, often in a very simple and intuitive way. From this point of view the present development of the Web known as Web 2.0 (which will be discussed shortly) is simply, in some of its characteristics, a completion of the original project of information management from 1989. In all the interviews and lectures on the origins of the Web, its inventor always points out with great solemnity the absolutely central role of the community. And, as Berners-Lee underlines, in order to work like this, the community must feature the most diverse specialists, from scientists to sociologists, from jurists to biologists, etc. The community, therefore, is the same transdisciplinary community described above. One can see how this project is relevant for the digital humanist as a writer, curator and organizer of knowledge, its relationships and connections. It is evident from the original documents about the Web that the objective was to define a mechanism of an editorial nature that would favor content, and the ability to make it easily accessible in an organic fashion through associative pathways.

But while many of the properties of the Web were suggested by the existing infrastructure and ideas circulating at the time, it is also true that Berners-Lee demonstrated his own special skills in connecting the various components. The three elements that distinguish the Web were defined in his book:

> The art was to define the few basic, common rules of "protocol" that would allow one computer to talk to another, in such a way that when all computers everywhere did it, the system would thrive, not break down. For the Web, those elements were, in decreasing order of importance, universal resource identifiers (URIs), the Hypertext Transfer Protocol (HTTP) and the Hypertext Markup Language (HTML). (Berners-Lee and Fischetti 1999, 39)

He insisted, therefore, that the Web was simply a space where information could exist, be produced and connected. The realization of the project thus transformed the status of the most important element of its constituent parts. From the idea of the universal identification of the resources, there came a more prosaic "uniform resource locator"[9] (URL), a label that did not define a given resource in a universal way, but, more concretely, identified its location in a uniform and therefore unique manner. The next two stages of the development date from 1993. On 30 April of that year, CERN signed a document of just two short pages[10] agreeing with the legal department of the institution, in which they promised not to claim any royalties on the technological protocols developed by Tim Berners-Lee and his colleagues that were needed to run the Web. This was a historic step, because the Internet was beginning to take off at that time in the United States and the Web could use that infrastructure as an enabler for its development, provided that anyone could download programs and protocols that allowed machines to understand and connect hypertextual documents. To achieve this goal another small piece of the puzzle was needed: the creation of a browser, a hypertext-page viewer that was platform independent (i.e. independent from any operating system). Berners-Lee first sought European collaborators. He found a group who were working in the INRIA laboratory in France on a hypertext system written in SGML (standard generalized markup language) and asked them to develop software to display pages in HTML. The group, however, before beginning, sought assurances on the presence of European funds to finance the project. "They did not want to risk wasting time..." (Berners-Lee and Fischetti 1999, 49). Finally in February of 1993, the NCSA (National Center for Supercomputing Applications) at the University of Illinois made available a suitable browser, with all the most popular characteristics, easy to download and install and available for all platforms. It was Mosaic (the precursor to Netscape/Firefox), which was developed by a student, Marc Andreessen, and a staff member, Eric Bina. The Web now had almost everything it needed to grow and spread. It lacked only one last thing: governance. Thus, in 1994 Tim Berners-Lee agreed, after careful reflection, to move to MIT, at Princeton in the United States, to found an international institution to guide the Web, the *W3Consortium*, whose purpose was to "govern the World Wide Web to its full potential by developing protocols and guidelines that will ensure the long-term growth of the Web."[11] The consortium still unites institutions, countries and private companies operating on the Web and proposes and establishes rules for civil coexistence. Its objectives include the definition of standards accepted by the entire community to ensure its homogeneity.[12] It also focuses on the preservation of the heart of the Web as a public thing, a collective good, since there are no royalties to pay to the inventors. Tim Berners-Lee is still guiding the consortium, and retains all the authority it had when he established it with a few other collaborators. Even now that the WWW has matured and is autonomous, he continues to believe that it needs the coordination and integration that only an international, non-profit organization can provide. In his speech to the 20th anniversary conference,[13] he pointed out the primacy of democracy and consensus, and confirmed that the W3C was working to increase sharing and joint participation. In his speeches, he recognizes that the activity of the W3C is political, even when it deals with the definition of technical standards. He has stated quite clearly that "The Web, and everything which happens on it, rest on two things: technological protocols, and social conventions. The technological protocols, like HTTP and HTML, determine how computers interact. Social conventions, such as the incentive to make links to valuable resources, or the rules of engagement in a social networking website, are about how people like to, and are allowed to, interact" (Berners-Lee 2007, 7). The relevance of the social and human aspects of the Web cannot, in his view, be underestimated. For this reason, his projects involve, for example, the creation of institutions where scholars can meet to create "an intellectual foundation, educational atmosphere, and resource base to allow researchers to take the Web seriously as an object of scientific inquiry and engineering innovation" (ibid., 8). The Web Science project (http://webscience.org) starts from the premise that, for the future of the Web, it is necessary to adopt a "systemic" approach like that of biology, in which not only technological aspects are taken into account, but also effective strategies for understanding "social machines" in action (Hendler *et al.* 2008). In 2009, he further revised his position regarding the future of the Web and found that Web science was not enough: more than 80% of humanity, to which the Web is dedicated, is not connected; and many of the most popular Web-based tools are culturally focused on habits and customs of the average American, without regard to the rest of the world. To this end he is still advocating the creation of the www Foundation (http://webfoundation.org). Its purpose is to study the diversity of conditions in which the Web can be accessed: for example, cultural differences, (it does not make much sense for someone in an African village to interact with others using tools such as social networking, which are designed for young Westerners), technological differences (in developing countries access is, in most cases, via a mobile phone), and language differences.[14] If the *gap* that separates two thirds of the world's population from the Web cannot be bridged, all the effort in favor of humanity will have been wasted, and will end up bringing further discrimination. One aim of the digital humanist should therefore be to address all problems related to social and political traditions, and to help define a common ground for action.

2.3 Web 2.0 and beyond

As Tim Berners-Lee likes to say, the Web is not something that is completed: it is a constantly evolving tool that must be redesigned periodically to remain in the service of humanity. However, it is not always clear whether, and in what way, technology can remain in the service of humanity, rather than serve only one part of it, usually the richest, most efficient and most organized from a certain cognitive point of view, as Wiener had warned, about 60 years ago (cf. § 1.4). At this point it would be useful to temporarily suspend the discussion of history and to look at the present, and try to form hypotheses about what will happen in the near future.

"Web 2.0" is a successful label invented by Tim O'Reilly (2005) (cf. §§ 3.6–8). This was the name he gave to a series of conferences organized by his publishing house in 2004, and it was an unprecedented marketing success. Wherever one roams among Web applications, there is not one that cannot be understood in the framework of Web 2.0. Giving the Web a new title was intended to revive a sector affected by the collapse of the dot-com bubble at the beginning of the century, as a result of the excessive aspirations of Web services companies. So O'Reilly, using the well-known numbering system of major software releases that implies a simplification and resolution of problems, relaunched the businesses of the Web from a new perspective. The thread of his discourse, as traced by the Italian sociologist Carlo Formenti (2008, 248), describes a scenario that differs from the original as imagined by Berners-Lee. O'Reilly's Web seems to be a sort of caricature. The objectives of Web 2.0 were summarized in a few bullet-points: focus on the offering of services rather than software, consider the Web as an architecture of participation, develop strategies for the exploitation of collective intelligence, with particular regard to the possibilities of remixing services in new combinations. Questioned on the subject in 2006, the inventor of the Web said that Web 2.0 was a "piece of jargon," and that besides wikis, blogs and social networks (the focus of the Web 2.0 era) there were many other ways for people to collaborate and share content (Berners-Lee 2006). However, the instrumental nature of Web 2.0 and its commercial interests are fully transparent in O'Reilly's project. User-generated content is presented in different forms and organized to make it more attractive to the advertising market and other related business models. In summary, the common good, as represented by digital content, is put to the service of private business. This is a kind of capitalism 2.0, where whoever owns a platform for sharing information with friends, and can post videos and photos, will not have to worry about paying for content, and can sell advertising on the attention it generates, as well as widen the audience for investors. Online, in fact, you can buy and sell small amounts of advertising space, so that even small advertisers can have their own little place in the sun.

In an article published in *Scientific American* on the anniversary of the launch of the www, Tim Berners-Lee (2010) expressed his concern about the risks to which the project had been exposed in recent years. The lines of evolution considered most problematic are related to the development of the more commercial aspects of Web 2.0. He identified some critical areas for the universality of the service due to the tendency of some operators to take ownership of the content published by users on the platform (Facebook, LinkedIn, etc.) and to prevent them from being exported to other sites, even although they were produced by the service's users. Also at risk, in his analysis, is the place of open standards, which he believes are the only way to produce continuous innovation. The use of proprietary protocols such as that of iTunes to sell copyrighted music and videos is thus considered problematic. These proprietary tools not only lock up information and prevent the creation of links to protected data, but they also produce an even more threatening long-term effect: the interruption of investment in services that take advantage of open protocols. Indeed, if technologies become proprietary, they do not become standardized, and nobody wants to risk producing applications for proprietary protocols that are not widespread.

Another critical point raised by the inventor of the Web is the issue of Net neutrality. The original idea that each packet is equal before the network is set to crumble, not so much for the simple Internet connection, but certainly in mobile and broadband, where, as will be seen below, there exist situations of privilege related to the economic strength of various users. The loss of this principle would seriously harm the environment of the network as a place of equal opportunity for all users, if only from the theoretical point of view. In practice it is clear that, due to the topological structure of Internet and the practical facts of visibility, some content and some nodes are privileged above others (cf. Ch. 5). In short, the transparency of Internet access would be threatened not only by the mechanisms of network self-organization, but also by the will of some of its commercial players (see the Google-Verizon agreement, substantially accepted by the American Federal Communications Commission (FCC), [Stelter 2010]).

In conclusion, the phenomenon of Web 2.0 can be described critically as the progressive entrance into the field of Internet services of a new, and sophisticated class of brokers who earn money in their capacity as organizers of collective content. All of this takes place with the blessing of the content producers (i.e., *us*), whose personal details they are using. The era of "zero comments," as defined by the Net critic Geert

Lovink (2007) is fast approaching, when the writer on a network usually does not reach a position of visibility and recognition that would enable him or her to acquire the status of an "author." Web 2.0 is considered the realm of the amateur. There are almost no professionals and, when there are, they are treated as if they were not (i.e. they are not paid for their services) in a sterile celebration of the wisdom of crowds that simply becomes an excuse for a new generation of Web businesses that have no interest in developing ways to finance intellectual production. There is much here for the digital humanist to reflect upon. On the other hand, these new intermediaries have not yet removed the previous ones (the telecom companies, industrial producers of content, the large television networks and publishing groups) but have instead come alongside them, sometimes in conflict, but more often seeking agreements to establish some form of revenue sharing that would secure the interests of both sides.[15] Chapter 3 investigates the positive side of Web 2.0 as a set of tools for creating personal identity through writing and collective sharing. Another possible positive attribute of the phenomenon is the fact that through its instruments, it is now much easier to implement marketing strategies for individuals (the five minutes of fame that everybody can achieve after posting personal performances online) or for small groups who previously had to maintain visibility through traditional media. The first chapter of Clay Shirky's book (2008, 3–20), which tells how the services of Web 2.0 allowed a woman to recover her lost mobile phone, found by someone else on the seat of a taxi, by building a community who sided with her, is an exciting representation of the power of Web 2.0. It is beyond doubt that some of the tools of Web 2.0 can help people (famous, rich, or talented) to bounce off the traditional media, and then provide a springboard for a career in show business or other fields through the publication of suitable information. Indeed, it has been argued that the recent efflorescence of the digital humanities worldwide owes much to the development of Web 2.0 (Jones, 2014). On the other hand, the weak (the unknown, poor, and or less clever) will never be able to use these products to their advantage and their hopes will be easily crushed. And if success still passes through the traditional media, then what is so new about using the Web as a way of penetrating the agenda of the media circus?

An exception in the grand landscape of Web 2.0 can be made for the activities of social tagging or cataloging. These applications, such as Delicious, LibraryThing and Connotea, are services that allow users to establish collective descriptions, in the form of labels, or keywords (tags), for certain components of the Web, (e.g. pages, personal books, or digital resources).

All of these applications for the categorization and sharing of online content take the name of *folksonomy,* the contraction of the words "folk" and "taxonomy."[16] A successful example of a social filter, originating back in June 1998 (in very difficult times compared to Web 2.0), is the Open Directory Project (dmoz.org), which has become the Google directory. A special mention may be made of the use of the social Wiki technology to create a collectively-edited encyclopedia. The result of the project was wikipedia.org,[17] currently one of the most updated and reliable reference works, which has come to rival the most prestigious encyclopedias. There are also plenty of other examples of social software currently in use to access, organize and categorize Web resources.

However, there is another group of tools for archiving and retrieving information useful to the community. These allow the organization and sharing of the knowledge by each member of the community, provided there is some way to propagate trust and distrust (Guha *et al.* 2004). In social data-mining systems (cf. Ch. 4), which represent an advanced version of collaborative categorization, it is not even necessary for users to be explicitly involved in order to contribute. The system exploits the behavior of surfers to find information implicit in the description of their activities (Amento *et al.* 2003). An efficient and successful example of this strategy is the Amazon knowledge management system, the largest online retail shop. This site keeps track of customers' behaviors and uses the information to provide them with advice on any articles of interest, based on similar preferences by other users. This mechanism is particularly effective at producing suggestions consistent with the real interests of customers. The system also takes advantage of the sense of belonging to a virtual community based on the common interests of clients, who sometimes also actively contribute by writing reviews and offering assessments of books and other items for sale. These tools are more problematic because users do not know that they are "serving" the community, often for the profit of the mediators. In the case of Amazon, the aim is to offer those articles that fit as closely as possible to those desired by the user to maximize revenue. Categorization and collective filtering are a resource of the Web, which should be protected and defended from purely commercial interests, because they belong to the commonwealth of the Web.[18]

2.4 Leibniz's *Lingua Characteristica* and the Semantic Web

The machine built in the 1940s was the confluence of various ideas that came from far away. One can recognize in the debate about the intelligence of the machine the discussions of the 17th and 18th centuries between the rationalistic and empiricist approaches to knowledge and its creation. Could perhaps the machine solve all problems by calculating the solution, as Leibniz would have suggested? As mentioned above (cf. § 1.2), according to Gottfried Wilhelm Leibniz (1646–1716), one of the most prominent scientists, politicians and philosophers of his time, the best method to obtain certainty through knowledge was the creation of a system called *Characteristica Universalis,* which would allow all the people who used it to "calculate" the solution for all the scientific and philosophical problems. The system consisted of two modules; one was the *lingua characteristica,* a sort of universal language that permitted the expression in unequivocal form all the necessary and useful ideas in science or philosophy. The second module was called *calculus ratiocinator,* it was a method that allowed everybody to "deduce" via a calculus the correct conclusion for all possible premises that were expressed correctly using the universal language.

The use of this system, according to Leibniz, would avoid all possible mistakes and guarantee that all the conclusions were sound and true. The project was first envisaged when he was only twenty years old, but he kept on thinking of it for the rest of his life. In a letter to one of his many correspondents he declared:

> I am convinced more and more of the utility of this general science, and I see that very few people have understood its extent .... This characteristic consists of a certain script or language ... that perfectly represents the relationships between thoughts. The characters would be quite different from what has been imagined up to now. Because one has forgotten the principle that the characters of this script should serve invention and judgement as in algebra and arithmetic. This script will have great advantages; among others, there is one that seems particularly important to me. This is that it will be impossible to write, using these characters, chimerical notions .... An ignoramus will not be able to use it or, in striving to do so, he himself will become erudite. (Letter to Jean Galloys December 1678, translated from French in Davis 2000, 16)

In this letter, he showed the major advantages of the new "script" to his correspondent. First of all, it offered the guarantee that only the "real" concept could be represented in it, and secondly it forbade ignorant people to use it, or alternatively they would become savant in the effort to master the method. Such a language would also allow perfect correspondence of the relations among thoughts and would also help the user to have clear and correct thoughts, adequate both to the external world and to the true consequences of all axioms. All these results could be obtained by using a calculus similar to algebra or to arithmetic, which meant that once the notions were represented with the language symbols, it would be very easy to "calculate" the right conclusions. This project was only one on the long list of the dreams of reason by which human beings tried to control knowledge creation, by guaranteeing the correctness of every conclusion that was driven by correct assumptions. The birth of the computer and of the consequent "dream" of creating a mechanical intelligence could be considered just another scene of the same drama: the hope that truth and certainty were achievable exclusively by performing the right calculus. It will be shown shortly below that Semantic Web and AI share a lot of common beliefs.

On the other side of the epistemic range lies the work of David Hume (1711–1776), the philosopher who could be considered the champion of the empiricist tradition in the 18th century. He discussed knowledge and its characteristics in the first volume of *A Treatise of Human Nature*. Here, among other crucial questions, he stressed the central role of the association of ideas for knowledge creation, declaring:

> This uniting principle among ideas is not to be consider'd as
> an inseparabile connexion; for that has been already excluded

> from the imagination ... but we are only to regard it as a gentle force, which commonly prevails, and is the cause why, among other things, languages so nearly correspond to each other .... The qualities, from which this association arises ... are three viz. Resemblance, Contiguity in time or place, and Cause and Effect. (Hume 1978, 10–11)

The basic characteristics of the association of ideas are the contingency of the connections and the central role of imagination in the creation of the links between them. Both these principles are central in Bush's description of the operation of the mind as it accesses and connects thoughts together. The relationships between the association of ideas and logic are not necessarily rigorous. There are many different reasons why ideas unrelated to the logical inference between concepts cannot be connected. One of the consequences of the use of the association of ideas in the paradigm of the communication machine was the introduction of *hypertextuality* (see § 3.3) as a new writing method that allowed the association of different ideas to each other, without following a linear train of thought. The non-sequential writing model that was used in the human–computer interface research environment had a remarkable impact on the development of information technologies, whose consequences are still difficult to describe and foresee in detail.

According to Michael Mahoney (2005), the design of the computer was based on a confluence of contributions not only by different communities, but also from different philosophical approaches. Identifying these various influences and professional attitudes would be a challenging research project, but it is necessary to explain not only the history of computing but also the actual epistemological status of the various fields of information technology. The digital age did not come about as an achievement only of engineers, but represents the merging of many professional influences and models. Such an investigation may produce surprising results, and would in any case help in determining both the multi-faceted nature of the computing machine, as well as the opportunities, risks, threats and future directions of computer science.

In thinking about the development of the Web, it is important to recognize that different positions were being taken up that undoubtedly related to the general epistemological standpoints of rationalists and empiricists, who had different ideas about computers and the other devices that were being developed from the end of 1960s when the network was still in its infancy.

As described above (cf. § 2.2.2) Tim Berners-Lee's model of hypertextuality was inspired by Ted Nelson and Vannevar Bush, who believed that associations of (especially free-thinking) ideas, would lead to the creation of new knowledge, and enhance our mental capacity in building cognitive links between different scenarios. In spite of this influence, Tim Berners-Lee did not wed himself to the empiricist philosophy that lay behind it. In fact, at the same time as the Web was being launched, he admitted that he wanted to create another project, which was much more ambitious and philosophically quite different. This was the Semantic Web. The idea was, as he explained, to add a layer of logic to the Web (Berners-Lee 1998, Berners-Lee *et al.* 2001) that would identify every single online resource through a set of tags, or metadata, which would then allow the machines to "read and understand" the descriptive "semantic" layer of the Web. Under this scheme, the network would not be able to maintain its characteristic spontaneity in the publication of data and resources, but would have to be built as a database of structured information, organized according to specific types.

Today, this idea of categorization is completely different to the Web that Berners-Lee created. The idea of openness and serendipity is central to its working, founded on the free association of resources. In 2006, through the famous article *The Semantic Web revisited,* Berners-Lee and other authors reflected on how the future of the Web should look, and clarified their position. They admitted that "a Web of data" would be very different from the operation of the actual Web, first because of the presence of structured data, expressed in machine readable and context-sensitive formats, and second because intelligent agents could handle that data independently in a generalized way. They did, however, claim that the W3C and the Internet Engineering Task Force "has directed major efforts at specifying, developing, and deploying language for sharing meaning. These languages provide a foundation for semantic interoperability" (Berners-Lee *et al.* 2006, 97). These languages, such as RDF, SPARQL and OWL, like some languages used in artificial intelligence, can describe objects or events via properties and a function associated with each element (for example, if it was a number, an event, a film or a novel and so on). Each of these typological characteristics had in turn their own properties that had to be described in each instance of the type. To make them usable it was necessary to proceed with standards of composition that would allow the creation of ontologies suitable for any context in which you might want to provide a description. So this was just what Leibniz wanted: a representation of the world through a unique language, and an inference engine capable of extracting all the knowledge implied by each definition. The Semantic Web thus presents a precise vision of science and, more generally, of a system in which all knowledge can be described in a hierarchical manner starting from first principles, following a few simple rules of inference — a sort of a pyramid in which everything is organized, connected and perfectly consistent. However, that is not the way things always actually are. In the first place, the definition of standards for representing objects, events and ideas is not without its own problems. When a tag is chosen, using English of course, it represents a certain concept that in some way describes and therefore affects its content. From that moment on, the specification must be slavishly respected by all other actors in the process. The Semantic Web or Linked Data, as the project came to be known, can be considered as a system for data classification of online resources. At the start of any project of classification, it is assumed that it can guarantee some minimum standards, e.g. that: "there are consistent, unique classificatory principles in operation .... The categories are mutually exclusive .... The system is complete ...." However, one might also agree with the position that "No real-world working classification system that we have looked at meets these 'simple' requirements and we doubt that any ever would" (Bowker and

Leigh Star 2000, 10–11). If this is so, then it is very important that when designing a classification system one takes into account the arbitrary, culturally biased character in any organization. Tim Berners-Lee and his collaborators have strongly underlined the importance of openness in setting standards: "the construction of a standards body that's been able to promote, develop and deploy open standards" (Berners-Lee *et al.* 2006, 100). But one should not forget that they are also subject to the same cultural pressures as anyone else, and that such standards are also the fruit of specific historical and temporal situations, which perfectly reflect classification as a social and cultural act. A standard can be defined as "any set of agreed-upon rules for the production of objects. ... It has temporal reach as well, in that it persists over time. ... There is no natural law that the best standard shall win ... Standards have significant inertia and can be very difficult and expensive to change" (Bowker and Leigh Star 2000, 13–14). These considerations should not be seen as good reasons not to create standards, but they do underline the need to remain aware of social conditions and the collective and constituent dimension they represent. The impression of the authors, however, is that the process of the Semantic Web/Linked Data has been activated without reflecting on the cultural aspects of each binding and limiting decision that produced the classifications that were adopted. The interpretation offered by the team gathered around Tim Berners-Lee of the activities of categorization seems devoid of any problematic aspects. It appears to be objective and free from any reference to the cultural or political issues connected with the social group most strongly represented by the bodies responsible for establishing the agreed names for categories, known as types. "Areas such as epistemology and logic are to some extent operationalized in computers and computer infrastructures. Knowledge representation and ontology engineering are about trying to capture aspects of shared conceptualization" (Berners-Lee *et al.* 2006, 101). Here is where Leibniz's universalizing dream resurfaces, with the idea that it is possible to "operationalize" logic and epistemology without the impact of time, of the history of subjectivity that enables practice. It would be too complicated here to account for the close relationship between the epistemological project of artificial intelligence that emerged and developed in the 1960s to the 1980s and that of the Semantic Web/Linked Data. However, the connections are explicit:

> AI will be one of the contributing disciplines. AI has already given us functional and logic programming methods, ways to understand distributed systems pattern detection and data mining tools, approaches to inference, ontological engineering and knowledge representation. All of these are fundamental to pursuing a Web Science agenda and realizing the Semantic Web. (Berners-Lee *et al.* 2006, 101)

Although the universal dream of the Semantic Web is far from being achieved, one might recall that in Spanish, the same word is used for sleep and dream: *sueño*. In interpreting Francisco Goya's ambiguous phrase "*el sueño de la razón produce mon-*

struos" one could substitute *sleep* by *dream* to suggest that monsters are also produced when the dream of reason comes true.

☙

2.5 Social and cultural inequalities on the Web[19]

The preceding paragraphs attempted a critical assessment of Web 2.0, and argued that humanists should be aware of both its creative applications and its potentially manipulative agenda.[20] Before concluding this second chapter, however, it is time to take a broader view of the Internet, and to consider some of the issues that stand in the way of a more democratic and genuinely multicultural development of digital humanities. This may be termed the *Digital Humanities Divide*. It breaks down into five interconnected problems:
1. A digital divide may exist within or between countries, and possess different internal and external dimensions, e.g. geographical, sociological, economic, cultural, etc.;
2. the governance of digital infrastructures (from local institutions to worldwide organizations, like ICANN, IETF, IAB, W3C, etc.);
3. the development of standards (again, from large organizations like the Unicode consortium to more focused and smaller scholarly communities like TEI[21]);
4. the "code hegemony," i.e. the semiotic and technical dominance of multinational private groups, from Microsoft to Google, from Apple to FaceBook;
5. and finally, how all this relates to problems of governance structure, multicultural and linguistic issues, gender, and the representation of minorities (including alternative methodological views) within current DH organizations.

The main issues regarding point 4 will be discussed in Ch. 5, but the other problems will be dealt with here in order.

2.5.1 The digital divide
As described above, since Licklider and Taylor (1968) introduced the concept of the computer as a communication device, it was clear that, although the potentialities of the tool were tremendous, the central critical issue was how access could be controlled and distributed. Although in the US[22] and in the rest of the Western industrialized world, the access problem seems to be at least reasonably resolved, other criteria must still be taken into account in assessing the digital divide.[23] By the end of 2015, the Internet has an estimated 3.2 billion users: about 40.3% of the world's population, according to UN agency ITU,[24] and 40.7% according to the World Bank. In 2014, approximately 83.8% of people living in the 27 high-income OECD member states had access to the Internet.[25] In comparison, 50.2%, 38.3%, and 19.2% of the populations of Latin America and the Caribbean, the Middle East and North Africa, and Sub-Saharan Africa, respectively, had access to the Internet.[26] The data gathered by the World Bank (see Figure 2.1, overleaf) provides a snapshot of the situation by

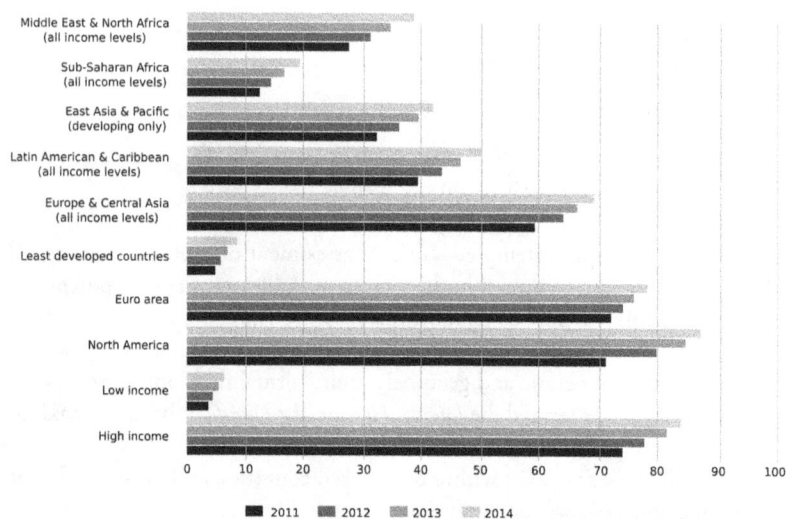

Figure 2.1. Internet users per 100 people in selected geographical areas (http://databank.worldbank.org/data/reports.aspx?source=2&Topic=9)

geographical region and income level, and shows the existence of a persistent and expected digital divide at the global level. However, as already mentioned, the digital divide cannot be reduced to a mere economic inequality between states, but is an internal problem within each individual state, based on age, education, type of government, ethnic group, etc., as is clear in the case of the US. The bitter conclusion of two experts like Witte and Mannon is that a technology "designed to be decentralized and democratic ends up maintaining and even expanding inequality" (2010, 127).

Data released in 2015, provided by the ITU, shows that Internet penetration in developing countries stands at 35%, but is only 10% for least developed countries. In developing countries 34.1% of households have Internet access, in contrast with 81.3% in developed countries and only 6.7% in least developed countries. As regards mobile broadband, the percentages are 86.7%, 39.1% and 12.1% respectively. In the case of Africa, with an estimated population in 2015 of 1.166 billion people (about 15% of the world's population), only 0.5% have a fixed broadband Internet subscription, although 17.4% have access to mobile broadband. However, the digital divide is not simply the result of geo-economical inequalities. According to Eurostat,[27] Europe seems to be a good example of issues relating to both access and exploitation of the Net. In the level of Net penetration, a clear dividing line can be drawn between Nordic countries, including Germany and France, on the one hand, and southern and eastern countries on the other (i.e. Italy, Spain, Greece, Portugal and Romania). Northern countries show a percentage of Internet usage similar if not superior to the US, while southern and some eastern European countries lag seriously behind. The EU Information Society database provides the relevant data.

Starting with Figure 2.2, there is a distinct gap between northern and southern European countries in the number of households with Internet access. In the second

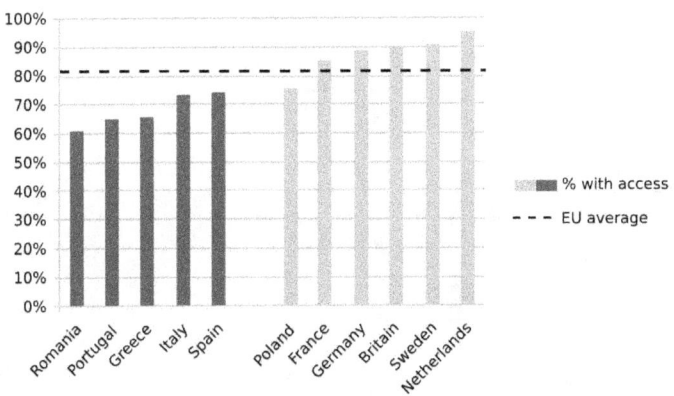

Figure 2.2. Percentage of households with Internet access (http://ec.europa.eu/eurostat/tgm/table.do?tab=table&init=1&language=en&pcode=tin00134 &plugin=1)

category "Individuals — Internet use in the last 12 months" (Figure 2.3 overleaf), Romania drops to 54%, Italy to 62%, and Poland to 67%, while almost all the other countries mentioned increase their percentages or remain the same. The values for weekly access are lower: Greece and Italy 59%, Portugal 61%, Spain 71%, France 80%, Germany 82%, Britain 89%, etc. The final interesting data worth mentioning are the interaction of citizens with their governments via the Internet, as shown in Figure 2.4 (overleaf).

Here the division between southern and northern Europe increases: all the old continent falls behind the EU average, while the northern countries pull ahead.

In conclusion, not only do the differences among European and OECD countries remain large, but age, income, education, family structure, and gender, in individual countries, all play a role in determining computer adoption, Internet access, and the level of digital literacy (Dobson and Willinsky 2009, 295–298). By "digital literacy" is meant not only basic computing skills, but also what Jeremy J. Shapiro and Shelley K. Hughes in 1996 called *information literacy*:

> A new liberal art that extends from knowing how to use computers and access information to critical reflection on the nature of information itself, its technical infrastructure, and its social, cultural and even philosophical context and impact — as essential to the mental framework of the educated information-age citizen as the trivium of basic liberal arts (grammar, logic and rhetoric) was to the educated person in medieval society. (Shapiro and Hughes 1996)

But in order to realize the ambitious curriculum of Shapiro and Hughes, the multiplicity and pitfalls of those digital divides must be addressed. According to Witte and Mannon "in a country in which some form of Internet access is becoming com-

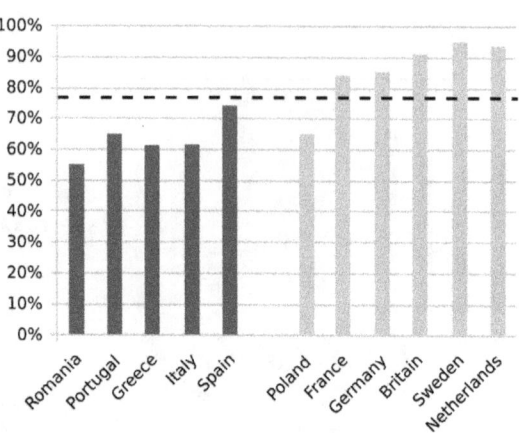

Figure 2.3. Percentage of people who accessed the Internet (http://data.worldbank.org/indicator/IT.NET.USER.P2)

mon, we also need to examine how individuals participate in and benefit from the Internet in distinct ways" (2010, 145). Their analysis seems particularly useful to the DH scenario. The authors combine three different perspectives to define the effects of inequality produced or introduced by the use of the Internet in US society. Only two of the three proposed views will be examined here: the Marxist and cultural perspectives. The former argues that inequality is not only preserved, but increased by the Internet habits of different social and cultural groups. The Marxist vision rests on the idea that in a capitalistic society the dominant class uses its assets to increase and maintain its advantage with regards to production:

> Recent theorists define skills as a kind of asset. In today's information-based economy, Internet access and use can be understood as an asset used to maintain class privilege and power. Second, capitalist relations of production can only be maintained if the inequalities upon which they rest are reproduced from one generation to the next. (Witte and Mannon 2010, 81)

Turning to the cultural perspective (inspired by the German sociologist Max Weber), and the extent to which education and income affect Internet literacy, Witte and Mannon underline that

> ... occupational prestige and family background channel individuals into differential lifestyles, which in turn mark culturally enduring social divides. One of those cultural markers is Internet use. ... Better-off and better-educated Americans left online footprints many time larger than the poorest and the least educated segments of American society. Moreover the online

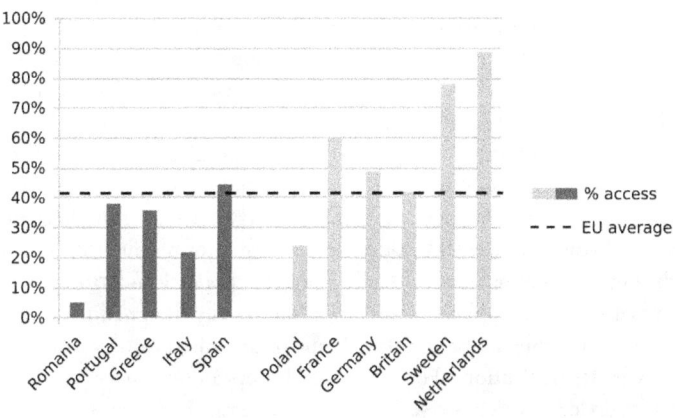

Figure 2.4. Internet use: interaction with public authorities
(http://ec.europa.eu/eurostat/tgm/table.do?tab=table&init=1&language=en&pcode=tin00105&plugin=1)

footprints for more privileged members of American society were more extensive, indicating online activities associated with consumption and production, as well as information and communication. (ibid., 113–114)

It can thus be concluded that the cultural and socio-economic characteristics of a population have a direct impact on the visibility, efficacy and pervasiveness of Internet use. If this perspective is accepted, some examples of the theoretical, cultural and political biases lying at the core of the nature and origins of the Internet may be given, since these have the potential to increase the asymmetry of the network and its players, including the world of DH.

2.5.2 *Geopolitics of the network*

The revelations of former NSA contractor Edward Snowden in 2013 have shown to a global audience, among other things, the *geographical* dimension of cyberspace, in other words that "where technology is located is as important as *what* it is" (Deibert 2015, 10). Governance and standards go hand in hand, and there is always a *symbolic* level implied in a *political* (let alone *technical*) decision: "classifications and standards are material, as well as symbolic," and their control "is a central, often underanalyzed feature of economic life" (Bowker and Leigh Star 2000, 15; 39). In their studies Bowker and Leigh Star show how the classification techniques (and the standards generated from them) have always played a fundamental economic and socio-cultural role. Current digital technologies standards appear to be the result of a double bias: the technical one and the cultural one (geopolitical). These two biases are entangled and it is almost impossible to discern where the technological choice begins and where the cultural prejudice ends. Although the socio-cultural origins of the Internet have often been discussed (cf. Ch. 3), the impact of these origins, and their symbolic and cultural implications are rarely taken into consideration. Thus, the vast cultural consequences of tacit choices made by a group of English-speaking pioneers often pass unnoticed. And once again, *where* we are tells often *what* we do. An example is the structure of the addressing code rules that use the 128 ASCII (American standard code for information interchange) to describe all the servers on the Internet. The same techno-cultural bias affects most of the services and instruments of the network, such as the domain name. In the last forty years it has not been possible to use accented vowels in the URL address, and in spite of recent IETF and ICANN efforts[28] the new internationalizing domain names in applications (IDNA) system can only be implemented in applications that are specifically designed for it, and it is rarely used in Latin alphabet-based URLs. Some of the initial top-level domains can be used only by US institutions. For example, a European university cannot use the top-level domain .edu, which is reserved for US academic institutions.[29] The domain .eu was only added in 2006, and applications for top-level domains using characters outside ISO-Latin were only recently invited (requests were open from 12 January to 12 April 2012). ICANN (the Internet Corporation for Assigned Names and Numbers) finally allowed the opening up of top level domains to Arabic or Chinese characters, included in Unicode, but every decision has so far rested in the hands of an organization under the clear control of Western industries and governments (Hill 2015). The request procedure is very complicated, many of the rules are described only in English, the cost of an application for a top-level domain is $185,000, and the application does not guarantee that it will be granted. The applying institution needs to show a clear technical and financial capability that must be certified at the discretion of ICANN itself. The problem is that ICANN, a "not-for-profit public-benefit" corporation, has always taken decisions of global relevance, but still lacks a clear institutional and multi-stakeholder accountability.[30] According to Richard Hill, president of the Association for Proper Internet Governance and former ITU senior officer, "for the most part the narratives used to defend the current governance arrangements are about maintaining the geo-political and geo-economic dominance of the present incumbents, that is, of the US and its powerful private companies" (Hill 2015, 35).[31]

The Domain Name System (DNS), one of the technical backbones of the network, is another example of the "centralized hierarchy" of the Internet. In March 2014, in the wake of Edward Snowden's revelations, the United States agreed to relinquish control of the DNS root zone. But even now, the system of root name servers, according to the IANA Web site, is still operated by thirteen organizations: ten US-based institutions or private companies (led by VeriSign), two European entities, and one Japanese company. As noticed by Laura DeNardis, "there is a physical geography of the Internet's architecture as well as a virtual one", and "root servers are the gateway to the DNS so operating these servers is a critical task involving great responsibilities in both logical and physical management" (DeNardis 2014: 50). Despite this change, the geopolitical set-up of the DNS root zone is still based on a network governance paradigm of the "West and the rest". Many of the Internet standards were set at the beginning of its history and were obviously conceived by, and made for conformance with the small community involved at the time. The character set standard was clearly designed from a legitimate mono-cultural point of view, but today we are still dependent on those choices as an international and multicultural community. The data for Internet access[32] reveals that users in the Western world (Europe and the US) represent only 34% of the total, while Asian users represent 45%. However, as suggested by Tim Berners-Lee in the presentation of his Web Foundation, "creation of locally-relevant content on the Web is impeded in many places, not by lack of the Internet, but by a lack of knowledge."[33] Figures suggest that these differences are due not only to a lack of skill and competence of people in developing countries, but also to a specific cultural orientation of contents and opportunities. Although it is true that Internet adoption in Africa and Middle East is not comparable to that of developed countries,[34] it has been widely acknowledged that the 2011 Arab spring benefited from the use of social media such as Twitter, particularly in Tunisia (Howard and Hussain 2011; Bettaïeb 2011; Meddeb 2011), and Facebook, particularly in Egypt (Ghonim 2012). It is not possible here to discuss the opposing views of cyber-utopians and cyber-sceptics about the so-called "Facebook revolution in the Middle East,"[35] however it is clear that the role of social networking was a crucial element (although not the only cause) in organizing and informing people about what was going on in the streets, even if the same tools were also used by antidemocratic political powers to trace and repress their opponents.[36] Social networks certainly cannot be ignored after what happened in 2011 in North Africa or in 2013 in Turkey (Durdağ 2015), but what should be kept in mind is that the role of technology is always mediated by the people and their capabilities to transform the potentialities of the tool (Etling, Faris and Palfrey 2010). It is still a matter of skill to exploit the medium for revolutionary purposes, not a property of the technology itself.

2.5.3 The value of cultural and linguistic diversity
Although today Chinese and Spanish are increasingly used on the Web,[37] access and control of the Internet are firmly in the hands of select Western (and mainly anglophone) authorities. Discussions on identity, ethnicity, gender, etc. on the Internet abound (Siapera 2010, 183–197), but the mix of technical, methodological and linguistic biases of Internet resources and tools defy current analyses. José Antonio Millán is a linguist, net analyst and Spanish blogger who left university twenty years ago to dedicate himself entirely to the study of digital textuality and digital media. His blog "Libros y bitios" (http://jamillan.com/librosybitios) is known as one of the best online resources in the Hispanic DH world. Millán in 2001 published an important book, which is still a valuable source of information, and at the same time an effective manifesto of the "digital margins" of the world.[38] His work helps to substantiate with researched examples the geopolitical scenario outlined above, by closely analyzing the production and spread of all Internet technologies that concern language. According to Millán, there are many products and services which derive from these technologies, all of them of strategic value, and all in "alien" hands: operating systems, search engines, intelligent agents, distance learning, electronic commerce, the copyright industry, etc., Each of these areas presupposes or stimulates specific

research sectors. These range from automatic translators to syntactic parsers, from terminological databases to software for speech recognition, etc. Even though the estimated burden of linguistic technology for each product and service analyzed is low (see Table 2.1), the result is astonishing: for an audience of 61 million Spanish speakers, the annual business turnover was estimated in 2001 to be something like 91 million Euros (Millán 2001, 148–149).

Product/ service	Weight in linguistic technology
Electronic Commerce	0.01
Copyright industry	0.01
Tourist information services	0.03
Operating Systems	0.05
Distance Education	0.07
Word processing	0.10
Teaching material for Spanish as SL	0.10
Information services (non-touristic)	0.10
Editorial platforms	0.20
Search engines	0.30
Information managers	0.50
Intelligent agents	0.80
Teaching software	0.80–0.90
Terminology assistant	0.90
Translation software	0.90

Table 2.1. Linguistic technologies and products: weight per product or service. In this list the author omits the technology of voice recognition, which is dealt with in Ch. 9 (Millán 2001, 134)

The author concludes by saying: "while networks are the highways of digital goods and service flows, technologies linked to the user's language are their compulsory tolls" (Millán 2001, 140). Thus, at the roots of economic, social, political primacy one does not find "just" technology, but rather the mix of copyrighted algorithms and protocols that manipulate and control languages. Presiding over both natural and artificial codes has become a profitable business: not investing in this sector presently means being forced to pay to be able to use one's own language. Unfortunately, the problem of cultural primacy overflows linguistic boundaries: the pervasiveness of cultural representations and metaphors belonging to the Anglo-American context in all technological appliances and computing tools is a well-known tendency since at least the 1960s. Many familiar elements borrowed from everyday US and Western life were exported to the computer world. Beyond programming languages or algorithms, where deep semiotic and cultural biases are intrinsically evident (An-

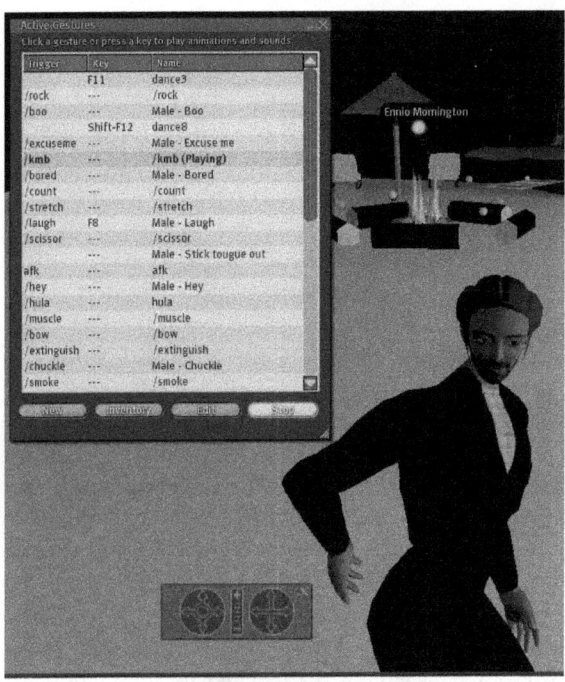

Figure 2.5. "Kiss my butt" gesture in Second Life

dersen 1997; Chun 2011; Kittler 2008), ideologies extend to the "superficial" (and not less subtle) world of icons and graphical interfaces (Selfe and Selfe 1994; Ford and Kotzé 2005; Galloway 2012). One example is the manila folder, a ubiquitous object used in all American offices that owes its name to a fiber (manila hemp) commonly used in the Philippines for making ropes, paper products and coarse fabrics. An object coming from a removed colonial past suddenly, thanks to the Xerox Star desktop,[39] became later the metaphor for any computing content: a symbol that conceals the bureaucratic origins of the desktop computer and its unique ties to the cultural imagery of the average US customer. Examples of symbolic digital colonization are Second Life facial expressions and user-playable animations, where we can find body language gestures which can be only deciphered by expert American native speaker.[40] Take for example the famous "kiss my butt" animation (see Figure 2.5), where both the verbal expression and the body posture would suggest (at best) deceptive or vaguely alluring meanings to most of Latino or Mediterranean cultures.

This list of aggressive US iconic settlements in the global world could continue, but a more important example of representational bias that directly affects the work of humanists, is the important work carried out by the Unicode consortium.

First, two words about the organization itself. Unicode is a non-profit organization "devoted to developing, maintaining, and promoting software internationalization standards and data, particularly the Unicode Standard, which specifies the representation of text in all modern software products and standards."[41] The Board

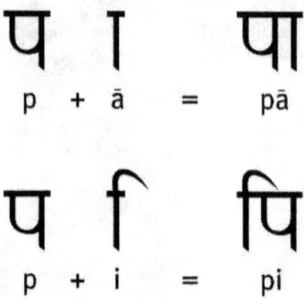

Figure 2.6. Two graphames of Devanagari Indic script as shown in Perri 2009, 735

of Directors of Unicode is currently made up of people from Intel, Google, Microsoft, Apple, IBM, OCLC, and IMS Health.[42] Not very different is the make-up of the Executive Officers (the president is a Google engineer since 2006). Apart from one or two exceptions, universities, public or research institutions are not represented. As a matter of fact, Unicode is an industrial standard made and controlled by industry. And claims about the geopolitical neutrality or impartiality of this organization appear to be at least questionable.[43] Localization still matters, and the researchers of the Language Observatory Project (http://www.language-observatory.org/) noted that, although Unicode is recognized as a step forward for multilingualism, "many problems in language processing remain":

> The Mongolian language, for example, is written either in Cyrillic script or in its own historical and traditional script, for which at least eight different codes and fonts have been identified. No standardisation of typed fonts exists, causing inconsistency, even textual mistranslation, from one computer to another. As a result, some Mongolian web pages are made up of image files, which take much longer to load. Indian web pages face the same challenge. On Indian newspaper sites proprietary fonts for Hindi scripts are often used and some sites provide their news with image files. These technological limitations prevent information from being interchangeable, and lead to a digital language divide. (Mikami and Kodama 2012, 122–123)

The Italian linguist and anthropologist Antonio Perri has offered convincing examples of the bias inherent in the Unicode system for representing characters, showing the concrete risks of oversimplification and erasure of the "phenomenological richness of human writing practices" (Perri 2009, 747). Perri analyzed a number of encoding solutions proposed by the Unicode consortium for different problems relating to Indian sub-continental scripts, to Chinese, Arabic and Hangul (Korean writing). In all these cases, in addition to being excessively dependent on visualization software, which raises problems of portability, he showed that the Unicode

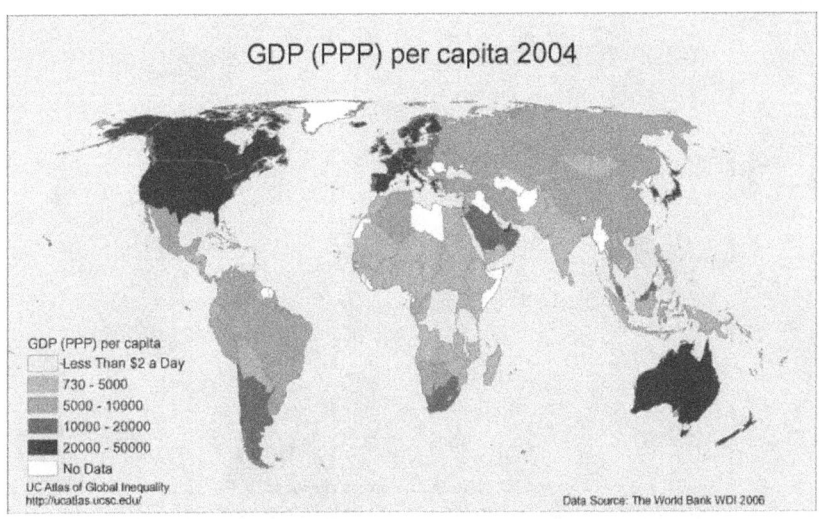

Figure 2.7. World Gross Domestic Product in 2004. (http://ucatlas.ucsc.edu/)

solutions were based on a "hypertypographic" concept of writing, i.e. Western writing embodied in its printed form and logical sequencing. By neglecting the visual features of many writing systems this view overlooks their important functional aspects. Perri gives a striking example of this bias when discussing Unicode treatment of ligatures and the position of vowel characters in the Devanagari Indic script.[44] Often in Indian systems aspects of a graphic nature prevail over the reading order of the graphemes.[45] As showed in Figure 2.6, in the second glyph the order pronunciation/graphic sequence is reversed. Unicode experts, however, argue that Indic scripts are represented in its system according to a "logical scheme" that ignores "typographic" details.[46] Perri concludes:

> But why on earth should the order of characters corresponding to the phonetic segment be considered logical by an Indian literate? Who says that the linearity of Saussure's alphabetic signifier should play a role in his writing practices? ... It is therefore all too evident that the alphabetic filter, the rendering software and the automatic process of normalization of Indic scripts are the result of a choice that reflects the need for structural uniformity as opposed to the *emic* cultural practices of the real user. (Perri 2009, 736; our transl.)

One last example is a comparative experiment based on two graphic representations. The first image (Figure 2.7, overleaf) is a map of world income inequalities from the University of California Atlas of Global Inequality database. The second world map (Figure 2.8, overleaf), a Wikipedia image based on Ethnologue.com sources, repre-

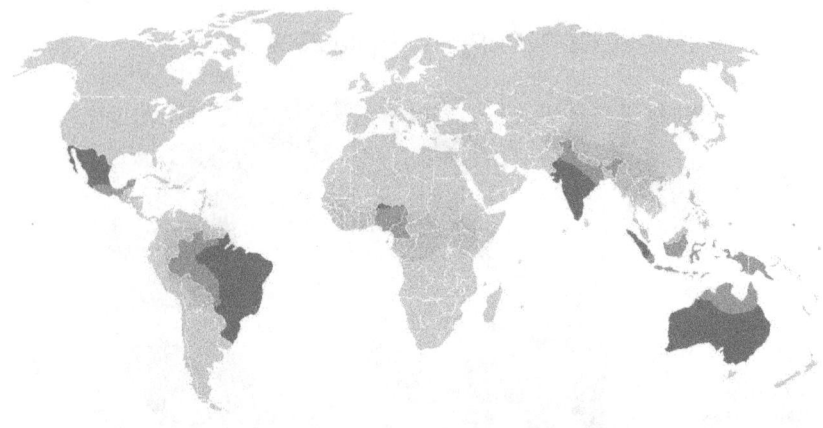

Figure 2.8. Linguistic diversity in the world
(http://en.wikipedia.org/wiki/Linguistic_diversity#Linguistic_diversity)

sents linguistic diversity in the world: in red are shown the 8 megadiverse countries that together represent more than 50% of the world's languages, and in blue, areas of great diversity. By overlaying these two maps, one can notice that — excluding Australia, where the linguistic diversity is in any case that of the aboriginal inhabitants before settlement by the British in the 18th century[47] — the lower income countries of the first map in many cases fit the areas of greater linguistic diversity. Over the past decade the idea began to emerge that linguistic diversity is inextricably linked to biodiversity (Maffi 2001). The Index of Biocultural Diversity adopted in 2004 by a group of interdisciplinary scholars, who later would found the international NGO terralingua.org, shows that three areas of the world "emerge as 'core areas' of exceptionally high biocultural diversity: the Amazon Basin, Central Africa and Indomalaysia/Melanesia" (Maffi 2010: 6).

> Instead, a lowering of both cultural and biological diversity has been found to correlate with the development of complex, stratified and densely populated societies and of far-reaching economic powers. ... From ancient empires to today's globalized economy, these complex social systems have spread and expanded well beyond the confines of local ecosystems, exploiting and draining natural resources on a large scale and imposing cultural assimilation and the homogenization of cultural diversity. (Maffi 2010, 8)

In other words: cultural and biological richness does not necessarily match material wealth.[48]

Unsurprisingly, the world income map also overlaps with the "Quantifying Digital Humanities" infographics flatland produced by the UCL Centre for Digital

Humanities.[49] Although that survey was generated from spontaneous inputs from anglophone scholars, and not from a systematic research and data collection, it is interesting to note how powerful is the tendency of this community to self-represent itself as The Digital Humanities world, without any kind of geographical, linguistic or cultural restriction. As observed by Chan (2014), these kinds of universalizations are very common in the West.[50] As already pointed out, regions and countries with ubiquitous Internet access tend to think of the rest of the world as having similar coverage, and this "first world" outlook contributes to the reassurance of representing the entire globe.

The issue of the over-representation of anglophone institutions and people in the DH international organizations has been discussed in Fiormonte 2012 and Dacos 2013 (cf. Conclusions). Most of the "international" organizations are monolingual, and the rhetorical structure of their websites and official documents does not leave space for anything except the "inner" Anglo-American rhetoric and academic narrative (Canagarajah 2002, 109–27). All this seems to confirm Millán's hypothesis of the strict relation between economic hegemony, technological concentration and linguistic impoverishment, and raises the as yet untackled question of the internal and external *digital humanities divide* in Western countries.

Although confirmed by recent studies (Amano *et al.* 2014), the comparison between the two maps proposed here does not intend to suggest easy conclusions. However, it is legitimate to hold that in some of the poorest areas of the world, in the deserts, jungles, and mountains at the margins of our globalized society, a handful of communities continue to cultivate the last resource still entirely in their own hands: biological and cultural diversity. The significance of language diversity and of its present loss in a digital world cannot be underestimated (Harrison 2010). Digital humanists cannot ignore this multiform dimension if they want to build inclusive digital resources and tools, and become more conscious about their role as knowledge gatekeepers and producers.

2.6 The challenge of open knowledge

The issues of inclusivity, access and diversity call for possible solutions. Is the variegated galaxy of *open knowledge* a good candidate for addressing some of those problems? As we will see, many DH projects embraced it successfully, and from many points of view the idea of knowledge as commons (Hess and Ostrom 2007) can be a powerful antidote to some of the negative effects of globalization. But let's start from the beginning of the practice, as abstract definitions will not help here.

In 2006 Ilaria Capua, an Italian veterinarian and researcher, refused to share her research about the H5N1 avian influenza virus with a private database in Los Alamos (NM). Instead, she decided to release her findings to the public domain, and later helped to launch the database *Global Initiative on Sharing Avian Influenza*

Data (GISAID) (Armstrong Moore 2009). Her decision attracted the attention of the world's media, and in 2008 she was included among the five "Revolutionary Minds" by the American magazine Seed. Today she is considered one of the leaders of the open science movement, based on the idea that all scientific data relevant to society (including but not limited to public health) should be openly accessible. This chapter will sketch a brief overview of the influence of this movement on the digital humanities, and show how some aspects of the open science/open data remain controversial. One problem is that there are many overlaps between open knowledge, open data and open science, and sometimes it is hard to separate the genuine impulse of the scientific community to share its knowledge from the commercial interests of companies that have embraced the open content model.

Web 2.0 may be a problematic term, but many of its positive aspects can still be welcomed, as agreed even by the once skeptical Tim Berners-Lee (cf. § 2.4). Previously, only documents were shared online. Now it is also possible to share other forms of data. The open data movement proposes making data from all areas, from chemistry to genetics, from medical trials to physics experiments, from grammar to geography available to all, open and non-proprietary.[51] There are already some shared databanks, and others are being developed.[52] The project's aim is to produce quality content socially, to make it freely available to all, and to allow the data to be updated and cross-checked with other archives using the same architecture.[53] As mentioned earlier (cf. § 2.4), Linked Data is the new brand name for the Semantic Web, but it also reduces the idea to a form that is easier to implement. It is "a set of best practices for publishing and connecting structured data on the Web" (Bizer, Heath and Berners-Lee 2009, 1). While the Semantic Web proposed the addition of a semantic layer to make the Web "readable or understandable" by machines, Linked Data only considers data on the Web that is already in structured form. However, this change in perspective has not altered the basic principle, which is to continue to increase the amount of data, to label it consistently with "meaning," and then to find ways to make it interoperable. That Linked Data is a more practical and limited version of the Semantic Web can be seen from the official declarations of the project's working group:

> The first step is putting data on the Web in a form that machines can naturally understand, or converting it to that form. This creates what I call a Semantic Web — a Web of data that can be processed directly or indirectly by machines. Therefore, while the Semantic Web, or Web of Data, is the goal or the end result of this process, Linked Data provides the means to reach that goal. By publishing Linked Data, numerous individuals and groups have contributed to the building of a Web of Data, which can lower the barrier to reuse, integration and application of data from multiple, distributed and heterogeneous sources. Over time, with Linked Data as a foundation, some of the more sophisticated proposals associated with the Semantic Web

vision, such as intelligent agents, may become a reality. (Bizer, Heath and Berners-Lee 2009, 17)

The bar thus appears to have been lowered. There is no more talk about adding a layer of logic to the entire Web, but only of making structured data already on the network interoperable, or working on the development of an appropriate vocabulary for schemas, or query tools. All this is evidently based on good will and the ability to build reliable networks for shared data (Bizer, Heath and Berners-Lee 2009, 19–20).

The availability of so much data on the Web, including personal information made available by social network users, has led to the development of other methods of data processing—for example, the analysis of user sentiment in relation to a certain brand or idea. These analyses, which are becoming less common, because of simpler tools such as the "like" button on Facebook or the +1 of Google+, make use of sophisticated linguistic computational analysis to evaluate the emotional orientation of the public to a new product or idea (Wilson *et al.* 2009). The management of user data derived from clickstream analysis, from active network participation, from personal information supplied about religious beliefs, political or sexual inclinations, literary and personal tastes, makes up the rich mine of Web 2.0 data. It can be exploited in various ways, but always with surprising accuracy by the biggest data collectors, who are also the most successful service providers. This data-mining business is a key activity of the social dimension of the Web, and one of the most interesting and risky novelties of business in the Web 2.0 world.

2.6.1 Big Data[54]

A new hype surrounds the "Big Data" phenomenon. According to some scholars (Barabási 2010; Mayer-Schönberger and Cukier 2013) access to such a huge amount of information will revolutionize the way scientific results are obtained, particularly in the field of social sciences and humanities. This promise is very attractive to media companies that store all the data, but alarming for users, whose freedom is threatened, not only in terms of privacy. In fact, the data mining techniques used to manage and interpret information derived from the digital footprints of users are based largely on the same techniques adopted to analyze corpora or to interpret texts by literary scholars in the digital humanities.[55] So digital scholars face a dilemma: do they want to participate in the epistemologically and ethically problematic activities related to the use of Big Data? This is still an open question with no easy answer.

The collected digital traces left by almost any human activity, such as organizing a trip abroad, or starting a love affair, will allow researchers to manage not only statistical data on a population, but people's real lives. According to other scholars (Boyd 2010, Chun 2011, Gitelman 2013), however, the excitement around the change of perspective of human sciences due to the manipulation of Big Data is completely overestimated. According to Boyd and Crawford "Big Data offers the humanistic disciplines a new way to claim the status of quantitative science and objective method. It makes many more social spaces quantifiable. In reality, working with Big Data is still subjective, and what it quantifies does not necessarily have a closer claim on objective truth — particularly when considering messages from social media sites" (Boyd and Crawford 2012, 667). So it is imperative for digital humanists to maintain their critical attitude towards those quantification techniques that appear to give their disciplines the appearance of objectivity. From the epistemological point of view, humanistic studies offer a privileged perspective to assess the awareness that "raw data" does not exist (Gitelman 2013). The reasons for the critical approach to big data are complex and various. One argument relates to the incompleteness and dirtiness of the data that form the basis of data-mining procedures. People are unaware that they are recording data on themselves when they participate in social networks, and, as a result, they may record false or incomplete information about themselves or their friends, which are then stored in the database and considered true. One of the reasons for this, according to Wendy Chun (2011, 93–94) is that people are always inconsistent in describing themselves, and any self-produced data design can only provide a misleading understanding of the subject and an inadequate prediction of his/her future preferences and actions. Others, like Jaron Lanier (2013), critique our current digital economy, making a case that links rising income inequality to the spread of what he calls "Siren Servers," or data-gathering companies:

> ... progress is never free of politics ... new technological syntheses that will solve the great challenges are less likely to come from garages than from collaboration by many people over giant computer networks. It is the politics and the economics of these networks that will determine how new capabilities translate into benefits for ordinary people. (Lanier 2013, 17)

In fact, Big Data raises a lot of critical issues relating to control and access to private information, as is clearly shown by the data protection saga unleashed by the publication of documents by whistle-blower Edward Snowden and the New York Times, Guardian and other media during the summer of 2013. The details of the multi-million dollar programs managed by NSA (National Security Agency) and its British equivalent GCHQ (Government Communications Headquarters) show that PRISM and other tools are used with the (overt or covert) help of the "big four" (Hotmail/Microsoft, Google, Yahoo! and Facebook). From email to texts, from mobile traffic to social network data, everything is collected and processed to prevent the potential risk of terroristic activities. The approach of English speaking intelligence agencies is based on the theory that it is better to know everything, than to miss information that may be relevant to a potential enemy action. The normal balance between the right to privacy and the right of executive power to protect society against violence has been completely subverted, given both the commonly misperceived level of risk in social networks, and the power of new brute-force decryption technologies to decipher formerly secret information. The opportunities offered by technology, together with the social perception of risks, has already changed the boundary between the permitted and illicit public exercise of power.

All these new applications of Big Data and intensive information extraction techniques raise enormous social and political issues that should be addressed by digital humanities scholars, considering that they are among the few experts who possess both a humanistic and a technological background.[56] Digital humanities skills provide a unique opportunity to assess the ethical and social constraints placed on information technologies by a society that aims to maintain a consistent and plausible sense to the term "democracy" (cf. §§ 5.5, 5.6 and 5.9).

It is hard to accept a tool for understanding social behavior that forces us to accept that "the current ecosystem around Big Data creates a new kind of digital divide: the Big Data rich and the Big Data poor. Some company researchers have even gone so far as to suggest that academics should not bother studying social media data sets" (Boyd and Crawford 2012, 674). Big Data sets out to change the rules of what was once the reproducibility of experimental results (regarded as one of the foundations of the scientific method) and the accessibility of data, which would provide the controls needed to validate those results. If the data in question are controlled by a few companies who do not need to share it, or who can decide who to share it with, then an aristocracy of data-owners will be able to define the rules and hypotheses of social knowledge beyond the scrutiny of any external authority. According to Kristene Unsworth, what is needed is an "Ethics of Algorithms" to ensure their neutrality with respect to responsible data use and interpretation.[57] As suggested by Wendy Chun, Big Data represents a challenge for digital humanists "not because they are inherently practical, but rather because they can take on the large questions raised by it, such as: given that almost any correlation can be found, what is the relationship between correlation and causality? Between what's empirically observable and what's true?" (Chun and Rhody 2014, 21). In his work Databasing the world, Geoffrey Bowker underlines that "the most powerful technology ... in our control of the world and each other over the past two hundred years has been the development of the database" (Bowker 2005, 108). Computers and networks have shaped the knowledge and standards of database design. But the greater the need to put together data from different fields and contexts, the greater the need to find an agreement, or a standard for the relevant form of that data. "The point is that there is no such a thing as pure data" (Bowker 2005, 116). With Big Data the problem is no different, although the discussion shifts to the different methods needed to process such a large amount of data. It is always necessary to find and define a context, a standard, and an interpretation hypothesis that makes sense of the data. According to Culturomics[58] and distant reading of books, the fact that we have millions of books that can be read together changes the perspective and the possibilities for interpretation. For example, Ngrams (an application that can be used to find the statistical frequency of terms within the corpus of Google Books), which is one of the tools used within the Culturomics project,[59] enables the distant reading of many books arranged in historical or linguistic categories. Although it seems necessary to keep a critical eye on this project, the applications proposed by researchers in the field of Culturomics are new and promising.

2.6.2 Open data and the humanities

Open data is, according to the Open Knowledge Foundation,[60] "data that can be freely used, reused and distributed by anyone." But for this to work in the digital humanities there must be freely available tools to operate on that data in typically used formats.

One of these is TaPoR,[61] an open-source set of text-analysis services, which can be used either online or in-house. Another suite of tools for reading and analyzing texts is Voyant,[62] which can be used on any corpus of textual data to obtain a quick summary of the rhetorical characteristics of the corpus, including word-frequencies or word-trends within a text. The interesting perspective adopted by this tool-suite is that it focuses on representing texts not only at their intrinsic textual level, but also at the metalevel. One of its objectives is to study how computer-assisted text analysis works.

But because the format of data is often dictated by the needs of the research that gave rise to it, even open data is not always as open in practice as it is supposed to be. One example is the so-called e-Government 2.0 delivery model, which represents the results of transparency and collaboration by public institutions and governments with its citizens. The US federal administration in 2009 launched a portal for participation in the life of Congress, where it became possible to leave comments and discussion on the laws under debate (http://www.regulations.gov). In the summer of 2009 the then prime minister of the United Kingdom, Gordon Brown, asked Tim Berners-Lee to collaborate on the creation of an instrument to increase the transparency of government activities, and facilitate communication with its citizens.[63] However, one may still question whether such public data is truly open. Although software can be developed to understand it, only citizens with a technical education will be able to use the programs needed to analyze the data and obtain suitable results. In spite of the transparency rhetoric, many open government initiatives thus still risk transforming public information archives into private data mining exercises (Birchall 2011a, 2011b, 2014).

2.6.3 Open access

The open data movement is also connected with open access. According to one of its main exponents, Peter Suber, "Open-access (OA) literature is digital, online, free of charge, and free of most copyright and licensing restrictions" (Suber 2007). The basic idea is that science and knowledge should be accessible to everyone without restriction and, therefore, it is necessary to break down barriers such as the cost of printing. The cost of scientific journals since the 1980s has increased by at least four times the rate of inflation, increasing the strain on university libraries, which has led to a reduction in the budget for monographs (Van Orsdel and Born 2009; Pochoda 2013).

The main argument in favor of open access for scientific articles is the fact that much of the research is publicly financed, with the result that the institution pays twice: once to finance the delivery of results and again to fund libraries to buy the journals in which the results are published.[64] Since the 2003 Berlin Declaration on Open Access to Knowledge in the Sciences and Humanities,[65] many things have changed. Some publicly funded institutions in the US and abroad are now adopting a policy of requesting that studies published with their contributions must be available in open-access journals and repositories.[66] In times of economic crisis, it is natural that public research institutions will lose some of their financing. The reduction in funds available to libraries, along with the indiscriminate increase in the costs of journals, is making open access an almost obligatory choice,[67] though also fairer and more democratic. Even paywalled journals are gradually changing their strategies. Some are now maintaining their own repositories of preprints that authors have allowed to be open access. Others have started to convert themselves into open access journals. It is not at all the case that open access journals should side-step the peer-review process, or host any kind or quality of content. Nor is it the case that an open access journal cannot be an efficient business, since the costs of digital editing and publication are much lower than those for traditional print media.[68] But in spite of these advantages, a full conversion to the open access model still seems unlikely. The vast majority of high-prestige journals are still subscription-based, and for the authors, once they pass the peer review process, publication is essentially free. Laakso (2011) has charted the increasing popularity of open access publishing, but progress has been modest, and by 2009 only 7.7% of articles were published using the open access model. The reason for this slow take-up is that open-access journals simply shift the cost of publication from the libraries through subscription fees onto the researchers. *Digital Scholarship in the Humanities,* the flagship journal of the field, currently charges authors $3000 to publish an article with open access.[69] Fees for other journals vary greatly, from nothing to $3,900, the average being $660. The cost to the publisher is harder to determine and varies widely, though it tends be around $200–$300 per article and in some cases is much higher (Van Noorden 2013). But the open-access movement has at least made it possible for authors to directly compare costs, which should lead to greater competition that will drive down prices.

Public archives are another component of open access. These are either theme-based or belong to the university where the researcher works.[70] From an author's point of view, authoritative studies show that open access articles are cited more often than those behind a paywall.[71] This is important because in the world of royalty-free publication (scientific literature in which the authors are not paid for what they produce) what matters is only the impact and dissemination of research. Even in terms of the authoritativeness of content, an open-access channel running parallel to paywalled journals is possible, without surrendering control and evaluation of articles.

Gloria Origgi and Judith Simon in 2010 edited "Scientific Publications 2.0. The End of the Scientific Paper?" a special issue of Social Epistemology where authors try to analyze and challenge the current practices and systems of scientific publishing and scholarly communication. Their perspective is that, while the official strategic evaluation of scientific works is based on the need for peer-review to increase the value of scientific publications, "epistemic vigilance" tells a different story. Digital open knowledge practices weaken the distinction between "certified" academic entities and the public, reduce the time lapse between when an idea is created and when it is publicly accessible and citable, allow a more relaxed conversation among interested parties, and remove the boundaries between scientific and non-scientific subjects. As a result, "a system of norms for publishing that encourages today's researchers to submit to peer-reviewed journals while discouraging them to write for Wikipedia is an epistemically irresponsible system that should be challenged by researchers" (Origgi and Simon 2010, 146). However one should be aware that the open access and Web 2.0 scientific practices cannot alone resolve the problem of cultural and linguistic inequalities in the evaluation and transmission of knowledge. As pointed out recently by the Indian economist C.P. Chandrasekhar, the "distribution of recognized knowledge tends to be extremely uneven, with that unevenness being geographically stark," and open access does not yet challenge "either the for-profit framework or the problem of North Atlantic domination. The result could be the magnification rather than attenuation of currently prevailing distortions in the control over the nature of knowledge" (Chandrasekhar 2013). Scientific citation indexes are biased by many different variables (not least a linguistic bias, see Gazzola 2012), tend to increase popularity of already popular authors and institutions, and depend on the centrality of the paper positioning within mainstream knowledge.[72] So why rely on such evaluation methods while disregarding other social recognition of scholarly work? According to the scientist Michael Nielsen (2011), collective intelligence activity is definitely changing the methods, evaluations and results of science. In his book on networked science he describes how the practice of producing science in an open environment is transforming science itself, its objectives, and its accepted methods.

While this is true in general, and especially for the humanities, the value of humanistic research is intrinsically difficult to quantify or measure. The critical faculty and the diversity of approaches that form the basis of the humanities disciplines require independent judgment and a change in perspective from mainstream beliefs. DH should take into account such changes resulting from the open access model as applied to the study of culture and science, and support discussion of such delicate issues as measuring the validity of scientific outputs. As argued by Roopika Risam, "Rethinking peer review in the age of digital academe is a task that goes beyond the question of medium or platform to a question of epistemology" (Risam 2014). A new approach to digital scholarship is reflected by projects like DHCommons (http://dhcommons.org/) whereby DH scholars put together resources, data and projects in order to cooperate and benefit from a mutual collaboration in research and the sharing of results. However, as in the rest of the sciences, much still needs to be done to overcome the problem of the under-representation of DH research produced in less visible languages, and by more marginal institutions and countries.[73]

The funding of digital humanities projects and their assessment is rather complicated because it involves different competences and skills that need to cooperate together in order to achieve desired goals. For this reason, the presence of institutions eager to fund and to sponsor DH projects is fundamental to consolidation of the field. Open access projects can be funded by various institutions, particularly within the Anglophone countries. Looking at the projects funded in 2014 from the various grants of the National Endowment for the humanities[74] (http://www.neh.gov, the US agency which funds humanities projects) it is clear that many of the projects belong to the area of open access digital humanities research. Moreover, an increasing number of DH journals are now published as open access: Digital Humanities Quarterly, (http://www.digitalhumanities.org/dhq/, published since 2007), *Digital Studies/Le Champ Numérique* (http://www.digitalstudies.org, published since 1992, though irregular until 2009), and the Journal of the Text Encoding Initiative (http://journal.tei-c.org/journal/, since 2011).

The digital humanities community has another open space to discuss and assess DH projects: the already mentioned DHCommons project (http://dhcommons.org), sponsored by CenterNet — an international network of DH centers.[75] DHCommons is a hub for people and institutions to find collaborators and a space to discuss ongoing projects. The DHCommons also publishes an open access journal, the *DHCommons journal*. The scope of this journal is to represent and give voice to the multilingual, multidisciplinary activities of the DH community; "to certify the scholarly contributions made by digital projects-in-progress, helping scholars articulate the interventions of their digital work; ... to foster an innovative, truly developmental model of peer review." (http://dhcommons.org/journal).

The objectives of this open access DH journal underline the difficulties faced by the scholars in the field in obtaining a fair assessment, and academic acknowledgement of, their multidisciplinary work.

The permanent crisis of the humanities has pushed these disciplines towards new strategies for communicating with the general public, finding new sources of funding, and assessing the value of the projects produced within their departments. The humanities, in fact, as opposed to science, medicine or defense, do not enjoy the same access to private or national agencies for funding resources. This permanent underfunding condition forces every scholar to justify his or her engagement with research. There is also a problem in the lack of communication infrastructure and in the technical abilities of humanities researchers, as suggested by Alan Liu (2012, 496). The skills of digital humanists could help the humanities develop digital tools such as blog or content management systems that merge platforms for publication as Open Journal Systems with other devices, such as text analysis and extraction tools, as in the case of Simile Exhibit and Timeline (Liu 2012, 497).

It is important, however, that DH maintains a critical attitude and does not become ancillary or subsidiary to the humanities. This is the essence of Liu's heartfelt claim about the need for DH to become a leading advocate for the humanities (Liu 2012, 495–498).[76] But the risk is that DH scholars may fail in their goal to deliver tools that increase awareness in the use of digital technologies by only automating existing processes. As suggested by Liu "... the appropriate, unique contribution that the digital humanities can make to cultural criticism at the present time is to use the tools, paradigms, and concepts of digital technologies to help rethink the idea of instrumentality. ... The goal is to rethink instrumentality so that it includes both humanistic and STEM (science, technology engineering and mathematics) fields in a culturally broad, and not just narrowly purposive, ideal of service" (2012, 501). The critical attitude that characterized the study of the humanities for centuries should also be directed inwardly towards their own methods and results.

Wendy Chun's approach is similar: "the blind embrace of DH ... allows us to believe that the problem facing our students is our profession's lack of technical savvy rather than an economic system that undermines the future of our students. ... The humanities are sinking ... because they have capitulated to a bureaucratic technocratic logic" (Chun and Rhody 2014, 3–4). She underlines the desire to give humanities students a technical education, as if this could let them escape the crisis of the humanities, without any critical attitude towards which technologies are needed to face the crisis and to find satisfying job opportunities.

Open journals could thus be one of the key tools to escape the old, traditional procedures for assessing the merits of the scholars. However, tension still exists because "the position of being a scholar and that of being a blogger" (Fitzpatrick 2012, 452) are too different to permit a single, adequate publication policy for ideas. Open publishing journals do not offer a definitive solution to this dilemma. The peer review policy is not in line with "publish, then filter" proposed by Clay Shirky. According to Fitzpatrick, "the self-policing nature of peer review, coupled with its reliance on the opinions of a very small number of usually well-established scholars, runs the risk of producing an ingrained conservatism, a risk-averse attitude toward innovation, and a resistance to new or controversial approaches" (Fitzpatrick 2012, 454). This imposes a strong tension between the traditional peer-reviewed practices of academic journals (including the open publishing selection strategies) and the kind of authority definition advocated by Internet blogging and posting practices, which relates mainly on the effect of visibility and success through readership, not retrospective filtering. Hence digital scholars find themselves in a continuous struggle between two contrasting trends. On one hand, they need to get an academic position, like all other scholars, according to the traditional authority-oriented evaluation practices of departments; on the other hand, they are eager to participate in the on-going digital debate, whose engagement rules are based on a scarcity of attention, rather than limited printing space.

Although this kind of new digital authority has its own bias and positive reinforcement effects, these are mainly due to the readily adopted hegemonic practices typical of online publication. However, online communication uses measurements and parameters that are completely different from the traditional publishing methods of the academic press. So it is important to find a balance and to openly discuss the changes that digital publishing are bringing to assessment policies. A suggested by Gary Hall, one of the founders of Open Humanities Press (OHP), the Open Publishing movement, which until now has mainly worked just in the field of Science, Technology and Medicine, must engage with the practices of the humanities. "... the humanities could help prevent the OA movement from becoming even more moralistically and dogmatically obsessed with maximizing performance, solving technical problems and eliminating inefficiencies than it already is .... The humanities could help the OA community to grow, precisely by forcing scholars to confront issues of politics and social justice" (Hall 2010).

In turn, the humanities can offer added value to the open publishing movement, by limiting the rhetoric of efficiency, and at the same time discussing the meaning of "openness" in a more critical perspective than is normally adopted by scholars of the "hard sciences," who generally support this publishing practice.

The expertise of the humanities thus has a lot to offer the discussion about open press and the open access movement as a whole. It can play a leading role in an open and dynamic discussion of the crucial issues of this new way of assessing knowledge and enhancing science. It can say something relevant, for example, in the debate about the establishment of a new system for evaluating authority in open and traditional presses, and it can make a crucial contribution to the loss of author-recognition, and to the risks related to the lack of responsibility for assertions made in a scientific environment.

Summary of Part I

In the introduction of his famous paper History of Science and its Rational Reconstructions *Imre Lakatos remarks: "Philosophy of science without history of science is empty; history of science without philosophy of science is blind" (Lakatos 1971/1978, 102). Lakatos' apophthegm may serve as the underlying theme to the first part of this book, which investigated the historical background of the digital humanities from a different perspective. One of the objectives of this first chapter (*Technology and the humanities: a history of interaction*) was to show that, from its inception, computer science was built around a new form of symbol manipulation, which led in turn to a renewed representation and organization of knowledge. The various components of the electronic revolution: its foundations in logic, computability theory, cybernetics, artificial intelligence, human–machine interaction, and the theory of communication and information, all contributed to the discourse and rhetoric that informed and guided the birth of the digital humanities.*

The central issues of our new discipline were also, interestingly, major points of discussion at the origins of computer science. But the pioneers of that early era cannot be so clearly discerned as humanists or computer scientists as they would be today. As suggested by Wiener (1948, 2), it was a discipline that started to colonize the "no man's land" between the various established fields that contributed to its birth. Looking back at the key events that made the computing and communication technologies possible, it is clear that many of the important scientific problems their inventors faced were already being discussed openly within the humanities. These included the organization of information, the ethical responsibilities arising from the creation of machines for processing it, the development of databases for scientific or everyday use, communication between humans and machines, the definition of intelligence, and the representation of interactions between the human mind and what Licklider called the "fund of knowledge" (1965).

The answers to these crucial and substantially "pre-scientific questions", not only shaped the core of computer science, but also informed and directed the birth of humanities computing, and later digital humanities. Our aim was to describe the debates that not only animated the first years of computer science, but also cast their shadows on the present discussions about the digital humanities (Gold 2012).

The possibility of describing the human activity of computing as a succession of elementary steps that could be written down (Turing 1937) lay the foundation for the invention of first the Turing Machine, and then the Universal Machine. When, almost ten years later, the computer was realized by the combined effort of a group of engineers, linguists, physicists and mathematicians, the Turing Machine came to embody a certain notion of computability as the manipulation of symbols in accordance with a set of definitive and precise written rules, which would allow the machine to be controlled.

The next step was unforeseen: that symbols manipulated according to precise rules could be used to represent any kind of content, whether linguistic or mathematical. The victory of the digital over the analog representation of information was based on the argument that the digital approach allowed for a more precise handling of content that would be more suited to obtaining a rigorous set of responses from the same inputs. The concept of the black box, borrowed from cybernetics, was central to the definition of this new kind of machine: a device whose internal function need not be understood by its users so long as it guaranteed a certain behavior within a given limit of reliability. The end-users were thus not in complete control of their machine, but were still able to communicate precise orders and illicit the semblance of a precise and adequate response. The outcome of the struggle for technological success was thus a new paradigm for a machine based on the concepts of communication, control, feedback and information-processing.

The "computer as a communication device" (Licklider and Taylor 1968) became the new paradigm for this next generation of machines. Its definition started with the work of Licklider at the beginning of the 1960s, including some of the analog criteria within the digital computing environment, which was the key to its sudden success. Licklider was the leading figure who was able to create a precise and convincing agenda for the emerging paradigm: the human–machine symbiosis. A human operator, who could perform his/her[2] gestures within the constraints of the digital device, represented the analog component of the symbiosis, and could exploit all the capabilities of the machine within the new frame of communication. This scenario, based on the possibility of interaction, and on the rhetoric of "augmenting" human intelligence, differed from that of artificial intelligence, whose goal was the complex simulation of human capabilities by a machine (see Franchi, Güzeldere 2005, I).

The perspective supplied by Norbert Wiener differs from that of the other pioneers, by including ethical, political and social issues raised by the new control and communication paradigm, which had been completely disregarded by Licklider and his colleagues at the Information Processing Technologies Office (IPTO), and by the Arpanet project. Wiener was unhappy that new solutions, based partly on his work, were being used in military or private sector projects. His behavior suggests an opposition to the major transformation of science that was taking place at the end of World War II, as suggested in one of his books, published posthumously, Invention: The Care and Feeding of Ideas (1993).

According to Wiener, the Human use of human beings (1950/1954) would include a different attitude to the use of technology. His critical attitude can also be regarded as a recommendation for the digital humanities: that we should not lose sight of the true "soul" of the humanities disciplines that that were being transformed by the introduction of computing technology. Wiener's inheritance is that he considered technology only as a means to an end, and not as a goal in itself.

Another interesting topic for the digital humanist is Wiener's insistence that machines should be under the control of human operators, even when they could operate autonomously. Wiener's perspective was based on an equal understanding of the fields of technology/science on the one hand, and of humanities on the other, and of the potential risks and benefits for interaction between the two. He did not want to oversee a reduction of the human element in decision making. The machine was incapable of making responsible choices, even though it was technically able to choose between alternative behaviors. In other words, one cannot ask the machine to decide on our behalf, even though it may be consulted when solving problems.

These are exactly the kinds of issues being discussed by digital humanists today. The historical debate thus highlights not only the importance of these events, but also their *relevance to current debates within the digital humanities. Beyond technical arguments about which methods should be adopted in the processes of digitization, the scope of the discipline should also include the ethical, political and social consequences of using digital techniques to reassess our critical vision of literature, the visual representation of poetry, or the analysis of Big Data and social media (Kitchin 2014). What cannot be denied is the crucial role played by representing, organizing, archiving, retrieving and classifying content for the creation of new knowledge, or in defining priorities for research. If digital humanists truly want to be key players in the transformation of the new "texts" (in the broader sense of the term), they cannot avoid questions like these, which are their most natural research objectives.*

The second chapter (Internet, or the humanistic machine) offered a critical account of the history of the Internet from a humanistic perspective. It used examples of trends and tools that exemplify the social, economic and cultural biases inherent in current technological choices, and how they shape the use, organization and practical rules governing whether the Internet will become a common pluralistic space, or a controlled and elitist environment. In order to extend and strengthen its positive social and economic effects, the issue of a genuinely democratic governance of the Net, and the creation of tools and opportunities to support and strengthen cultural differences must be addressed. Digital humanists can play a strategic role in meeting this challenge because they have historically been trained to recognize, understand and empower cultural diversities. Digital representations — both visual interfaces and textual — embody and reflect the spatial and temporal layers of cultural difference:

> *... cultural diversity, which includes identities, experiences of, and encounters with difference, is always* mediated, *that is, constructed, (re)presented, and experienced through the media of communication. (Siapera 2010, 5)*

Digital humanists are responsible for managing these representations. DH *institutions and international organizations should renew their agenda on issues of multicultural diversity. But simply opening conferences to foreign projects and authors is not enough. They must also demonstrate that research in this field can be independent of the interests of industry, from the governmental obsession with control, and that the* DH *community is able to propose new critical solutions, and not merely reproduce or utilize state-of-the-art software and databases. It is clear what ducking this responsibility might mean. At a time when Western cultures are setting about translating (and transforming) their own knowledge into digital formats, the need today, as five centuries ago, is clearly that of elaborating a new paideia: the creation of a multicultural and multilinguistic community able to train the trainers.*

Among other issues, this chapter also traced a map of the opportunities and risks provided by open knowledge from a theoretical, critical and social standpoint. It discusses the challenges in overcoming and discussing various kinds of resistance, from the strictly organizational to the political. It focused on the relationship between open access and open publishing within the DH *community, and described the positives and negatives in the use of open tools. It also highlighted the possible epistemological, critical and economical outcomes of an overly enthusiastic endorsement of open Big Data.*

The last part of this chapter attacked the familiar characterization of the origins of the Internet as a lost paradise of freedom and opportunity, destroyed by the interests of commercial, marketing, military and intelligence organizations. It offers instead a multifaceted reconstruction of its history, in which the opportunities and risks of the technologies involved were present from the very beginning.

One important goal of this book is to argue that technological innovation is never neutral. A "way back machine" cannot be applied to return society to a former state once innovation and transformation have taken root. But history shows that the consequences of technology are not always inevitable. Everyone involved in the process of transformation should be aware of the potential risks, and can accept or reject the new tools. Managing the effects that new technologies have involves political and social choices as well as an accurate assessment of the potential benefits. As digital humanists, we have a responsibility to discuss how we use the new tools, and not to blindly accept the latest technical fad without any critical assessment of its "meaning," or of the epistemological and cultural biases it introduces.

PART II

THE THEORETICAL & PRACTICAL DIMENSIONS

Chapter 3
Writing and content production

3.1 Writing, technology and culture

About a century ago, in a remote region of Central Asia, on the margins of the former Soviet empire, an expedition of psychologists and anthropologists arrived from Moscow. Both disciplines, psychology and anthropology, were little more than embryonic sciences, but the expedition was planned by two individuals who would go on to make history: Alexander Romanovich Luria and Lev Vygotsky. The objective of the expedition in Uzbekistan and Kyrgyzstan, a land inhabited by men and women immersed in an illiterate society, was ambitious: to study the processes of cross-cultural differences in cognition, or — to put it another way — to analyze the thinking styles and categories of perception in archaic populations, comparing them with those of other local groups that were socio-economically more advanced. Luria does not attempt to conceal the difficulty of the task, and refers to the unique possibility offered by this historic moment of transition between the old social structure and the new order that the Soviet reforms were bringing about (Luria 1979). Research at the time worked within a complex Marxist framework, and they set out to find the material (i.e. the historical and cultural) roots of the mind. The basic question raised by Luria and his colleagues was therefore: to what extent are we the result of the material conditions and historical circumstances of the tools and techniques we use?

Attempting to answer this basic question, Luria conducted experiments and tests, some of which remain well-known to this day. The following example illustrates the kind of reasoning he used. Rakmat, a thirty-year-old illiterate peasant from an outlying district, was shown drawings of a hammer, a saw, a log, and a hatchet.

> "They're all alike," he said. "I think all of them have to be here. See, if you're going to saw, you need a saw, and if you have to split something, you need a hatchet. So they're all needed here."
> ...

> "But one fellow picked three things — the hammer, saw, and hatchet — and said they were alike."
> "A saw, a hammer, and a hatchet all have to work together. But the log has to be here too!"
> "Why do you think he picked these three things and not the log?"
> "Probably he's got a lot of firewood, but if we're left without firewood, we won't be able to do anything."
> "True, but a hammer, a saw, and a hatchet are all tools?"
> "Yes, but even if we have tools, we still need wood. Otherwise, we can't build anything." (Luria 1979, 7–8)

Luria's conclusion after this long series of interviews was that "words for these people (the illiterate) have a completely different function." They are not used to insert objects into conceptual patterns but "to establish practical correlations between things." In other words, "processes of abstraction and generalization are not invariant in each stage of socioeconomic and cultural development," but they are themselves "products of the culture" (ibid. 10–11). This emphasis on the role of culture in the development of the mind, in part inspired the early works of social science (Durkheim 1982), would be one of the foundations of cultural psychology, developed in the second half of the twentieth century by Jerome Bruner and his school. The debt to the reflections of Vygotsky (1978; 1934) was also acknowledged: "the genius of Vygotsky was that he recognized that the intellectual power of the individual depended on the ability to appropriate human culture and history as tools of the mind" (Bruner 1998, 22). Cultural analysis and the analysis of cognitive processes are therefore inseparable.

Luria's analysis and above all the responses of the Uzbeki peasants have exerted a powerful influence over the years, leading scholars in various disciplines (psychologists, anthropologists, philosophers, etc.) to use it as a basis for quotation and commentary. The most prominent of these commentators, the cultural historian Walter Ong, wrote: "an oral culture simply cannot think in terms of geometric shapes, abstract categories, formal logic, definitions or even inclusive descriptions or articulated self-analysis that all derive not simply from thought itself but from thought conditioned by writing" (Ong 1982, 55–57). Recent studies on the role of literacy in the development of abstract categories and logical reasoning have undoubtedly led us to reconsider the significance of Luria's experiments, as well as the somewhat peremptory conclusions offered by Ong (Denny 1991; Roburn 1994; Olson 2012). Many years have passed since the mission to Uzbekistan, and much in the meantime has since been understood and discovered about the relationship between technology and language. The profound questioning of ethnographic methods also raised doubts about studies hitherto considered the cornerstones of research on the development of literacy, like those of Jack Goody on African peoples or Eric Havelock on the birth of writing in Greece. To give an example, Goody's (1987) attempt to demolish the myth of the orality of the Homeric poems, setting aside the positive value of his argument, was based on a comparison with the poetic traditions of some modern African populations that today would be regarded as questionable, since any attempt to define orality in an absolute sense collides with the modern understanding of the oral dimension as historically, socially and culturally determined; indeed there no longer exists *one* orality but *many* oralities which are diachronically and synchronically incommensurable (Duranti 2007).

Yet the original question, namely, what is the relation between *artifacts* and the mind, between material tools and cognitive processes, is still of crucial importance today. The villages of Uzbekistan or Kyrgyzstan have become the global village, and everyone is like the illiterate peasant Rakmat, immersed in a transition between the old and the new. Another revolution has invaded, less visible but no less disruptive than the Russian: the digital revolution. This revolution is forging new tools and using the new "firewood" of digital information, a brand new fuel that does not just feed knowledge, it transforms it.

Luria and Vygotsky underscored the role that artifacts play in cognitive mediation, arguing that the perspective from which we observe reality changes, depending on the conceptual tools and materials in our possession. The recognition of the obvious is not obvious. Even a circle is not recognized as such if our relationship with it is mediated by the environment and the tools we use (for Rakmat it's just a plate). Obviously the point is not whether a circle is a circle or a pot but to try to understand how digital objects create new receptive-perceptive spaces, showing us "new" things and making others "disappear." Born-digital writings occupy an important place in this scenario. They look and feel "immaterial" to us, but at the same time digital inscriptions can be more persistent and durable than usual physical supports (Kirschenbaum 2008, 58–71) So they show elements of continuity, but also strong discontinuity with the past, challenging established categories of modernity such as education, norms, identity and literacy.

3.2 Writing from the margins

It should also be borne in mind that the very concept of "lower classes" must be viewed differently depending on the type of society under consideration: one still largely late medieval, like between the fourth and sixteenth centuries, or a society entering the age of the first Industrial Revolution. In the first case it will be a patchwork of different and ill-defined categories: artisans and traders, farmers, street vendors, servants, beggars; in the second, in large part, a few farmers and the urban proletariat.

> Different situations, then, and different people, yet in both cases we are dealing with phenomena of sociocultural marginalization that laps at the world of written culture, that attacks and,

> sometimes in special circumstances, penetrates it. Knowing how, when, how and why this happened seems to me to be very important. (Petrucci 1998, 311).

The period framed by the Italian palaeographer Armando Petrucci is the diffusion of the printed word. A little later the student will discover that the movement of these social strata towards writing is not directly related to the flowering of the culture of humanism (i.e. as was the case with the intellectual elite), but that "the need for writing was due to an increasing number of increasingly complex administrative and accounting practices" (Petrucci 1998, 314). Perhaps it is not legitimate to establish a parallel with the modern situation, and yet mass technologies, such as mobile phones, seem to reproduce in different ways the situation of pressure in which even the marginal and the underling, the migrant worker and the homemaker, the windscreen-cleaner and the unemployed young adult, approach reading and writing. The most obvious difference between the modern situation and the early diffusion of print technology is that the device in the hands of these subalterns is an object that already implies a kind of technological literacy. And the relationship between writing as a technical artifact, and its medium, also composed of written codes, remains unexplored (Lughi 2006). So in what sense can a seventh grade boy who still does not fully command the codes of writing and communication, but uses Facebook and WhatsApp be defined as "subaltern" to the dominant culture? Who and where are the *domini*,[1] the stakeholders and hegemonic forces in this intricate process?

The only possible (and obviously incomplete) answer for the moment is that today we are all potentially *writing from the margins*. The global wave of neo-literacy in technology clashes with the local currents of illiteracy. The results of this collision are uncertain. The norm is no longer linked to the fate of the language, but also to the languages and dialects of technology that describe and circumscribe the boundaries, that mold rather than transform. The dominant forces of writing, instead of schools, universities and educated elites, are Google, iPhone/iPad and the social networks: the first is a symbol of access to the network, the second is connectivity and the mobile media, and the third is user-generated content.

As in the past, a Babel of dialects exists. But there is something new: that even those who are not fluent composers, can and in some cases "must" publish. There is no supervision, no control over this mass of voices, and it is not possible to apply to them the culturally-literate standard of "quality." Meanwhile, in the babble of this "lack of quality" outside the rules, new non-texts, *pastiches* in hypermedia, collective writing, computer-generated writing programs, mutant writing, are all taking shape. Five centuries after the spread of printing applications, Petrucci's questions have returned in a new form: who are these subordinate writers now? What will be preserved from the traditional practices of reading and writing, and what is new about these new languages? But most of all: how can digital technology provide an opportunity rather than a threat to writing? At the end of his analysis, Petrucci seems to move towards self-criticism regarding a progressive vision of the processes of literacy, catching, perhaps unconsciously, a glimpse of the future:

> The too-schematic mantra, "From the people who subscribe to the people who write" was supposed to symbolize the passage from the limited and exclusive semi-literacy of the medieval period to the more complex and significant period of writers and mass readership, which occurred in Europe during the modern age. In fact the process through which that step is taken, where and when it happens, is not only complex, uncertain, uneven, but simply in many places and circumstances has not yet happened, and very likely will not ever be accomplished, at least not in the forms and ways that we have known. (Petrucci 1998, 318).

If the end of that process is never reached, then perhaps more credit can now be given to writing. In the past it was relatively easy to find the "sources" and the voice of the writer, as media, authors and performers (from medieval copyist to modern typographer) were mostly distinct categories and protected by separate production cycles. But what happens when the copyist is the "legitimate" creator (see § 3.7) and not just "contaminating" (Segre 1988, 29–30) the texts of others, as classical philology claims? What happens when the stone-mason does not inscribe the word of the present lord, but makes himself master, controlling the technique that generates it? And what does it matter if he does so with more or less awareness of his means? He simply does it, and it is this doing which marks the distance between the time when rules were laid down in the high places of knowledge and the material time of everyday writing.

3.3 Modes of production: layers, forms and genres

The challenges facing humanists and written communication professionals affect their role as producers and scholars, and as textual analysts. They are called upon to make sense of texts, but every day they are forced to interact in the digital dimension, and to find in it new remedies and solutions. Since there is no room to discuss here more than a small sample of the different kinds of electronic writing, a simple fourfold division will be used (see Figure 3.1, overleaf), not as an attempt at classification, but to help the reader orient him- or herself. The map moves from the more familiar forms to those, as it were, "external" forms of textuality, to the most complex and implicit. What fails to fit in this two-dimensional pattern are of course the other dimensions; for example, it is clear that a blog or a wiki intersects on the levels of *encoded text* and *processed text*. So rather than concentrating on the apparently hierarchical aspect of such a presentation, one should think of digital text as more like an onion (or a "wheel"[2]), potentially made up of all layers and not necessarily organized sequentially. Text, and especially the digital text is, in short, a space-time *travel machine*.

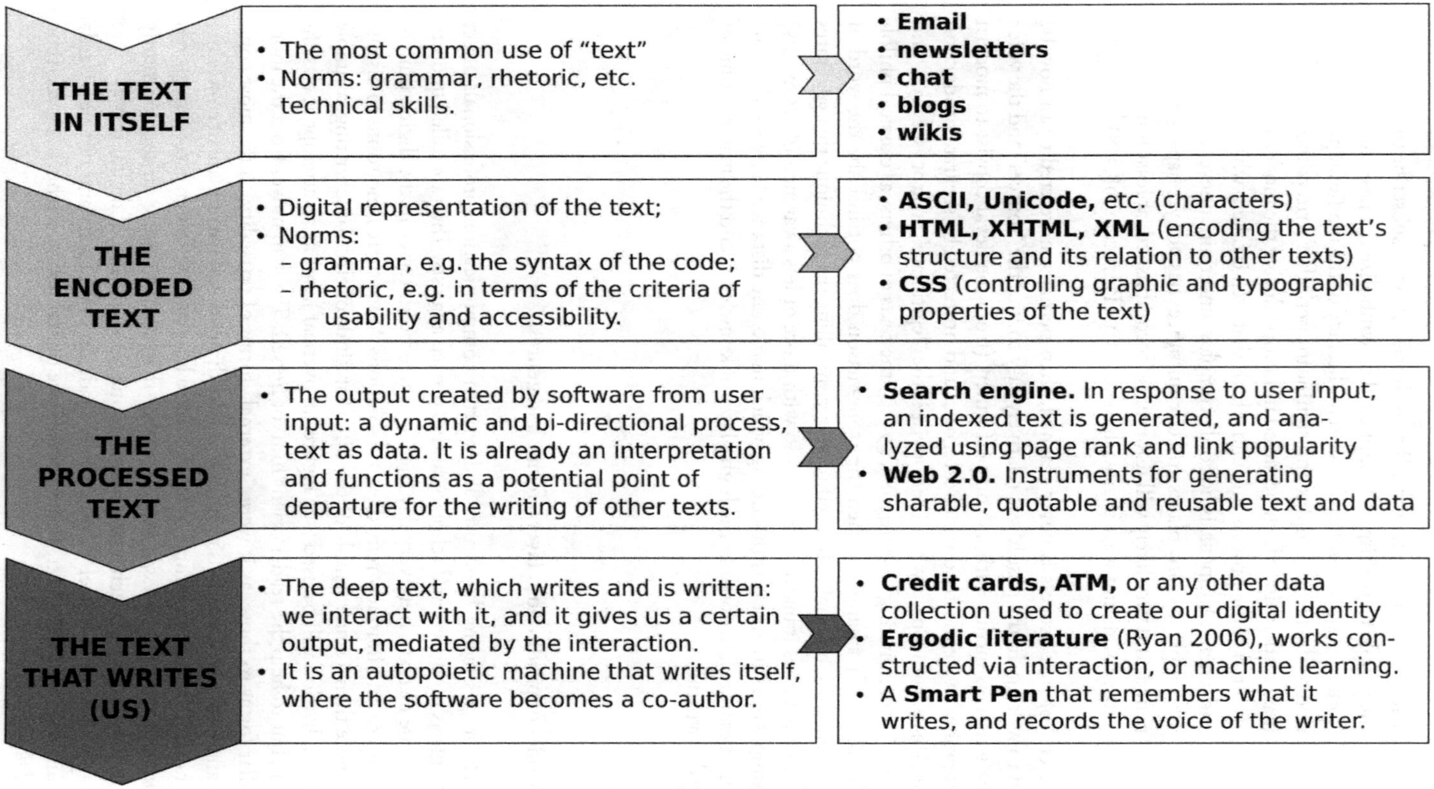

THE TEXT IN ITSELF	• The most common use of "text" • Norms: grammar, rhetoric, etc. technical skills.	⇒	• Email • newsletters • chat • blogs • wikis

THE ENCODED TEXT	• Digital representation of the text;
	• Norms:
	  – grammar, e.g. the syntax of the code;
	  – rhetoric, e.g. in terms of the criteria of usability and accessibility.
		⇒	• **ASCII, Unicode**, etc. (characters)
			• **HTML, XHTML, XML** (encoding the text's structure and its relation to other texts)
			• **CSS** (controlling graphic and typographic properties of the text)

THE PROCESSED TEXT	• The output created by software from user input: a dynamic and bi-directional process, text as data. It is already an interpretation and functions as a potential point of departure for the writing of other texts.	⇒	• **Search engine.** In response to user input, an indexed text is generated, and analyzed using page rank and link popularity • **Web 2.0.** Instruments for generating sharable, quotable and reusable text and data
THE TEXT THAT WRITES (US)	• The deep text, which writes and is written: we interact with it, and it gives us a certain output, mediated by the interaction. • It is an autopoietic machine that writes itself, where the software becomes a co-author.	⇒	• **Credit cards, ATM**, or any other data collection used to create our digital identity • **Ergodic literature** (Ryan 2006), works constructed via interaction, or machine learning. A **Smart Pen** that remembers what it writes, and records the voice of the writer.

Figure 3.1. Forms and genres of digital textuality

The first layer, the text-in-itself, is the outer skin of the onion, and represents the most common kinds of digital writing as they appear to the user. Each of these has codified a set of communication standards, and has its own rhetoric that has evolved over time.

The encoded text is the layer below the text-in-itself. From a historical point of view, it has been used to identify a moment of rupture in the transition from word-processing to hypertext writing, although in fact the theoretical development of hypertext precedes the first word processor by about thirty years (Engelbart 1962; Nelson 1965). However, one can say that the spread in the 1990s of HTML as a hypertext language marks a watershed — if only a chronological one — in the history of electronic text. From that moment on, it is difficult to split the encoded text from the text-in-itself, because although it is true that one can write a wiki or a blog without knowing HTML, to maximize the potential of this form of text one needs to acquire technical skills. As will be seen later (§ 3.4), it is only by combining stylistic and rhetorical skills with technological ones that it becomes possible to understand how far we can push our creativity as techno-rhetoricians (Barry 2000). Encoded-text is therefore the mark-up language or metatext (Fiormonte 2008a) that flows beneath the writing interfaces, sequences of alphanumeric characters able to determine and describe both the appearance and the logical structure of documents. To manage the tangled relationship between the communicative and technical levels of websites, the concept of "usability" was born. In § 3.5 below, it will be seen how usability is a set of norms representing a convergence of technical and rhetorical elements, since it aims to reconcile the rigors of informatics with the design of effective communication.

In the third layer, the processed text, there are two rather distinct trends. On the one hand, the text is processed through catalogs, indexes and archives generated by machines, as in the case of search engines or databases every time we interrogate them by inserting a character or word. Normally, therefore, it is a text of outputs based on our inputs. However, it also conforms to the representation of knowledge contained in a certain repository (from the entire Web to a single site). This is the model of information retrieval: *text as an information structure.* Early in the history of computing, in fact, the text was a single piece of linguistic data to be saved, retrieved or analyzed. Only when the network and the first interfaces appeared, did electronic text emerge from its infancy as a statistical-linguistic elaboration and become not just an object, but a *subject* of communication. This evolution started with the development of tools for the production and editing of text, although as early as 1965 there was already Ted Nelson's Project Xanadu, the hypertext and collaborative writing system considered by many (but not by Nelson himself) as the embryo of the modern Web (Nelson 1987).

On the other hand, processed text nowadays refers to the way in which the tools of Web 2.0, from Facebook to YouTube, from Delicious to aNobii, allow the network to share data, information and records by inserting them automatically within other contexts, and by allowing them to be manipulated. In this case the processed text (i.e. text reworked by the machine), as will be seen, is not the result of a simple cut and paste, but creates, as Nelson foresaw, a new intertext that undermines in an even more problematic way the concepts of "quotation," ownership and authorship of the digital object.

The fourth level is quite an unexplored field, where various aspects blend together. The *"text that writes (us)"* is written every day, in the daily operations of machines: by receiving and reading codes, the machine tracks our movements in space and time and articulates and constitutes our identity as consumers, but not only as consumers. We are entering what Geoffrey Bowker has termed *dataverse* (Bowker 2013; cf. §§ 5.8–5.9), that material but invisible space "independent of any particular container. It is everywhere. Institutionally, politically, socially and culturally" (Hand 2014, 7). *Who is writing* when Amazon, reading the history of past purchases, suggests (often guessing) new books for us to buy (cf. Ch. 2)? Does the machine interpret or possess us in perhaps a more plausible way than other human beings do? The traces left by our passage in cyberspace are likely to become more real and tangible than reality itself.[3] For this reason, Bruce Sterling, the inventor of cyberpunk, some years ago spoke of the "end of cyberspace" (Thomas 2006): what is the point in continuing to distinguish between inside and outside, between virtual and material? The production cycle of objects, events and actions is now so bound up with the digital that materiality, along with our experience, cannot be interpreted or even exist without it.[4]

In this phase, new objects and practices make their appearance, objects born of an era of transition, where the different levels and areas of communication overlap. This is the case of the SmartPen, as illustrated by digital ethnographer Michael Wesch (http://mediatedcultures.net): a pen that writes and records our voice, but also reads our writing, attaching what we pronounce to the signs we trace. A demo on YouTube shows other applications of the instrument (the musical notation or the Chinese characters that are "sounded" when you pass the pen-reader over them is particularly impressive), but, as Wesch says, we can hardly begin to imagine the future uses of such tools.

This continuous process of reading/writing of machines is flanked by experimentation in human–machine interactions. What is meant, in Figure 3.1, by the term "autopoietic"? *Autopoiesis* is a concept introduced in the 1970s by the biologist and philosopher Humberto Maturana (Maturana and Varela 1980), whereby living systems are capable, by interacting, of self-organization, self-transformation and constant self-redefinition:

> We need instead to be concerned with process, with the paradox of development by which any organism has simultaneously to *be* and to *become* .... The central property of all life is the capacity and the necessity to build, maintain and preserve itself, a process known as *autopoiesis*. (Rose 1998, 18)

Machines as living things? Not exactly.[5] However, this resort to biology is necessary because semiotics, sociology, philology, literary theory—in short, the humanities in general — are no longer able alone to explain what is happening in the digital dimension. Even the new science that will explore these new objects needs the "epistemological pluralism" that Rose calls for in biology. As mentioned above, there are two phases that mark the history of the relationship between IT and language: the first is characterized by the efforts to formalize computer language and the second by the introduction of man-machine interaction (see Ch. 1), or perhaps more accurately, man-machine-man interaction. Under closer inspection this double track does not simply reflect certain technological choices made in different historical periods, but a different conception of language and ultimately of knowledge. On one hand a model of consciousness formalized "linguistically" (i.e. syntactically), and on the other a concept related to pragmatics, in which knowledge emerges from interaction and *conversation* (Duranti 1997). But if these are explanations of how history unfolded, how far can one push the analogy between biological systems and new forms of network communication and conversation? On the surface this leads to an apparent paradox, which must be tackled in an orderly fashion.

As the philosopher Rocco Ronchi (2008) has noted, the question of what is and what is meant by "communication" is an epistemological problem that has been examined throughout the entire history of philosophy:

> But what kind of *process* is communication? The standard model offers an explanation that is completely indebted to the Aristotelian explanation of becoming ... The standard theory of communication is a hyper-simplification of the Aristotelian theory of *kinesis*. ... It assumes a change in the category of "being somewhere." Communication is a kind of *phora*: a mobile, the "message," passes from source to receiver, a "mobile" moves from here to there. If there is communication, it seems quite clear that *something* must be communicated. ... Such an instrumental hypothesis serves as a true paradigm whenever a phenomenon is taken into the category of "communication." But we must ask whether this is evidence or a reconstruction of the phenomenon due entirely to a metaphysical assumption. (Ronchi 2008, 197)

According to Ronchi, this Aristotelian prejudice permeates the paradigm of the standard theory of communication: a theory that ultimately would exchange the "dead body" of communication for its "living body"; that is, something that, when examined, is nothing other than "communication" (Ronchi 2008, 198). The origin of "this exchange of the abstract for the concrete, the dead for the living" should be traced not only in information theory, "but in the changes in human experience attendant on the introduction of the alphabetical algorithm" (Ronchi 2008, 199).

The territory this argument is venturing into has suddenly become slippery. However, an attempt at clarification, or at least connection, should be made. The "living community" that opposes the model of Shannon and Weaver (1949), according to some, would be in conflict with the alphabetical algorithm of the machine. Giuseppe

Longo, a mathematician and computer scientist, was among the first to declare (and to clarify) what we humanists dared openly only to whisper: "the digital machine is first an alphabetic machine, then a logical and formal one" (Longo 2009b). This detailed and reasoned affirmation puts itself beyond the limits of digital simulation and modeling. Just as the alphabet made discrete the continuum of spoken language, creating the "insignificant atoms" that are letters, so abstraction from meaning — the making discrete — is the nucleus that allows the machine to operate: it is precisely because they have no meaning on their own that letters can be encoded. But, as Longo says, "no natural process calculates":

> Yet, following a path that went from the invention of the number, of course rooted in pre-human, animal practices of "small-scale counting," and from the writing of the number and of the alphabet, which alone enabled us to conceive the numeric codification of meaningless letters, we have achieved the masterpiece of formalising the alphanumeric Cartesian dualism which is the Turing Machine. (Longo 2009b, 57)

The paradox referred to above thus lies in the proposal of an analogy between forms of digital communication which are new and "alive" when the origin of this communication is in fact an object, the computer, which "shapes our way of constructing knowledge," but is hardly able to grasp the change and dynamism of the living (Longo 2009b, 55). Although the discussion here is not of models and simulations of biological systems, it is clear that attempts to build new forms of digital communication are challenges to literature, art and languages, which are repositories and, at the same time, sources of those discontinuous, non-linear and dynamic processes, whose complexity is often comparable to that of living forms. For some time now humanists have begun to use concepts such as variation (Boyd 2009; Fiormonte 2011) and process temporality, which has exposed the limitations of previous models and approaches, including those that currently model both temporality and variation via linear coding languages (Fiormonte, Martiradonna and Schmidt 2010). So while Ronchi and Longo are right in denouncing two different and parallel historical obstacles (the alphabetical order of the computer and the "dead body" of the standard theory), the paradox is that only with this "Aristotle-Turing Machine" (Longo 2009b, 47) have humans built the most formidable tool to test the limits of the alphabet. Networks of alphabetical machines connect people, and this is what allows one to relaunch and exceed the "living experience" that is trapped (made discrete) in the alphabetical algorithms.

Unfortunately there is insufficient space here to examine these issues, and also because at the fourth level, the text becomes just one component of a phenomenon of communication that crosses and merges with other arts (Balzola and Monteverdi 2007). On the one hand, a return to the iconicity of writing has been observed (Harris 2000; Valeri 2001), a trend that confirms a visual and iconographical colonization of cultural processes; on the other hand there is still a lot of writing (even in the traditional sense of the word) behind the visual experience and in particular much reflection on the mechanisms of language. The sum of these new forms of expression are *dynamicity* and *process,* not only rhetoric but also pragma: a space where writing, both that of machines and of man, is acted out in time. There have been interactive representations (not exactly video games) such as *Façade* (http://www.interactivestory.net) by Michael Mateas (Mateas and Stern 2005) or the hundreds of experiments that fall under the unstable definition of digital literature (Hayles 2008).[6] *Screen* (http://www.noahwf.com/screen/index.HTML), one of the works that puts this process into practice, was made some years ago by Noah Wardrip-Fruin (2007) at Brown. The viewer-participant enters into a room called the Cave wearing only a pair of plastic glasses similar to those worn for 3D cinema. One difference to traditional virtual reality is that the participant sees his or her own body, not an avatar. On one of the three walls (there is nothing at your back) a poem is projected and read by a voice. Soon after this the interaction begins. Words and sentences are detached from the walls like a film and come floating up to you, floating; the feeling is vaguely ectoplasmic, until with a special "magic wand" (a sort of oblong mouse) you "touch" the words that immediately rebound onto the wall, where they fill the gap left by other words. The result will be a different text: a compromise between your choices (by clicking on this or that word or phrase) and the empty spaces of the wall/page. Even having seen and interacted with the work, it is still hard to describe in words the semiotic, musical and kinetic intensity of the experience. The impression one has, however, is that these applications (forms of writing? Of art? Of multimedia?) represent the future.

3.4 Rhetoric and the Internet

Figure 3.1, as already mentioned, has the disadvantage that it is unable to explain the overlap between the various levels. What should be clear, however, is the intention to show that the digital text, although used, as it were, "horizontally" — reflects a production cycle that is active on several levels. This poses a problem that the humanist or writer cannot ignore, namely how to demarcate the parallel layering of skills and competence needed in the production of digital text. Although the current practice of companies and institutions seems rarely to take this into account, it seems unlikely that in a single individual the various strata of knowledge regarding software, encoding systems, content management systems and perfect editing abilities will be adequately combined. Increasingly, therefore, writing for the Internet is emerging as a collaborative skill, not unlike laboratory activity or fieldwork in the human sciences such as sociology, anthropology, psychology and, of course, all the natural sciences. Such diversification therefore urgently raises the issue of training, given that currently the humanistic sciences are not yet designed (with rare exceptions) to deal with the conversion of skills needed by the new humanist.

Although the preceding argument has concentrated only on writing skills and, in particular, on the Web as a publishing platform, it should not be forgotten that in the digital dimension the author–*dominus,* whose identity was formerly based on the idea of a single human writer, now resides in the plurality of instruments and the collective paths of the network. The chirographic ideal born at the dawn of Humanism in the work of Francesco Petrarch is the model against which digital practices form lines of continuity and discontinuity. A point of contact between the two practices is that reading and writing is an activity materially inseparable from a spiritual-intellectual process; there is a close relationship between the content and the *form* of writing (Storey 2004). But if this point coincides with the current image of the work of the writer-programmer (Marino 2006), it is clear that Petrarch was among the first to tackle questions related to the role of the individual in writing, setting out the theoretical cornerstone of the uniqueness, originality and authorship of the text (Pinto 2005, Geri 2007). This paradigm remained largely unchanged until Romanticism and the confirmation of the identity of the author (usually male) and the work (or even vice versa). It is only with modernity that the scheme falls into a crisis of authorial identity, and finally today involves not only a "productive identity" but also a formative identity. And the teacher's "loss of aura" requires a reconfiguration of the teacher-student relationship.

3.5 Time in writing

The Romantic ideology, which still permeates literary culture, has popularized the notion of writing as the external result of an "internal dialogue" (Jaynes 1976), and not as a process that develops in time and space. It is only with studies on typography that began in the last century that literature officially entered into the material realm, and writers and scholars have found that the formal structure of the text was as important as its content (McKenzie 1986). Indeed the format of the book, its layout, fonts, modes of segmentation, etc. were all "items that carry an 'expressive function' that contribute to the construction of meaning" (Chartier 1991, 9). Starting in the 1990s, however, with the spread of computers (Bolter 2001), the metaphor of space began to spread and to undermine the Romantic metaphor of "internal time."

In fact, the impression is that text on the Internet extends more in space than in time: from online newspapers, condemned to eternal updates, to that apology for the fleeting moment that is Twitter, the present seems the only possible time for the Internet.

A sophisticated reflection on the dialectic of space-time in modern culture, and its relation to the network, is contained in an essay by literary critic and scholar Raffaele Pinto (2005), where the author compares the positions of the philosopher Frederic Jameson (1991) and Pier Paolo Pasolini's ideas on film theory (Pasolini 1967). To state his case briefly, Pinto sees an opposition between the time of modern literary works and the space of the literary text. On the one hand there is a modernity based on the *time* of narration, on the other a postmodernity characterized by space: "memory (the dominant feature of the work) presupposes the principles of totality, interpretation, thematic order, temporality, and narrative; forgetfulness (the dominant feature of the text) presupposes principles of fragmentation, representation, uncertainty, disagreement, space, and instantaneity" (Pinto 2005, 256; our transl.). Pinto assumes, therefore, that on the Internet "memory can be an impediment to navigation in texts and therefore an obstacle to the perception of its peculiar form, which is too elusive and uncertain as to make memory an instrument for understanding it."

Certainly, in terms of practical Internet communication, it is difficult to identify such clear contrasts. Yet this reflection helps to explain the underlying causes of current trends, for example, the fact that from a normative point of view, the efforts of designers are focused, as will be seen below, on the "architecture" of information. The metaphors of interaction revolve around all the semantic fields of space and movement: files are "shared," "loaded" and "downloaded," links are "gateways" (or "windows"), communities are "areas," a collection of webpages is a "site" but also a "portal," and so on.

3.5.1 Technology and textuality

What, then, has text become or what is it becoming in the digital dimension? And how is the relationship between space and time, between processes and products developing? Before attempting to answer this question a working definition of text is needed.

> At this point, only a frame-definition is possible. It goes more or less like this: a text is a coherent and consistent sequence of linguistic signs, placed between two notable interruptions in communication. In oral communication, a notable interruption might be, for example, rather a long pause … ; in written communication, the interruptions might be the two front and back covers of a book. Even arbitrary cuts create, in this sense, notable interruptions (almost meta-linguistically) in communication. In this way, even if the help of a determining "speaking situation" is not given, we can have very short texts: the lower limit is formed by two linguistic signs — as the minimum units of signification; there is no fixed upper limit. (Weinrich 2001, 23; our translation)

Weinrich's definition, coming from a Romance philologist and one of the European innovators in textual linguistics, is based on the role and consistency of the "pause" (or rather on the *time of the text*). This definition will be revisited in the conclusion to this section, but meanwhile it can be shown briefly how linguistics and semiology have addressed the issue of digital textuality.

Several attempts have been made to analyze and classify digital texts from semiotic (Cosenza 2008; Petöfi 2005; Scolari 2004; Zinna 2004), rhetorical (Landow 1991, Rosati and Venier 2005), linguistic-pragmatic (Garzone 2002; Prada 2003) and educational (Maragliano 2004) standpoints.[7] The grid proposed by Prada identifies five (or maybe six) common features of Web text: "being *transmitted* (or *diffused*), *mobile, composite* and *hypertextual, multimedia* and *interactive*" (Prada 2003, 251). An important observation is that "Web text ... is a transmission available only through a specific technical interface." Analyzing the last category, interactivity, Prada concludes that "electronic text ... may end up only existing virtually, as a result of a combinatorial strategy that makes the text mutable, allowing it to be changed even without the direct intervention of the author" (Prada 2003, 253–254). This is an important emphasis, because it highlights the re-shuffling of the roles of reader and author, not only in terms of visibility and identity of the two — an aspect of digital text on which theorists have long reflected: cf. Landow (2006) and Bolter (2001) — but also in terms of the mechanisms of text-production itself.

Moving from the specific area of computer-mediated communication, Giuliana Garzone (2002), in her study of e-commerce sites, while sharing these ideas about Web text, suggests a field-test of the seven criteria of textuality identified by De Beaugrande and Dressler (1981). Of these, the first two criteria come into the ambit of the scholar: cohesion and coherence. It should be immediately noted that if the above mentioned characterization of Web text is accepted, alphanumeric text can only be considered as one component of the communication process active in the digital medium (in this case the webpage), and it will thus not be possible to allow textual cohesion to depend solely on lexical or grammatical features (De Beaugrande and Dressler 1981, 18–19). This is because the alphanumeric text on the Internet is typically discontinuous. And as mentioned above, the analysis of coherence should also include hypertextual coherence. The coherence of a Web text may depend greatly on effective design and writing of links (Pellizzi 1999; Pajares Tosca 2000; Miles 2002). For a link does not simply provide access to content: it also configures an action and thus has pragmatic significance. But, in conclusion, the categories of De Beaugrande and Dressler, with some necessary extensions, survive, according to Garzone, "the proof of the Web." And the potential anarchy of a hypertext page is led back to its roots in the analysis of multimodality (Garzone 2002, 287), a phenomenon of "semiotic synergy" (Held 2005, 51–52) already noted in other forms of communication.

But to return to the definition of Weinrich, according to whom the text is the "filler" between two "voids" of time: here again that "dead body" of communication as theorized by Rocco Ronchi resurfaces (see above, 2.1), the ghost of a communication-object that has a separate existence from its real user-producers. Paradoxically it is founded, or substantiated, on the concept of emptiness, on the absence of enunciation. At first glance Weinrich's definition seems to apply also to the structure of hypertexts. For example, the term *lexia* (borrowed from Roland Barthes, 1970) — or units of hypertextual text — would correspond, *mutatis mutandis,* to the spatial-temporal concept of Weinrichian coherence: the page as a material interruption in space and the spoken word as a pause in time. However, this concept of coherence is not sufficient in situations where the meaning of the text lies in interaction (for example, web-links) or in its being shared (for example, remixed code: cf. 3.6). Weinrich is simply not interested in the productive and performative aspects of writing-reading, which reside, so to speak, "downstream" of the text. He considers that the relationships it maintains (or would maintain) with the outside world cannot disturb or change the structure of communication.

Ultimately, both in theoretical and practical analysis, linguistic and semiotic studies pay the price for their allegiance to a specific conception of textuality — or perhaps, one could say, of language. Although it is impossible here to summarize the complex history of studies into the relationship between language and its media, it seems certain that the epistemology of linguistics, the line extending from Ferdinand de Saussure to Noam Chomsky, has never shown great interest in the material cycle of the sign. This materiality, in fact, is specifically relegated to a theoretically inferior level, or even misunderstood: "the concept of text, thus, includes not only the text in itself, but also the medium of writing: that which philologists work on" (Fabbri and Marrone 2000, 7). But is it possible to define a text independently from its medium? It is basically the same formal construction that underlies structural linguistics, as in the case of the expression/content dualism (Hjelmslev 1943), to project the place of signification into a space of external relations, detached from their contingent vehicle, and to render the bond between signification and its media opaque (now relegated to the "vile mechanics" of the text, archaeology and philology). Yet, in the dimension of digital communication it is clear that it is the specific tool (such as markup languages, see below, 6.3) that provides the framework within which expression becomes possible. Chatting on Skype[8] is not the same as chatting using IRC (Internet relay chat), the online text tool in vogue in the early 1990s.

In other words, too much theoretical brilliance ends up obscuring the role of the medium as a *producer of meaning,* and especially as the *text in itself* (see above, § 3.3), which breaks in from a less reassuring semiotic universe such as informatics.

Outside of the work of Giulio Lughi (2006) and the revaluation of media carried out by the founder of integrationism, Roy Harris (2000), the exception to this trend is the work of Alessandro Zinna. His use of a structuralist (and Hjelmslevian) framework does not prevent him from underlining the importance of "material media," and defining the field of "objects of writing" (Zinna 2004, 88–89). While it is not possible to go into detail here, it seems relevant to introduce his concept of interface (but cf. Johnson 1997) as applied to textuality, which explains how each mechanism of semiosis related to digital writing is understood and analyzed as a stratified phenomenon, i.e. composed of layers that interact among themselves to form the object-text that in the end we read and interact with:

> Common sense has always intuitively separated objects from writing. In contrast, the technologization of the means of expression shows that the two are converging more and more. If it is true that objects have a functional and pragmatic character, while texts and manuscripts are distinguished primarily by their

cognitive aspect, the birth of electronic objects ... showed how these two universes were close to each other. (Zinna 2004, 119)

In order to apply linguistic and semiotic analysis to conquering the territory of the new media, it is suggested that the sociolinguistic model be integrated with a fifth axis of variation, the diatechnical axis. The root *technē*, without necessarily interfering with the diamesic dimension (the means of communication), would reflect the internal features of languages and technological tools that generate or even *are* the digital text: they are elements that circumscribe, and at the same time actualize, their own semiotic possibilities.

3.5.2 Paratexts, microtexts, metatexts

Summarizing what has been said so far in terms of practice and application, writing for the Web means, in the first place, knowing how to plan. On the Internet, texts live only through the network of relations that surround them. The environment consists of text, images, sounds, and of course, links. This is the short explanation of the magic word "hypertext," or an editorial interface in which "every act of reading contains in itself the possibility of writing, and every act of writing increases the possibility of reading" (Maragliano 2004, 53). Writing for the Web, then, means designing these possibilities through the acquisition of specific skills: both "traditional" publishing skills and, inevitably, technological ones. As already pointed out, knowing how to write is not enough.

In summary, due to the special nature of its organization, experts and techno-rhetoricians recommend some rules to follow for writing texts on the Web:

— avoid titles that are overly complex, ironic, paradoxical or flowery. Instead, use short titles that are descriptive and contain keywords;
— use simple sentences, avoiding the use of complex syntactic constructions and figures of speech;
— divide the information visually, using the white spaces or other graphics that identify the independent blocks of information (e.g. paragraphs);
— begin each paragraph with a brief presentation of the concept; "the inverted pyramid"(see below);
— use proper formatting of the text by highlighting relevant words or content, and avoid creating visual confusion or logical or hierarchical inconsistencies in the text.

Most of these rules of thumb are meant to improve site navigation, which in turn depends on an adequate design for the paratext, the most "architectural" element of writing for the Internet. It is no coincidence that this spatial element plays a central role in creating usable sites (see below, § 3.6). The transition from text to hypertext does not imply the disappearance of the former, but a paratextual rearrangement, stratified on three interacting levels.

1. *Paratext*. According to Genette, this can be defined as a "zone of transaction: a privileged place of pragmatics, a strategy, and an influence on the public" (Genette 1997). Indexes, notes, titles etc., are the classic paratextual elements

of print media, which are reborn in new forms on the Internet. The most interesting part of Genette's definition is that, because of its role as a dynamic border (as a connection, support, means of access etc, to the main text), the paratext constitutes an area of negotiation between author and reader: "These comments on illocutionary force, then, have brought us imperceptibly to the main point, which is the functional aspect of the paratext" (Genette 1997, 12).

But the functional boundaries outlined by Genette can be expanded and refined by the introduction of two further categories.

2. *Microtext* (or *microcontent*) (Nielsen 1999). This refers in general terms to those texts (maximum 40–60 characters in length) that usually perform some function of synthesis, definition, direction, or illustration within webpages, but which can (and in fact must) make sense independently. It would seem that the idea of microcontent reshapes the "classical" functionality of the paratext in print media as understood by Genette.

3. *Metatext*.[9] This is the "deep" text of the Web. It can be further subdivided into two types that may have quite different functions and outcomes: a) metadata (see Ch. 4), i.e., those snippets that are not visible to the user, but provide information (for example) to search engines, influencing access to the Web resource by the end user; b) the file names, text labels (for example, HTML tags), scripts, and all those textual forms used by a programmer or Web editor. Although not immediately visible or accessible to the user, they may play a descriptive and practical role within the site.

Every typological classification, however, may encounter some difficulty in the digital dimension, where several types may overlap in the same object. For this reason, it may be useful to refuse such an external classification even in accordance with the "pragmatic operations" (Flanders and Fiormonte 2007, 3) that characterize para-micro-metatexts (PMMs).

1. *Descriptive.* The descriptive function is reflected primarily in the construction of a (visible) signposting for the user and in the realization of textual descriptions (not visible to the user) to facilitate the traceability of information. Most metadata, as already noted, are forms of descriptive PMM. So, for example, the results of any Google search provide the user with a paratext from an internal metatext built by someone else (a library, business or individual user) and by Google's own internal system of page analysis and selection (see Ch. 5).

2. *Normative.* Many PMMs were created to bring order to the semiotic chaos of the Internet: for example, the accessibility initiative of the W3C, or the many guidelines on readability and usability of documents. Most of these rules focus on microcontent, establishing how a Web resource can be built that is accessible even to disadvantaged users, unlike the case of Web usability, which will be discussed in the next section.

3. *Dialogical-transformative.* This is the interactive aspect of PMMs — for example, the above-mentioned links — but it is also present in other "deep" forms of metatext, as well as in all those embedded objects (Javascript, ActiveX etc.)

that are inserted into the Web document and interact with the user, expanding or modifying the contents and so simulating real forms of dialogue.

These three functions do not cover all the features of PMMs or Web textuality, but they are probably the most important. Here is where the first distinctions between the various hypotheses of the authors who have dealt with this issue begin. According to Genette, paratexts are "those liminal devices and conventions both within and outside the book" (Genette 1997, book jacket). But on the Web, as has been observed (Scolari 2004, 103, Tomasi 2005, 714), the situation is reversed, not only in terms of quantity, but also in terms of the cognitive aspects of reading, since for the user the PMM may be on the same level as the "primary" text. The process of reading, as well as the fragmented structure of hypertext, explains the insistence on the model of the inverted pyramid — "starting with the conclusion," as outlined in Nielsen (1996) — in which the paratext becomes the protagonist, acquiring in the process a new name: *microcontent*. Thus, although catalogs, archives and libraries tend to consider the digital paratext as an extension of the paratext in print media, it seems hard to speak of the PMM as "a discourse that is fundamentally heteronymous, auxiliary, and dedicated to the service of something other than itself that constitutes its *raison d'être*" (Genette 1997, 12). On the Internet, we are, above all, readers and users of PMMs and Genette's suggested expression "P < T" ends up being turned on its head.

3.6 Content usability and accessibility

The terms "usability" and "accessibility" are used to refer to a complex of ideas, rules and guidelines for the creation of interfaces, websites and multimedia content that can be easily and effectively used by as many users as possible. Although sometimes mistakenly used interchangeably, usability and accessibility follow different routes towards the common goal of making the Web a global space available to all users. While usability refers to a set of instructions on how to create a website to meet the user's information needs quickly and effectively, by accessibility is meant a range of standards and technical requirements for designing Web sites that are accessible to as many users as possible, with particular reference to users with disabilities. Note, then, the main difference between the two concepts revolves around the user and, although both are user-centered, one moves from an exclusive model (the best communication for users of that site) and the other follows an inclusive model (better communication for all potential users of that site). Usability may be thought of as the communicative and specifically rhetorical and pragmatic side of the Web, while accessibility could be described as striving to expand the scope of the entire community of Internet users.

The historical origins of usability are to be found in two different areas: on the one hand, ergonomics and human–computer interaction as conceived by Donald Norman (1998, 2007) and Jakob Nielsen (1999), and on the other, industrial design by Bruno Munari (1968, 1971). Usability was therefore born as a hybrid and as a multi-disciplinary field, merging aspects of engineering with psychological, semiotic and "applied art" (a term that hardly manages to express the composite skills required by the designer). But any complex phenomenon has deep roots. And at the center of this plot, it is not difficult to perceive the path opened by the avant-garde art of the twentieth century:

> Russian Constructivists and Productivists referred to their creations as objects ("vesh," "construktsia," "predmet") rather than works of art. Like their Bauhaus counterparts, they wanted to take on the roles of industrial designers, graphic designers, architects, clothing designers and so on, rather than remain fine artists producing one-of-a kind works for museums or private collections. The word pointed toward the model of industrial mass production rather than the traditional artist's studio, and it implied the ideals of rational organization of labor and engineering efficiency which artists wanted to bring into their own work. ... In the world of new media, the boundary between art and design is fuzzy at best. On the one hand, many artists make their living as commercial designers; on the other hand, professional designers are typically the ones who really push the language of new media forward by being engaged in systematic experimentation and also by creating new standards and conventions. (Manovich 2001, 39–40)

The Dutch designer Paul Mijksenaar argues that design involves three components that are inextricably linked: durability, usefulness and beauty (Mijksenaar 1997, 18). These three features (taken from the Bauhaus) are reworkings of the ideals of the Roman architect Vitruvius (ca. 80–70 BC): *firmitas, utilitas, venustas* (stability and structural materials, functional utility, aesthetics). Mijksenaar translates them into a "practical formula," applying them to design: reliability, usefulness, satisfaction. Since the weak point of digital architecture is durability (consider, for example, the issue of software obsolescence, cf. Ch. 4), *firmitas*/durability/firmness can be translated as the need for transferability and portability of programs over time and content, as well as their virtual localizability, e.g. the URI (uniform resource identifier). These are aspects that stray into the question of accessibility, demonstrating the overlaps that exist between the two areas.

This genealogical excursus was needed to highlight the links that the concept of usability weaves especially with space: "navigating," "surfing," "exploring," "visiting" etc. are therefore not only metaphors, but also descriptive of an (inter)action in the network, moving us to places where there are objects, events and people. It is for this reason that one talks about information architecture, and even defines it as an "ecology of content." Information architecture recognizes among its ancestors classification systems of libraries (for example, the Dewey system), tools that allow the librarian and the user to track a resource in space (in this case a physical library). But one can get lost as easily on a website as among the shelves of a messy library: and therefore, information architecture provides the tools and methodologies for rationally structuring and organizing access to content.

So far the discussion has been about space. But what about time? And what is the relationship between writing and usability? Another stage of the excursus reveals that it is precisely in the space of large urban centers (Luzzatto 1988, 207) that rhetoric, and the theory of discourse, which to the ancients was how communication was taught, originated and developed. That is where urban space and the time of digital writing form their first alliance: in interaction and dialogue. If the epic extends over wide areas and vast expanses of the tribal spirit (migration, war, conflict), rhetoric comes from the need to mediate in the city, or to codify the "peaceful" verbal transactions that animate its spaces: courtrooms, political arenas, temples and markets. The approach of the ancients to rhetoric did not conceive discourse as something static. Written or oral, the text was immersed in the flow of time. In order to arrange itself and operate in different contexts and in different situations, the *ars scribendi* developed a set of rules, models and exercises, but mostly focused on what is now called the "user."

> Rhetoric falls into three divisions, determined by the three classes of listeners to speeches. For of the three elements in speech-making — speaker, subject, and person addressed — it is the last one, the hearer, that determines the speech's end and object. The hearer must be either a judge, with a decision to make about things past or future, or an observer. (Aristotle, *Rhetorica* I 3, 1358a-b)

The contact point between rhetoric and usability therefore lies in persuasive speech. That is not to say that the art of speech can be equated to marketing, as often happens (the logical leap from user to consumer is common), but only that the audience, with its needs and expectations, is made central. What Richard Lanham (2006) calls the "economy of attention" is the mass media's bombardment of our senses. Their most valuable asset is the attention of the user; this is why rhetorical techniques have come back into vogue. In fact, returning to Aristotle, who is "the hearer" if not the reader-user?

In conclusion, the interdisciplinary nature of usability is particularly interesting because its field of action is neither a mere "object," nor purely a discourse (text), but a stratified semiotic phenomenon that is the scene of a constant negotiation between programmed objects, users and producers (and increasingly user-producers: cf. § 3.7). Online writing, as noted above, is squeezed into the present. The objective of usability is to create artifacts whose usefulness and readability depend primarily on a careful design of the rules of space.

3.6.1. Elements of "interaction design" for the Web
Although most experts are in agreement about the theory and objectives of the usability paradigm, in practice there are different schools of thought. One the most celebrated figures is the above-mentioned Jakob Nielsen (1999), who defines usability as "the practice of simplicity." Behind this apparently simple and intuitive slogan, Nielsen has developed over the years a large body of methods and rules of composition, available in his books as well as on his website (http://www.useit.com/papers/webwriting). Nielsen expounds the heuristic principles he has constructed through a factor analysis of 249 common errors identified in several previous studies. He identifies 10 factors, which can be divided into 3 main areas of concern.

1. *Orientation and Navigation.* Make available and understandable all the tools that allow the user to immediately understand where he is, where he came from and where he can go within the site. Sections of the site and directions to separate sections must be presented in a clear manner, using meaningful and comprehensible names and avoiding the use of unclear metaphors. In addition, the information must be structured according to the user's understanding, allowing him maximum freedom of movement, with clear guidance on how to go back and how to return to the main page.
2. *Prevention and Management of Errors* without being alarmist and using common language. Errors should first be prevented, says Nielsen, but if this is not possible, the user must always have the ability to go back, and always have what is happening explained in plain language, avoiding technical messages from the server. This becomes especially crucial in cases of bad links, of data entry into forms, of purchasing procedures and registration for online services. Working on this is the responsibility in the first instance of the technical staff in charge of the site, but also of the designer: the management of errors should be reported via a language close to that of the end user.
3. *Internal consistency,* adherence to standards and constraints of the Web. The whole site must be defined in a consistent style, not confusing the reader with changes in typeface, size, color and layout without a compelling semantic purpose. In other words, changes in shape should always correspond to changes in content or logic. As for standards compliance, links should be in blue text and, if possible, various types of links (navigation bar, menu, external links, etc.) should be differentiated. The constraints are mainly related to the size and format of the graphics and HTML pages, which we must ensure are compatible and usable without any major problems on as many devices as possible.

Beyond these principles, Nielsen also lists some strict, all-encompassing usability warnings, such as "Do not use frames," "Do not use Flash," "Links should be blue and underlined," and many others. Such statements should always be limited to a specified context of use and to the precise objectives of the site, and not taken apodeictically. In fact, usability concerns the interaction between a particular user and a cognitive artifact, and is not an abstract property that can be measured automatically. One must certainly be attentive to the rules, but also able to ignore them in favor of approaches linked to the objectives of individual sites and specific cultural environments, rather than aiming for a uniformity that does discourage communication. According to many authors, in fact, the great success (and, paradoxically, limits) of Nielsen's work is that he has transformed the idea of usability into something measurable, something from which to derive rules and precepts, when in fact it was developed in an open and multidisciplinary context. Although the original aim was to adapt "things" to humans through the analysis of cognitive artifacts and their relationship to humans and the external environment, now usability is understood in a prescriptive sense. The aim risks being turned on its head: the adaptation of man to machine.

3.7 Digital ethnographies

3.7.1 Cultural interfaces and the ethnoscience of writing
With the term "digital ethnography," Michael Wesch, professor of cultural anthropology at Kansas University, not only managed to win the coveted title of "Professor of the Year 2008" (http://www.usprofessorsoftheyear.org) and attract the attention of the Web, but redefined the field of digital writing studies. Wesch's site (http://mediatedcultures.net) is the best place to observe that "dialogic dimension of fieldwork" (Rabinow 1986, 245) in which roles, traditional teacher-student functions and their assessment systems are placed into crisis by the use of technology. The engine of this reversal, for Wesch (as with other champions of Web 2.0: see Ch. 2), is the multi-directional flow of the network, or the ability to create, organize and share content that is mutually and collectively manipulated and rewritten.

The paradigm of "rewriting" is not a recent invention in the field of new media,[10] but Wesch's model in particular has grown roots in post-modern ethnography that advocates

> ... a cooperatively evolved text consisting of fragments of discourse intended to evoke in the minds of both reader and writer an emergent fantasy of a possible world of commonsense reality, and thus to provoke an aesthetic integration which will have a therapeutic effect. (Tyler 1986, 125)

Ethnography is defined as a border area (Clifford 1986), setting itself the objective of exposing the codes and representations of Western cultural anthropology through reflection on writing. If in fact the subject of social anthropology was "the life of signs within social life" (Lévi-Strauss 1960), from the late 1970s a large interdisciplinary movement focused on the critique of the methods for collecting, constructing and processing experiences and ethnographic data. And at the heart of this critique will be these "texts."[11]

Ethnography is not alone, however, in this work of "disclosure." In what follows, four conceptual nodes are identified, as are their links with the characteristics and processes of cultural transmission. Around them revolves the work of identifying the *constructive instability* of the phenomena of writing.

1. The overthrow of the postal model of communication and the observation of the inherently "distorting" nature of the phenomena of communication pursued by cultural (Hall 1980) and ethnographic studies. In Stuart Hall's interpretation, the sender not only consumes but produces communication.[12] Indeed, cultural studies, which in the United States emerged from the debate on communication studies (Carey 1992, 37–68), formed a strand of self-reflection on the relationship between technology and culture (Slack and Wise 2005).[13]
2. Reflection on the "cultural representations" which underlie Lotman's semiotics of culture (Lotman 2006; Uspenskij *et al.* 1973) and of ethnosemiotics. This area is particularly useful for the analysis of tools for digital representation, such as encoding languages, which may be considered in all respects true metalanguages. Digital rhetorics (Anderson and Sayers 2015; Sano-Franchini 2015) and code studies (Manovich 2013; Marino 2006 and 2014) can also offer important insights to the cultural analysis of digital discourses and the underlying encodings.
3. The development of semiotics and its encounter with the sociology of science and with science and technology studies (Bijker *et al.* 1994; Latour 1988; MacKenzie and Wajcman 1999) have generated another area which focuses on the analysis of so-called "technical objects" (TO) or the study of "the practices in which the 'operational cycle' of artifacts unfold" (Mattozzi 2006, 12). This is an important area because, as opposed to dualist ergonomics (Mattozzi 2006, 19–20), the semiotics of TO define the human–machine interaction as a process of mediation from which meaning emerges. This approach prompts a rethink of the theory and practice of designing writing interfaces (Zinna 2004) (see above 4.1).
4. Finally, a number of authors from various disciplines, ranging from cognitive anthropology (Sperber 1996) to cultural psychology (Bruner 1990), from literary theory (Boyd 2009) to neurosciences and biology (Changeux 2003; Jablonka and Lamb 2005), have helped to establish a model of diffusion and transmission of cultural processes based on the principle of "variation":

> In every phase of the process, the variants are not a "plus one" or worse, a useless set of faulty versions, but the very condition of survival of history. The non-occurrence of variants means the end of evolution and we must believe that it spells the end of that form of life: whether it is a species of plant, *animal,* or man or his stories. (Sobrero 2009, 72)

Instability is a phenomenon inherent in the processes of knowledge transmission: in other words *there is no cultural transmission without variation.* All of these trends taken together, as well as strengthening the ethnographic approach to the study of digital textuality (and in particular online writing), would perhaps justify the need for a broader framework, like that suggested by the title *the ethnoscience of writing*, which may be understood as a field of study that includes the modes of production, reception and use of communication.

3.7.2. The Machine is Us[14]

In a video lasting four minutes and thirty seconds entitled "The Machine is Us/ing Us,"[15] Wesch shows that the machine is made of text: it is written. Starting on the surface from the blue and underlined text that activates the lowest level of hypertexuality and interactivity, to reach the depth of the code (HTML, XHTML, XML), and leaving aside its growing multimedia, the Web rests the foundations of its development, its operation and its expansion on a series of alphanumeric characters that model pages, connections and meaning. We write and the machine learns to read. The machine reads and humans discover new readings — to be rewritten. When we save a bookmark to Delicious and tag it with some keywords, we perform an operation within the confines of our personal productivity. We publish content on the Net to be read by other web-surfers and other applications, which can reproduce, modify and represent it in a new context to a new audience of readers.

There is not one bit on the Net today that is not shared with Web 2.0. It was this idea that caused Tim O'Reilly (2005) to coin this name, in a series of conferences organized by his publishing house in 2004 (cf. Ch. 2). With a simple numerical label that the world of software uses to mark the transition to the next version, O'Reilly offered a new horizon for those who still believe in the driving (and creative) force of the Internet. Under closer examination, the aspects picked out by O'Reilly — interactivity, sharing, common authorship — were already inherent in the nature of the Web, at least according to the original vision of Tim Berners-Lee. And yet the American publisher's marketing operation had such a "novelty" (and necessity) about it that it managed to create a break, if only a psychological one, between the "old" and the "new." The following pages provide a brief survey of this "new" world, by looking at a few concrete examples.

3.7.3 Goodbye Windows?

Reading newspapers, commercial transactions, banking, finding information, sending communications, producing documents, writing personally, seeking entertainment: all these computer-mediated activities, whether they are real or virtual, are moving from our desks and converging on the Web: the network is now an operating system or, rather, an operating meta-system that needs no installation of proprietary software, but only a browser. From Google Docs (http://docs.google.com) to Diigo (http://www.diigo.com) or Backpack (http://www.backpackit.com), from Picnik (http://www. picnik.com) to Stereomood (http://stereomood.com), Web 2.0 has incorporated spaces of production and entertainment that are typically thought of as being offline, such as word processing or calendar organization, photo-editing or listening to the radio. And the digital tools of the researcher and teacher are evolving beyond the desktop, thanks not only to meta-search engines (see Ch. 5) and online archives (see Ch. 4); but also to tools that aid the collation and annotation of sources, directly integrated into the browser, such as Zotero (http://www.zotero.org). Only ten years ago, each of these activities would require the download (or CD) of a program of considerable size tailored to a specific operating system, with observations about which features were supported in a given version. Moreover, the availability of the documents would remain tied to the computer on which they were recorded: sharing would be done via floppy disks, CDs or ad hoc uploads.

Today, everything produced via the network is shared, standardized and interoperable by its very nature, because the Web is based on standard languages.

3.7.4 Behind the screens: the languages of the Web

The birth of the Web was guided by the principles of knowledge sharing and accessibility of information (cf. Ch. 2). Tim Berners-Lee (1999) knew what he wanted from his creation and HTML (the hypertext markup language) was the lingua franca that allowed large numbers of Web users not only to follow hyperlinks, but to create them (Kelly 2005). Reading the source code of a HTML page and understanding its simplicity and reproducibility invited a new generation of writers to the Internet, writers who had previously been kept away by technical barriers. Throughout the history of the Web, the principle of universality has often given way to market-driven compartmentalization, which has complicated access. For many sites built in the 1990s, "Best viewed with Internet Explorer 5" was the phrase that marked the intrusion of a monopolistic operating system onto the Web.

Once it had entered the arena of a commercial battle (the Web according to Netscape versus the Web according to Microsoft), the lingua franca destined to represent the simple structure of a hypertext document, valid for every application that could interpret it, became an inextricable hybrid of standard and proprietary tags, which were for the most part exclusively presentational. As Jeffrey Veen asked, "What did the tag <font> mean for the text marked with it?</font> Nothing of importance." (2001). Paradoxically, just when there was only one absolute ruler remaining on the Web, the WBC released CSS (cascading style sheets), a language for the graphical display and printing of webpages, to allow HTML to return to its original organizational, structural and logical function, free from the presentational burdens accumulated during the browser wars. It is no coincidence that during those years the WSC added an "x" to the hypertext markup language (XHTML), to mark its close relationship with the then emerging XML (extensible markup language), the heir to IBM's behemoth, SGML (standard generalized markup language). More recently, the W3C have redefined HTML5 independently of both XML and SGML, as a language in its own right, and the W3C's shorthand semantic tagging standard for HTML, RDFa, has likewise removed its compulsory dependency on XML. And the differences in the behavior between modern browsers have now been largely eliminated by increased compliance to Acid3, and by a standardized Javascript in the form of jQuery.[16] HTML, it seems, has become too important a framework in its own right to depend on the existence or failure of someone else's technology.

With the support of the Web Standards Project (http://www.webstandards.org), who, with a small semantic trick, has begun to define and disseminate as standards things that were in fact only recommendations of the W3C, the World Wide Web is a better place once more: shared and interoperable, not least because the market has started to come to terms with Google. Today, the market is asking for some order to be put into the billions of pages and documents on the network. It wants to find, classify and retrieve them. The separation of the structure of contents from their presentation is convenient, although not entirely perfect.

3.7.5 The seduction of discretion
With a structure separated from visual representation, search engines can focus on an effective indication of the actual content of a page, assigning value to the chosen markup. Consequently, the results are also classified based on those choices, and the markup may leave room for the description of the content. However, separating the content from its presentation and reducing it to a discrete structure also means alienating it from the context of its production. This is perhaps the biggest innovation since the age of modern printing techniques and the photograph (Benjamin 2008): both were reproduced and serialized, but without losing their connection with the material sources of their production. Instead, now they are turned into bits: for a computer there is no difference between Picasso's *The Bathers*, *A Love Supreme* by John Coltrane and the *Nine Stories* by Salinger. In memory of the machine, the representation will in all cases become an anonymous sequence of 0s and 1s. In HTML an article in a newspaper or a blog post is a (hyper)textual organization of headings, paragraphs and links. The machine can export this structure and make it available in other formats for other applications, regardless of their source or original destination.

News feeds via RSS (really simple syndication) or the Atom publishing protocol, which allow you to follow the updates of a news site or blog without navigating to it, come from this precise logic: publish once, distribute anywhere. Anywhere may be, in addition to the site of origin, a news-reader, a browser or an email client. This is all about keeping up with the wonders promised by the push of technology (Negroponte 1995). Instead of going to the newspaper, the press clippings arrive in the email. But along with newspapers, you can also find your favorite videos, the articles of the most popular bloggers, communications and invitations from friends or books recommended by passionate readers. If the Internet shares the same code and the same language, then the contents can be shared, exported, aggregated, and reproduced in all the different contexts that interact on the network — that is, the whole Web.

At an even deeper level of the code, just below the phenomenology that allows the sharing of data via XML or, increasingly, JSON (javascript object notation), and produces HTML pages readable by humans, the various Web 2.0 applications can talk to each other via their application programming interfaces (APIs). A Google map can be published on any website, manipulated and customized, since Google releases free access codes to their application libraries. And through Javascript, another standard language of the Web, services of that application provided by Google feed page n of m sites in the form of HTML code.

3.8 Identity on the Web

The original idea of the Memex (Bush 1945) and Xanadu (Nelson 1965) has perhaps found its first credible incarnation (cf. Ch. 2). But memory media are not "intimate" as envisioned by Vannevar Bush: they are public. Regardless of the level of privacy that can be set, all traces left on the hypertext Web are readable, understandable and (re)writable: a post or comment on a forum, the composition of a link, the upload of a photo on Flickr, the ranking of video popularity on YouTube, a vote on Digg, a bookmark recorded on Delicious, a review posted on aNobii; all come together to make up a fragmentary but all-encompassing work of self and identity, of which the navigator/author is more or less aware. Whether we like it or not, our simple entry onto the Web and serendipitous navigation writes software and a story that others can read (Weinberger 2007, 163). There is no such thing as a closed and private edition: in the end everything is connected on the Internet: the texts, the machines, the people.

Just fifteen years ago, having a presence on the Internet meant having a website, perhaps through a free service, like that offered by GeoCities. But, despite the efforts of simplification of Tim Berners-Lee, HTML remained a bugbear for the average user. The work of selection, preparation and organization of content in a coherent architecture and presentation was the (offline) job of the author. Nowadays, it is enough just to have an account on one of the many social networking applications. The machine does it all through an elegant graphic interface: it organizes the content, presenting it in attractive templates and fitting it into the context of representation (the home page, "about" page, etc.). The website is ready in a few clicks. Making websites is easy: my photos, my favorite books, my network of friends, my blog.

But what is a real website? And whose is the voice of the site?

3.8.1 My Website, outsourced
In a post titled *The Vanishing Personal Site,* Jeffrey Zeldman explains Jody Ferry's site (Zeldman 2009). As in the 1990s, there is a welcome page, without any promotion of content, with a link to the author's email and a navigation menu composed of four links: Linkedin, Flickr, Delicious, Twitter. Whereas, in a classic website, the links would lead to four sections/pages within the site itself: one for a resume, one for photo albums, one for links, one for updates. The site connects instead to four external resources that perform those exact same functions. Why? Outsourcing, of course, is convenient because it saves effort and resources. In addition, these applications offer a focused service of a quality you would have to be masochistic not to use.

Furthermore, membership of a social network offers all the benefits of sharing and integration, and increases visibility. All of these are good reasons.

But can Jody Ferry's website be called a "real" website? Maybe "world domination" is not among an author's concerns, but the control of his or her identity should be. Especially if these traces, personal data, text, and navigation choices are not only used to make search engines smarter, but also to understand who we are and to guide (determine?) our purchasing choices, or even to assess our ability to fill a professional position. Analyzing the phenomenon of the first iMac, the see-through plastic computer, which promoted the fortunes of Apple, and introduced the idea of the PC as a part of home design rather than as a bureaucratic ornament, Marcel O'Gorman has spoken, not by chance, of a false transparency (O'Gorman 2000). The illusion of the perfect interface (invisible or, indeed, transparent) is sold at the cost of renouncing a deep understanding of the mechanisms that govern our relationship with the computer. Web 2.0, something to which the term "misleading participation" could be applied, has proven that the thing is not knowing how to "to use computers" so much as the management and control of information that we now produce and disseminate daily through the Internet. When an aspiring filmmaker opens his free channel on YouTube, he signs a contract whereby, among other provisions, he becomes an author for a publisher called YouTube, which belongs to Google. If you add to this knowledge a mastery of the platform and the means for publishing and distributing his/her work, the author has a good chance of improving the conditions of that exchange, or even of becoming independent.

The introduction of iCloud, the application launched by Apple in June 2011, quickly followed by rival services from Amazon, Microsoft and others, raises new problems. We no longer need the memory of our computers because everything we write, photograph and record will be saved in the "cloud" or on a server somewhere, which we can access anywhere in the world. The cloud will follow us everywhere, allowing the user to download data to our tablets, smart-phones and laptops. The idea of getting rid of the PC and doing everything on the Net is hardly a new one. In 1997 Netscape, the old-school leader in Web browsers, worked on Constellation, a system that would make it possible for a user to work on their data from any computer. Whereas previously we had to connect to a computer remotely to manipulate our data, now, cloud storage allows us to manage our data in an infinitely more convenient way so that it is synchronized across our growing collections of information appliances. The fact that we no longer having direct control (and in some cases, even possession) of our information will not only have immediate legal and ethical implications, but it will also help us develop a different perception of ourselves.

3.8.2 Digital literacy

The new digital literacy starts from the Web. Various authors have spoken of new media literacies (Jenkins 2006; Dobson and Willinsky 2009), which can be seen as a revision of information literacy, the formative manifesto of Jeremy J. Shapiro and Shelley K. Hughes (1996), discussed in the previous chapter. This is a liberal art aimed at a critical and deep understanding of the dynamics, functioning and social impact of computers and new technologies, as essential in this era of information as grammar, logic and rhetoric were for the city of antiquity. As developed by Fabio Metitieri (2009, 142), the curriculum includes "publishing literacy," the ability to develop and publish research and ideas in electronic format, text and multimedia. Because, again thinking of Walter Benjamin, one cannot ask whether personal identity dies under the attacks of Twitter or Facebook, but rather how the nature of personal identity changes.

Code Writing. To learn how to talk on the Internet with one's own voice, and try to make it heard with some chance of success, today as in 1994, the dawn of Netscape, one must first know the basics of the Web and its language of hypertext markup. Without understanding that communication works because of code sharing, our webpages, whether they are self-produced or outsourced, will remain unheard — and depersonalized. If we want to put information into the computer so that other people can talk with us, we must speak HTML. When we use a what-you-see-is-what-you-get (WYSIWYG) interface for a webpage, the visual editor writes labels — on our behalf— designed to render the text correctly for browsers, and to ensure that the page will be correctly indexed and found by search engines. Even though, from a graphical point of view, the <hn>, <i> and <p> elements of HTML may conceivably have on the published page the same appearance in color, size and weight, from a structural point of view, search engines evaluate the marked words differently. The choice of which button or icon editor to use thus influences the effectiveness of the metalanguage and has an impact on aspects of representation and translation, because the Google web-crawler (like the software in a browser) is just one reader among many.

Compared to fifteen, or even five years ago, the instruments for developing that code and communicating in HTML have changed a great deal. The production of a website has moved from the desktop to the network. If people can write to other people on the Internet, and web-based applications can write to each other, and people can write using web-based applications, why make a website using an offline application? The current problem of Dreamweaver, a historic WYSIWYG program (but with an excellent interface for working with code) for creating webpages and sites, is that no matter how professional, it is still an application created for the desktop. And if it is always true that no site is an island, it is even more true that the connections, relationships and additions that are possible today have increased exponentially. Above all, as evidenced by Jody Ferry, the few pages of our website are not enough to contain a complete representation of ourselves. If our identity lives as so many fragmented and socialized *lexias* on the Net, what sense can it have to redesign ourselves in isolation from our effective operating system?

Content Management System: E pluribus unum. As already explained, the Web can be considered a management hypersystem for personal content: news, books, photographs, videos, songs, appointments, contacts, notes, diaries and calendars. Writing on the Internet in a way that creates an identity must therefore pass through a meta-application that integrates the tracks scattered through social applications and brings them together into a space for publication: the space of a conscious author. Rewriting identity needs a convergent editor. Content Management Systems (CMS) for the Web were born in the late 1990s for the management of large sites, built using a database rather than individually stored HTML pages. These systems were used by companies and major projects, not forgetting that before the advent of open source solutions (which tend to, but are not necessarily free), CMSes were created based on ad hoc commercial needs. The explosion in popularity of blogs, which coincides chronologically with the ever-increasing number of open source CMSes, implies, from a purely technical point of view the development of simplified online content management systems. Through the browser, the aspiring blogger is registered to a service, obtains a username and a public Internet address, accesses a restricted form in which essentially two fields are filled in (title and content of the post), clicks "Publish" and then suddenly the aspirant becomes a practitioner. The same operation can be repeated n times: the CMS does everything for him/her: chronologically organizes the posts, publishes the most recent item on the homepage, builds the archive pages, maintains space for comments, produces RSS feeds, etc. In four movements, the blogger becomes a (potential) protagonist in the great conversation.

With blogs, content management systems come fully into the realms of social software: no application that manages content for a website can do so without a mechanism to produce feeds, release its APIs, make use of third party software, or provide the space for user feedback on specific pages. The website turns into the Web 2.0 mashup.

As the Macintosh was to desktop publishing, so has the blog been for the Web, managing to bring to the network that "digital lifestyle" that Apple sensed again immediately after introducing iMac applications like iTunes and iPhoto, then iMovie and GarageBand, and iWeb, all brought together now (with the exception of iTunes) in a package called, of course, iLife. But if the integration of Macintosh software with Apple hardware (to which are strategically added the iPod and iPhone) is seamless, the integration of iLife with the Web stops when a multinational corporation's ideas of property and locking clashes with the logic of the open source Web. For today's Web, the new PageMaker is Wordpress. Tomorrow may see new software, new platforms, new machines, but what seems clear is that digital writing is definitely out of the infancy of word processors and "static" intertexuality, making for the cooperative and polyphonic dimension predicted by ethnographic science (Tyler 1986).

3.9 Transitions. The edited human

> Assuming that we are dealing with an author, is everything he wrote and said, everything he left behind, to be included in his work? This problem is both theoretical and technical. If we wish to publish the complete works of Nietzsche, for example, where do we draw the line? Certainly, everything must be published, but can we agree on what "everything" means? We will, of course, include everything that Nietzsche himself published, along with the drafts of his work, his plans for aphorisms, his

> marginal notations and corrections. But what if, in a notebook filled with aphorisms, we find a reference, a reminder of an appointment, an address, or a laundry bill, should this be included in his works? Why not? These practical considerations are endless once we consider how a work can be extracted from the millions of traces left by an individual after his death. Plainly, we lack a theory to encompass the questions generated by a work and the empirical activity of those who naively undertake the publication of the complete works of an author often suffers from the absence of this framework. (Foucault 1970, 323)

This quotation from Michel Foucault's famous address to the Collège de France in 1969 is considered one of the leading introductions to deconstructionist criticism. Reading that "millions of traces," how can one not think of what has been said so far? The text of the French philosopher inaugurated the concept of the ethnography of writing, in the sense of identity through the written record. Today the question is no longer how to define "the work," but rather the mapping of an almost unlimited area: the written representation-encoding of the individual, which goes far beyond the borders of the material self. It goes beyond the body and combines with the eternal flow of digital data that precedes, surrounds and envelops us. So one can no longer (simply) ask what is the work, but *what is the individual* in the digital age?

And what exactly is a document today? Conserving documents that have been handed down for centuries has been the purpose of one discipline that has functioned more than any other as an interface to our "cultural identity": philology. The crisis in this discipline coincides with two interrelated factors: first, the discovery of the material and cultural (ethnographic) dimensions to discourse and the artifacts connected with them (Benozzo 2007), and second, the impact of information technology, which is nothing other than a new instrument and medium for the storage and transmission of discourse. This impact has not gone unnoticed and, as mentioned in the introduction, some philologists (Crane, Bamman and Jones 2008) have spoken of the need for a *cultural informatics,* which could be a discipline that goes beyond the current structure of the *digital humanities.* The heart of the argument is that philology is evolving towards a digital model in which machines will be able to learn from user input. Through the continuous analysis of feedback, software will be able to affect the very *act of reading,* modifying the characteristics of the hermeneutic process. As a result, the fusion of the ethnographic ethos and new technologies can redefine the epistemological framework of the disciplines of the document. But what will happen to the sciences of the document (of which philology is the core foundation) when the document exists only in digital form? Today, scholarship is dedicated to the preservation and dissemination of content born in the world of paper: but will this be the philology of the future? The ethnosciences of writing evoked at the beginning of the chapter are currently the only feasible alliance for implementing in the future the critical edition of human-work, where the term "edition" refers to the historical reconstruction of the memory of an event.[17]

Foucault's question, therefore, extends its scope: not what to publish or save, but how to define an online event? What is the boundary between one's own work and that of others? *Who* — not just *what* — are we talking about? Will there be a memory in the future that is not collective, that is not "social"? Raul Mordenti, writing from a philological-literary point of view, notes:

> If we no longer had the Author (and his intentions) we would have the text anyway, and even if we no longer had the text (and its intention) we would, in any case, have the tradition of the text, that which represents the specifics of philology and criticism, and their *raison d'être*. This is the sense of text (Mordenti 2011, 680).

The polemical target is the "hermetic drift" of deconstruction, which would have waived any claim to find meaning in the text. But it seems that the postmodern critique, and in this case Foucault, hurls itself against the notion of "tradition," showing how it was always the product of specific historical and social conditions and contexts — contexts where the choices made were often (and still are) a direct emanation, reproduction or reassertion of dominant authorities. In other words, the principle of power is not neutral with respect to the principle of tradition. The object of deconstruction, in our view, is not the meaning of the text, but the "tradition that is": the cultural system that transmits, translates and betrays.

But in the *continuum* of the digital trail, represented in part by the examples discussed so far, the question is not whether it has any meaning, but rather how to reconfigure its scope by asking more pertinent questions. Who is the owner of the discourse? Who manages it? Who chooses and creates, who guarantees access and use? Even the meaning of deconstruction, with such a horizon, appears outdated. Author, text and work are no longer the center of the processes of cultural transmission, but it is the *processes themselves,* as in biology, that require the establishment of a new epistemological framework and, consequently, a new hermeneutic.

The next chapter will introduce the third part of the digital trivium: the techniques and methods used in the digitization of documents and their collection into broader repositories of digital "objects." These technologies arbitrate our control over the past, present and future of our written culture. Understanding their limitations and possibilities for recording and preserving written cultural objects is part of the essential skills of the modern digital humanist.

Chapter 4
Representing and archiving

THE PREVIOUS CHAPTER examined the processes behind digital text production: the new forms, genres and structures that emerge from the meeting between writing and digital computing. This encounter is causing the humanistic skill-set to realign in new directions, but it is not the only reason for change.

In order to understand how these changes affect the work of the humanities scholar, it is necessary to look further afield, into the larger world of digital representation and preservation of cultural heritage. This chapter will investigate strategies designed to minimize the risk that time will alter our cultural memory, or make it inaccessible. This extends beyond merely preserving in digital form previously non-digital objects, such as books and other analog objects, but also increasingly what is already digital. Here texts occupy a central, although not an exclusive, position. Our *Digital Cultural Heritage* can thus be seen as represented by a set of "digital objects." In this context the concept of digital object is understood, broadly, as part of an integrated multimedia approach, where each type of object is represented digitally, and all the objects in the collection can be referred to and searched uniformly.

Digital objects may be derived from printed texts, manuscripts, archival documents, photographs, but also paintings, museum pieces, works of art and architecture. Resources may be *born digital* (originally created *in* a digital medium) or they may have to be first digitized from an analog primary source. To be useful, resources need to be accessible in virtual spaces, principally on the Web. They may also be augmented by user-generated content (UGC), through secondary material such as recordings of interviews and scholarly articles, subject indexing and annotation.

There are also individual collections in specific digital formats, and, increasingly, miscellaneous collections consisting of closely associated objects, such as the transcriptions of texts and their facsimiles (e.g. the textual version of a manuscript and the image of the manuscript itself), or documents and videos (e.g. from the archival object to the video that tells the story of its formation), or 3D objects and sound re-

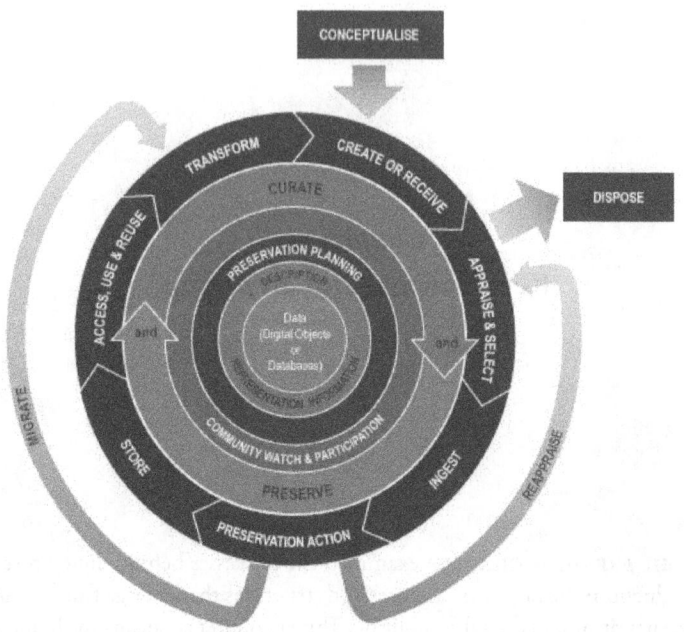

*Figure 4.1. DCC (Digital Curation Centre) Curation Lifecycle Model
(http://www.dcc.ac.uk/resources/curation-lifecycle-model)*

cordings (e.g. from the virtual reconstruction of an Attic vase to the audio narration of its finding).

The issue of the digital preservation of cultural records has long been the subject of study and reflection and has led to the flourishing of various initiatives, mainly originating in the field of library and information science. Universities and institutions dedicated to conservation have undertaken several projects to investigate the state of digital collections in libraries, archives, museums and in the arts generally, in order to improve their understanding of current best practice for preserving our digital cultural heritage, including born-digital content produced in modern social media.

But preservation nowadays has to be understood in a more critical and expansive way. "Digital curation" is the selection, preservation, maintenance, collection and archiving of digital assets. It thus involves maintaining, preserving and adding value to digital research data. A more holistic look at data is to visualize it as belonging to a process in which it is "curated" throughout its life-cycle (Figure 4.1).

A digital object is an association between data and metadata. Data is the primary source in digital form of its various potential manifestations (text, static or moving image, 3D models, audio or video files, potentially related to one another). Metadata is information about that source, its description, management and retrieval.

For digital objects to be properly preserved, they must be created using formal, standardized and portable formats. To be portable and interoperable a file must be readable by various hardware platforms and software systems, which can understand its structure and semantics.

For original textual sources, the focus in this chapter will be on XML as a language for representing not only the content, but also the metadata, because this is one of the most effective strategies for their preservation.

Another important question is where such materials can be stored. On the Web the concept of *repository* refers to an organized collection of digital content accessible to users. Two reference models of such virtual places for storage, archiving and access are digital libraries and open archives.

Connected with these issues are two key terms that characterize the landscape of the modern Internet: Web 2.0 (cf. §§ 2.3 and 3.7–3.8), which treats the Web as a collaborative and participatory platform, and the Semantic Web (introduced in § 2.4), which aims to redefine the systems of production, representation and management of knowledge.

☞

4.1 The longevity of digital information

One problem that anyone who works with digital technology has to face is the relentless march of time.[1] Regardless of whether the material is already in digital form (either digitized from an analog source or born digital), or still in an analog form (e.g. a vinyl record, a celluloid film), time has powerful effects on the technologies used to record these objects, both at the hardware and software levels. Being aware of what each phase of technological transition means is fundamental to developing an understanding of how to create, store and archive knowledge. It is also important to remember that different kinds of digital objects, from texts to images, from audio to video, were created using different systems, and thus need to be stored and distributed in different ways. Resources may be stored in the form of a webpage, as collections of data in a database, or as a set of files produced by proprietary software, and still others were created by open source applications, which are needed if they are to be viewed or played. All of these forms that knowledge can take contribute to our notion of cultural heritage.

There are thus two levels of data preservation to consider:
1. different physical media for storing the data;
2. different languages and/or software used to create and utilize digital objects.

This apparently simple division, however, brings with it a series of problems that must be worked out on different levels. Humanities scholars need to be aware of their role in the production and archiving of resources.[2] And they must not forget that the strictly technical aspects of conservation are concerned with a theory of knowledge management in the digital world, and that each of these media and

Figure 4.2. The monster footprint of digital technology (http://www.lowtechmagazine.com)

technologies possess and reflect a historical and cultural *bias*, in other words they become the carriers of specific values and visions of the world (cf. § 2.5). Procedures for creation/utilization and systems of storage thus represent two crucial elements in the process of conservation of digital objects. The following sections will now examine these elements in more detail.

4.1.1 Degradation and obsolescence

The first consideration is what type of medium was used. Every medium (CD, DVD, HDD, floppy disk or flash memory) is subject to some form of degradation. Once physical media deteriorate, any damage suffered may cause data loss, which compromises access to the information. Storage systems used for physical preservation must therefore be adjusted to suit the nature of the material. In addition to degradation of physical media there is also the problem of technological obsolescence of the data itself, which has the secondary effect of forcing changes in the systems of conservation and storage. This involves hardware as much as software: there is a constant evolution not only in the physical technologies of storage, but also in the software applications through which the material can be read and interpreted, and in how the two interact. So the first defense against technological obsolescence is an awareness of technologies used to create and maintain digital content. Beyond preservation techniques that may slow physical deterioration, the adoption of open source technologies may provide a partial solution to the problem of software obsolescence. Making the code of an application for reading a certain kind of digital object available to the community resolves at least some of the problems, since any problems that arise may be fixed by the community (not hidden in a fixed proprietary form). However, there the danger remains that the software itself will eventually become obsolete if it is not maintained, since the software environment in which it runs will continue to evolve.

The Task Force on Archiving Digital Information (Garrett 1995) represents the first important step in resolving these difficult problems. Its objective was to think about ways to design systems for preserving materials already in digital format, in the face of the twin threats of media deterioration and technological obsolescence. A commission made up of archivists, librarians, researchers, editors and government representatives produced a landmark report in 1996, chaired by Donald Waters and John Garrett, which they called *Preserving Digital Information*.

4.2 Balancing tradition and innovation

After the Task Force made its report there was a flourish of studies and initiatives addressing the problems of digital aging. Many conference papers and scientific articles have since addressed this issue, and there have also been other initiatives such as collaborations between institutions or conservation experts, designed to coordinate activities related to the production of digital resources, or to provide guidelines for the creation of durable and lasting digital objects (cf. below §§ 4.6–4.7).

One of the most searched-for terms on the subject of digital objects on the Web is *digital preservation*. This involves conserving our collective digital memory in the form of a communication exchange, where the end user is also an active producer, not just a passing reader. This goes beyond simply conserving the data, the binary sequence of 0s and 1s, and extends to the information carried by the documents themselves (Buzzetti 2006).

What, then, should be preserved? Or put another way, what is meant by a digital object that is worth preserving? Ensuring access to digital objects over time involves a variety of processes because digital objects are themselves multifarious, and cannot be tied down to a single well-defined notion or model.

In some cases, the information content can be found in a single file, but in other cases several documents might be needed. An image might be inserted into a document, or a website may be composed of several pages, or even different versions of files, in different formats, or different documents created at different times, but with the same content. Those who create digital objects are increasingly using multimedia systems to guarantee the completeness of the information they carry. This stratification of media, in the form of various data formats (text, image, video and audio files) has become an essential strategy in the communication of knowledge. Any program for preservation must therefore tackle digital objects on four fronts (Webb 2003):
— as physical objects, sequences of bits loaded onto a physical medium (the problem of media deterioration);
— as logical objects, i.e. as code, not tied to a physical medium, but necessarily in machine-readable form (the problem of hardware and software obsolescence);
— as conceptual objects with content and meaning, usable by a human reader;

– as a collection of elements that help determine the content of the digital object.

In short, a digital object must be considered as an entity with many layers. Each layer requires specific strategies for conservation to be put in place. These layers may be considered as different facets of one object, whose overall integrity must likewise be preserved. So a possible definition might be that the conservation of digital resources means putting in place activities and procedures, and developing or using tools and methods designed to ensure long- and medium-term access, use and identification of information as complex digital objects. One could say that:

> The polymorphism of digital information means that even the apparently basic issue of what is it that is to be preserved is not a given, but involves choice: should we preserve what was displayed in a given instance or the data, structures, controls, and functionality that enabled the presentation, or both? In order to decide on appropriate choices, we have to consider not only the characteristics of the data objects and presented objects, but also the dynamic context in which digital information exists. (Thibodeau 2012, 3–4)

4.2.1 Proposals for preservation

In the current literature, it is possible to find many solutions, both technical and practical, that have been proposed for the long-term preservation of digital objects. The most commonly mentioned solutions revolve around:

1. *Maintenance* — the conservation of obsolete hardware and software for the reading of specific digital objects. This proposal leads to high costs and little guarantee of success.
2. *Refreshing* — the copying of data from one medium to another, for example from 5.25" floppy disk to 3.5" floppy, or from CD to DVD. This technique aims to tackle the problem of hardware obsolescence or physical deterioration of media.
3. *Use of standard formats* — moving digital objects from their original format to a standard format. This can only be a temporary solution, since no standard is immune to change.

The most popular solutions in the literature that deal with technical obsolescence of the information content are the following:

4. *Migration* — transferring digital objects to a new platform (hardware and software) before the old platform becomes obsolete. This goes beyond simple "refreshing" since the digital object is recoded to be compatible with the new hardware and software. However, this process is not always perfect and information may be lost.
5. *Emulation* — emulating obsolete systems on new systems. Here, the digital object is preserved along with the software and technological environment in which it was produced. In any operating system it thus becomes possible to

call up the digital object together with the software needed to read it on the emulator of its native platform (Rothenberg 1999).

None of these models has found universal appeal or undivided consensus. And all of these approaches, particularly migration and emulation — the two most exhaustive — admit of limitations that prevent them from being considered sufficient to solve the whole problem of digital preservation. This suggests tackling the problem on another front: the production of electronic documents already designed with preservation in mind.

4.2.2 The role of languages and metadata

Digitization is a procedure designed to convert an analog object (such as a printed text or manuscript, a painting or architectural work, a document or museum object) into a digital one. The process works on two levels, both of which must be taken into account: which format the document will be saved in, and how to add information to make it accessible in the long term. On the first level the focus must be on portable and standardized languages, rather than specific software, and on creating files in readable, non-proprietary formats. Although standards change with time (cf. § 4.2.1 point 3), their use helps to guarantee exchangeability, portability and interoperability with other resources. On the second level use must be made of metadata, i.e. information added to the digital object to identify, describe and manage it — to help us understand the how, when and why it was created. Metadata persists across the evolution of platforms. The following sections will deal with these two levels, languages and metadata, with one proviso: by concentrating on markup languages, as an instrument capable of assigning a descriptive level to the content carried by a digital object, it should not be forgotten that preservation strategies are not limited to the use of such languages.

If an image can be annotated and therefore described by metadata, it can at the same time be subject to quite different computational operations than those applicable to text. Systems for the virtual restoration of damaged manuscripts (through ink spills, foxing, discoloration, abrasions, tearing and burning), and automatic recognition of constituent elements through pattern recognition, are some[3] of the more interesting systems for the extraction of information from images. Systems for digital image processing are designed to improve the quality of the source or, at least, to increase its legibility: once the source is legible and recovers its status as a cultural object it becomes more accessible to the end user.[4]

Image search and retrieval can also succeed without the need for explicit textual annotation or metadata. Since the 1990s tools supporting *content-based image retrieval* (CBIR) also known as query by image content (QUBIC) have emerged.[5] These systems use different techniques and algorithms to describe and extract iconic information from the visual and external features of an image, such as shape, color and texture. In this way, the user can perform different tasks at both a material and cognitive level, e.g. searching for visual similarities among images without the need to use textual attributes or descriptions.[6] For example, the QUBIC color and layout searches realized by IBM for the Hermitage Museum allows the user both to select colors from a spectrum and use geometric shapes for locating artwork within the digital collection.[7]

CBIR/QUBIC systems thus offer a different approach to the handling of multimedia objects, which is perhaps more respectful of the epistemological status of non-textual artifacts. In the past few years the study of images has expanded beyond the humanities and social sciences, and has included contributions from cognitive psychology and the neurosciences. This boom was perceived and described by some scholars as an "iconic turn" (Bohem 2007; Burda *et al.* 2011), as opposed to the "linguistic turn" identified by the philosopher Richard Rorty in 1967. The turning point, however, seems to have only partly involved the DH community, which was in a certain sense "condemned" to its own success: the increasing creation of large textual repositories and its related tools, with few exceptions,[8] has dominated its intellectual and technological achievements. Some DH scholars were nonetheless aware of the existence of an "image divide":

> ... images have not generally yielded to the same kind of regularized manipulation of electronic text, where the humanities computing community has achieved reasonable success to date in using descriptive encoding schemes to build robust textbases for structured search and retrieval. Indeed, computationally speaking, the divide between image and text remains all but irreconcilable ... This computational divide in turn reflects and recapitulates certain elemental differences in the epistemology of images and texts. (Kirschenbaum 2002, 4)

4.3 Markup standards and languages

One possible solution to the problem of preservation might be the use of standard, readable and non-proprietary languages for creating files. Standard technologies, recognized by organizations of experts and by the scientific-academic community, represent a solution to the problem of data portability and also, partly, of data preservation. Archivists and librarians have always counted on the use of standard systems to create digital versions of cultural objects, and have specified guidelines for the creation of durable digital objects. A digital object may be termed portable when it can be interpreted regardless of the computer and operating system in use. But at a higher level, for a digital object to be readable means that it can be interpreted without the need for a specific piece of software. An object's portability is linked to its data format, which is determined by the language in which the file was produced. Obviously, standard file formats vary according to the type of digital object being created. An image will use a format adapted specifically for it, different from an audio or video clip, and use different strategies for conservation from those best suited to a text document. Every medium will therefore have one or more standard formats that guarantee portability. In the area of multimedia it is precisely the dialog between data formats that ensures the function of the system. A multimedia system must therefore provide for the integration of different elements that together determine the nature of the digital object as a complex entity.

For text, Unicode is an example of a portable code, since it can be read on different platforms.[9] A file in a plain text format is encoded at the character level. No additional information is implicated in the process of file creation. All software, and hence all hardware, that is able to read Unicode can read plain text. Plain text is therefore both portable, because it works across hardware and software platforms, and durable, because it will remain accessible in the long run, provided it is migrated to storage media that are readable in the current technical environment.

4.3.1 Marking-up a document

The set of features preserved by "plain text" has evolved significantly over time, from the original 5-bit characters in 1931 used for telegraphic transmission (MacKenzie 1980) to the modern 32-bit representation of Unicode. What we regard today as "text" in fact contains many fossilized codes from the dawn of the computer era: obscure control codes such as "ring the bell" (ASCII character 7) or characters common on US keyboards in the 1960s, such as # or @ (originally the price "at which" a commodity was sold). What we regard as "text" should thus not be restricted to this changing technological notion of encoded characters, but to the abstract notion of all those attributes of a document chosen for preservation (Sahle 2013, 277f). Plain text on its own does not resolve the problem of how to represent those features of a document that cannot be expressed through mere characters, its formatting (text color, font, justification, styles) or its structural components (title, paragraph, sections, chapters). To this end, markup languages have been created (Coombs *et al.* 1987). In markup descriptive labels are usually embedded into a document to explicitly denote elements of structure or layout in a machine-readable way (cf. §§ 3.7.4, 3.7.5 and Figure 3.1). Logical markup, in particular, permits the creation of a document model determined by a series of abstract elements that will eventually be assigned certain characteristics in the output.[10]

The description of the document via logical or "generalized" markup can be regarded as a way of maintaining information over the long term. For if, like the content, the markup itself is also expressed via a plain text format, then readability and therefore the preservation of the text and its structure will be guaranteed.

By "syntax" is meant a set of rules that govern which markup tags may occur and where they can appear; they must also be clearly distinguished from the plain content of the document. If two applications utilize the same syntax they can exchange digital objects without loss of data.

The most common way to markup a document is to "embed" descriptive tags into the stream of characters that represent the content. However, it is also possible to store the markup externally using a "standoff" representation, which preserves the same syntactic structure as the embedded form, but stores the markup tags in a separate file (Grisham, 1994). Another possibility for representing external markup is to use "standoff properties," where the markup is applied to the text without the tags having to conform to a specific syntax (Piez, 2013, Schmidt, 2012). This form of markup is also used in annotation systems where documents need to be commented on by users without changing the underlying text (Sanderson et al, 2013). These alternative approaches may overcome some of the inherent limitations caused by embedding tags directly into the documents they describe.

4.3.2 XML and the OHCO theory

The most widely used form of embedded markup in the digital humanities is XML (extensible markup language, http://www.w3.org/XML/). The XML project began in 1996, through the Activity wing of the W3C, and was officially recommended in February 1998, XML is a metalanguage: it provides a set of rules that can be used to create a potentially infinite number of markup languages. It is a subset of SGML (standard generalized markup language), the first standard language for marking up electronic documents in machine-readable form. SGML was created in 1986 at IBM by Charles Goldfarb as a generalization of the earlier GML (Goldfarb, 1996). SGML was mostly used in publishing. Its big success came when it was used by Tim Berners-Lee to define the first version of HTML, which went on to become the *lingua franca* of the Web (Berners-Lee and Fischetti, 1999, 41–42). XML was a later simplification of SGML that required a stricter adherence to the proper nesting of tags, and so could optionally dispense with the SGML requirement for an external grammar definition (or "DTD"). The XML specification was co-authored by Michael Sperberg-McQueen, a digital humanist and German-language philologist who graduated from Stanford in 1977. Sperberg-McQueen, who worked for an extended period at the W3C, won the XML cup, the prize for the most significant contribution to the development of XML, in 2003.

With XML it is possible to create digital objects that are interoperable between applications that understand a given XML format. An XML file consists of plain textual content and tags that conform to a certain grammar. The tags are defined in an application-independent way via named "elements" (blocks of content) qualified by "attributes" (name-value pairs), which facilitate interchange.

The underlying principle of all markup languages based on XML is the precise notion of "well-formedness," whereby a text is structured as a strictly hierarchical organization of its constitutive elements. The syntax of a markup language determines the logical structure of the document, and corresponds to a tree-graph, ordered by content. This theory, known as OHCO (ordered hierarchy of content objects), was first presented by a group of American scholars (Renear *et al.* 1992/1993). The original OHCO thesis stated that texts were predominantly hierarchical in structure, reinforced by the fact that such structures were readily computable. Markup languages thus seemed at the time to conveniently provide a rigorous definition of the structure of text as it "really" was, or should be. However, given the number of exceptions noted by Renear *et al.*, the original thesis was in fact rather tentative, and its authors later distanced themselves from its stronger formulations (Renear, 1997). Since then

Figure 4.3. What does "markup language" mean?
(http://www.computingverticals.com/496/what-does-markup-language-mean)

it has come to be generally recognized that texts are not fundamentally hierarchical (McGann 2001; Buzzetti 2002; Schmidt and Colomb 2009), even though in certain cases a strong hierarchical organization may be used by their authors (e.g. in plays). There is no denying the efficacy from a computational point of view of casting texts as OHCO objects, even though this often means settling for only an approximation of the desired representation. But neither does this mean that non-hierarchical forms of markup are necessarily *in*efficient.

One could say that markup is a self-descriptive process, because it describes the structure of the text through the system of writing itself, and makes explicit what is otherwise implicit. But encoding is never a neutral act, starting from the choice of which text is to be transcribed, followed by which attributes should be recorded, and then which tags should be used to express them. Hence every encoding represents an interpretation of the text by its transcriber on multiple levels (Sahle 2013, 277ff). Such hypotheses affect the reading of the text, but also the understanding imparted to the end user. Encoding, at whatever level, even when the intention is purely conservational, or structural, is concerned with contextual manipulation or typology; it is always a semiotic activity, because it functions on the basis of a precise theory of the text expressed in a formal language.

Although a word processor allows the formatting and structuring of a page through a friendly graphical interface of buttons and menus, and *invisible* codes, XML provides the means to perform more or less the same operations at a different level of analysis, by using a visible textual code. This enables any computer that can understand XML to read that file and understand which portions are text and which are tags. It is no accident, therefore, that among the techniques of preservation (cf. § 4.2.1) migration to an XML format is often considered as a possible strategy for conservation (Potter 2002), not simply to facilitate exchange. However, exchange is not limited to embedded forms of XML. Even standoff forms of markup can also be expressed in XML or in other languages, such as JSON (javascript object notation).

4.3.3 XML Schemas and the "document type" approach

XML itself only provides rules of syntax, and the tools for marking up a document, but does not indicate which names should be used to give any part of a document a certain interpretation. That is, it does not specify the properties that can be used to describe blocks of text, or the rules for their combination and nesting. For this, schemas are needed. It should be pointed out, however, that in XML the use of schemas (formerly DTDs or document type descriptions) is entirely optional. Although a schema-less XML document is guaranteed to be well-formed (for otherwise it wouldn't be XML) it doesn't guarantee a consistent use of markup. A schema is an XML vocabulary or grammar, which regulates the names of elements and the hierarchy within which they reside; it is a kind of lexicon for XML. While XML explains how to markup, the schema provides the words to perform this operation. Thus interchangeability and portability are ensured, at least at the syntactic level, in the sense that two systems that exchange files in an XML format can communicate by understanding the syntax and structure of a document, though not its semantics. The world of XML has recently seen a shift in the concept of semantics (cf. § 2.4), which no longer applies to the idea of negotiation as implied in natural language, but more as a description of contents. Schemas contribute to enabling a first level of vocabulary sharing, but this does not mean that computers will be able to interpret the meaning of an element of information or of an entire document (cf. the Semantic Web). In fact, a schema on its own does not actually assign a semantics. This situation has lead to projects designed to assign semantics to XML (Renear *et al.* 2003, 119–126).

Although XML does not require the use of a schema, using one increases the value of the document in terms of interchangeability. Documents produced in this way can easily be "validated" or checked against the declared syntax for inconsistencies. Schemas for XML can be created on an ad hoc basis, mostly for a single type of document. But the use of standard schemas is also possible, and should be encouraged. HTML and XHTML, already mentioned, are both markup languages defined by their own schemas.

The concept of *document type* or class is a fundamental property of the language. Based on a "declarative" type of markup, XML allows the definition of a set of markers to carry out the primary job of a standard, by allowing the markup of a document's structural logic. Each schema specifies the features of a class of textual documents, all sharing the same structural characteristics. By class or type of document is meant a group of documents that share certain properties: poetry, narrative, and drama are three classes or types that have their own logical structure. A poem will therefore by marked up according to the properties of the class "poetry."

Specifying a schema means defining a set of element names for interpreting the phenomena that distinguish a given class. Working out which features need to be recorded in a class of documents is called modeling, and has significant semiotic and cultural implications (Fiormonte 2008b). The model to which a text refers defines those aspects of the source that may be subject to interpretation, and their associated vocabulary. It is interpretative because the definition of a schema and the choice of elements to use are both parts of the ad hoc modeling used for a certain source. Such a model is determined both by the type of the source and therefore by its class (e.g. a manuscript, a printed text, a poem or a piece of prose), and by the objectives of the researchers who are marking up the source.

4.3.4 TEI: A standard for the humanistic domain
Among the schemas for XML, the one that has dominated in the field of humanities is TEI (TEI P5 2008), a lexicon of elements and attributes useful for the description of cultural objects and artifacts. The TEI project originated in 1987, following a conference organized by the ACH (Association for Computers and the Humanities). During the conference, the need to define a standard for the digitization of text inspired the ACH, along with the Association for Computational Linguistics (ALC) and the Association for Literary and Linguistic Computing (ALLC) to establish the first guidelines for the encoding and exchange of texts in electronic format.

In 1999, the TEI Consortium was founded with the aim of maintaining, developing and promoting the Guidelines. Literary texts, whether in prose, verse, or drama, find in the TEI Guidelines a ready set of elements for the description of all necessary phenomena suitable for interpretation: from the definition of the elements of a document's logical structure to the specification of people's names, places and dates, from the description of a manuscript to the recording of phenomena peculiar to an edition (such as the apparatus of a critical edition), from linguistic analysis to hypertextual linking. TEI is also a project in continual evolution. From version P1 in July 1990 (an initial draft, and not published, 89 tags) it has evolved to P5 (2007–2015, version 2.8.0, 550 tags).

The TEI Guidelines are widely used as a standard instrument for the digital representation of content in the humanities. It is used in projects such as the collection of texts from literary traditions to the production of literary hypertexts, from digital publications to linguistic analysis (on this last aspect see 4.8.2). Projects based on TEI offer a variety of interpretative solutions, which attest to its strong support among the traditional humanistic disciplines. From digital editions of single texts to archives of documents united by a document type or a period, the catalog of projects using TEI (TEI P5 2008) currently numbers 157. This list is regularly updated, and there are doubtless many other projects that use TEI.

Not only are there increasing numbers of projects based on the use of TEI as a useful tool for conservation and interchange, but there are new centers of research emerging that use TEI as a reference model for the creation of texts in a digital, portable format. The TEI consortium also investigates the evolution of new technologies, and ensures compliance with the new languages, formats and models of the Web. There are also special interest groups or SIGs for the different areas in which the Guidelines are used: from ontologies to manuscripts; from libraries to correspondence; from linguistics to scholarly publishing (for the complete list see: http://www.tei-c.org/Activities/SIG/). The TEI also organizes an annual conference (http://members.tei-c.org/Events/meetings), and runs the journal jTEI — Journal of TEI (http://jtei.revues.org/, Issue 1, June 2011) and a mailing list (tei-l@listserv.brown.edu).

The TEI developers do not force users to adopt the all of the TEI framework. TEI Roma is a tool that allows the customization of the TEI schema for specifical applications: "A TEI customization is a document from which you can generate a schema defining which elements and attributes from the TEI system you want to use, along with customized HTML or PDF documentation of it. The schema generated can be expressed in any of DTD, RELAXNG W3C Schema or Schematron languages." A TEI customization is informally referred to as an ODD (for "One Document Does it all").

However, not everyone in the DH community recommends use of the TEI Guidelines (e.g. Buzzetti, Fiormonte, Schmidt). The large number of elements and the fact that it is continuously growing are two factors that have, in their view, impaired its function, and have made it less useful in practical projects.

4.3.5 Schemas and namespaces: why we need formal vocabularies

The TEI schema is not the only vocabulary of XML in use by digital humanists. For example, the metadata tags used to describe digital objects often include names from, e.g., Dublin Core (cf. § 4.4.4) and the Friend of a Friend schemas.[11] However, some of these names conflict with the TEI vocabulary. For example, the TEI schema defines a header that contains metadata, which may include <title>, <date> or <source> elements; so does Dublin Core (DC). In order to use the DC versions in TEI documents namespaces must be used. A namespace is just a reference to an external schema, via a URI (uniform resource identifier, cf. § 4.4.1). For instance, the URI http://dublincore.org/documents/dcmi-terms is used as an identifier for the dc-terms metadata tags. An abbreviated form of the URI is declared in the document and then elements from that schema can be used by prefixing them with the abbreviated name. So an element called <dc:title> would denote the Dublin-core version of title, not the TEI one. Similarly, in a non-TEI document, the tag <TEI:title> would mean that the element "title" is defined according to the rules of TEI. This provides a measure of interoperability, since elements defined using exactly the same names (taking into account the prefix qualifier) in different documents can be considered to contain the same kind of information.

Although TEI documents contain metadata in their headers, to assist compatibility with other kinds of digital object (which usually lack embedded metadata), external metadata is normally added whenever digital documents are gathered together in a repository. This is also usually recorded using an XML schema. The most commonly used XML metadata formats for this purpose are MODS and METS.[12] MODS describes individual digital objects, whereas METS acts as a wrapper linking them together.

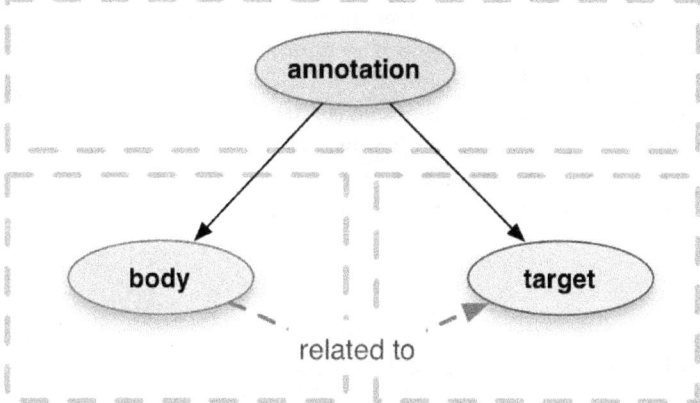

Figure 4.4. The Open Annotation Data Model (http://www.openannotation.org/spec/core)

4.3.6 Beyond text: using annotations

While mark-up generally refers to the process of adding strings to text, annotation refers to the action of adding information to any kind of digital object.

Annotation is one of the most ancient activities of the humanities scholar (Tomasi and Vitali 2013). Many of the books written by Alexandrian scholars around 2,000 years ago were commentaries on existing literary works. Each comment consisted of a lemma (a quotation from the original text being commented on) and a body, which could explain the meaning of the passage, or provide additional information about people or places mentioned, or describe textual problems. Comments also often contained links to other works. Modern annotations are surprisingly similar. When we comment on a news story on the Web we are effectively annotating it. The target is not changed by the annotation because, like the ancient commentaries, annotations refer to objects externally. They do this by pointing to target resources, which can be in any format: XML, HTML or plain text, or even parts of images and videos. The body of the annotation likewise can be in any format: it could even be an image. The author and time of the annotation might also need to be recorded, and the exact position and extent of the annotated text or image. An annotation thus can quickly become a fairly complex bundle of information. In the Open Annotation model each part of the annotation is given an identifier, and the annotation itself simply links them together (Sanderson *et al.* 2013). One advantage of this approach is that it is easy to find annotations that refer to particular objects or types of objects.

All commentary supplied by the user about a video, audio clip or image (for example, a character in a video, a melody in a song, a certain detail in a digital image) can be assigned an identifier, and so can itself become a searchable item — for example, all videos in which a certain city appears, all images in a certain collection featuring a flower, etc.[13]

Many projects are now focused on the problem of annotating media. For example, ResearchSpace at the British Museum (http://www.researchspace.org/) and Europeana (http://pro.europeana.eu/thoughtlab/user-generated-content#EConnect) are working on annotating multimedia objects, that is, not only images but also audio and video, to enrich their semantic power. The Pundit project (http://thepund.it) developed by Net7 is an example of an open source tool for semantic annotation of resources that has been used in several projects in the Digital Humanities domain. Hypothes.is is another annotation tool, based on the W3C Open Annotation specification (http://www.openannotation.org/spec/core/).

4.4 Metadata and the description of the document

Creating digital objects means creating units of information that are to be conserved, unambiguously identified, or which carry content comprising both the data (the document itself) and information about that data, its metadata (Arms 1995).

4.4.1 The unambiguous identification of resources

Unequivocal identification is the first aspect to consider in attempting to understand the meaning of metadata. Standards for unambiguous identification are necessary if digital objects are to be searched and accessed. A URI (uniform resource identifier) is an object that allows a resource to be found regardless of its physical location. It is not the same as a URL (uniform resource locator), which specifies the physical address of a resource, whereas a URI allows for changes in location. Because it is a persistent, conventional name, it represents a first level guarantee of the identification of an electronic resource. It is a distinction between an object as a flow of bits (identified by a URL) and an object as a logical entity (identified by a URI). Tim Berners-Lee saw the URI system as fundamental to the World Wide Web (cf. § 2.2.2), and as a key element in the construction of a distributed environment for the dissemination of content and access to digital objects in the form of Web resources.

Other standards have also been created to this end, with the aim of setting objects free from their location. The URN (uniform resource name) is based on the definition of a schema for the assignment of names to resources; the DOI (digital object identifier) provides a mechanism for attaching numeric strings to each digital object. In general these identifiers (also known as "handles") are fundamental because the ability to find an object is vital to the conservation of information. They might serve different purposes, but the important thing is that they all use a system that allows unambiguous identification, just as the ISBN (international standard book number) did for a printed book.

4.4.2 Metadata and modeling

An identifier is a fundamental piece of metadata for describing a resource. A general definition for metadata might be any added data that serves to describe a certain digital object, to assist in its management and retrieval. In this sense one could say that even embedded markup tags are a kind of metadata, in as far as their function is to add something (for example, the tag <p>) that can be used to describe something else (i.e. a paragraph). Hence the idea of modeling, that is, the assignment of descriptive elements or properties to a document's individual characteristics, is a concept that can also be applied to metadata.

When a single digital object or collection of objects must be described, a model of reference should first be established to declare which characteristics of the object or collection are considered relevant.

The example most often used to explain metadata is that of a library catalog. Books represent the objects and data, and the metadata is the information in the catalog that describes them, such as a book's title, name of the editor, year of publication, etc. This is no different from what happens when describing a digital object except for the kind of characteristics that are being described. Metadata models are used because every digital object, and every collection, will have different metadata. Depending on the resources to be managed, different characteristics will need to be assigned: a digital text is one thing, a video file is quite another. And depending on the nature of the collection to be described, different features will have to be emphasized.

However, a model can never be exhaustive; it is always an abstraction, which expresses a certain view of a set of digital objects. For example, the metadata for a collection of manuscripts might include a codicological description, or describe all the illuminations in the codices, or add information about the holding institution, or the people who have consulted certain manuscripts. Each point of view of the collection will determine the modeling procedure and thus an individual choice of characteristics, which will potentially give rise to a varied set of metadata.

Although, in an extended sense, markup may be considered as a kind of metadata, the usual function of metadata is to provide a description of an electronic resource so that it can be managed and retrieved. To achieve this, other information will need to be provided to answer questions such as who created the document, what its state is, who owns it, when it was created, where it has been stored, in what format, how big it is, etc.

The convention is to classify types of metadata on three levels:
1. *Descriptive metadata* — the bibliographic description of the electronic resource (and its analog counterpart), resembling an OPAC (online public access catalog) entry.
2. *Administrative metadata*. Because of the different ways in which digital objects are managed, at this level the metadata can be subdivided on a further three levels:
   — technical metadata: formats and parameters used in digitization;
   — preservation metadata: procedures and technologies used to digitize and maintain the digital document;
   — rights management metadata: intellectual property rights, access and copying restrictions, licenses for use of the resource.

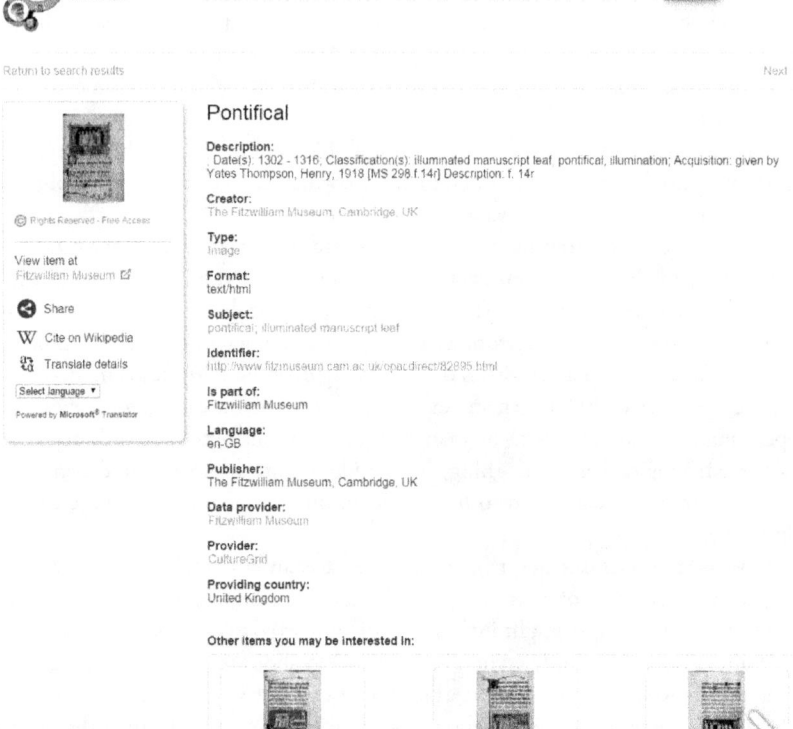

Figure 4.5. A set of metadata from the Europeana collection the description of an illuminated manuscript (http://www.europeana.eu/)

3. *Structural metadata.* The function of this level is to describe the structure of a digital resource, such as the list of files that make up the object or the different digital versions of the same file. This kind of metadata allows for different materials to be compared, for example, by specifying that an illumination is present in a certain codex, or an image in a particular document. But it can also relate different versions of the same material: for example it can specify that a given .jpg file is the compressed version of the same object in .tiff format. This is an important point because, as mentioned previously in § 4.2, objects may be stored in different formats but with the same informational content, and that is why the metadata is important.

This tripartite division is the most common, but it is not the only one. Depending on which aspects of a resource are considered most important, a different set of metadata might be chosen, or they might be classified differently. There are in fact several standards for metadata, created by different institutions and organizations. They differ in their goals, in the level of detail they consider most pertinent (descriptive, administrative or structural) and by the type of resource they are designed to describe.

As far as preservation is concerned, metadata has the function of unambiguously identifying a resource (through its URI, for example), and of providing information on the provenance of the data, the context of its production — in what technological environment it was produced — and the kinds of mechanisms put in place to ensure its authenticity, including rights management. PREMIS (preservation metadata: implementation strategies) is an activity promoted by the Online Computer Library Center (OCLC) and the Research Libraries Group (RLG) that has seen the involvement of archives, libraries and museums in various European and North American countries, in the desire to create a data dictionary for preservation. The PREMIS data model includes the concept of an intellectual entity, as distinct from a digital object, in the content of a document:

> Intellectual Entity: a set of content that is considered a single intellectual unit for purposes of management and description: for example, a particular book, map, photograph, or database. An Intellectual Entity can include other Intellectual Entities; for example, a web site can include a web page; a web page can include an image. An Intellectual Entity may have one or more digital representations. (Premis 2008)

The next section will examine one of these standards for metadata in detail.

4.4.3 A Model for understanding metadata: FRBR

A suitable starting point for discussing metadata is the FRBR (functional requirement for bibliographic records) standard, a model for creating catalog records. FRBR treats digital objects as complex entities, composed of different aspects that led to its creation: from the language used to the format it is stored in, from the model it is based on to the technology used to produce it, from the hardware in use at the time of its creation to the software best suited for processing it. Metadata must therefore be calibrated with this in mind and able to document the decisions taken and the results obtained.

Even if FRBR is mostly used in the bibliographic domain, the conceptual model that it implies helps to describe a digital object as a stratified entity on different levels.

— When associating metadata with a source, the following points should be considered: whether there is an analog version of the digitized resource that needs description;
— the digital version of an analog resource requires declaration of the specific features of the languages and formats used to create it;
— there may be several digital versions of the same analog source;

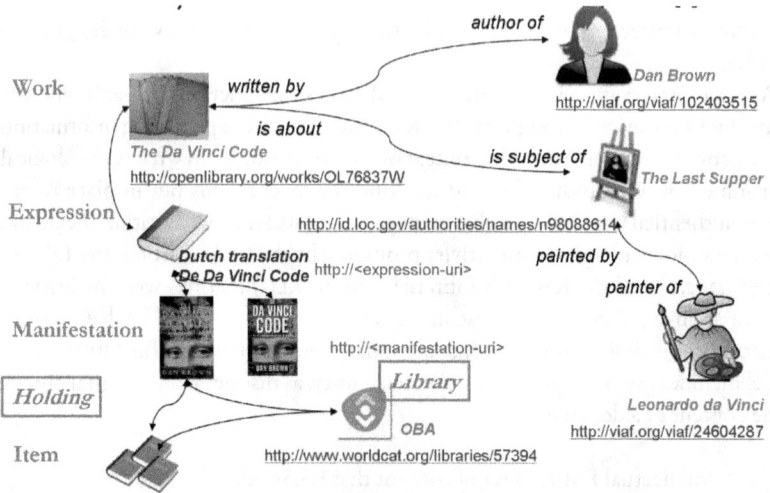

Figure 4.6. A sample of the FRBR approach (http://commonplace.net/tag/frbr/)

— the digital object being created might be related to other digital objects with the same content, but made using other languages or formats, or based on a different analog version.

As an example, consider a digital version of Dante's *Comedy*:

— there must be a print edition, considered the most representative, on which to base the digitization;
— the digital object may take the form of a text, a collection of images, an audio file or a video;
— other digital versions of the same text may also be available online;
— these other versions may be based on the same or on a different print edition, and may or may not have been created using the same technologies.

In these terms, FRBR defines the concepts:

— WORK: the artistic, intellectual creation; an abstract entity. It is realized in the
— EXPRESSION: the intellectual and artistic "realization" of a work. The work exists only within the community of content that exists through the various expressions of the work. The expression takes material form through the
— MANIFESTATION: the physical embodiment of the work, represented in the
— ITEM: single instance of the manifestation.

In the given example, the *Comedy* (the work) is "realized" in various editions (expression) that can be digitized in a number of ways using various techniques (manifestation) to create a digital object (item).

Using FRBR as a model for metadata might seem a daring move, and the example provided might not correspond exactly to the conceptual model of FRBR. However, this model provides a way of thinking about the digital object as a complex entity, on several levels, that can be documented via metadata.

4.4.4 Tools for metadata: the role of Dublin Core
In general using metadata means thinking about it on three levels:
1. the syntax for writing it;
2. the reference schema for the names of its elements;
3. zthe names of the elements for describing the various characteristics of the document.

Metadata may be expressed in a variety of formats, including many based on XML or, increasingly, on JSON (javascript object notation). The choice will depend on implementation details, such as how the metadata is to be used in a given software environment.

At the schema level the standard vocabulary has become Dublin Core metadata (http://dublincore.org), which is designed to provide a list of minimal descriptive tags for digital resources.

The name comes from the idea of the project being a "core" of interesting meta-information for any given resource, and because it was born out of an initiative by librarians, archivists, content providers and markup experts, who met in 1995 in Dublin, Ohio. Through Dublin Core, the description of an electronic resource becomes more like the description of a simple bibliographic resource.

The importance of Dublin Core is bound up with the need to guarantee the interchange of information. For if digital objects can share a single vocabulary through their metadata then they can be mutually understood. If combined with agreement at the syntactic level, this can also guarantee a basic level of interoperability.

This emphasizes again the importance of standards as tools of communication and interchange. Every community, including archives, libraries, museums and art galleries, has built custom vocabularies with the aim of constructing the best possible set of metadata to describe their own collections of physical objects, such as books, manuscripts, museum artifacts or paintings. However, working with digital objects which can so easily now be gathered together from heterogenous sources has underlined the need for a common metadata standard.

With this same aim in mind, there have been numerous projects for mapping between different metadata schemas to promote information exchange. These mappings use tables of correspondence that permit the establishment of relationships between various schemas, by equating the names used by each metadata set (Day 1996). The possibility of using such a mapping makes it practical to limit the discussion here to Dublin Core.

Dublin Core proposes a set of fifteen descriptive categories, which make it possible to describe a digital resource in any format. Using a namespace, metadata can be assigned to a digital resource. If an instrument such as Dublin Core allows for the standardization of the set of descriptive categories, with the aim of true semantic interoperability, then it follows that the description of the resource, and the values associated with it, are also standardized. For example, the Dublin Core category "subject" might be used to describe a new subject created for a resource or an already standard one, such as those commonly in use in libraries. Making use of shared schemas — official vocabularies — provides a guarantee that the metadata created in dif-

2000: Growing the vocabulary

Elements	Refinements		Encodings	Types
1. Identifier	Abstract	Is referenced by	Box	Collection
2. Title	Access rights	Is replaced by	DCMIType	Dataset
3. Creator	Alternative	Is required by	DDC	Event
4. Contributor	Audience	Issued	IMT	Image
5. Publisher	Available	Is version of	ISO3166	Interactive
6. Subject	Bibliographic citation	License	ISO639-2	Resource
7. Description	Conforms to	Mediator	LCC	Moving Image
8. Coverage	Created	Medium	LCSH	Physical Object
9. Format	Date accepted	Modified	MESH	Service
10. Type	Date copyrighted	Provenance	Period	Software
11. Date	Date submitted	References	Point	Sound
12. Relation	Education level	Replaces	RFC1766	Still Image
13. Source	Extent	Requires	RFC3066	Text
14. Rights	Has format	Rights holder	TGN	
15. Language	Has part	Spatial	UDC	
	Has version	Table of contents	URI	
	Is format of	Temporal	W3CTDF	
	Is part of	Valid		

Figure 4.7. Dublin Core Metadata Initiative (DCMI) — Learning Resources. The DC in the year 2000 (https://glennas.wordpress.com/2010/01/31/dublin-core-metadata-initiative-dcmi-learning-resources/)

ferent places can be mutually understood. This is no different from what happens in OPAC, where interoperability, which allows the searching of many catalogs from the one portal, makes use of a shared system of cataloging using a standardized language, syntax and vocabulary. For example, LCSH (Library of Congress subject headings) provides lists of subjects, and the Dewey decimal classification offers hierarchical lists of descriptors as subjects. For authors' names there are authority lists, which ensure that a given author's name is always written in the same way.

The Dublin Core model is similar to a classification system designed by the Indian mathematician and librarian S. R. Ranganathan around the middle of the 20th century called "faceted classification." In this system, each book is assigned a series of attributes, called facets, designed to record different characteristics through which the object may be analyzed. Even if this system is little used in traditional libraries (since a physical book can only be in one place), it is an approach that has been often used on the Web because it permits the examination of different aspects of a collection or a resource. For example, using Dublin Core, one can explore a collection by language, format, author and so on, for the entire series of labels.

From this brief reflection on metadata, it is clear that assigning a series of categories to a given resource is not a straightforward and objective process, but results from the careful consideration of which aspects of the resource, or collection, are of interest. However, knowing the names of these categories in advance (through modeling) facilitates the assignment of values to the appropriate tags.

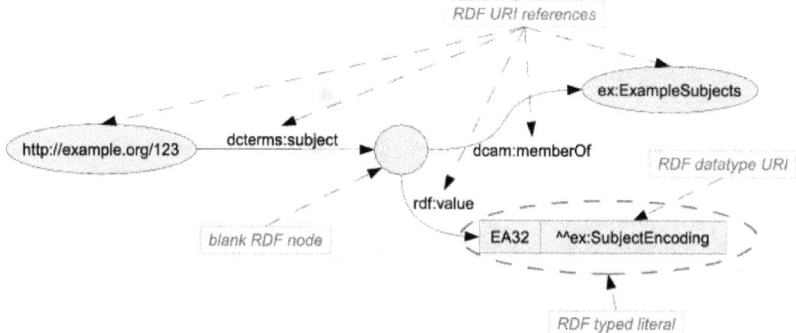

Figure 4.8. Expressing Dublin Core metadata using the Resource Description Framework (RDF). (http://dublincore.org/documents/dc-rdf/)

4.4.5 Expressing metadata formally: RDF

This view of metadata leads naturally to the description of a new model that is establishing itself as a tool for formally expressing metadata. This is RDF (resource description framework), a W3C project born out of research into new languages for online content. According to this model, the creation of metadata is based on "triples," which are composed of:

— a subject about which the statement is made. This is usually a resource, such as one or more webpages, or a resource that might not be actually online, so long as it has a URI;
— a predicate, which could be a property that describes the subject (for example, the name of a category in Dublin Core);
— an object: the value associated with this property. This can be a literal or another resource.

Namespaces, schemas, URIs, and RDF are some of the key elements of what is commonly referred to as the Semantic Web. Tim Berners-Lee, the inventor of the World Wide Web and the man behind the concept of the Semantic Web, had the idea of creating webpages that could be understood by a computer. The objective is for the machine to be able to help in gathering information needed by the end user.

RDF could be described as a data model based upon the idea of making statements about resources (especially web resources). A collection of RDF statements intrinsically represents a labeled, directed multi-graph. But there are in use several common serialization formats of RDF (i.e. Turtle, N3, RDF/XML). Another approach is the related RDFa standard (Adida *et al.* 2013). This uses simple attributes (about, property, rel) that may be added to XML or plain HTML documents so they can record RDF triples, which can also be chained together into a full RDF graph.

When the document is searched for information the relationships between resources can be discovered and useful information deduced. For example, if the user was looking for the text of Dante's *Comedy*, and the metadata on the page referred to other texts online, or other versions, other formats, or libraries that have manuscript

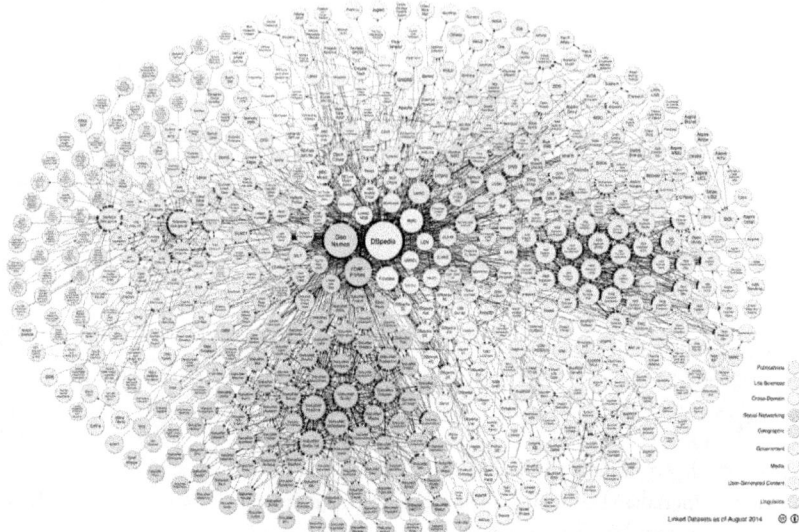

Figure 4.9. The Linking Open Data Cloud Diagram 2014 (http://lod-cloud.net/)

copies or digital images of those manuscripts, then this related information could be returned.

In a global system of information on the Web, it will be possible to relate data from different environments, stored in different places, or using different technologies. One project involved in this is Linked Data, an evolution of the Semantic Web:

> Linked Data is about using the Web to connect related data that wasn't previously linked, or using the Web to lower the barriers to linking data currently linked using other methods. More specifically, Wikipedia defines Linked Data as "a term used to describe a recommended best practice for exposing, sharing, and connecting pieces of data, information, and knowledge on the Semantic Web using URIs and RDF." (http://linkeddata.org/)

Standardizing the procedures for creating webpages might be an important step forward in this direction, by helping computers exchange information. This is why it is necessary to:
— always associate metadata with a resource;
— use RDF as a model;[14]
— use Dublin Core as a possible dictionary for the properties of the metadata;
— employ controlled vocabularies for the values of the properties.
On this last point, some expansion may be required.

The Digital Humanist

Research

Research Home ▶ Tools ▶ Art & Architecture Thesaurus ▶ Full Record Display

Art & Architecture Thesaurus® Online
Full Record Display

New Search   ◀ Previous Page   ? Help

Click the 🔺 icon to view the hierarchy.

Semantic View (JSON, RDF, N3/Turtle, N-Triples)

ID: 300265436   **Record Type:** concept

🔺 **arrow vases** (vases, vessels (containers), ... Furnishings and Equipment (hierarchy name))

Note: Refers to a type of globular Chinese vase with a long cylindrical neck at the top of which are two tubular loops or lugs. They were used as targets in the competitive game in which arrows were aimed into the mouth or, better yet, the lugs.

Terms:
    arrow vases (preferred,C,U,English-P,D,U,PN)
    arrow vase (C,U,English,AD,U,SN)
    pijlenvazen (C,U,Dutch-P,D,U,U)

Facet/Hierarchy Code: V.TQ

Hierarchical Position:
🔺   Objects Facet
🔺   .... Furnishings and Equipment (hierarchy name) (G)
🔺   .... Containers (hierarchy name) (G)
🔺   .... containers (receptacles) (G)
🔺   .... <containers by form> (G)
🔺   .... vessels (containers) (G)
🔺   .... vases (G)
🔺   .... arrow vases (G)

Additional Notes:
    Dutch ..... Verwijst naar een Chinees type globulaire vazen met een lange cilindrische hals aan de bovenkant waarvan zich twee buisvormige lussen of oren bevinden. Ze fungeerden als doelwit in een wedstrijdspel waarbij pijlen werden gericht in de mond of, beter nog, de oren.

Sources and Contributors:
    arrow vase............ [VP]
    .... Fleming and Honour, Penguin Dictionary of the Decorative Arts (1989) 41
    .... Savage and Newman, Illustrated Dictionary of Ceramics (1985) 31
    arrow vases............ [VP Preferred]
    .... Getty Vocabulary Program rules
    pijlenvazen............ [RKD, AAT-Ned Preferred]
    .... AAT-Ned (1994-)

Subject: ..... [RKD, AAT-Ned, VP]
    .... AAT-Ned (1994-)
    .... Fleming and Honour, Penguin Dictionary of the Decorative Arts (1989) 41

Note:
English.......... [VP]
    .... Fleming and Honour, Penguin Dictionary of the Decorative Arts (1989) 41
Dutch .... [RKD, AAT-Ned]
    .... AAT-Ned (1994-)
    .... Bureau AAT, RKD

Figure 4.10. The Getty Art & Architecture Thesaurus. The concept "arrow vases"

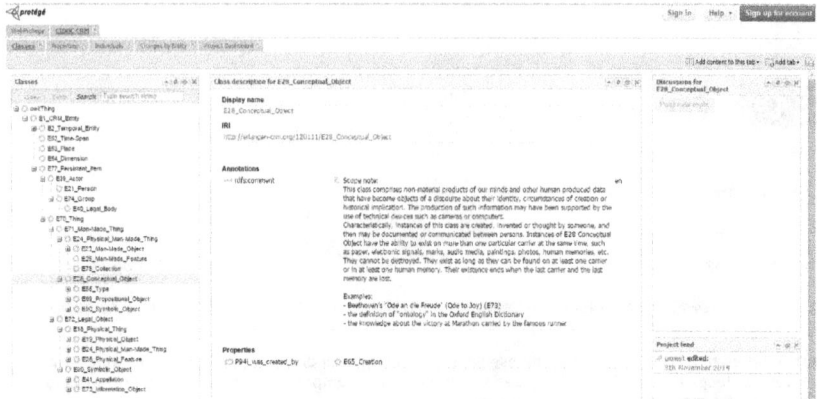

Figure 4.11. A portion of the CIDOC-CRM Ontology on Protégé Web, a tool for creating ontologies (http://webprotege.stanford.edu)

4.4.6 Taxonomies, thesauri, ontologies: towards semantics

The majority of values associated with properties can and should be acquired from a controlled list of names. Thesauri and taxonomies created by different institutions, principally libraries, museums and art galleries, are tools for limiting the polysemy of natural language.[15] Given that everyone uses different words to describe the same concept, the use of controlled lists makes it possible to think in terms of a single concept for each synonym. This also facilitates the establishment of links to other concepts. A synonym is one such case, but by using hierarchical relationships other possibilities may include hyponyms (subordinate terms) and hypernyms (superior terms). Although a taxonomy is just a hierarchy of concepts (like the Dewey decimal classification noted above), a thesaurus also establishes equal relationships between terms: equivalences, synonyms, and associated terms (like the LCSH noted above).

Reasoning in terms of properties, controlled values, relationships and hierarchies leads naturally to a fundamental concept of the Semantic Web: the conceptual model of an ontology. In a given area of interest (e.g. a collection of books) an ontology might be defined as the shared conceptualization of the classes it contains (i.e. the books), their possible sub-classes (author, title, publisher, year etc.) organized hierarchically, the properties of the classes (the author will have a name and a surname) and the relations between classes (the author's "has written" relationship to the title). An ontology is also based on a set of rules that govern the construction of concepts and their attributes.[16]

An ontology will be populated with objects from its area of interest. One might say that the ontology allows the expression of metadata so it can be automatically used by a computer. If RDF can provide a formal representation for the structure of metadata, ontologies permit the establishment of semantic relationships that allow inferences to be made within its domain.[17]

The Digital Humanist

4.4.7 Metadata and folksonomy: the user experience
Among the new characteristics of Web 2.0, there is now a new way to describe content, which differs from the ontological approach. "Tagging" is the application of a tag by the reader in order to describe the content of a webpage. This is the "social tagging" referred to above (cf. Ch. 2 and 3). In contrast to the use of formal, rigid, and pre-established classifications, it is the user who is the author and describer of the resources that he or she visits and uses (Dattolo *et al.* 2009). Known also under the term "folksonomy," this is an approach quite different from that of the Semantic Web, where metadata is assigned in accordance with a rigorous, formal and controlled set of properties and values. The folksonomy approach is open at all levels, in terms of the choice of useful properties for a resource and also in the values associated with them. It is, however, only a first level of cataloging that can serve as a point of departure for metadata in a system of collaborative tagging. The end user thus plays the role of being not only an active producer of content, but also a cataloger of the same content. This is the age of blogs and wikis, social bookmarking and social tagging, music, audio and video sharing or livecasting, CMS (content management systems) and distributed editing, and some of the most eminent "social" projects of production and free annotation of content in the fields of collaborative production and multimedia. These are social projects that use tools, such as Blogger, Wordpress, YouTube, Facebook, Delicious and Google Docs just to name a few, which demonstrate the democratization of knowledge that Web 2.0 has brought about. The user, who in Web 1.0 was (in theory) a passive consumer, has become a "prosumer" — a producer and consumer at the same time. The fundamental role of the prosumer is recognized also in the remote systems that increasingly utilize knowledge created by users through their choices, selections, options and tags. Every activity on the part of the end user becomes a mine of information that can be used by web-oriented applications. Collaborative filtering is a good example. This makes suggestions to the user based on similar preferences expressed by other users,[18] although it requires careful management to avoid being seen as a way of suppressing the user's individuality and of controlling his/her choices (for a complete discussion of these issues see § 5.5.)

As already described, markup languages and metadata are necessary tools for the creation of portable, lasting digital objects. In this way files can be created in a non-proprietary format, adequately described, unequivocally identified and searchable. However, so far no mention has been made of where these digital objects can be kept, so as to be accessible to users (principally on the Web). Access to digital objects means access to their contents (data) and to the elements needed for their identification and management (metadata). The next two sections will examine the archiving and dissemination of such digital objects: open archives and digital libraries.

4.5 Open archives

Where can these digital objects be placed so that data and metadata can be retrieved and preserved? Repositories are organized deposits of digital content, whether texts, images, audio, or video collections. These are virtual spaces, mostly available over the Web, where digital objects are collected, stored and generally made available to users. Every digital object in the repository must be unambiguously identified so it can be found regardless of its physical location.

Repositories might host a complete digital object or only its metadata. The metadata may either be incorporated into the document (embedded metadata) or stored in a separate file connected to the resource (external metadata). This latter model splits the data (document, image, audio file or video) from its metadata, allowing it to be queried separately. From a single interface, it thus becomes possible to access the metadata of different collections that can then be connected with the actual resource. Instead of just one repository, there may be several, communicating among themselves because they use the same metadata standards and protocols.

In open archives copying and transferring of files can be done autonomously and voluntarily, using the principle of self-archiving for public access on the Web. Indeed, the open archive is nothing more than a purpose-built place to store digital objects, with a view to making them publicly accessible.

The adoption of shared architectures such as open archives is becoming a reference model for the dissemination of digital content. The usual design is to create different repositories, each consisting of a group of autonomous collections with shared standards for metadata to guarantee interoperability between groups (cf. Conclusions, §2).

4.5.1 The open archives initiative

The OAI (open archives initiative) model of self-archiving, mostly arising from collections of e-prints, pre-prints and post-prints, is now becoming established in the field of distributed metadata associated with collections of cultural resources.[19]

OAI was designed for the dissemination of metadata in a shared environment, through the use of centralized repositories, that integrate heterogeneous resources in a unified service. Instead of offering a digital object from a dedicated repository, only the metadata is supplied, which can then be used to retrieve the actual resources via a URL or URI.

According to the OAI model, each producer of digital objects (a "data provider") can transfer metadata, generally in a portable format such as XML, single objects and collections, to an open archive (the "service provider"), and thus make them generally accessible on the Web.

One of the OAI's current projects is the open archive initiative protocol for metadata harvesting (OAI-PMH), which should allow for the automatic collection of metadata. Harvesting is the technique that search engines use to index webpages (cf. Ch. 5). As soon as the data provider makes standardized metadata available (for example, in Dublin Core), harvesting is automatic, and the metadata of various repositories will be integrated into a single environment, a collective OAI, and made accessible to the end user.

The key concepts already raised, such as the unambiguous identification of resources, the use of repositories as accessible archives online and the data/metadata distinction, also form the basis for the architectural design of open archives.

In particular, Robert Kahn and Robert Wilensky (1995/2006) were the first to study a theoretical model of an infrastructure able to integrate different digital information distribution services. This theoretical model led to development of the already-mentioned "handle" (cf. § 4.4.1), an indispensable tool for identifying digital objects, and focused on data and metadata as the necessary building blocks of the digital object, which is understood as a complex entity.

4.6 Digital libraries

If open archives are one model for the dissemination of digital objects on the Web, another is the digital library. It is unclear exactly where one ends and the other begins, but it has to do with the type of software applications used in their creation. In both cases, the tools are based on portable languages, unambiguous identification systems and sets of metadata.

There is still much variation in the practices of libraries, and no real standard that clearly distinguishes between what is classified as a digital library or digital repository. But a digital library seems to be more than a mere collection of digital objects. What then is meant by the term? There are several published definitions, and there are often large differences between them. One way to think about digital libraries is to reflect that their role is not much different from that of a traditional library. A digital library must allow for the creation, conservation, description and access of digital materials. A few of the key concepts appear to be that:
— the materials produced, conserved, described and made accessible may be texts, images, audio or video files;
— the formats must be standardized, both for "born digital" and explicitly digitized items;
— each item must be augmented with appropriate metadata at different levels of representation;
— there must be an OPAC, or a catalog for the digital library, to allow the repository to be searched;
— the items must be accessible through a Web interface;
— and, above all, strategies must be adopted that allow digital libraries to exchange data with one another (interoperability) and conserve information for the long term (preservation).

The first step towards the creation of digital libraries arrived with the first projects to digitize cultural objects in institutions such as libraries, museums, art galleries, universities, etc. The digital library contains not only electronic books, articles and periodicals, but also historical catalogs, collections of manuscripts, photographs and printed books, all of which are collected and searchable on the Web. While libraries and institutions have started projects directed towards physical preservation, the Google project is more like a collection of digital images of books than a digital library in the usual sense.

Institutions concerned with conservation have reflected on the requirements of preservation, and as a result projects have been initiated to share information about the principles of preservation on the theoretical, methodological and technical levels. Some examples include the ERPANET (http://www.erpanet.org) and DELOS (http://www.delos.info) networks of excellence, projects such as CASPAR (cultural, artistic and scientific knowledge for preservation, access and retrieval, http://www.casparpreserves.eu) and DPE (digital preservation Europe: http://www.digitalpreservationeurope.eu).

For the true preservation of digital objects, recognizing and establishing the model that underpins digital libraries has become a particularly urgent task. In other words, planning and realizing a digital library also means using a platform for the creation, archiving and distribution of digital materials that answers certain requirements.

In particular OAIS (open archival information system) is a project that proposes a logical model for the creation of digital libraries. This means specifying which characteristics a digital object must generally have for it to be stored in a digital library. OAIS does not, in fact, say anything different from what has already been said above, but it does formalize it in such a way that software developers can create applications based upon it. The theoretical basis for the model is that every digital library must have systems for dealing with the intake, archiving, and management of digital objects, as well as user access and administration.

The key concept in OAIS is that of the information object (IO) — the digital object — is made up of data and metadata. Digital libraries subscribing to the OAIS principles use various components to administer each digital object: systems for archiving (storage), data management, and presentation to the end user (transformation and dissemination). Information objects are classified in accordance with three types of information packages (IP), and with three modes of access to the digital object:

- SIP (submission information package), is data sent by the producer according to a pre-arranged policy;
- AIP (archival information package), is the long-term archiving of the data;
- DIP (dissemination information package), is a package intended for distribution at the request of a user. A DIP can be adapted to the specific requirements of the end user. Every user will have different requirements according to his or her cultural and social background, but also according to the specific requirements of the queries and search results. It then makes sense to think in a user-centric way, by giving each user profile a DIP that corresponds to his or

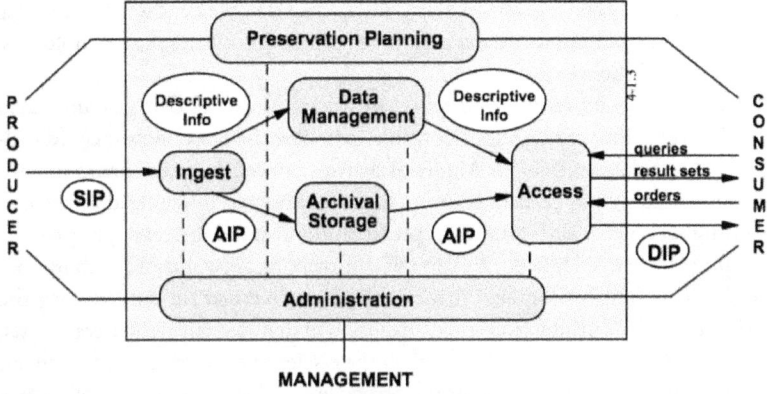

Figure 4.12. Reference Model for an Open Archival Information System (OAIS)[20]

her informational needs. Figure 4.1 shows clearly the theoretical formulation of this model.

OAIS can therefore be seen as a solution defining the infrastructure of a digital library and constitutes the model for the creation of environments regardless of the types of digital resources, disciplines, formats, and the syntax and vocabulary adopted for the expression of meta-information. But it is not the only available model. Another possible architecture is the Kahn-Wilensky model mentioned above. Beyond these various proposals it is at least clear that a solid infrastructure is a necessary condition for the construction of digital libraries that conform to the requirements of the preservation of digital objects.

4.7 Semantic repositories and networking

This chapter will conclude with some thoughts on the dominant new paradigm in the field of digital archives and libraries: the application of Semantic Web and social networking technologies to the building of environments for the dissemination of digital objects. The Semantic Web only makes sense if the underlying technologies and principles can be applied to existing repositories, and to the reality of the Web. If the application of the technologies mentioned above — the use of metadata, Dublin Core, XML and RDF — find a place in projects for creating collections of cultural objects, a truly efficient and effective system of resource interchange can come about. Already the OAI-PMH protocol has established some rules for the production of metadata so they can be written in a form that permits harvesting. This is not quite yet the Semantic Web, but rather Web 2.0: or even Library 2.0. The Web is still being considered as a universally available environment for the transfer of digital objects, produced by collaborative activity. In order to take the next step towards the Semantic Web, digital libraries must describe their resources using the technological models described above.

This may be a good moment to reflect on what a protocol that guarantees exchanges between different repositories would look like, and hence how it could realize the goal of the Semantic Web. Modes of sharing and collaborative environments, and relying on networks to help coordination and integration will lead to the creation of digital objects with long-term preservation in mind. Increasingly, projects are insisting on the need for coordination in constructing networks of collaboration. Projects such as *Bamboo* for sharing services and *Interedition* for constructing the infrastructure for the production and distribution of digital versions of literary texts, *TextGrid* and *Grid Computing,* that work in the e-science networking environment, are some examples of how important the principle of collaboration really is.[21] These projects tend to constitute a new model of scientific research where the researcher is able to manage every stage in the production of knowledge, from the acquisition of sources to their manipulation and publishing, without ever abandoning the digital environment, and sharing with others the various stages of the research process (cf. Conclusions, § 2).

The architecture of the digital library will determine the success of this new vision, with technologies like Fedora (flexible extensible digital object repository architecture),[22] or DLMS (digital library management system) within the Delos project.[23] In conclusion, what is proposed here is a possible model or "evolutionary" path:

— Web 2.0: collaborative production of digital documents and the use of shared annotation systems.
— Web 3.0: the Semantic Web, including the adoption of technologies such as Unicode, URI, XML, schemas, RDF/Topic Maps and ontologies.
— Web x.0: a semantic-based environment for building collaborative distribution networks.

In the Web of the future there will be two dominant models. The first is collaborative and distributed production. Increasingly, the term "cloud computing" is being applied to systems for producing and archiving digital objects online (cf. Ch. 2 and 5). This content results from production through participation, where the concept of "author" becomes fluid and complex. The second is the concept (or the *dream,* cf. § 2.4) of the Semantic Web. The problem of the enrichment of semantic webpages is the subject of various projects and experiments. It is not only the above-mentioned HTML5 that is trying to assign "content" to webpages through new, more explicit elements to "describe" strings, but projects like Microdata for HTML5 (http://www.data-vocabulary.org/) are attempting to augment content objects with an additional interpretative substrate. Analogously, proposals like Microformats (http://microformats.org/) or RDFa (http://www.w3.org/TR/xhtml-rdfa-primer/) aim to reach the same objective of the semantic enrichment of markup. As will be seen in the next chapter, the search engines are in favor of these developments, and increasingly they will be able to return to the end user exactly what he or she is looking for. The announcement from Schema.org is challenging:

> ... a collection of schemas, i.e., HTML tags, that webmasters can use to markup their pages in ways recognized by major search providers. Search engines including Bing, Google and Yahoo! rely on this markup to improve the display of search results, making it easier for people to find the right web pages. (http://schema.org/).

However, before focusing on search engines, it is necessary to briefly introduce a theme that runs through all the topics covered in this ideal digital *trivium* (and in this particular case *quadrivium*) to act as a bridge between data representation, data archiving, and Web search. The topic is text analysis and text mining as applied to humanities data.

4.8 Text analysis and text mining

Text analysis in the humanities reaches to the core of philology, which itself lies, according to Nietzsche, at the heart of historical studies. In fact, in his 1874 essay *On the advantage and disadvantage of history for life,* Nietzsche maintained that "historical knowledge" is fundamentally responsible for manipulating the past, and hence puts the present both at risk and on hold.[14] Whether or not one agrees with Nietzsche, one cannot deny one of his points: no analysis, recovery or reconstruction of the past can ever be a neutral process. And the consequences of Nietzsche's attack on the methodology of historical studies "from within" seem at times no less dramatic than the potential effect of informatics and its tools on the reconstruction/deconstruction of the history of text reception and interpretation. The operation of text analysis and data recovery/management is not merely a "gearing up" of classic philological methodologies that has only technical and mechanical benefits — but in fact lays the foundations for new directions in literary criticism and philology. It is no surprise then that this meeting of computer and humanistic studies has its roots in the work of Father Roberto Busa, in his project of digitization of the complete works of Saint Thomas Aquinas.[25] It is at this stage, in word-computing, that the "new philology" foreseen by Robert R. Dyer in 1969 was born. His words could be taken from a modern DH textbook:

> I do believe we are at the threshold of the most exciting science which man has yet envisioned. .... Yet the study of the mind at work through the written and spoken word fits badly in linguistics or in psychology. For it is one of the great branches of human study — it is, I suggest to you, still philology. ... I propose that we urgently need large research centers where the computer can be applied to this analysis of tradition and originality in the

expression of ideas in words. ... In these centers we will work alongside behavioral scientists, linguists, psychologists, statisticians, electronic engineers, neurophysicists, and biochemists; and our students will acquire scientific training in these disciplines. Here philology and the study of man as creator of words and ideas will become a science, and humanism will finally learn that its bases as a pursuit are as open to scientific formulation as any other search to conquer human experience. (Dyer 1969, 56–58)

Although three generations of digital humanists have been almost literally repeating Dyer's words, to this day his vision still seems a thing of the future. For many years computer-assisted philology has dealt with pre-established categories: co-occurrences, indexes, lemmatized indexes, rhyming dictionaries and other items that belong to the classic tradition of philology.[26] What has changed in recent years? What kind of attitude should modern philologists take (or be expected to take) when confronted with this discipline? Once again, it is the attitude of critics and philologists who aim to explore literary works, to interrogate them and make them talk: not unlike those eighteenth century poets who, upon discovering the classics of the Greeks and Romans, turned to their silent tombs, apparently mute and crystallized by time. Such crystallization is the effect of centuries of critical work on literary texts, a concretization that prevents the recovery of their original integrity and at the same time establishes the limits and forms of their reception. Today it is worth asking whether literary works can talk "more" when questioned with new digital tools, or whether they have already given up all their answers, and if that is not the case, whether such hidden answers could only be brought to light with new tools. An archaeologist would probably ask similar questions when dealing with new scientific and technical developments: the same questions will be asked here and the answers will be put in a positive light.

4.8.1 Performance or character string?

In his article *What Is Text Analysis Really?* Geoffrey Rockwell recalls the historic debate between two founders of the field of DH, Allen Renear and Jerome McGann in 1999 on the concept of text and the theory of textuality. The positions each adopted explored the concept of text from two very different perspectives (Rockwell 2003). This debate is worth remembering, as it shows how textual analysis is an interpretative approach to a literary document, with all the semantic complexity that the concept of text entails. Interpreting text as a string of ordered, hierarchically representable, characters or as a "performance," as a product of a reader's reading, forces a clarification of what kind of responses an electronic text will be able to provide.

In general terms, text analysis is a process by which a number of applications work to extract words — defined as strings bounded by spaces — present in a text, establishing the number of times each string occurs. This results in the analysis of vocabulary in terms of nouns, adjectives, verbs, conjunctions, adverbs and prepositions, and thus permits inferences to be made based on the author's lexicon. But the complexity of language systems (not only at the syntactic level, but also at the possibly ambiguous semantic level) means that not only are more sophisticated tools needed to analyze texts, but also intervention in the form of descriptive procedures (what may be termed markup) will be needed if a computer is to make automatic inferences about the use of language.

Computational linguistics is the discipline that first addressed the issue of *natural language processing* (NLP), a set of practices that aim to create tools for accessing the digital content of linguistic data. Beyond the level of the simple string recognition, the manipulation of strings, automatic analysis of texts and the extraction of information from such data are now becoming the new tools for using digital content. The ultimate goal is to acquire new knowledge from texts: or rather, while the organization of data is a means of conveying information, the ability to reprocess this information makes the acquisition of new knowledge a real possibility.[27]

Particularly in the field of literary studies, analysis systems allow the researcher to consider different styles and themes, fixing their attention on the lexicon and syntactic style of the author. This even allows anonymous, apocryphal or unattributed works to be associated with their true authors through stylometry (Holmes 1994, Craig 2004).[28] There is thus a need for a tool to allow the humanities scholar to move from simple text retrieval to full text analysis, and to explore the implications and possible benefits of text mining.

4.8.2 From text retrieval to text analysis

At the level of text retrieval it is possible to generate formatted data from a text, either in the form of an index or a list of concordances, and measure their frequency using frequency lists.[29] This is one point of departure for the exploration of a text, allowing the extraction of a certain type of information.

The reader might also use indexes, frequency analyses of a certain term or a concordance to interpret the text. Of course, this is simply using computers to perform tiresome tasks and calculations in which there is a high risk of human error. It is still up to the user to interpret the results. On the other hand, studies on word counts and frequency analyses have been used to attribute works definitively to certain authors (Hoover 2008). Stylometric analysis, by providing a "stylistic fingerprint" of a writer, can, by measuring the length of words and sentences, or the frequency of a certain kind of word, identify characteristic features in an unattributed document. Stylometry can also help researchers establish the chronology of an author's work.[30]

Increasingly, the frequency analysis engines added to online corpora of literary texts offer information in the form of indexes, frequency lists and concordances, often making use of the output to make structural divisions.[31] Knowing the number of times a given word, a combination of words or collocation occurs in a text can help elucidate a certain expression, and therefore aid semantic analysis. However, just as was the case for text retrieval systems, it is still the user who must interpret the results. The question then becomes, can the computer meet the information needs of the reader, without incorporating elements of the user's interpretation on top of the automatically retrieved data?

From the string recovery phase, the process moves into the real analysis of the text, the information retrieval phase. If the first step in the analysis of a text is represented by the compilation of a list of word-occurrences, then the objective of the next step must be to acquire linguistic information (at the morphological, lexical, syntactic and semantic level) by using other tools.

Normalization, lemmatization, *part of speech* (POS) tagging, parsing, synonymity and homography reduction, automatic keyword extraction and semantic categorization: these are some of the processes normally associated with natural language processing (NLP).[32] These processes can only be partially automated, since human intervention is crucial to obtaining valid results, starting with the selection of the corpus to be analyzed (on the correct construction of corpora cf. Ide 2004). This means that it is necessary to pre-process the text or corpus in order to normalize it. In order to obtain reliable results during the text-analysis phase, it is especially important to intervene in text markup. Marking-up a text means adding information on various aspects (in this case linguistic aspects) that reflect the purpose of the analysis. In this situation the role of the humanist is key, because knowledge about the assignment of identification strings to the linguistic data requires knowledge of its context. Software tools supporting these kinds of operations work by automating the normalization and markup processes, but the quality of the results is still fundamentally dependent on the human operator. The most common way of marking-up a text is by assigning tags to the items to be identified on a morphological, syntactical, or semantic level. These indicators are generally expressed using a formal language with a standardized vocabulary, such as the TEI-XML schema (cf. § 4.3).[33] The information can be added directly to the body of the text — as inline or embedded annotation — or it can be defined in a separate file, to be inserted later through linking (*stand-off markup*). However, many existing corpora are marked up according to the Eagles XML *corpus encoding standard* (XCES), an XML-TEI-based standard created specifically for corpus linguistics and the management of linguistic annotation systems (available at http://www.xces.org/). An annotated corpus, or treebank, greatly enriches a text and the kinds of information that can be extracted from it. Such a corpus may be queried not only at the level of character strings, but also through its annotations. Assigning a grammatical or syntactical value to a string enables it to be queried for its morphology, and this facilitates the recognition of nouns, verbs, adjectives, etc., so as to satisfy a specific interpretative need (for example, to determine the frequency of an adjective used attributively). Likewise, annotations on specific vocabulary items can facilitate the search for names of people and places, as well as geographical or spatial information.

4.8.3 Towards text mining

The next step in information retrieval of a corpus analyzed in terms of vocabulary, morphology, syntax and semantics, is information extraction: the examination of pertinent data, its extraction from the document and its presentation in a certain format. The new boundaries of textual analysis can be found in the use of various processes that can conveniently be called "text mining," or the extraction of knowledge from unstructured text. The difference between this process and markup systems is that with text mining, hidden, not pre-recorded data can be discovered and knowledge, rather than information, is produced. Through clustering techniques and classification of semantic usage, one can find unexpected things for literary purposes. The potential uses are manifold. Here is one example, offered by http://mininghumanities.com/:

> The question we'll think about is this: "How does the portrayal of men and women in Shakespeare's plays change under different circumstances?" As one answer, we'll see how WordSeer [a text mining application] suggests that when love is a major plot point, the language referring to women changes to become more physical, and the language referring to men becomes more sentimental.

One of the recurring considerations in DH is that there are millions of marked-up texts and some way needs to be found to make use of them effectively (Crane 2006). Among the most important text mining projects are those initiated by John Unsworth (2009), who has received substantial funding for projects related to systems for extracting knowledge from literary texts. Unsworth has established three projects aimed at developing text-mining applications to help students and scholars in the analysis of texts. The first of these is SEASR (software environment for the advancement of scholarly research, http://seasr.org/), an infrastructure that focuses on the development of leading-edge digital humanities initiatives: "Developed in partnership with humanities scholars, SEASR enhances the use of digital materials by helping scholars uncover hidden information and connections."

The second is the NORA project, "a two-year project, now finished, to produce software for discovering, visualizing, and exploring significant patterns across large collections of full-text humanities resources in existing digital libraries." NORA has now been replaced by MONK (metadata offers new knowledge — http://www.monkproject.org/), a continuation of the NORA project with co-PI Martin Mueller, of Northwestern University, now available as a library service to faculty staff and students at all CIC institutions.[34]

One interesting case study linked to the NORA project is a survey of Emily Dickinson's erotic poetry (Plaisant *et al.* 2006). Working from Dickinson's correspondence, the authors were able to find data hidden in the corpus ("undiscovered knowledge"), on the theme of erotica: while the classification was previously made manually, the researchers showed that automatic classification was possible. Such classifications can be born spontaneously from the text, allowing the researcher to discover unexpected thematic situations.

Another interesting project comes from collaborative work between the ARTFL Project at the University of Chicago and the Linguistic Cognition Laboratory at the Illinois Institute of Technology on one subset of the technologies required for a future global digital library: the intersection of machine learning, text mining and text analysis:

> ... The ARTFL Project has developed a set of machine learning extensions to PhiloLogic, ... a full-text search and analysis system. PhiloMine replaces the notion of "searching" a database for one or more words with "task" submission. (Argamon and Olsen 2009)

So, using data/text mining techniques, search engines are able to return data to the user not only in the form of character strings or information derived from pre-cooked annotations, but also new knowledge. Concepts and new content that are not initially evident to the reader thus become available through the use of computer algorithms.

The clustering of documents on the basis of their content allows them to be transformed into information, and from there, into knowledge. This kind of operation is greatly facilitated by the availability of documents which may be marked-up and/or subjected to morpho-syntactic and semantic analysis. The final objective of language processing systems will lie in the acquisition of knowledge from the application of NLP systems and from the further examination of text using techniques such as text mining. With these methods uncovering the hidden connections between fragments of content will throw new light on the study of literature and other fields.

☙

4.9 New applied technologies in the digital humanities

Before moving on to our last major topic, the searching and organizing of information, a few words should be devoted to describing new emerging paradigms in the DH domain. Certain technologies are showing their potential to connect the problem of production of resources to the retrieval of information as a fundamental activity for both users and machines. However, this is not really a question of describing new technologies that have already been described in the preceding pages, but is more about changes in methodology that represent a new theory of research.

The basic question is this: are other disciplines able to enrich DH research? In a discipline that is already recognized as being an integration of various closely-related disciplines, can methods developed in apparently distant research fields offer new opportunities for research in the digital humanities?

For example, Maps, GIS, and interactive methods developed in geography open the the possibility of locating documents in their temporal/spatial axis. The very activity of reading documents — texts and images — as historical sources, naturally shifts attention towards people, dates and especially places through a graphic view of cultural heritage (see for example the Geolat project, devoted to "make accessible Latin literature through a query interface of geographic/cartographic type"). In this field, automatic entity recognition, as developed within NLP, represents a change in direction towards the automated extraction of information.

The current focus on describing people arises from the new social networking paradigm. Social network analysis (SNA) is basically the study of relationships between people through network theory. First used in sociology, it has now become popular in many other disciplines, with a growing group of enthusiasts in ancient and modern history.

SNA focuses on any kind of relations between the actors rather than on them individually. Through visualization of the network graph and network statistics, information can be derived about the structure of the network and the roles of the individuals in it. (http://snapdrgn.net/archives/category/social-network-analysis).

The SNAP project (standards for networking ancient prosopographies) is a sample of this approach adapted to work in the propospographic domain.

Statistics, sociology and network graph theory have suggested new approaches to research in DH. Discovering relationships between documents may reveal their authenticity, declare unexpected social, political or cultural connections, or derive personal profiles. The Google "Knowledge Graph" aims to move from strings to things, from information to knowledge, by interrelating concepts in a global environment (http://www.google.com/insidesearch/features/search/knowledge.HTML).

Another new methodology is Distant Reading (Moretti 2013). Moretti's aim is to to open humanities research towards "a growing field of unorthodox literary studies," to the adoption of "quantitative methods," the systematic empirical investigation of observable phenomena via statistical, mathematical or numerical data, or computational techniques.

But just as Moretti champions the broad explanatory power of quantitative literary analysis, he overestimates the scientific objectivity of his analyses, while undervaluing the productively suggestive stories of doubt, failure, and compromise that lend nuance and depth to his hypotheses. Combative, absorbing, highly topical, and unevenly persuasive, Distant Reading embodies both the optimism of early digital literary studies and also its perils (Ross 2014).

Finally, topics such as "gamification," "digital storytelling," "transmedia web editions" and "content curation" may soon become new methodologies/technologies for research in the digital humanities.

Chapter 5
Searching and organizing

5.1 The paradox of search according to Plato

Since antiquity, Man has struggled to organize and access information to assist in the creation of new knowledge. Investigation of the problem and its possible solutions goes back to the earliest discussions on the nature of thought. Plato, for example, was perfectly aware of it, as can be seen from this discussion in the *Meno*:

> Meno And how will you enquire, Socrates, into that which you do not know? What will you put forth as the subject of enquiry? And if you find what you want, how will you ever know that this is the thing which you did not know?
>
> Socrates I know, Meno, what you mean; but just see what a tiresome dispute you are introducing. You argue that man cannot enquire either about that which he knows, or about that which he does not know; for if he knows, he has no need to enquire; and if not, he cannot; for he does not know the very subject about which he is to enquire. (Plato, *Meno,* 80d–81a [1948, 105–106])

Plato's solution to Socrates' dilemma is to assume the existence of a kind of foreknowledge of our future discoveries, based on our previous experience of ideas, which allowed us to understand what we do not yet consciously know, because "all inquiry and all learning is but recollection." Although our condition at birth is gradually forgotten, it could guide us through the memory of a remembrance of ideas, first vaguely, then more clearly. Eventually, we recognize and reconnect our findings to this original knowledge.

Of course, Plato's theory of knowledge is complex, but from it can be drawn the simple notion that new knowledge does not arise from nothing, but from the interpretation of a preliminary reference model, which helps us to make sense of the phenomenon under investigation. Cognitive processes are often based on methods for the creation of knowledge that allow the integration of experimental data into a model to produce an initial hypothesis. The choice of model, although an inevitable element in the cognitive process, is never neutral with respect to the construction of consciousness. This idea, that existing knowledge must first be organized before new knowledge can be discovered, is supported by the French 17th century philosopher René Descartes in his *Rules for the Direction of the Mind*. In his thirteenth rule, he states:

> ... however, though in every question something must be unknown, otherwise there is no need to raise it, we should nevertheless so define this unknown element by means of specific conditions that we shall be determined towards the investigation of one thing rather than another. (Descartes 1985, 166)

Descartes suggests that the search for new understanding starts from a clear idea of what must be found, even if the details are unknown. Therefore, the cognitive process does not begin in the dark, but is based on what is already known, and hypotheses about the unknown.

This chapter aims to show that the model of representation and organization of knowledge adopted by search engines only respects part of the communal, associative and polyvocal nature of the Web, and produces some inevitable distortions in information access. It will describe the mechanisms by which its information is structured, and demonstrate its lack of neutrality. It will also identify possible corrective strategies to be applied in the finding of data, and utilize that critical attitude characteristic of the *studia humanitatis*. Its starting point will be studies of the theory of networks, which seek to provide a detailed topological description of Web content. The aim is to outline the procedures needed to accurately scan a webpage, which is essential for the proper functioning of search engines. It will also underline how searching for information on the Web has transformed and continues to transform the way content is produced. From print-based journalism, to audio and video production and the publishing industry, no production model or business strategy has been spared by the entry onto the scene of powerful intermediaries like search engines, social networks and other tools for sharing in the so-called Web 2.0. In order to understand how this new intermediation of content works, the investigation cannot be limited to observing how search engines operate in response to a query, but must also examine the entire reorganization of the production, use and ranking of content. The television industry in the past used to argue that "content is king and technology is queen." Now the roles are perhaps reversed, unless the software and hardware that control the dissemination of content, by allowing their production and reproduction, are now regarded as a kind of content in their own right, and hence as kings of the production process. But what must be described first is the ecosystem in which digital content and its producers/users are immersed and interact.[1]

5.2 Web topology and the (in)equality of nodes

Arpanet, as described above (cf. §§ 2.1 and 2.2), was created to prevent the isolation of scientists and to encourage the sharing of available technological and knowledge resources. The Web improved communication further, not only in scientific development, but also as a general tool for increasing interaction between man and machine (cf. § 2.2). However, the very network that should have made human relations more efficient and democratic, on closer inspection, turns out not to be so democratic after all. Studies in network theory, on the topological description of networks like the Internet, have produced unexpected results.

The research group at Notre Dame University under Albert-László Barabási developed an historical experiment aimed at mapping the Web. Using methods commonly used in statistical mechanics, they analyzed a small fragment of the Web in terms of topography, and applied the result to the network as a whole, based on the assumption that relations between the nodes on the network would maintain the same structure. Through this experiment, they were able to measure degrees of separation[2] on the Web, establishing that there were, on average, nineteen steps between two randomly chosen webpages (Barabási 2002, 32–34):

> The most intriguing result of our Web-mapping project was the complete absence of democracy, fairness, and egalitarian values of the Web. We learned that the topology of the Web prevents us from seeing anything but a mere handful of the billion documents out there. (Barabási 2002, 56)

Perhaps the reference to democracy in this context is risky, but it can be said that the structure tends to create an asymmetric system that continues to reward those who are already well connected in the market and to damage newcomers or nodes that, for whatever reason, attract few links. The ease with which sites already rich in links attract clicks, indicates a system that is unfair, at least with respect to the establishment of new links.

The Web seems to behave like a dynamic ecosystem in which pages are constantly created, change address, die, move, change, etc., following a distribution that follows unwritten power laws (Barabási 2002, 67). If the Web were a casual construct, on average every page would have more or less the same number of connections and nodes would be distributed on a *Bell Curve* (Figure 5.1, overleaf). The *Power Law Distribution* instead creates a scale-invariant distribution in which a few nodes have many connections and the majority of nodes have few (Figure 5.1, overleaf, right).

Although distributed online, information is not equally accessible in the same way because, among other things, its typical topography is a directed graph (Broder *et al.* 2000), which produces a bow tie of nodes (see Figure 5.2, overleaf).

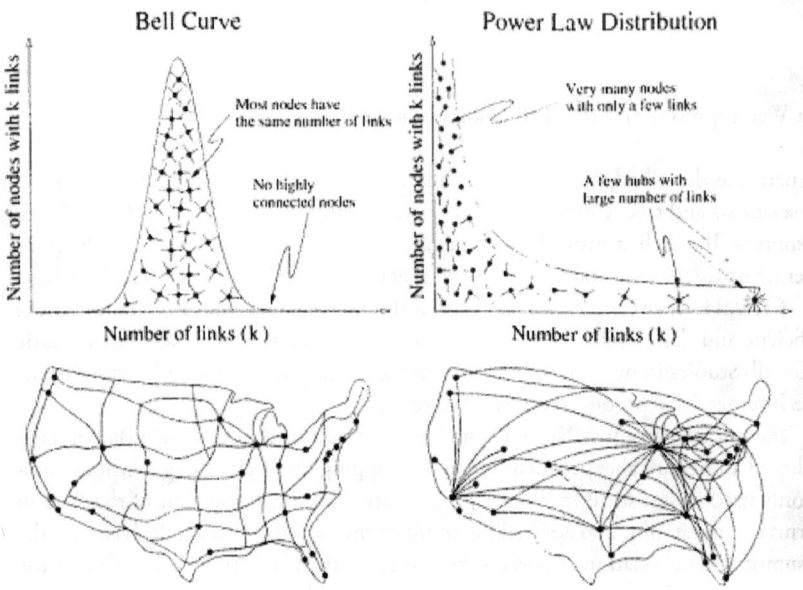

Figure 5.1. Two examples of distribution, bell curve and scale-invariant (Barabási 2002, 71).

Only some of the "continents" of the Web can be easily navigated, as can be seen in Figure 5.2, while the majority of nodes (more than half) remain hidden from the user, who has no direct access to the addresses of these zones. The idea of the Web as a tool giving access to all the information published online now seems a little naïve. The latest research into network theory has shown that the situation is not as clear as first appears. Social networks, including those on the Web, are dominated by certain hyper-connected nodes, or *hubs*; and this can be considered as the strongest argument against the utopian vision of cyberspace as egalitarian.[3] Things are no different in the blogosphere, as studies on link data using Technorati[4] show, and it is also clear that scale invariance also dominates social networks. The problem of node distribution is closely linked to the ability to find content.

5.3 The role of search engines on the Web

According to a survey by the Pew Research Center carried out on November 2012, many American school teachers believe that search engines have changed "students research habits" and "what it means to do research":

> Teachers and students alike report that for today's students, "research" means "Googling." As a result, some teachers report

The Digital Humanist

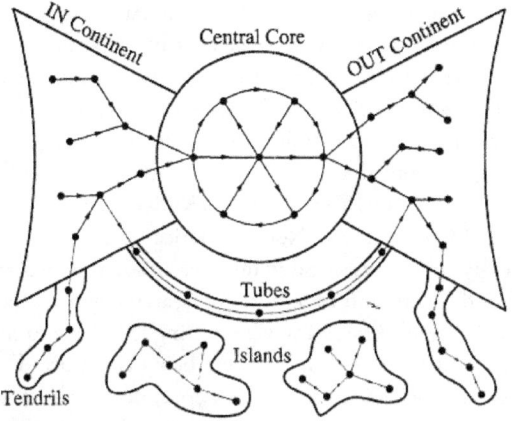

Figure 5.2. The bow tie structure of a directed network (Broder et al. 2000).

that for their students "doing research" has shifted from a relatively slow process of intellectual curiosity and discovery to a fast-paced, short-term exercise aimed at locating just enough information to complete an assignment. These perceptions are evident in teachers' survey responses: 94% of the teachers surveyed say their students are "very likely" to use Google or other online search engines in a typical research assignment, placing it well ahead of all other sources that we asked about. (Purcell *et al.* 2012)

Therefore, the access of information to students (and not just teens as reported by Pew Research) is mediated by search engines, and particularly by Google, and this trend seems to support Vaidhyanathan's assertion that education is completely and pervasively dominated by the "the ideology of 'access' and 'findability'" (Vaidhyanathan 2011, 191). But the situation is similar for other categories of users.

Search engines are the filter, the Web's magnifying glass, or, as the inventors of Google state, their goal is even more ambitious in the medium term: "to organize the world's information." In a more recent survey, US citizens affirm that they feel better informed thanks to the Internet (Purcell and Rainie 2014). In this report there is no clear reference to search engines, but it is clear that they are playing a relevant role in this feeling of satisfaction about information access. Another interesting study published in 2008,[5] analyzed the behavior of the *Google generation* — those born after 1993, and who therefore grew up with the Web. The research aimed to survey the search practices and attitudes of young people currently in higher education in the UK, in an attempt to predict the future of search and research, and the role played by libraries in this new context. The results were rather discouraging. Around 90% of subjects began their journey with search engines and were happy with the results they obtained. In addition, the research showed that there were no typical attitudes towards search in the Google generation. The result can be summed up by saying that we are all becoming part of the Google generation, regardless of age. Researchers, in fact, tend to have similar attitudes. They trust search engines, are indifferent to other methods that work more slowly, download a lot of material and use it carelessly. The logs of virtual libraries indicate that articles are, at best, quickly scanned and rarely read with attention. The picture painted by these surveys offers some ideas with which to ponder the future. The IAB and GfK Media 2014 survey dedicated to online professional video content in North America (IAB — GfK 2014) reported that on an average day Americans spend 37 minutes on social networks applications, such as Facebook and others, and 23 minutes on search engines pages.[6] Already in 2010 it was clear that, though Americans were turning to Google to check their own online reputations,[7] and these reputations were being constructed through social media, such as Facebook or Twitter, as if these were closed worlds where they could access the most interesting information offered by their "friends." The fact remains that, with all the difficulties search engines present, they continue to represent a filter that is perceived as efficient, neutral and appropriate for accessing information, even for students or researchers: users who should be more aware of their research instruments. These filters, while being considered more impersonal than social networks, maintain a strong centrality in determining the survival, spread and visibility of online information, while being able to produce an efficient and profitable business model. They are also set up to find information within other services such as social networks and applications and this gives them, together with other players, a central role in the political and social arena. This chapter will show how the topology of the Web, along with some techniques used by ranking algorithms (i.e. Google's), can have a serious impact on how we find resources and evaluate the efficiency of search engines.

Before discussing PageRank, Google's ranking algorithm, mention must be made of an experiment performed by Steve Lawrence and Lee Giles in 1997 and repeated in 1999 to monitor the quality of search engine results. Comparing the pages found by various search engines in those years, the two researchers found that each engine could only manage partial coverage of all webpages. Commenting on their results, they raised some concerns as to the methodologies of search mechanisms that we might share today:

> The Web is a distributed, dynamic, and rapidly growing information resource, which presents difficulties for traditional information retrieval technologies. Traditional information retrieval systems were designed for different environments and have typically been used for indexing a static collection of directly accessible documents. The nature of the Web brings up important questions as to whether the centralized architecture of the search engines can keep up with the expanding number of documents, and if they can regularly update their databases to detect modified, deleted, and relocated information. The an-

swers to these questions impact on the best search methodology to use when searching the Web and on the future of Web search technology. (Lawrence, Giles, 1998, 99)

A user's Web-browsing cannot be very complicated or frustrating. Search engines play a delicate role of mediation between the mass of information available — an amount that is now impossible for humans to handle — and relevant answers to their questions expressed in the form of queries.[8] It acts as the user's mentor, and protects against the excess of information by presenting a list of results to satisfy his or her curiosity. However, it is impossible to measure the efficiency of a search engine, due both to the absence of suitable metrics for its assessment, and because there is no alternative substantially equivalent to use in evaluating the results (Belew 2000, 34–36). A resource that is not mentioned in the results of a research is destined to remain unknown, and this often also applies to those resources relegated to the third or fourth page of the listing.

Even Google managers agree that much remains to be done. In answer to a question by Charlie Rose about the possibility that search technology could still be in its infancy, Marissa Mayer, one of the most prominent public faces of Google, and vice president of Location and Local Services, replied:

> Very much so. It was interesting for our engineers to see that early index and see how far we've come in ten years. But when you think about what would be the perfect search engine, what is an answer as opposed to a result? Why are we handing you just links and URLs? You know, what does it mean to try and synthesize a video or an image or a diagram that better explains your answer or maybe even grabs facts from all the different pages and helps you do comparisons. There's just a lot of different things we can do.[9]

5.4 How search engines work

At this point, it is appropriate to ask how reliable is the description of the Web offered by search engines in response to our queries. To answer this question requires a brief analysis of the activities and components of a typical general search engine when it indexes and organizes its results on the composition and structure of webpages. Of course, this overview will not be exhaustive, both because there are too many variables in the equation (Google claims to use more than two hundred variables to build its lists), and also because the mechanisms are kept secret by the Mountain View company. Nevertheless, it is still possible to produce a rough map of the tools in use.

First, there are the crawlers or *spiders*. These are software agents employed by search engines to explore the Web. The engine uses them to acquire information from webpages. Their role is to acquire web content, by visiting pages for which the URL is known, and moving from one page to another via the links they find. From the moment they enter a page using only access provided by other pages, or "inbound" links, they are mostly navigating the best connected parts of the Web, and hence rarely visit other zones, where they might be unable to move on. Even without the problem of interconnections, there will always be some parts of the network that remain unexplored. Crawlers are unable to access online forms for a catalog, as, for example, in a library, so they are excluded from an important part of the information on the Web. There are also pages that are inaccessible for technical reasons (e.g. a host that does not support automated queries), or because of company policy. To this category belong, among others, dynamically generated pages, such as the pages obtained in response to our queries to search engines. In conclusion, there are areas hidden by necessity or by choice from crawlers in their efforts to acquire information, which represent the natural "senses" of the search engine. However, it should be emphasized that in the last few years search technology has overcome a series of technical obstacles, for example, the scanning of pages not in HTML format (PDFs, Word, Excel and PowerPoint docs, etc.). Even pages created by a database can be now found as long as they have a stable URL that the crawler can find.

Once the crawler has acquired the information, it is stored in a page repository (see Fig. 5.3). This contains all the indexed data pages, which can then be associated with the user's keywords. In an engine's repository there is thus a copy of the indexed page (or cache) from the last time the crawler accessed it. Thus it is possible for a page to be no longer directly accessible on the Web, but still be available through the cache. It is interesting to note that when searching the Web with a search engine, what is actually being searched is that part of the Web that has been copied to the engine's repository. Based on this information an "inverted index" is generated. What does that mean? When an engine indexes a page, its URL is associated with all the words it contains, in the form of a vector, or a kind of tray, made of sequences of letters that form words. What users want is a URL to be given in response to their query. So the index, as initially constructed, is inverted, by associating every word with a list of URLs that contain it. In the repository are performed all those operations needed to turn each page into a vector of all the relevant strings (words with meaning in a given language) that appear in the text. Words are evaluated also by their position on the page (a word contained in the title or in the metatag — cf. below, Ch. 3 — is considered more relevant in characterizing that page[10]). In short a kind of automatic lemmatization of pages is performed, preserving only the list of terms associated with words on the page. This deletes all minor words such as conjunctions, articles and other "stop words" present in texts, and they do not contribute to the assigned meaning of the page. All this happens on a purely syntactic level, but that does not mean that this operation is any less relevant from the cognitive point of view. No operation carried out on the representation of pages by a search engine is neutral with respect to certain queries (Arasu *et al.* 2001).

Before moving on to the *ranking* algorithm, the heart of the search engine's selective activity, the concept of *query* needs to be examined. This is a word or sequence of words supplied by the user to instigate the search. Most of the time it is not an actual question, but only one or more keywords. If the query is limited to two or three words, the selective ability of the search engine is obviously rather limited, and the result of the query is a list including thousands or even millions of links. However the user may employ an exact phrase query to obtain more precise results. For example, take a line of poetry from T.S. Eliot: "April is the cruellest month." In this case, quotation marks can be placed around the query to indicate that an exact wording is wanted.

In the last few years, the main search engines — Google, Yahoo, Bing and Ask — have begun to use the method of query suggestion. This is used to carry out searches or to correct typing mistakes by the user, or to suggest more popular synonyms for the search terms. Needless to say, this behavior is an attempt to redirect the user's search based on the historical experience of the engine. It shows a willingness to assume a cognitive ability in interpreting the user's real needs, and is driven mainly by considerations related to the engine's main source of income, which is keyword advertising.

But by suggesting queries, how is the background knowledge necessary for this interpretation and its connection with our experience constructed? As will be seen below, the engine directs not only the answers it provides to questions but also how queries are formulated. Especially in the case of a young user or non-expert in the subject of the query, a search engine has the power to manage searches, and so has a considerable influence on what information is returned.

The final element of this quick analysis of the search engine is the ranking algorithm.[11] PageRank, in particular, has been very successful for Google. Before beginning an analysis of the algorithm, however, it should be pointed out that exactly how it works is known only to a few Google employees. It is known to be constantly modified to improve its efficiency and to combat spamming[12] caused by certain techniques of search engine optimization, of which more will be said later. However, the way it works was outlined in an article written by its inventors, Sergey Brin and Larry Page (1998). The idea behind this page-ranking algorithm is the exploitation of the interconnections among webpages as a valuation of the authority of those same pages. The rank of a page is based on a mixture of its authority and its relevance to a precise query, which is computed on the basis of its presence in the vector of that page, its location, and its frequency of use.[13]

The authority of a page is not a value in itself, but is constructed in relation to the links that point to it (inlinks). The more a page receives links from other pages, the more authoritative it will be considered. Google's ranking system is therefore recursive: the more links a page receives from authoritative pages, the more authoritative it will become. Thus if a page is very authoritative its own links will carry more weight of authority to the pages it links to. For example a page that has an authority rank of ten, and has five outbound links will divide its patrimony of authority between its linked pages, giving each two points of authoritativeness (Brin and Page

1998, *passim*). The idea of PageRank is to attribute to every in-link the value of a positive reference and then regard it as a favorable mark from the page on which the link originated. This mechanism functioned better when the Web was only limited to the world of research and science in general. The algorithm was adapted from library science and was originally intended to determine the impact of a published article on the basis of its citation index. If this was problematic enough in the case of library science,[14] things get much more complex when the number of citations, or links, increases dramatically. The situation became uncontrollable when the network grew much larger in the second half of 1990, when the algorithm was tested for the first time. The great success of this kind of algorithm has had, in fact, a huge influence on the way in which the Web is organized. The winning technology has modified the production habits of those commercial webpages, which have an interest in being as visible as possible.

Before moving on to describing the problems associated with this way of organizing digital information, it will be instructive to tell a short story that shows how in 1990 there existed a body of research similar to that which led to the invention of PageRank. There were several articles published around the same time that showed "family" resemblances. They were not all destined for the kind of commercial success enjoyed by Google, but this was not because of technical inferiority. As mentioned by Brin and Page (1998), Massimo Marchiori was the author of one of these algorithms. His idea was to have an engine that took account not only of textual information on a webpage, but also information from hypertexts (Marchiori 1997).[15] The Italian researcher says that Brin was happy with his results and asked him many details during the breaks in a conference they both attended. According to Marchiori, Brin and Page's solution was not the best possible, but it was the simplest.

At about the same time as PageRank was being developed, Jon Kleinberg (1999) was working on another algorithm called Hits (*hypertext induced topic search*). Instead of giving a unique rank to each page, this algorithm was based on the search query itself. It produced not one score but two, one for authorities (which attributed a score for recognizing authoritative pages) and the other for *hubs* (collections of links that were not necessarily authoritative in themselves, but which linked to many authorities). Further examination of these algorithms would not be relevant, but it is interesting to note how hard it is to identify the reasons why one of these mechanisms for evaluating has had so much success in organizing research on the Web. Google has certainly shown great capacity for marketing, and has been innovative in making search financially viable through *Adwords* and *Adsense*,[16] and above all has been able to keep pace with the growth of the Web, adopting a policy of massive and continuous investment in technology and innovation.

The system on which the storage of data is based is extremely interesting, and has allowed an enormous and abundant repository to be built up, guaranteeing the greatest security on the Web. The technology used is of course the famous "cloud," and consists not so much in the use of very large and powerful machines, but in the networking of thousands of machines of relatively low performance. In addition, there is a system of redundancy of data that allows various copies of the same

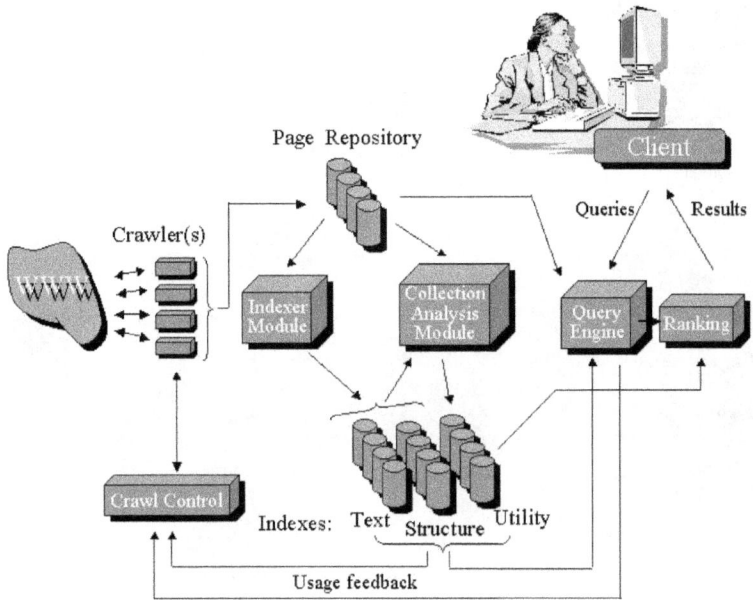

Fig. 5.3. A general schema of the workings of a search engine (Arasu et al. 2001, 4).

data to be spread over different sites of the engine's data centers. Although the relatively small market for search engines in 1997 and 1998 allowed a newcomer to enter the market and outclass its competitors, nowadays the cost of entry into the sector in terms of technological investment and human resources would make "doing a Google" very difficult.

In concluding this brief investigation into search engine operation, it is worth noting that the techniques of information retrieval are derived from those of database search, which is characterized by an extreme structuring of data, which must be precisely queried. When the Web became the largest data warehouse in the world, the only reliable methods available to organize information were those of database management, as pointed out by some experts:

> Many of the search engines use well-known information retrieval (IR) algorithms and techniques (Salton 1989; Faloutsos 1985). However, IR algorithms were developed for relatively small and coherent collections such as newspaper articles or book catalogs in a (physical) library. The Web, on the other hand, is massive, much less coherent, changes more rapidly, and is spread over geographically distributed computers. This requires new techniques, or extensions to the old ones, to deal with gathering information, making index structures scalable and efficiently updateable, and improving the ability of search engines to discriminate. (Arasu *et al.* 2001, 2–3)

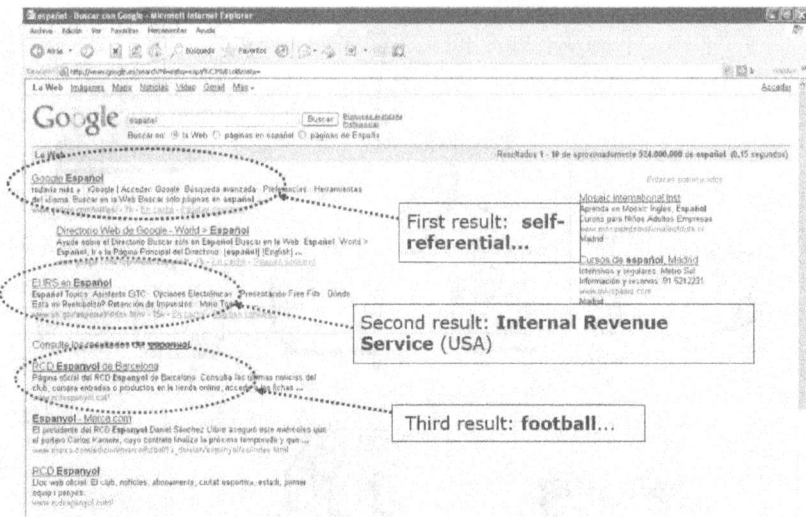

Figure 5.4. "Español" according to Google.es in 2008

It may therefore be inferred that current Web search techniques are not fully able to take into consideration many of the peculiarities in the complex organization of information on the Web, and are thus likely to suffer from dubious interpretations of information, and to keep relevant data hidden from the unsuspecting user. Since the 1980s, in fact, it has been clear that the management of databases is not a true paradigm for the extraction of information from unstructured collections of documents. In databases search gives results that are completely predictable. In the case of Web documents, however, the mechanisms for querying systems are based on trial and error, and responses to queries retain a character of unpredictability, since they cannot in their turn be structured or predicted in advance (Blair 1984).

As Vannevar Bush anticipated (cf. § 1.3), the associative and distributed character of the global hypertext, of which the Web is composed, cannot be represented in a database without a clear loss of information. At best, it can only be used to search through a snapshot of its current state. After all, Bush was thinking only in terms of the personal archiving of data, not of instruments for providing large-scale search services.

5.5 The trouble with search engines

Although the PageRank system is particularly suitable when the user searches for popular nodal pages or resources, the mechanism works less well when searching for "niche pages." If the information you seek is not well known or popular, or is written in a language that is not widely spoken, it is much more difficult to obtain the

Figure 5.5. "Español" according to Google.es in 2015

desired result (Cho and Roy 2004). Although the protection of minorities is not a central concern for the Web user, it is very important to ensure the greatest chance of visibility for every site, in as much as it is a tool for spreading information. There are many reasons why a search may be made. A user may be trying to find something already known (for example, the location of an article with a given title), or to better understand the searched-for item. In the first case PageRank is perfect because, by entering the key words of the title of the article and the author's name, it can be certainly retrieved, provided it is available online. In the second case, however, the user is unsure exactly where he/she wants to end up, and here PageRank's choice has an enormous effect on the result. One may never know if what was found was really what was needed, or how satisfactory the given list of information may be. The user will probably think no more about it, and so not reflect on the discrimination that the algorithm has made in consulting the available resources, by rejecting items on the basis of language, date of publication, type of document, etc. Figure 5.4 shows the results of a Google search made with Google.es for the term "español" in 2008. It is worth noting that in 2008 Google search was still largely dependent on the mechanisms described above (authority generally based on number of links, etc). But Google's algorithms have evolved in response to changes in the Web, and expansion into new markets. It has also developed in line with the behavior of users, and is becoming more sophisticated and less self-referential, as is demonstrated by the same search made seven years later (Figure 5.5).

According to Google engineers, PageRank takes more than 100 other variables into account. It is thus inevitable that the solution proposed by the system is outside the control of any human authority, except for explicit choices by the optimization team. One of the parameters taken into account is local personalization. If you connect to the Internet from a different country than usual you will not receive the same results for the same query, and the track record of your search history will affect the results.

Search results are also influenced by browsing history, and preferences, once expressed, will influence future behavior, in ways that are impossible to anticipate or deny. The user is in no position to ask Google or any other search engine to disregard past preferences or past clickstream when computing the desired or anticipated results, and exactly how such information is used by the system itself is impossible to articulate.

But to return to the big picture of the search ranking method: by attributing a positive vote to every link, ranking algorithms, and especially PageRank, are mistaking popularity for authority. Even if a standard were established for the operation of search mechanisms, it would be an open invitation to manipulate the Web in order to be considered superior according to those same means of evaluation. Using Google, or any other search engine, as the only route into the Web brings with it a series of inevitable risks, partly as a result of the success of the engine itself. In order to reach the top positions in a search result, well-known *ranking* techniques can be used. It may be appropriate to give a little more detail at this point on the complex and controversial phenomenon of search engine spamming.[17] It is known that there are agencies who sell their ability to make a webpage more visible. They practice what is known as *search engine optimization* (SEO). To the search engines, these services represent competitors for the advertising budget of companies. Apart from very simple techniques designed to reorganize content to appeal to the ranking algorithms and the peculiarities of certain engines, there are others who aim to make use of automation to increase the visibility of their clients' pages.

Some of these techniques of the second type are worth examining, because they might be able to explain how the promotion of information on the Web is evolving. There are two main areas: *boosting* techniques and *hiding* techniques. The first consists of amplifying the relevance and importance of some pages by acting on the text or its connections, while the second attempts simply to hide from the human user the techniques used to increase the relevance of a certain Web object (cf. Gyöngyi and García-Molina 2005). Suffice it to say that *hiding* intends to show a crawler a different webpage from the one a human user will see when connecting to a given URL. The server knows how to distinguish a user from a crawler and can manipulate its data, by activating a different document for the second kind of visitor.

As far as *boosting* is concerned, the methods for improving the relevance of a page based on its text are popular and quite well known. The trick is to increase the number of terms for which you want to gain relevance, especially in those areas of the document that are considered most important for the representation of content, such as titles, metatags, descriptions etc. Less well known are the techniques based on increasing connections in order to improve the authoritativeness of pages. This activity, known as *link spamming* consists in the construction of mechanisms that will increase the number of links back to the page in question, or in increasing the authority of pages that link to it. Various systems are used to realize this goal. Among the most impressive are: *the honey pot,* a page that provides useful content (for example, information about a popular program) and so attracts a lot of connections. The page also contains a hidden link back to the site to be promoted. The promoted pages find themselves heirs to the authority of this authoritative page, and so quickly climb in rank. Another way to achieve the same result might be to infiltrate a directory that has a high authority, or to insert many comments on a blog, or on an unmoderated forum, or to access a successful wiki and insert the desired links. All these strategies help to quickly increase the visibility of a page by circumventing the control mechanisms of the search engine, or even by taking advantage of its features. Search techniques have thus impacted on how pages are organized in order to acquire the much sought-after visibility.

The spread of these techniques is mainly due to the existence of a true oligopoly of technologies for research on the Web: there are only a few engines: three or four at most, in the Western world, which are currently competitive and two of them — Yahoo! and Bing — made an agreement to combine in July 2009. The most successful technologies share a number of characteristics, such as the use of a crawler to access the pages, a central repository and sorting mechanism that defines authority on the basis of page connectivity. If there were many different methods for accessing online resources, each based on different philosophies and research technologies, it would be much more difficult to try to "play" the services with their different mechanisms, and a more equal and democratic Web would probably result. More solutions would also be in line with the collective and shared nature of the Web. It is worth noting, however, that according to the empirical measurements of some experts, the presence of search engines improves the *status* of less popular pages, despite the ranking system that would indicate the opposite (Fortunato et. al. 2006). Now, it is difficult to gainsay the value of empirical research, especially when it states the obvious: that it is better to have search engines than to search the Web by oneself. It is about understanding how and to what extent it is possible to improve search results and to evaluate them in a balanced way.

One final issue is personalization and how it affects our cognitive capacity and the scope of our research. This feature is present not only in search engines, but is also extensively found in social networks and all e-commerce sites where suggestions for purchase are made based on our buying habits, or those of consumers like us. Pariser (2011) argues that gradually, the phenomenon of personalization places us in a sort of bubble in which we are no longer exposed to news and general situations of the world around us, but only to those things that, according to our habits, we explicitly declare to be interesting, or which are chosen for us by the system. This goes beyond mere generic filters based on the location of users, or general categorizations of ethnic or national interests. It is rather a radical process of more or less surgical precision through which the system of rules governing the ranking algorithms keeps track of our behavior and explicit preferences (as in the case of social networks), and presents us only with messages that we will (supposedly) appreciate. This makes searching more comfortable by saving us, for example, from seeing advertisements or material we dislike, or in which we are not interested. But even if "the filter bubble still offers the opportunity for some serendipity," there is still an insidious danger that "there will tend to be fewer random ideas around" (Pariser 2011, 97). The risk is that the personalization of searching may cause us to lose out: "as a result, living inside it [the filter bubble] we may miss some of the mental flexibility and openness that contact with difference creates" (Pariser 2011, 101). The problem is that the system is not "tuned for a diversity of ideas or of people" and a significant side effect is that the "personalized Web encourages us to spend less time in discovery mode" (ibid.).

There may be some risk involved in lending too much weight to the algorithms used to draw a picture of each user's needs, but creating a "locked-in" (Lanier 2010) view of the world around us may paradoxically lead to a progressive homogenization of users in their consumer niches, by eliminating or putting into the background every possible "external" intrusion. Evidently, the delirious omnipotence of the personalization mechanisms can be seen as controlling phenomena, as evoked by Gilles Deleuze in his *Postscript on the Societies of Control* (1992).

5.6 Ethical and social implications

In 1986, almost ten years before the birth of the Web, Richard Mason, a pioneer in the field of computer science ethics, identified four key challenges of the information age:

1. *Privacy* relates to information people are willing or forced to disclose, and to what they prefer, or can, keep to themselves.
2. *Accuracy* involves the assessment of resources and the determination of liability in the case of error.
3. *Property* is about who owns the rights to information, who can claim authorship, and how and to what extent they can be spread with or without charge.
4. *Access* can be understood not only in the sense of the digital divide[xviii], but also more generally as the conditions needed to acquire and use information, including information literacy.

All four of these challenges are still just as relevant today, and are all central to the function of modern search engines. There is no space here to go into the ethics and socio-politics underlying the use and centrality of search engines in information access and transmission (or loss) (cf. Witten *et al.* 2007). However, the predicted loss of importance for intermediation arising from the spread of digital communication does not seem to have occurred. At least in the case of search engines, the new intermediary appears to be in good health, even undermining traditional mediators, such as libraries and newspapers. It is obvious that access to information and the ability or opportunity to evaluate it now depends largely on the satisfactory operation of search engines.[19]

The question remains as to the cognitive and social effects search engines have on our searches. The list of the first ten or perhaps twenty links provides the context and the representation that the engine gives to a term or the concept attached to it, ignoring the grave issue of linguistic ambiguity, and accepting that a unit of meaning can be isolated in a keyword. By querying an engine with a certain awareness and a greater detachment than usual, one notes immediately cultural and cognitive effects in the way the preferred engine chooses to respond to requests (see the examples given above in Figures 5.4 and 5.5). Not only is it the single point of access to the richness of the Web, acting as a kind of funnel or mediator in our experience of the network, but its presence is also by no means transparent, and its interpretations are at best questionable. An experiment worth trying is to insert the same word in different language versions of an engine, Italian, French and American. Searching for a term like "Italy" on Google, for example, will give quite different results in the English version of the site from that of the Italian. In the latter case one obtains a series of links of an institutional character, and in the English version a series of pages about tourist information and travel. This shows that Google and the other general engines present results based on, for example, geographic location. Not only do they construct a grid of responses by following mechanical strategies, they also calibrate the results based on what is already known when the query was made, even if the search pages themselves have not been personalized. This makes one think of the engine as a machine for the silent attribution of meaning — a process with which one can have no kind of dialog (despite the rhetoric of Web 2.0).

The search engine has become the arbiter of meaning in our searches and at the same time a powerful generator of cultural representations, as shown by the recent UN Women campaign (Figure 5.6, overleaf).[20] It produces an output in response to users' inputs in an opaque way. It is a real machine for giving names to concepts, for convincing the user that he or she is satisfied: the opposite of the biblical God, who instead of creating objects and then naming them, assigns to every *query* an uneven and yet precise conceptual shortlist of the response's first links. Of course, there is no point in undermining how useful search engines are — indeed this book would not have been possible without their help. But it is worth pointing out some of the cultural, ethical and political implications that especially humanities students should keep in mind — and hopefully help to solve in the near future.

5.6.1 Copyright

Some popular sites have changed from being archivers of content, to hosts of user-generated content (such as YouTube or Flickr), or of quality data generated on the same platform that meets the needs of both authors and publishers, as in the case of Google Book Search (for more on authorship see Ch. 2). The significance of this change is that they are no longer trying only to filter information found on other servers, but to use their own servers as a repository to access what is often user-generated content. This takes advantage of the collective production environment to sell advertising and increase revenue, without having to pay for content. The case of Google Book Search is rather unusual. Google relies on the collaboration (paid in

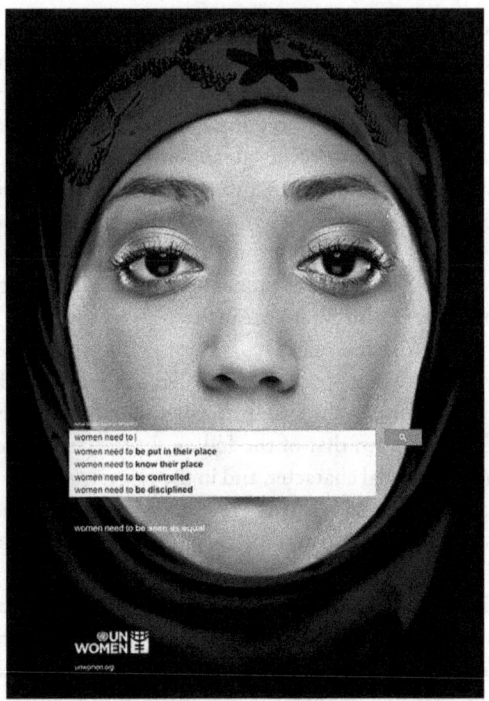

Fig. 5.6. Ad series for UN Woman: the bias of Google's autocompletion.

full) by participating libraries to increase the quality of content on the Web, especially on its own servers. In fact, books represent a source of higher quality information than the average webpage. The reason for this, beyond the rhetoric of the donor, is quite simple. Selling advertisements requires the user's attention, and the best way to attract it is through quality content. Besides, the project allows Google to be the Provider (with a capital "P") of content on the Web. Finally, the commercial role of Google Books was clarified by Google's entry into the eBook market with their eBookstore, where the private company will retain the right to be the sole seller of so-called orphaned books and other texts for which they have obtained permission from publishers (but not necessarily from the authors). This project was so legally controversial that Google proposed paying American authors and editors up to $200 per book to settle damages. The settlement proposed by the parties (Google and the Authors Guild and the Association of American Publishers) in 2008 was rejected by a district court in Manhattan,[21] and subsequent attempts to come to an agreement failed. Then in late 2013 Judge Chin dismissed the entire lawsuit, arguing that Google's book program complied with all the legal requirements for "fair use."[22] However, the Authors Guild appealed the decision in 2014, and that case is still before the court. The question of ownership of the content may still therefore be regarded as open. The tendency of service providers (who use servers to store content) is to consider that they have the right to appropriate content residing on their machines, to the detriment of its authors. Even the content of the books scanned in libraries across the world is considered in some sense owned by Google, although no author has expressly allowed them to keep a copy. The core issue remains that of ownership and usage rights for any form of content. Who can say who has that ownership? The person who produced it, or the company who keeps it on their servers? Should the rights-owners have to opt in to the service, or opt out, as Google would have it? In the case of user-generated content (i.e. YouTube, Flickr or Facebook) it is clear from the service terms of use that users have agreed to sell their ownership of documents, videos and photos that they upload. Only the service managers have the right to determine the removal of those files, in case they are incompatible with copyright laws, or for some other reason. A profound discussion about the figure of the author, and his or her prerogatives, is a matter of some urgency for the Humanities. The impact of changes occurring in the processes of online and offline content production must be thoroughly investigated (cf. Ch. 2). As Lessig (2004) suggests, unless it is clear who holds the right to exploit a certain piece of content, the risk is that the software will dictate which law applies. On the positive side, this translates into the possibility that certain objects may be enjoyed by all. But the management of common resources is very complicated and it can mean that, if the rules are not defined and respected, then the stronger parties, in this case the provider of the hosting and digitization, can have the content for free. Of course there are no simple or unequivocal answers to this problem. Digitization brings new agents into play, in the use, construction and distribution of content, and for this very reason humanists, the traditional guardians of knowledge transmission, can and should play a more central role.

5.6.2 Privacy

The importance of protecting online privacy is hard to underestimate. Maintaining a balance between privacy on the one hand and public control of socially dangerous behavior on the other has always been problematic, and has required continuous adjustments to both legislation and social practice. On the Web the ability to control is exercised not only by the police and their discretionary powers, but also by other Web agencies acting autonomously, such as search engines and the providers of other kinds of network services. Also now a large part of the monitoring of user behavior is carried out via social networks that, even outside a user's own network, can monitor preferences and choices, as with Facebook's "like" button (or the Google +1 button). User behavior can also be traced through the so-called *clickstream,* the trail of information that everyone leaves as they surf the Web, but it is also true that Google is in a privileged position in terms of contacts, downloaded pages and numbers of unique users.[23] This makes its user database particularly (and worryingly) complete. Furthermore, Google's privacy and personal data rules, accessed via a small link from its homepage, are not reassuring. In a nutshell it says this: Google won't pass out personal information, except when necessary, if the police ask for it, or it is needed to improve their services. And Google's cookie (an identification string stored on users' computers to re-identify them when they return) expires in 2038! Admittedly,

Google has promised the European Union that they will keep personal information only for one and a half to two years, but what if it is stored in the United States, which has very different legislation on privacy? Moreover, there is the very real risk that some hacker could steal sensitive documents without their owners realizing it. Google protects with a blanket of obsessive secrecy all significant events that occur on their servers. To take a trivial example of how much control Google's search tools allow: Google's books-service enables the browsing of a large number of books published and available in major libraries in the US and around the world. Google keeps track of all the texts that are downloaded, how many pages are scanned, and which ones were read with attention. In fact, to access the service, it is necessary to sign in with a Google username. In this way, the system holds all the details of a user's reading habits on its server. In a traditional library, no one could trace your behavior in such a detailed way. In reflecting on this power to scan and control our digital lives (although Google jealously guards its software), one cannot help but ask what is meant today by the terms "public" and "private." This question applies not only to engines, but also to social networks. Another privacy issue directly related to search engines is the practice of using them to look for information about people. The first page of results in response to queries about individuals becomes the very identity of those people, even though that list may contain outdated, disparaging or even false information. That is why services such as *Reputation* (http://www.reputation.com) have sprung up, designed to eliminate or downplay negative information on search engines, and to ensure that only information that does not damage their clients' reputations appears. Their clients often come from the world of entertainment or politics.

Another issue related to privacy is the so-called *right to be forgotten protection*. The European court of Justice delivered a sentence on the right to be forgotten protection on May 13, 2014.[24] Following the decision search engines are supposed to remove content that infringes the right to be forgotten of European people who feel that their reputation is damaged by the public access to links connected with their names in the search engines results. According to the European Court, the information should be deleted from the listing of search engines, which are considered the "controller" of the process, when it is considered incompatible with the protection of the right to be forgotten "not only from the fact that such data are inaccurate but, in particular, also from the fact that they are inadequate, irrelevant or excessive in relation to the purposes of the processing, that they are not kept up to date, or that they are kept for longer than is necessary unless they are required to be kept for historical, statistical or scientific purposes."[25] In a section[26] of Google Transparency report dedicated to the right to be forgotten sentence is all the data relative to the requests to delete links from the 21st of May 2014. Following the data published by the company in March 2015 there were 230,647 requests of removal, for almost 4 times as many URLs, and Google has agreed to remove 40.6% of these requests, deciding according to an in-house process of evaluation.

Google decided to create an Advisory Council of experts in order to obtain suggestions and recommendations on how to fulfill the task imposed by the European

Court. The experts and Google organized seven international meetings in European cities with the aim of listening to other experts and stakeholders opinions on the right to be forgotten protection. At the end of these conferences, on the 7th of February 2015, the Advisory Council together with Eric Schmidt and David Drummond, the Chief legal officer of Google, published a final report[27] in which they defined the rules according to which Google itself would proceed in the evaluation of European citizen requests. This procedure is very interesting and ambivalent at the same time. The European Court of Justice is effectively asking Google to be the controller, on behalf European Union, of the right to be forgotten, and Google itself that is defining the limits and the possibilities of its actions. But who is controlling the controller? And why did the European Judicial authorities acknowledge that Google and other search engines were in effect their executive arms in this matter, when they were themselves in charge of establishing the balance between the right of its citizens to be informed, and the right to maintain their privacy for past events?

The right to be forgotten and its complex protection is strictly related to the issue of censorship. It is in fact apparent that search engines have the power to decide what is included and what is not, according to rules and procedures that are completely beyond the reach of end users, and partially not even in control of their workers. The algorithm contains rules that are not subject to public scrutiny, unless the optimization section of Google decides differently, following a European Court sentence, or a foreign Country order, or a Company judgment that does not need to be discussed and democratically approved.

5.6.3 Politics and censorship

If privacy is a hot topic, censorship is no less so. In China, censorship of search engines means that not only do they have control over the behavior of their users, but they can also limit their access to undesirable information. All the major search engines have expended considerable effort to enter the Chinese market, and the three main engines have even sacrificed part of their democratic ethos to achieve their goals. For example, Google was willing to self-censor Chinese news (by not including information sources disliked the Beijing government in search results) and also general search (by excluding sensitive political or religious issues and discriminating against content deemed pornographic). Even this has not been enough to avoid the charge of spreading pornography, which led to the engines being blocked in some regions. He who lives by censorship, dies by censorship! Google's strategy with respect to China seems to have undergone a radical change from January 2010, after suffering serious burglaries and data thefts along with other companies on Chinese soil. The organization moved to Hong Kong and decided not to filter searches in accordance with Chinese government demands. The strategic choice of Google could be due to several factors, including not being able to break into the country from a commercial standpoint, since Baidu in China by 2010 accounted for around 60% of the Chinese search market. After the China affair and Operation Aurora, Google seemed to change its general political strategy in favor of search transparency. Following Google's decision, the US Secretary of State Hillary Clinton gave a speech,

"Remarks on Internet Freedom" delivered January 21, 2010,[28] which compared the choice of a free Internet to the fall of the Berlin Wall, aligning the US government's endorsement of transparency to the choice made by Google. This situation made it clear that search engines act effectively at a governmental level, as agents of geopolitical choices that can influence decisions and reorganize the axes of economic and military interests. War can also be fought on the digital front through hacking and spying by both sides. Yahoo! and Microsoft have suffered hacker attacks on Chinese soil, and have chosen to support in various ways the positions of the repressive Chinese government,[29] although often companies that operate in China are based in the Special Administrative Region of Hong Kong, which has an independent legal system. But the issue that goes beyond China is the search engines' capacity to censor content at will. If a page is excluded from the engine, it no longer exists, except to those who know its exact address. Google has used this practice of censorship in the West against companies[30] that, according to them, has committed some act deserving punishment, for example, by adopting illicit techniques to increase visibility. Although it would be difficult to assess the merits of business decisions by Google and other engines, in a context of quasi-monopoly, the "punitive" choices made by Google and others appear to discriminate against certain Web sources. What if they were asked to conform to the demands of Western governments? Would they boycott the webpages of the Opposition? And what if they should become an agency with international policy interests that favor or harm other institutions, whether friend or foe? How could users defend themselves? In terms of technology, recent history shows that search engines have the ability to censor unwanted pages and individuals, and this can only be alarming. Perhaps what is needed is greater transparency in the procedures and strategic choices of companies who, while private entities, are working in the archiving and organization of a public resource like the Web. In order to achieve this, international political intervention is clearly necessary. Technology cannot be self-regulating; it needs social and democratic powers to become involved in its management. Google has made some efforts in the name of transparency, for example, through the publication in July 2009 of a report[31] on the number of content removal and data requests on behalf of governments. However, there are some entries missing and Google explicitly states: "These observations on content removal requests highlight some trends that we've seen in the data during each reporting period, and are by no means exhaustive."[32] So the private company, despite a major effort to account for what happens at the level of relations with states, explains that it has only made public what it wanted to. Even the incomplete data reveals some interesting facts. For instance, the US made 757 content removal requests from January to June of 2011, 63% of which were accepted by Google.[33] In the same time frame, 5,950 user data requests and 11,057 requests relating to accounts were made, and Google responded positively in 93% of cases.[34] The figure is interesting, considering that Google also reserves the right not to be exhaustive and remains vague about the type of data removal requested. The US is taken by way of example, but other democratic countries are no less active. In addition to these requests, countries with regimes employing censorship also place restrictions on search engines and other social network services that are considered dangerous, such as YouTube, Facebook, Twitter, Google Plus, etc.

☙

5.7 Cloud computing and the search for truth

Important as social and political issues are, they are often deeply intertwined with technical ones. To gain a better understanding of how the architecture of the Internet can impact on searching and the organization of knowledge, it will be necessary to analyze some of its technical components. The client/server architecture was developed in the 1960s when the idea of time-sharing was being developed (see above § 1.7). This technology appeared to allow every terminal to have access to the server, whereas in reality every task was queued and processed in order by the central computer. At that time, computational resources were a scarce commodity compared to the number of service requests, and the terminal/server paradigm allowed for a more direct relationship between user and machine even at a distance. This represented a notable step forward both in terms of performance and in human–machine interaction. The physical architecture and network protocols designed in this period are still largely those in use today. This organization of resources only allowed for asymmetric relations between the user's machine and the network server, similar to the conservation and organization of data by search engines. The 1990s saw a steady increase in the availability of computing and the emergence of increasingly user-friendly operating systems for electronic devices. At the same time, a new philosophy of interaction was being promoted by well-known cognitive psychologists such as Donald Norman (1998). Norman held that the extreme consequences of the virtualization of devices, as promised by Turing's universal computer (cf. Ch. 1), would produce a machine that was too complex for the end user. At that time, the commercial aim was to widen the market for electronic devices, to create specialized "information appliances" with a small and focused command set, which would help make the user's interaction with the device more intuitive.

Cloud computing is a blend of this asymmetric network architecture based on clients and servers and the commercial success of information appliances. By having several devices manage our data, each with its own specialization, it no longer makes sense to think of conserving the computer's hard disk storage; it simply becomes one of the many facets of our "digital footprint." The information appliance has become a tool for unifying a mass of personal data (music, games, photographs and documents) in the form of a "cloud" that follows us around.

But what exactly is "cloud computing"? The National Institute of Standards and Technology, in September 2011, proposed the following definition:

> Cloud computing is a model for enabling ubiquitous, convenient, on-demand network access to a shared pool of configu-

rable computing resources (e.g., networks, servers, storage, applications, and services) that can be rapidly provisioned and released with minimal management effort or service provider interaction.[35]

A cloud service is based first on virtualization: the subdivision of one powerful server into many smaller machines, so that computing processing power, as well as storage can be increased in line with demand; second, on the "replication" or backing up of data in various data centers so that it is always available; and third, on the increasing availability of connectivity, which means lower connection costs, and the ability to manipulate data at a distance. The data might only be for personal use (using a server to store your own personal files, placing the information in a virtual, always-on, always-accessible archive), or for corporate use, such as data management services for big banks choosing to use this method for storing their data. In the client/server model of the 1960s, it was evident that software and data had to be managed at a distance. Later, when machine performance increased, the acquisition of hardware and software for individual personal and commercial use became the dominant business model. Cloud computing, on the other hand, leads in a new direction, where personal computers are less powerful and more reliant on connectivity, and storage space and software are monetized. From the political or social point of view there is little difference between these two models, but the control the user has over his or her data is completely different. The party that holds and therefore can access any data we make public more or less knowingly, and also the data contained in our private files, will find themselves in a delicate position. The idea of search is at this point no longer limited to services explicitly oriented towards this function — the classic search engines — although Google offers a cloud service for those Android users who have a Google account. It concerns instead the capacity of all cloud services to guarantee access to our data, which we will no longer control. To access it, we will have to trust the retrieval capacities of those same services, who provide us with storage space and connectivity. Furthermore, it is likely that the spread of cloud computing will put the principle of Net neutrality at risk. According to this principle, all packets of data are equal with respect to the way they are sent and received, and no one can claim privileged access to the Internet. This means that service providers cannot prioritize or penalize content. However, in December 2010 the Federal Communications Commission (FCC) decided to endorse a set of rules that were most controversial in this regard (Stelter 2010). Although Net neutrality is guaranteed on the land-based network without exception, there is the possibility that mobile networks will be allowed to prioritize certain types of content. These rules, under which it will be possible to favor or discriminate in the routing of content on mobile networks, have been anticipated in an agreement between Google and Verizon. This agreement, signed in August 2010, has been particularly controversial because Google had previously been an ardent supporter of Net neutrality. Beyond mobile telephony, it is inevitable that the connections between users and their own data stored in the cloud will become the focus of attention, whether it is business data (in complex cases through dedicated connections) or personal data, where access to information will become vital, and therefore liable to exploitation by its controllers. The theme of Net neutrality, taken together with the issues of privacy and data accessibility should therefore become part of our political and social reflection on the use of modern technology.

In recent years, the miniaturization of components and the corresponding increase in computing power and decrease in cost, have offered the possibility of a network architecture less closely tied to its origins. There has been a rise in the use of the much-loved Peer2Peer (P2P) networks, used for file sharing, the collective and free sharing of content, even content protected by copyright. These systems, constrained only by the nature of equalized communications protocols, construct search, storage and access mechanisms for dynamic pieces of information that have nothing in common with those used by traditional search engines.[36] These mechanisms could provide a viable alternative to the now common phenomenon of cloud computing, in which a few companies manage, store and distribute the data of the majority of users. However, one must remember that technology does not only depend on the availability of efficient technical solutions, but also on the political, social and commercial appropriation and use of technological innovation.

Cloud computing is the theoretical and practical consequence of the traditional client/server architecture and the idea that on each user's device there should be nothing to impede their use of the service, whether or not its logic and complexity is understood. In fact the idea of things being made "for a user as if he or she must be stupid and not know it," is a gradual reduction in his or her capacity for choice and the ability to organize documents and files. The idea is that a user will be happy if their activity is simplified in exchange for ceding some of their organizational freedoms. The consequences of this are that the user finds him or herself in a walled garden, where the only services available are those condoned by the provider, whether that may be Apple, Android, Amazon or Microsoft, with the ever-present risk of lock-in. This results in a progressive diminution in the potential of software, in exchange for a stabilization of those services that win in the marketplace. All efforts are directed towards adaptation and conformance to the standard promoted by the successful provider and not towards creative innovation.

One of the features of the cloud is the spread of application programming interfaces (APIs) that allow programs to interact with the cloud, and to provide services within its framework. But for programmers, working with an API means working within a proprietary system that requires them to develop software according to the constraints set by the technology supplier, who is allowed to censor and control which services are right for their platform, and which are not. Even from a strictly technological point of view, innovation is put at risk because individual programmers are denied access to the system; they are allowed to offer services only within the constraints defined by the API. On the other hand, once software has been developed in conformance with a certain API, the programmer is pressured to stay within that system, because to leave would mean throwing away all his or her work. This system has given rise to the current craze for "apps," or applications closely linked to the use of APIs and cloud computing. The "core" of the cloud is locked into an inaccessible sancta sanctorum that can only be communicated with through APIs, made available to developers by its "rulers." This strategy, intended to stabilize the processes of innovation, actually slows it down. Jaron Lanier, the inventor of the term "virtual reality," maintains that the structure of the Internet is anything but virtual. It should be studied in terms of topology, on a nation-by-nation basis. Success is determined through economical, material, political and social measures, and the freedom of users can only be maintained through the exertion of control and governance (2010).

One of the main arguments in favor of using cloud computing as an infrastructure was the saving in energy terms compared to traditional in-house infrastructures. According to the big-data-cloud-computing rhetoric, companies who use cloud computing service providers to store their data can decrease their energy costs and hence contribute to a greener economy. However, in order to quantify the energy cost of a data storage infrastructure, the cost of energy transmission must also be taken into account. According to a white paper published in June 2013 by the Center for Energy-efficient Telecommunications (www.ceet.unimelb.edu.au) *The power of wireless cloud: an analysis of the energy consumption of wireless cloud,* the highest energy costs in cloud computing arise from wireless transmission itself. It is estimated that the use of wireless cloud energy will increase by 460% between 2012 and 2015, leading to a great increase in energy *wastage*.

The spread of technology has always involved a trade-off between new liberties and new regimes of control, in the commercial dimension, just as in any other. The problem here is to recognize who are the "controllers" of our data, and what it will cost us not to worry about keeping it synchronized. While the suppliers of film, music or telephony hold our attention for the moment and make us pay for this directly or indirectly, the data managers, who accumulate and retain our preferences, our tastes, our contacts and relationships, can use that data (officially or not) to guide our purchases and advise us on our own preferences. This is something more than simply keeping us interested. Their objective consists in grabbing our attention, memory and consciousness, and storing it in a cloud maintained who-knows-where and accessible by who-knows-who. As Pariser (2011) suggests in the title of his seventh chapter, personalization can get out of control and offer you "what you want, whether you want it or not." Molding our memories in this way amounts to orienting our present and determining our future. It may be worth considering whether the trade-off between the increased freedom to use any device, with our data stored in the cloud, and a corresponding loss of privacy is worth the exchange.

Such considerations are complicated by the natural impulse to take as real the image we would like to think most resembles us. Furthermore, the information comes to us in real-time, as cryptic as an online Delphic oracle. As the great Austrian novelist Robert Musil said: "The truth is not a crystal that can be slipped into one's pocket, but an endless current into which one falls headlong" (Musil 1996, 582). Reality cannot be constructed from an online analysis of our habits, from a list of products and services in which we appear to be interested. And we cannot hold that such a list represents our identity, like a crystal we slip into our pocket. Careful attention must be paid to the relationship between truth and inquiry, keeping cheap pretensions to knowledge separate from the struggle for truth as an experience of liberty.

☙

5.8 Google, AI and Turing's social definition of intelligence

Over the past few years, major Internet, hardware and software companies such as Google, Facebook, Amazon, Microsoft, and IBM have conducted considerable research in AI and robotics, and made substantial investments in firms that are active in those fields. For example, at the beginning of 2014, Google acquired DeepMind, an AI company based in London and co-founded by a former child chess prodigy, Demis Hassabis, for around £400m. In October of that year, Google also bought two other AI British spin-offs of Oxford University: Dark Blue, a company working on machine learning techniques for natural languages, and Vision Factory, who are working on computer vision. The Web search giant also launched a partnership between the Google AI structure and the AI research group at Oxford University. All these AI acquisitions, partnerships and investments followed a long list of acquisitions of robotics companies over the past few years. A major component of this list was Boston Dynamics, a company whose primary clients are the US Army, Navy and Marine Corps (Cohen 2014).

Google clearly needs this kind of technology to deal not only with their core business, but also with their more innovative developments, such as Google Glass, self-driving cars, etc. But why do AI and robotics appear to be so strategic to Google? Even their core business deals with language understanding and translation, both in processing texts to help formulate responses to query requests, and in understanding the queries themselves through speech recognition. Visual recognition is used in the retrieval of images and videos, and in the development of Google Glass and self-driving cars. All of these areas of interest seem to be covered by the traditional fields of AI that from the 1960s onward has promised solutions to the same kinds of problems that Google is trying to solve today.

Another potential area for AI is the management of Big Data, which, as argued above (cf. 4.5.1), lies at the heart of the marketing and profiling activities of the search engine. In order to process huge amounts of data, adequate correlation algorithms are needed, based mainly on machine learning techniques developed in the field of AI during the 1970s and 1980s. It is not by chance that the director of Research at Google Inc. is now Peter Norwig, a key figure in the field, who was co-author, along with Stuart Russell, of the classical textbook on AI, *Artificial Intelligence: A modern approach* since 1995.

According to the paper "Intelligent machinery," written in 1948 by Alan Turing, considered one of the fathers of the modern thought about AI, the key areas of the field were: "(i) Various games … (ii) The learning of languages, (iii) translation of languages, (iv) Cryptography, (v) mathematics" (Turing 1948/2004, 420). With the inclusion of modern image recognition, these still appear to be the main areas of interest in AI.

Any field in which the same projects remain unaccomplished for so long naturally raises suspicions. But Turing offered another interesting point of view to understand why the potential of AI deserves attention: "the extent to which we regard something as behaving in an intelligent manner is determined as much by our own state of mind and training as by the properties of the object under consideration. If we are able to explain and predict its behavior or if there seems to be a little underlying plan, we have little temptation to imagine intelligence" (Turing 1948/2004, 431).

As suggested by the title of the last paragraph of his paper, intelligence is an emotional and subjective concept, and depends just as much on the observer's own conception of intelligence, and on his/her mental condition and training, as on the properties of the object under investigation.

According to Turing, the definition of intelligence should not be considered too crucial because: "at the end of the century the use of words and general educated opinion will have altered so much that one will be able to speak of machine thinking without expecting to be contradicted" (Turing 1950/2004, 449).

The suggestion was thus that, in the 50 years following the publication of his paper, the transformation of conscience and beliefs of the general public would be extensive enough to elevate "machine thinking" to the level of the generally perceived notion of "intelligence."

These two assumptions taken together: the training and mental state of the researcher, and the change in the mentality of the general audience, form the main presupposition of AI. In future it will be agreed that what machines will be able to do will be a reasonable definition of machine intelligence.

The AI results obtained by DeepMind in April 2014 on the First Day of the Tomorrow Technology conference in Paris,[37] as described in (Mnih, Hassabis, *et al.* 2015), offer an interesting perspective on what may be considered intelligent, for a task achieved by a machine.

The video shows the AI computer program as it learns to play an Arcade game, Breakout, which belongs to the family of the earliest Atari 2600 games, prototyped in 1975 by Wozniak and Jobs (Twilley 2015). The aim of the game is to destroy a wall brick by brick, using a ball launched against it. The "intelligent" program behaves in a very progressive way: at the start it is not very clever, but it quickly learns. After half an hour it becomes as clever as a non-clever human, and after 300 games the program stop missing the ball, and becomes more expert that the most expert human.

According to the description — published as a letter in *Nature* on the 26th of February 2015 — behind the great success of the Deep Q-network (DQN) lies two different kinds of "intelligent" tools: the ability to create a representation of an environment using high-dimensional hierarchical sensory inputs, and the ability to reinforce learning strategies based solely on that environment, without any rearrangement of the data, or pre-programming of the learning strategies. DQN was able to develop a winning strategy by simply analyzing the pixels on the screen and the game scores: successful actions resulted from analysis of the sensory description provided by the deep neural network.

According to the description of the experiment: "To use reinforcement learning successfully in situations approaching real-world complexity, however, agents are confronted with a difficult task: they must derive efficient representations of the environment from high-dimensional sensory inputs, and use these to generalize past experience to new situations" (Mnih, Hassabis, *et al.* 2015, 529). The deep neural network was described by comparing its performance to human behavior. Part of the enthusiasm surrounding this achievement was attributed to the assumption, as declared by the AI experts who described the results, that game-playing expertise can be compared to that needed to solve real-world complexity problems. However this assumption could be called into question, considering the low level of complexity in 1970s arcade games. Their working environments look very different from real world problems, both in terms of the nature of the rudimentary task, and in the computer reconstruction of the limited sensory experience.

To successfully compare human strategies with the neural networks requires an interpretation and analysis all the metaphors used to describe the objectives and accomplishments of the Deep-Q network: "humans and other animals seem to solve this problem through a harmonious combination of reinforcement learning and hierarchical sensory processing systems ..., the former evidenced by a wealth of neural data revealing notable parallels between the phasic signals emitted by dopaminergic neurons and temporal difference reinforcement learning algorithms"(Mnih, Hassabis, *et al.* 2015, p. 529). This reveals an underlying assumption that there is a symmetry between the behavior of dopaminergic neurons, and the function of the reinforcement learning algorithm used by the DQN. When declaring this parallel the researchers did not provide any convincing argument to prove their hypothesis. To this may be added the doubts already mentioned about whether simple success in playing Breakout should be included in any possible definition of human intelligence. Despite these undemonstrated assumptions, many appear ready to appreciate and support the result as an outstanding progress of AI research. This fact may thus be one of the social transformations of the definition of intelligence anticipated by Turing's 1950 paper.

The current situation thus does not differ too much from that in the 1960s and the 1970s where the game-like problem solutions of AI software prototypes were rhetorically transformed into the first step in climbing the mountain of human-like intelligent performances.

Another noteworthy effect of this exploitation of the AI effect within Google is their creation of an "ethics board," as required by the DeepMind people when they were taken over by Google. However, it is surely a strange practice to appoint an in-house ethics commission aimed at self-regulation. The board's task is twofold: on one hand it aims to judge and absolve Google of any potential "sin" when managing AI software, and on the other hand it guarantees that Google is not doing any evil, when trying to emulate certain human abilities via software.

Google thus acts as if it were both the controller and the agent under control: it accepts no authority except itself, when discussing what it does that is right or wrong. This "affirmative discourse" approach (Bunz 2013) to international, social and geopolitical problems became very successful, and sufficiently convincing that other international authorities also accepted it, as suggested by the decision of the European Court of Justice on the right to be forgotten, published in May 2014.[38] The European Court attributed to Google the role of the European guarantor of the right to be forgotten. Google accepted the role, but at the same time published a report[39] written by the Advisory Council, also nominated by Google, describing how it may act as an advisory committee in performing the role of guarantor. The report suggests rules that the company should follow in protecting the right of some people to have their data forgotten, while maintaining the right of the rest of the Europeans to have their data both available and preserved. It is the same situation of the ethics board for AI: Google is asking itself to be the guarantor of the ethical control over its operations of technological advancement.

5.9 Communication and freedom

Well before the datagate scandal and Wikileaks attracted the attention of the global media, the controversial relationship between control and online freedom has been addressed by scholars like Alexander Galloway (2004) and Wendy Chun (2006). Although their approaches differ, they both note the interconnections between opportunity and risk in the access and spread of personal data.

Galloway's book analyzes network communication protocols and the duplicity inherent in their rules. He looks at how the TCP/IP (transmission control protocol/Internet protocol)[40] permits the free and unimpeded transmission of data packets, while the DNS (domain name system), organizes and holds, albeit using a distributed model, the numerical addresses of connected servers, and so controls access to their content. In this original ambiguity, written into the very functioning of the network, Galloway traces the origins of the controversial question of the relationship between the opportunities for freedom in spaces where information is distributed and easier to find, with the need to control the network. One could follow this line of reasoning and find, in the protocols of the mobile network, another layer of coercion, at least in the control of commercial users.

Wendy Chun, on the other hand, analyzes the interplay between freedom and control lying at the heart of the structures of technology. She notes that all positions, whether optimistic with regard to the freedom of the network or more pessimistic in face of the Orwellian power of control that technology has over us, betray a lack of balance. The reality of the network consists in a mixture of chances for free expression and the consequent possibility for surveillance and control. Chun emphasizes that true freedom cannot be determined by the possibilities of expression offered by the network; in fact, it has more to do with the responsibility to make choices. It is interesting to note that Manuel Castells, the Spanish Internet sociologist, identified the same close relationship between the worlds of communication and politics through a study of social networking between members of the boards of communications companies and political lobbyists (Castells 2009). His thesis is that politics, or power and the instruments of control, even in the democratic world, are in the hands of those who rule the most successful media companies, including those that operate mainly on the Web. He also argues that those who would act as antagonists can use the same spaces of communication, break into cyberspace, and provide counter-information. Castells' argument is particularly interesting because, in his earlier analyses, he had been much more persuaded of the "revolutionary" dimension of the new media. His change of opinion shows clearly how this idealized view of the Internet is coming to an end.

5.9.1 Corporate knowledge or the end of science?
Regarding the regimes of control within the framework of freedom (with particular regard to search engines), it is useful to compare Vaidhyanathan (2011), who argues that the complete trust placed in the ranking algorithms used by Google may cause a long-term loss of control over some of humanity's crucial issues. He also calls into question the validity of a management style based on engineering priorities:

> ... the company itself takes a technocratic approach to any larger ethical and social questions in its way. It is run by and for engineers .... Every potential problem is either a bug in the system, yet to be fixed, or a feature in its efforts to provide a better service. (Vaidhyanathan 2011, 8)

The situation could therefore be at risk in terms of ethics, politics and epistemology if users lack an understanding of the possible risks. Of course, responsibility lies not just with the company, but in the scarcity of social awareness on the part of users and institutions. One of the most sensitive issues which does require a degree of awareness is the relationship between knowledge and search engines. On this point, an intensive campaign of information literacy is needed to combat a trend that sees college students using the Internet as their primary source of information, and failing to assess resources in terms of quality, by treating the search engine as the only arbiter of relevance. Again according to Vaidhyanathan "The notion of 'library' and 'Internet' have merged significantly for university students in the United States" (Vaidhyanathan 2011, 190). Such a situation requires the institution to guide students "through the information ecosystem," but universities often do not provide their students with such skills, abandoning them to their uncertainties and impulses. This may represent an additional risk to the freedom of knowledge, since in combination with the effects of personalization in search engines noted by Pariser (2011), it could result in a society that leaves no room for diversity, innovation, or the spirit of research.

What may be most important to the digital humanist are the mechanisms attributing relevance and how they function. According to an often-cited article by the celebrated Chris Anderson (June 4, 2008),[41] the massive availability of data through search engines makes the scientific method of research, with its hypotheses, theories and experiments, effectively obsolete. Computers might be better placed to explain the vast amount of data collected and stored in various databases. Anderson cites Peter Norvig, Google's Research director, who said, after George Box, "All models are wrong, and increasingly you can succeed without them." According to this viewpoint, "correlation is enough. We can stop looking for models. We can analyze the data without hypotheses about what it might show" (Anderson 2008). This techno-fundamentalist position can only lead to dismay. Today more and more funds are being redirected towards planning technological infrastructures, while investments in research laboratories and the like are being reduced. As Vaidhyanathan suggests, "The knowledge generated by massive servers and powerful computers will certainly be significant and valuable — potentially revolutionary. But it should not come at the expense of tried-and-true methods of discovery" (Vaidhyanathan 2011, 197). Knowledge exists only in relation to freedom of inquiry and the diversity of the researchers' hypotheses. If these are subsumed and embodied by the computational power of a handful of companies, the threat to the future of knowledge as a common good might be considerable, by reducing the diversity of opinion and experimental verification. For this reason, research institutions and universities must pay special attention to, and promote awareness of the importance of research freedom, which is guaranteed only by the plurality of research groups and the diversity of methods they adopt. It would also be helpful to underline the difference between the manipulation of data in machine-readable formats that can only be controlled by other computers, and the definition of scientific theories and hypotheses tested by socially repeatable laboratory experiments. Two of the most prominent supporters of the "big data" revolution, Viktor Mayer-Schönberger and Kenneth Cukier (2013, 70–72) do not believe in the mantra of getting rid of theories. They support instead the perspective that big data offers a change in scientific method, but still relies on theory for its interpretation and interconnection. According to Lisa Gitelman in the introduction to her interesting book *"Raw data" is an oxymoron* (Gitelman 2013, 1–9). The very idea that data can be correlated without a theory is only based on the rhetorical argument that data can be analyzed without interpretation, and that it exists independently from our need to collect it.

Another consequence of the reorganization of science connected with cloud computing resources and the emergence of big data was the idea of the "googlization" of genes. According to the reconstruction offered in Vise and Malseed (2005, 281–292) in February 2005 a private dinner was held between Craig Venter (CEO of Celera Genomics, the company who mapped for the first time the DNA of its CEO), Sergey Brin (cofounder and technologic chief of Google) and Ryan Phelan (CEO of DNA Direct, internet company for DNA Internet texts). The subject discussed at the dinner was the possibility of googling our DNA for genetic information about ourselves and our families. Google could offer the technological facilities for the big data manipulation necessary for the linear mapping of the Human Genome. Even though biologists know very well that the linear data on a single genome is not a probabilistic map of the possible illnesses of each individual, the potential for the management of such data is a big temptation for private sector insurance companies and the proponents of big data. The genomics map says nothing for certain about variables that are influenced by thousands of factors such as life style, social and environmental relations, etc. But the potential impact of genomic text, and its mapping via computer graphics, has a strong influence on the imagination (Nowotny and Testa 2011, 43–48) and on the prediction of the future health of individuals. As yet it is unclear whether this representation of DNA data, within the frame of big data, will facilitate or inhibit the explanation of health probabilities based on the correlation of genetic, environmental and social factors, or whether, as in the film *Gattaca*, we will all be assessed in the future by our known genetic profile.

The next subsection will analyze the role of archival facilities to produce new knowledge and understanding. Building a grid of data implies embedding within it the information needed to interpret that data. "Raw data" is just an illusion that must be pierced like the "veil of Maya" to achieve data without interpretation, where correlations emerge from scratch.

5.9.2 *The power of the archive*

Search engines and other tools of the so-called knowledge society can also reveal something about the failure of the blind trust placed in science, the tragic anarchic pride of scientists and their unconditional faith in progress and in themselves. Google PageRank, which copied the peer-review process to evaluate webpages, is transforming evaluation methods within science itself through Google Scholar, one of its products — a curious circular effect that should give us pause.

The organization of all human knowledge, as well as being extremely difficult, also has potentially disturbing side-effects. It is clear that the ambition of the search engines is to become the archive of the Web, and therefore of all the information and knowledge of society. But the archive is not a neutral space where information can be collected without order or rules. Whoever constructs such an archive interprets that information and establishes both what can be found and retrieved and what will be irredeemably hidden and buried, regardless of the genuine intentions of the archivist or the reader/retriever. In short, the archive constructs the meaning of phrases that would otherwise have no organic structure. As Foucault writes in his *Archaeology of Knowledge*:

> The archive is also that which determines that all these things said do not accumulate endlessly in an amorphous mass, nor are they inscribed in an unbroken linearity, nor do they disappear at the mercy of chance external accidents; but they are grouped together in distinct figures, composed together in accordance with multiple relations, maintained or blurred in accordance with specific regularities. (Foucault 1969/1982, 145–146)

Therefore, the archive is the horizon of meaning that determines the possible knowledge of events, ideas or people. It determines the regularities that allow us to interpret, in each moment, the world around us and to establish what information survives and what will disperse as mere noise, by losing access to a defined and organized form. Far from being a dusty and forgotten place, the archive in all its forms is the beating heart of a civilization. The work of the search engines must be connected to this sphere, and it is clear that humanists should supervise the criteria, principles and "regularness" adopted by these technological instruments. Search engines expressly declare that they want to take on the role of being superarchives of all online knowledge, and ultimately, of all knowledge, period.

The actors of the archival scenario are not limited to traditional search engines, whose most successful instance is represented by Google: now also social networks like Facebook are entering the archival machinery. The end of the Web, which is one of the key elements of the walled-garden era of post Web 2.0, means that relevant archival sources can be stored in different cloud computing repositories. Facebook's Graph search, although still in beta form, represents a crucial transformation of the archival attitude of the social network. The crucial twist of this search tool is its semantic orientation. It searches sentences, which is the reason why it is so clumsy to customize in the different languages spoken within Facebook boundaries. It will be possible to search in past posts, comments, statuses and "like" recommendations. While before it was so difficult to retrieve information about the past, the promise of the new tools is to make the past just as accessible as the present. Among the different risks inherent in the retrieval strategies of Zuckerberg's tool is the abandonment of privacy by obscurity, which was supposed to placate the concerns of users when they post sensitive information in a public arena. Another risk is the perception that retrievals of our own post streams and those of others are complete and reliable. It is as if the list of statuses represents a fair substitution of our memory and a perfect function of our ability to portray ourselves, or the attitudes of friends and acquaintances.

According to Foucault, "The archive cannot be described in its totality" (1969/1989 147). It is clear that it needs an external world, an outside to refer to: there cannot be an archive without an outside-the-archive (Derrida 1996). It is just this outside-the-archive that we risk losing, unless we retain the critical spirit and vigilance of the humanities, and prevent technologies from taking over the spirit of research, by permitting a mechanical rule like the ranking algorithm, no matter how efficient, to pass unquestioned.

The phenomenon of the quantified self will result in those human characteristics that cannot be measured and represented as "data" being treated as irrelevant. What we truly are is thus becoming increasingly less connected with the production of the very data that allows us to understand ourselves and our environment. But as suggested by Geoffrey Bowker "getting more data on the problem is not necessarily going to help" (Bowker 2013, 171). While it would be better to admit that "embracing the complexity of inquiry as a generative process of collaborative remix can push us to accept that no matter how good our tools, algorithms, or filters, we cannot possibly explain the whole of any situation" (Markham 2013, 10). We need to refuse the blackmail represented by the objectivity and complete measurability of phenomena by the data-program-data cycles (Bowker 2013, 170) and start exercising our "strongly humanistic approach to analysing the forms that data take; a hermeneutic approach which enables us to envision new possible futures" (Bowker 2013, 171).

There is no easy solution to the problems raised by the information society and its tools of knowledge control, such as search engines and its connected big data mechanisms and facilities. The only possible antidote is to increase the standard and frequency of education in critical reason and e-literacy, in order to encourage the development of a multiplicity of sources and the skills needed to consult them. In this sense, and for many reasons, Peer2Peer dynamic indexes may be an interesting way to avoid the unique source effect. First, the architecture of these services represents a new approach with respect to the traditional client/server one, and is more reminiscent of the old style computing services and their hierarchical terminals. Second, the dynamic index is more compatible with the distributed richness of the peer to peer network.

Resistance to controlling society is a political activity and probably needs to be directed via new political paradigms. According to Deleuze (1990), the solution is resistance in "non-communicative" areas that are not susceptible to being controlled. In Ray Bradbury's *Fahrenheit 451*, people learned books by heart in order to preserve them from destruction. Resistance strategies can be learned from "weak categories," such as women in patriarchal societies: they were used to telling stories about their identity, their status, and their inner feelings, in order to preserve themselves from being canceled by the indifference of the patriarch and his heirs. A "privileged connection" between language and women is confirmed by the hypothesis of the anthropologist Dean Falk. In her fascinating study (Falk 2009), she argued that the origins of language could be traced back to the "singsong babbling," that special dialogue between mother and her infant that arose at the beginning of human history.

Summary of Part II

The second part of this book dealt with the writing of digital content, and the archiving, representation, searching and organization of information. Each of these activities has been deeply transformed by the introduction of digital communication technologies. So the previous chapters investigated these changes by analyzing the risks, challenges and opportunities they present in a typical humanities environment.

Chapter 3 (Writing and producing content) *examined the forms and genres of digital textuality from a cultural, sociological and rhetorical standpoint. It investigated questions such as: what kinds of writing are in use today, and in what ways have the roles of author, publisher and reader changed? As Michael Wesch asks, does the machine in fact "write us" rather than act as a mere passive agent in our minds? Social media and Web 2.0 practices have changed the author-publisher relationship, and are raising questions of identity, self-representation, autonomy, etc. Although social media are not quite as pervasive as is commonly perceived in the Western world, our daily life has become almost unthinkable without them. But all of these forms of communication have their own technical rules and rhetorical dimensions. Producing effective content for the Web now goes well beyond working with texts, and involves the use of images, sound, video, and scripting as part of a cohesive human–computer interaction design. Although this chapter focused on writing and producing texts, direct visual modes of cultural representation and production also play an important cognitive and expressive role (Kress and van Leeuwen 2006, 23). Finally, the space or "immaterial" support used for storage and retrieval of content (the "Cloud") has serious social and ethical implications for what it means to be an individual in the digital age.*

Chapter 4 (Representing and archiving) *investigated the forms and methodologies of digital representation and data storage of humanities artifacts, focusing on texts and written documents. It analyzed strategies for minimizing the risks of obsolescence that would limit access to our cultural memory. It also investigated the powerful reorganization brought about by the digital transition in the places where data is preserved, such as libraries and archives. The practices of archiving and representation are in fact not limited to paper-based media such as books or other non digital objects, but also include digital objects at greater risk of damage and data obsolescence. The representation at the metadata level of physical or digital objects also implies a number of technical, cultural and social problems. Digital metadata formats and the tools for manipulating them need continuous efforts to maintain agreement and relevance. Archivists and the users of these standards do not openly acknowledge these agreements, but the need for such an organization plays a crucial role in the success of the representation effort. This chapter also discusses some new strategies for data interpretation, such as semantic representation, textual analysis and text-mining, as new models for making sense of, and extracting information from, preserved data. The degree of effectiveness of all these methods also has a major impact, and a lasting influence on, the practices of searching, retrieving and filtering, which form the subject of the final chapter.*

Chapter 5 (Searching and organizing) *explored the complex field of search and retrieval practices with special regard to the mainstream search engines. It focused on the techniques and strategies of Google, which, since its launch, has transformed the field of information retrieval, both from a technical and a commercial standpoint. It described how information is organized to facilitate its later retrieval, and the lack of neutrality this entails. It also offered a critical perspective on the corrective practices for resolving problems, based on the research tradition of the* studia humanitatis. *This chapter also tried to show how the dominance of Google has led to a transformation in the production of content, which is now designed explicitly to optimize the ability of an artificial system to understand it.*

The research on social, political, ethical and epistemological issues raised by such efforts to arrange and sort information is based on the software studies approach (Chun 2011, Fuller 2008, Galloway 2012, Lovink 2007, Manovich 2013, etc.). The main idea behind this analysis is a vision of software as a cultural artifact in its own right, because it has a significant influence on the reshaping of the knowledge it manages. This opposition between the visible/invisible components of modern digital communication produces some strange effects, such as hiding behind the apparent transparency of the information the complete opacity of the underlying technology.

A critical approach is also appropriate to the management of social data by certain algorithms, whose function is likewise hidden from view, but which are used to make sense of that data. This issue is particularly relevant to the discussion of Big Data, which deserves special attention on account of the ethical problems relating to privacy and surveillance techniques that it raises. Moreover, it is important to investigate the epistemological and methodological strategies at work when Big Data deals with experiments in social science and humanities research.

All of the problems raised in this second part deserve special attention from humanities and social science scholars. Digital humanists are in a good position to understand, discuss, and criticize the forms and consequences of knowledge digitization, and to assess their social and political consequences.

The study of these critical issues should be regarded as one of the core areas within our field. The practices of DH need to shake off their current subaltern role in the humanities and information technology, and move towards a deeper engagement with critical theory and social critique (Chun, Rhody 2014). DH should be considered as a trading zone (Berry 2011, Liu 2012), and commence a conversation with other established historical and theoretical discourses on technology, for example, studies of science and technology. Although the critical attitude is a crucial asset of humanists, "the digital humanities have been oblivious to cultural criticism" (Liu 2012, 491). The effort here is to bring back into focus this critical attitude to help analyze and comprehend the digital world. Building on the past, oriented to the future, can contribute to the creation of a mature DH scholar, able to confront with equal competence both humanities and computer science experts as a credible and innovative intermediary.

Conclusions
DH in a global perspective[1]

1. The periphery-center effect

The preceding five chapters have attempted to offer an historical-critical introduction to the principal concepts, instruments and resources of DH. This structure has been described as a new trivium, as an essential introduction for the humanist and social scientist of the 21st century. The subtitle of this book is "a critical inquiry" because, apart from reflecting on the foundations of DH, it also focuses on the social and cultural problems afforded by the use of technology from a less Western-centric perspective. Beyond Big Data, mega-platforms and the mass archivation of data, the true innovation of the next decade of DH appears to be its geographic expansion and the consequent enlargement (and deepening) of these questions. The surprising global expansion of DH has led to a series of discussions on previously neglected topics: the different nuances of the linguistic-cultural problem (Clavert 2013; Golumbia 2013; Shah 2010), cross-cultural representation within the international organizations of DH (Fiormonte 2012),[2] the consequences of the anglophone dominance in the processes of discussion and factual evaluation (Dacos 2013), the hierarchical structure of the management and ownership of major archives and repositories (Sánz 2013), the relationship of DH to colonial and subaltern studies (Bailey 2011; Risam and Koh 2013; Morais 2013), and the need for a critical approach in connection with the social sciences and other less represented fields and practices (#transformDH 2012; Honn 2013; Lothian and Phillips 2013; Liu 2012, 2013; McPherson 2012; Presner 2012; Rodríguez Ortega 2013; Romero Frías 2014; Vinck 2013).[3] As in other events of the global scene, the growing awareness in the way that DH is practiced in different cultural contexts is changing the traditional hierarchical relationship between the center and the periphery:

> Methods that have worked effectively in one cultural setting may fail spectacularly in another (and vice versa) and certain reasoning of how things should work does not apply similarly

> to other frameworks. Models, surveys, truisms should be placed
> in context. Periphery countries can contribute by framing and
> stating more explicitly how and in what ways true collabora-
> tion can be achieved. I think that attitude is the keyword here.
> (Galina 2013)[4]

But are centers ready to learn from peripheries? Or are perhaps new definitions of "centers" and "peripheries" required? These tensions originate from profound global changes in the production and diffusion of knowledge (European Science Foundation 2011; National Science Foundation 2011; Stodden 2010), which are challenging the instruments and hierarchies of traditional forms of evaluation (peer review, impact factor, etc.), and demanding new forms of governance for shared and participatory knowledge (Lafuente *et al.* 2013). These needs are represented by initiatives like the Digital Humanities Manifesto 2.0, the THATCamp unconference network, and by projects like Postcolonial DH, DH Commons, Digital Humanities Now, etc. Although such studies and initiatives underline insufficiencies, inequalities and imbalances, they also bear witness to the vitality of the debate and represent a unique opportunity for DH to overturn traditional scientific practices. The next few pages attempt to provide a critical map of the main initiatives, organizations, centers and research projects scattered across various continents. It is not intended as an exhaustive panorama (various forms of systematic census can be found online), but to introduce newcomers to the geo-cultural complexity of DH.[5]

2. Research and teaching experiences

As explained in the preceding chapters, our interactions with technology require investigation beyond the mere level of its applications. From the 1980s to the present day, the job of DH has been to show the epistemological nature of the changes in methodology. It is not really about new instruments, but about a different way of representing (and accessing) knowledge and culture through digital instruments. After more than half a century of this confluence of computer science and humanities, what is the current state of play? This question can be examined on several levels. From the researcher's point of view, the creation of digital tools, resources and now "infrastructures" for the study, preservation, and dissemination of artistic and cultural heritage has become a key driver of economic and cultural development well beyond the Western world. Including the period after the 2008 global economic crisis, the investment in DH continued to grow in Europe and North America. In the United States, the National Endowment for the Humanities, the main financing body for research in the humanities, set up a specific section for DH projects, the Office of Digital Humanities, whose "primary mission is to help coordinate the NEH's efforts in the area of digital scholarship."[6] In Canada, The Social Sciences and Humanities Research Council (SSHRC) spends about the same amount as the NEH with one tenth the researchers to support.[7] In Europe, the Framework Programs (FP), that unite all of the EU's research finance programs,[8] have shown a fluctuating interest in the cultural heritage sector, for example, by distinguishing—perhaps artificially—between applications for digital archives and libraries, from those for education and teaching (e-learning, linguistic and cultural diversity, etc.). Perhaps this is why the successes of Europe have not yet quite matched those of North America.[9] The 7th Framework Program (2007-2013),[10] backed by 50 billion euros of funding, has simplified its eligibility criteria: now "Socio-economic sciences and the humanities" and "Information and communication technologies" appear on its list of key thematic areas. Apart from the usual (and questionable) amalgamation of the so-called "weak disciplines," such generalization seems to be a step backwards when compared to the specificity of previous programs, where research areas reflected strategic choices and priorities (e.g. the Sixth FP had the themes "Citizens and governance in a knowledge-based society" and "New and Emerging Science and Technology"). Nevertheless, what stands out in the 7th FP is the prominence given to networks of excellence, to projects that integrate resources, groups, workshops and institutions to create "virtual research centers." Horizon2020, the latest EU Framework Program for Research and Innovation is organized and structured in a different way.[11] Initially the humanities and human sciences disappeared altogether. It was only after a petition signed by 6,000 professionals from the cultural heritage sector (museums, galleries, libraries, archives etc.) that the European Parliament managed to include "Cultural Heritage" in the €70 billion Horizon 2020 funding program, starting in 2014.[12] In fact, the attention given to cultural heritage has always characterized the continental European version of DH.[13]

In the remaining cases the EU's choices reflect a global tendency: research has entered a new phase, the digitization of processes and infrastructures.[14] Many institutions, in the US, Europe, Asia, Australia, etc. have realized that the challenge of the future will be not only structured access to content, but the transformation of research into an activity whose various phases, from source selection to experimentation and publication, will be carried out entirely online. They are called research cyber-infrastructures[15] "shared distributed infrastructures" or more simply eScience or eResearch.[16] This trans-disciplinary tendency clearly indicates that the era of simply storing and conserving electronic documents is now connected with the end-result, and that, as some hope, an era of standardization of the technologies of access, utilization and storage of resources is now beginning. In Europe this strategy has seen the emergence of consortia and networks such as CLARIN (http://www.clarin.eu), DARIAH (http://dariah.eu), NEDIMAH (http://nedimah.eu) and TELEARC (http://www.noe-kaleidoscope.org/telearc). These initiatives (especially DARIAH, NEDIMAH and CLARIN) intersect thematically with DH, but their scope is more vast and their objectives more vague.

Infrastructures and platforms that are more specifically connected with research include TAPoR (http://portal.tapor.ca), NINES (http://www.nines.org), Interedition (http://www.interedition.eu), TextGrid (http://www.textgrid.de), CENDARI (http://www.cendari.eu), Huma-Num (http://www.huma-num.fr), HuNi (https://huni.net.au/), and Bamboo (http://projectbamboo.org [cf. Ch. 3]).[17] The first three of these (TAPoR is Canadian, NINES and Bamboo are American, Interedition and CENDARI are European, Huma-Num French, HuNi Australian, and TextGrid German) represent the prototype of how the humanities will work in the future: a virtual space where sophisticated research on peer-reviewed publications can be carried out, with annotated sources, shared material and software, and the ability to publish in various formats. From these scholarly networks, it is but a small step towards a super-infrastructure for research.[18] That is how Bamboo and similar projects originated, by going beyond a single subject (19th century Anglophone literature in NINES) or a single methodological concern (document analysis in TAPoR, textual editions in Interedition, research infrastructure for medieval and modern history in CENDARI, exchange and sharing of data in TextGrid), and imagining a future without physical or *conceptual* barriers, by removing the differences between research, production and the diffusion of knowledge. The next ten or fifteen years will probably see more changes to the research and teaching system — embodied in the 19th century by Wilhelm von Humboldt's new university model (Röhrs 1987; Nybom 2003) — than in the last two centuries. Certainly, not all that glitters is gold: beyond the claims of progressiveness, Bamboo was born out of the crises of educational institutions and their unsustainable costs,[19] and these infrastructures are seen as way of increasing collaboration while still cutting budgets.

But to return to the original theme of this concluding section: projects old or new, of the first or second phase, cannot develop without a proper use of human resources. Here the situation becomes more complex, since, while it is relatively easy to show that new infrastructures are necessary (or even inevitable), it is much more difficult to create spaces within academic institutions to develop the necessary training skills to implement this scenario. This gap between research and training opportunities is the most serious danger for the humanities at present. This is not only because humanists, without a new generation of digitally-trained colleagues, will be at the mercy of computer scientists, engineers and other technicians, but also, more importantly, because they will risk not being able to understand from the inside the actual mechanisms of knowledge productionxx. Of course "going tech" is not the easy answer to a historical paradigm shift. As argued by Wendy Chun, equipping humanities students with technical skills does not seem to be the answer either for the job market or for the future of the humanities:

Speaking partly as a former engineer, this promise strikes me as bull: knowing GIS (geo-graphic information systems) or basic statistics or basic scripting (or even server-side scripting) is not going to make English majors competitive with engineers or CS (com-puter science) geeks trained here or increasingly abroad. (*Straight up programming jobs are becoming increasingly less lucrative.*). .... So, the blind embrace of DH (*think here of Stanley Fish's «The Old Order Changeth»*) allows us to believe that this time (once again) graduate students will get jobs. It allows us to believe that the problem facing our students and our profession is a lack of technical savvy rather than an economic system that undermines the future of our students (Chun and Rhody 2014). Nonetheless the success of DH teaching programs throughout the world is evident. The overall situation in terms of teaching has evolved variously in different countries over the last four or five years. When in 2003, Willard McCarty could count a dozen teaching programs in total between the US and Europe (http://www.allc.org/imhc), today it is impossible to cope with the dizzying proliferations of initiatives.[21] After a few years of stagnation, there has been a growth in the number of specialist courses, summer schools, Masters and Doctorates in the US, Canada, Europe, and now also South America and Asia (Azali 2013). Less bureaucracy and a less centralized degree structure usually allows Anglophone countries to put together postgraduate courses with more freedom, but these courses have, compared to many of their European counterparts, rather high fees.[22] Especially in UK the answer for a number of institutions was to link teaching, research and consultancy services,[23] as in the King's College DH Department (http://www.kcl.ac.uk/artshums/depts/ddh) or the Digital Humanities at Oxford Group (http://digital.humanities.ox.ac.uk). However, it is hard to see a similar model being adopted in the rest of the world, especially in Europe, for two main reasons. First, there is the well-known rigidity of continental academic structures, where interdisciplinary courses are still difficult to set up and less profitable for traditional academic careers. Secondly, the project-funded center model does not seem to appeal to many traditional humanities departments. A research model linked to external entities and companies certainly entails a certain risk (for example, there may be a greater focus on practical application than on research) but it is undoubtedly true that interaction with private and public sector partners who work (as in the case of King's) in the cultural sector (museums, foundations, archives, libraries, creative industry, etc.) can help form new disciplines and resources, and so reinforce the central role of academia.[24]

Canada seems to reflect a mixed institutional approach to DH (half American-style, half European), but thanks also to its more flexible academic environment (O'Donnell 2013) the investment in DH has been growing steadily. Geoffrey Rockwell in 2009 has surveyed around thirty courses, from undergraduate level to graduate level (Master's and Doctorate) in which the digital humanities feature.[25] The most interesting are perhaps: 1) the Master's in Humanities Computing at the University of Alberta (http://www.huco.ualberta.ca); 2) Bachelor of Fine Arts (BFA) in New Media at the University of Lethbridge; 3) an interdisciplinary degree in Communication, Culture and Information Technology at the University of Toronto (http://www.utm.utoronto.ca/); 4) the Digital Humanities Summer Institute (http://www.dhsi.org/) organized by the University of Victoria.[26]

The United States is in a privileged position from many points of view. The flexibility of the American university system has allowed courses in computer science for the humanities since the early 1970s. "Computers and the Humanities," between the 70s and 80s, published periodic reports on teaching and a quick perusal shows that in 1972 about twenty-five American universities and colleges were offering courses on computing for students in the humanities (Allen 1974). Until a few years ago, the teaching on offer, at least as far as graduate courses were concerned, appeared undersized relative to the quantity and quality of the resources, projects and research centers present in the country (Zorich 2008). But in the last three to four years there has been a notable increase, and the majority of graduate courses appears to be advancing on three main fronts: "genuine" or explicit Digital Humanities (sometimes associated with Cultural Heritage), New Media or equivalent (e.g. MIT's Comparative Media Studies: http://cmsw.mit.edu) and Conservation and Library Studies, as in the case of graduate degrees offered by a number of library and information science programs (see www.ischools.org). Lisa Spiro started in 2010 a comprehensive Zotero collection focused on DH undergraduate, masters, and PhD programs, which shows the impressive range of DH-related teaching on offer in the US.[27]

Europe has recently seen a strong growth in the digital humanities at the institutional level. The recent spread of the Anglo-American term DH has succeeded, paradoxically, in unifying the various experiences of individual countries, and projects the semblance of a trans-European vision to the outside world. However, as in other cases, it is likely that the strong influence exerted by central and northern Europe is due to the German "engine." As seems clear from the survey conducted in 2012 by DARIAH Germany and the Center of eHumanities at Cologne, Germany is the country that has invested most heavily in a relatively short time: there are now more signs that public universities in Germany have active courses and teaching programs in DH[xxviii].

The digital humanities teaching programs (*Digitale Geisteswissenschaften*) are expanding across the board, especially at the level of modules offered in single departments and faculties (*Studiengänge*). Examination of the content of all the programs on offer gives the impression that the major driving forces behind DH in Germany are the information and library sciences. This is a characteristic also found in other contexts: after the pioneering phase comes the rearrangement of disciplines and fields of interest which, at least in western countries, ends up focusing on two economically important sectors: library and information science and, as already mentioned, cultural heritage.

In the French and German-speaking world the recent contribution of Switzerland stands out, with the interdisciplinary groups at Lausanne and Berne, who organized, among other things, the DH2014 conference and their first DH summer school (http://www.dhsummerschool.ch). One of the peculiarities of the Swiss case is especially the collaboration beween the social sciences, humanities and computer science (http://dhlausanne.ch). A similar strategy guides the debate on *humanités numériques* (or *humanités digitales*) in the French-speaking world (Dacos and Mounier 2014; Mounier 2012), led for the most part initially by social scientists (Wieviorka 2013), unlike in the UK, USA, Italy or Spain, where the birth of DH was led by philologists, literary and linguistic scholars. In France the digital humanities[29] are led by initiatives of international scope such as the *Centre pour l'édition électronique* of the CNRS (http://cleo.openedition.org). As far as regards teaching, there are various graduate programs (at Masters level) at French universities, which, although rarely adopting the label of digital humanities, are nevertheless associated with DH. The courses on offer are various, and one of the more prominent aspects appears to be the guiding role of information technology in the digitization of cultural heritage, rather than the opposite: humanists who become technologists, as happened in other countries. According to Florence Clavaud, author of the first French census, "most of these courses are young, they only have a few years of existence. ... The offer is multifaceted and various, but scarce, which means that all the disciplines in the field of humanities are not covered" (Clavaud 2012). The growing interest in DH in the French-speaking world is testified by the *Carte des digital humanities francophones*, an interactive map of research-centers and teaching courses created by Stéphane Lamassé and Georges-Xavier Blary (http://pireh.univ-paris1.fr/DHfrancophone/index.php). Among all the European countries France — perhaps especially by virtue of its recent interest — is one where the actors involved appear to be more aware of how each definition and practice of DH depends on various historical-cultural contexts:

> At the heart of the debate on the digital humanities there is a recurring or even permanent question: that of its definition. Do the digital humanities properly designate certain practices, methods, in short, a discipline? In the admission of certain of its practitioners, the term constitutes a kind of "floating signifier." The community has proposed some answers to this question, but it seems problematic to unify the domain without reference to a school, an idea, or a precise context. A good answer might have an historical flavor, and take account of institutional strategies. (Berra 2012)

Teaching of information science in the disciplines of linguistics and philology began in Spain during the nineties, thanks to the contribution of pioneers like Francisco Marcos Marín (1985, 1996). But apart from some important initiatives in the second half of the 2000s (for example, the Masters distance course in digital humanities at the University of Castilla-La Mancha, which was available until the end of 2010), the teaching of DH has not yet succeeded in developing a structure at university level, although recently there have been several exceptions, among them the *Máster en Humanidades Digitales* at the Autonomous University of Barcelona, launched in the autumn of 2013 or the 30 ECTS course *Experto profesional en Humanidades digitales* at UNED.[33] Also in the Spanish-speaking world, it appears clear (as also in the birth of the national associations, see § 3) that DH has been so far especially related to the philological-literary disciplines.[31]

In Italy, the growth in courses and degrees that emerged in the 1990s has suffered a setback in the latest of many reforms.[32] Perhaps uniquely in Europe, the reform of universities in the nineties made the teaching of information technology obligatory in all the humanistic disciplines (a course of at least 30 hours in the first year). This requirement paved the way for the teaching of digital humanities at many universities (Torino, Bologna, Milan, Florence, Pisa, Venice, Rome, Naples, etc.), allowing the Italian community, which had been active since the pioneering years of Father Busa, to develop a structure, centered around various centers, laboratories and degrees. Few of these are now left, although some are currently becoming Masters and specialization courses (i.e. Venice and Rome) and a new Master and joint Doctoral program was recently created at the University of Genova.[33]

Although it is difficult to make a selection, due to the differing cultural characteristics and didactic objectives that they reflect, the following teaching programs reflect the variety currently on offer around the globe: 1) the pan-Irish Digital Arts and Humanities (DAH) PhD program (http://dahphd.ie); 2) Cologne University's *Historisch-Kulturwissenschaftliche Informationsverarbeitung* program (roughly translated as "Informatics for Social Sciences") has an undergraduate degree at Masters and Doctoral level, founded by Manfred Thaller, one of the pioneers of German DH (http://www.hki.uni-koeln.de); 3) three Masters and a Doctorate offered by the Humanities Advanced Technology and Information Institute at the University of Glasgow (http://www.gla.ac.uk/subjects/informationstudies/); 4) the Masters in *Informatica del Testo ed Edizione Elettronica* ("Digital Texts and Digital Editions") at the University of Siena-Arezzo (http://www.infotext.unisi.it); 5) the Postgraduate Diploma in Digital Humanities and Cultural Informatics of the School of Cultural Texts and Records at Jadavpur University, India (http://sctrdhci.wordpress.com/); 6) The Master's in Digital heritage. Cultural Communication trough Digital Technologies at La Sapienza University in Rome (http://www.mdh.uniroma1.it/master); 7) The French École nationale de Chartes offers the Master's in *Technologies numériques appliquées à l'histoire* (http://www.enc.sorbonne.fr/master-technologies-numeriques-appliquees-l-histoire); 8) The Master's in *Literatura en la Era Digital* at the University of Barcelona, Spain (http://www.il3.ub.edu/es/master/master-literatura-era-digital.HTML).

There are also some Masters course in Europe that universities have joined together to create, aimed at developing the skills needed for the digitization of cultural heritage, such as the Masters in European Heritage, Digital Media and the Information Society (http://www.uc.pt/en/fluc/euromachs). Finally, one of the most promising recent research and training initiatives is the European network DiXiT (Digital Scholarly Edition Initial Training Network — http://dixit.uni-koeln.de), funded under Marie Curie Actions within the European Commission's 7th Framework Program. The principal aim of the network is to offer to young researchers from any country a coordinated training and research program in the multi-disciplinary skills, technologies, theories, and methods of digital scholarly editing.

Although the above selection might seems Euro-centric, as we will see in the next section, the participation and visibility of Latin American countries, China, India or Russia, is increasingly confirming, at all levels, the progressive erosion of the DH Global North hegemony. If postcolonial studies taught us how difficult it is to define and apply categories outside our own cultural settings, the situation of global DH is by definition fluid and dynamic. It would be very difficult to apply standard scholarly and intellectual categories to DH research and work (Risam 2014) or imagine language or countries as functional containers. For example, the collaboration between Latin American scholars often crosses geographical borders,[34] and other cultural areas, as Indian or Islamic and Arabic studies, flourish in different contexts and regions.³⁵ The Russian and Chinese scenarios appears also increasingly interesting (Garskova 2014; Niero 2013; Cultural Research 2013; Guo 2014; Yang 2012), but linguistic barriers and digital universalism remain a serious problem (Fiormonte *et al.* 2015). What kind of cultural, economical and social discourse does the label "DH" convey? It is difficult to consider it neutral. In his review of Anita Say Chan's book (Chan 2014), Henry Jenkins reminds us of one of the present risks of DH: "For others, the Web is an Americanizing force, one which has made English an even more pervasive language among the world's youth than ever before, one which is transforming governments and altering cultures without regard to the desires of local residents." (Chan and Jenkins 2015).

3. Associations, journals and centers

This section, apart from outlining the panorama of international associations, will discuss some of the main examples of research centers, publications and groups around the world. The objective is obviously not to be exhaustive, but to seek to map the complexity, diversity and richness of the DH phenomenon. Over the past few years international associations have sought to coordinate their efforts. Currently, the American Association for Computers and the Humanities (ACH), the European Association for Digital Humanities (EADH, formerly Association for Literary and Linguistic Computing), the Canadian Society for Digital Humanities/Société canadienne des humanités numérique (CSDH/SCHN),³⁶ the Australasian Association for Digital Humanities (AADH), and the Japanese Association for Digital Humanities (JADH) have united under the umbrella of the ADHO (Alliance of Digital Humanities Organizations). After a debate lasting several years, the Italian Associazione per l'Informatica Umanistica e la Cultura Digitale (http://www.umanisticadigitale.it) was founded in 2010, and the Spanish Humanidades Digitales Hispánicas followed in 2012 (http://www.humanidadesdigitales.org). The Red de Humanidades Digitales (http://humanidadesdigitales.net) was founded in Mexico in 2011 with a regional ambition (http://humanidadesdigitales.net), and a German-speaking association was also created in 2012 (http://www.dig-hum.de/). The latest additions, including the French-speaking association to which reference was made above, are the Portuguese-speaking Associação das Humanidades Digitais (http://humanidades-digitais.org), founded at São Paulo by a group of Brazilian and Portuguese researchers, and the Asociación Argentina de Humanidades Digitales.³⁷ ADHO is made up of "regional chapters," and, following the close of Computers and the Humanities, Literary and Linguistic Computing (now Digital Scholarship in the Humanities) the historic journal founded in 1973, became the main academic journal published on behalf of both the EADH and ADHO.³⁸ The ADHO umbrella also coordinates the most important annual conference in the field, Digital Humanities, and supports such initiatives as the online peer-reviewed journal *Digital Humanities Quarterly* (http://www.digitalhumanities.org/dhq/) and two introductory collections of essays published by Blackwells: the *Companion to Digital Humanities* and the *Companion to Digital Literary Studies*.[39] To these can be added four purely online journals: *Digital Medievalist* (http://www.digitalmedievalist.org), *Digital Humanities Journal* (http://journalofdigitalhumanities.org/), *Informatica Umanistica* (http://www.ledonline.it/informatica-umanistica), and *Humanist Studies & the Digital Age* (http://journals.oregondigital.org/hsda). To this group may also be added the Spanish *Caracteres. Estudios culturales y críticos de la esfera digital* (http://revistacaracteres.net) and the Swiss-led *Frontiers in Digital Humanities* (http://journal.frontiersin.org/journal/digital-humanities) founded in 2011 and 2014 respectively. They both represent a new wave of online publications reflecting the need to go beyond "classical" DH labels.

All these institutions and publications reflect the rich diversity of the field, but there remains the problem of the over-representation of the Anglophone sphere in terms of people, associations and resources (Fiormonte 2015). As of November 2015, the ADHO steering committee is composed of nine voting members of which six come from Anglophone institutions.[40] But, as already pointed out, the entire geography of DH is changing: the creation of numerous national associations and those sharing a common cultural background (Spain, France, Italy, Brazil, Argentina, etc.) will force a reconsideration of the geographical and cultural axes of DH, starting with EADH and probably also ADHO.

It is evident that regional or national associations reflect cultural and juridical practices that cannot be fully implemented within ADHO or EADH. The DH2014 "Code of conduct" declares that "ADHO works actively toward the creation of a more diverse, welcoming, and inclusive global community of digital humanities scholars and practitioners."[41] However it is not clear how ADHO could foster diversity while keeping a governance structure largely dominated by Anglophone organizations and cultural practices. No one is voted to be on the ADHO executive, and the founders (based in the US, Canada, Australia, Japan, and Europe) decide who can become a member, and the procedure for applying. For example, if the applicant was a German, Italian or Spanish association they would need to negotiate their participation through EADH. But what if the applicant was from Mexico, Russia or India? Can ADHO survive in a multipolar and multicultural world if it really wants to keep the brand of DH firmly in the hands of its six founding members? It is probable that in future it will be necessary to create a supranational organization based on the principle of "one head, one vote," as in many other similar aggregations and networks. Such an organism will have to renounce the supremacy of the proprietary lingua franca (English), at least in its formal activities, and seriously tackle the problem of gender representation. The more DH becomes a global phenomenon, the greater the need to have a democratic organization that genuinely represents all the cultures and languages of its members.

As for EADH/ALLC, what in the past may have been virtues (i.e. its geographic and cultural boundaries), in the present global scenario turn out to be limitations. Some of its weak points are the pyramidal governance structure, and the problem that until now its tradition did not reflect the current varieties of digital scholarship (although the change of name of LLC to DSH reflects the explicit intention "to broaden the interest and the scope in, of, and about the field" [Vanhoutte 2014]). However, these are just details that confront the fact that today there is probably not much point in characterizing DH on the basis of those old aggregations, but rather to have the courage to broaden the discussion, by asking ourselves what kind of future we imagine for our cultural heritage, for our languages and the "trail of digital exhaust" (Deibert 2015, 10) we leave behind us every day, and which already constitute part of our identity and our memory.

This, of course, is an issue that is not restricted to DH, and it would be unjust to accuse those working in the subject of complacency in this regard: in fact, initiatives like GO::DH (http://www.globaloutlookdh.org) and DH Awards (http://dhawards.org) show that a sensitivity to cultural and linguistic diversity is growing within the DH international community. As explained earlier (cf. Ch. 2 and 5), it must be remembered that in the field of the humanities, the creation of methodologies and technological standards is never neutral with respect to linguistic and cultural differences.

Since 2010 centers of research and laboratories that use the term "Digital Humanities" have multiplied almost everywhere in the world. Each of these initiatives reflect the institutional strategies and cultural identities of the countries or geographical areas where they are found, and also the traditional links with the historical development of the discipline, and the tensions inherent in a broadening of the traditional confines of DH. Alongside national hubs like the Digital Humanities Lab of Denmark (http://dighumlab.dk), eHumanities of the Royal Dutch Academy (http://ehumanities.nl),[42] the Laboratoire de cultures et humanités digitales at Lausanne (http://www.unil.ch/ladhul), DigiLab (http://digilab.uniroma1.it) in Italy, or the Transylvania Digital Humanities Centre in Romania (http://centre.ubbcluj.ro), there are also models that combine in an innovative way teaching with research, such as the Digital Humanities Initiative at Hamilton College (http://www.dhinitiative.org) or mono-disciplinary centers like the Centre for Digital Philosophy at the University of Western Ontario or the Institute for Textual Scholarship and Electronic Editing at the University of Birmingham (http://www.birmingham.ac.uk/research/activity/itsee). Increasingly sections dedicated to Digital Humanities can be found within already consolidated departments, as in the case of the Spanish MediaLab USAL at the University of Salamanca (http://medialab.usal.es/blog/humanidades-digitales). In Asia, expertise is linked to "traditional" DH, as in the Digital Humanities Center for Japanese Art and Cultures (http://www.arc.ritsumei.ac.jp/aboutus.html), but more often there are spaces and groups that intersect various sectors like the Centre for Creative Content and Digital Innovation at University of Malaya (http://www.3cdium.com), or the Centre for Internet and Society at Bangalore (http://cis-india.org). The Chinese and Indian scenarios are also on the move, as shown by the creation of the Research Center for Digital Humanities at National Taiwan University (http://www.digital.ntu.edu.tw/en) and the private Center for Digital Humanities at Pune (http://www.cdhpune.com).

Finally, one should mention the increasingly crammed realm of virtual study and discussion spaces, which, as in the case of HASTAC (http://www.hastac.org), focus on the aggregation of scholars and disciplines across traditional boundaries.

The *Survey of Digital Humanities Centers in the United States*,[43] lists only 32 centers of Humanities Computing in the US that meet their criteria, but the looser classification of CenterNet (http://www.dhcenternet.org/centers) records 196 centers (including some teaching programs) from "social sciences, media studies, digital arts, and other related areas"xliv. At present, there is no exhaustive and reliable survey that documents the complete global situation in Digital Humanities. For example, there are currently only five Italian centers and initiatives included in CenterNet's list, and a study by Romero Frías and Del Barrio García (2014) documented the exclusion of many others. Some are excluded because CenterNet compiles its list directly from centers expressing an interest, but also because it is not always simple to demarcate the borders of the discipline.

The desire of mapping and defining Digital Humanities in a more inclusive way is shown also by initiatives like *The Digital Humanities Manifesto,* assembled in Paris in 2010 and translated in 11 languages, including Arabic, Greek, Russian, etc. (http://tcp.hypotheses.org/category/manifeste).[45] A newcomer to the international scenario is the THATCamp un-conference series (http://thatcamp.org/), which is becoming a good opportunity for peripheral communities to share alternative views of what the digital humanities are or could be.[46] But after all, every survey or mapping (as Bowker and Star 2000 have shown for other fields) ends up by reflecting the focus of its creators and not the variegated multi-polar galaxy that more truly reflects the nature of the discipline.

In conclusion, a possible model for the future may be that adopted by the Center for New Humanities, launched by Rutgers University in January 2008.[47] The Rutgers project probably goes beyond what has been said here so far. The Writers House at New Brunswick (http://wh.rutgers.edu) is not just a new way of thinking about an informatics lab or a study room. The House is organized as a center for the production and sharing of multimedia content, where the idea of the classroom almost disappears, along with the concept of lectures and teachers. Here the teacher does not transmit knowledge accumulated according to the sender-receiver model and the students do not simply study, but produce. This is another of the big differences introduced by information technology: the use of productivity tools, often subject to continuous updating, puts student and teacher on an equal footing, and often allows the student to find solutions to problems as yet unimagined by the teacher. Places like these put up for debate the entire university system, as conceived in 19th century Europe (Leerssen 2012). Accustomed as they are to building their authority on the layers of analyses of cultural objects and their meanings as produced by history, humanists can only wonder about their future.

Notes

Preface

1. Fish, Stanley. "The Old Order Changeth." *Opinionator, New York Times* blog, December 26, 2011. <http://opinionator.blogs.nytimes.com/2011/12/26/the-old-order-changeth/>
2. See also Pannapacker, William. "The MLA and the Digital Humanities." *Brainstorm, The Chronicle Review* blog, Dec. 28, 2009.
3. See <http://tcp.hypotheses.org/411>
4. See Svensson, Patrick, "Humanities Computing as Digital Humanities," *DHQ*, 4:3, 2009, <http://www.digitalhumanities.org/dhq/vol/3/3/000065/000065.html> and "The Landscape of Digital Humanities," *DHQ*, 4:1, <http://www.digitalhumanities.org/dhq/vol/4/1/000080/000080.html>
5. Wang, Xiaoguang and Mitsuyuki Inaba, "Analyzing Structures and Evolution of Digital Humanities Based on Correspondence Analysis and Co-word Analysis," *Art Research*, 9, 2009, pp. 123–134.
6. Other prominent figures in the digital humanities in Italy include Tito Orlandi in Rome and Dino Buzzetti in Bologna.
7. This Preface is based on a review I wrote of the previous Italian edition in 2010.
8. See for example Willard McCarty's *Humanities Computing* (New York: Palgrave, 2005) which goes much deeper than *The Digital Humanist* into issues of what we do, but ultimately presents the field as an interdisciplinary commons for methods without any political agenda of its own. For that matter, my forthcoming book *Hermeneutica* (MIT Press) avoids political/cultural issues.

Introduction

1. See http://www.globaloutlookdh.org/working-groups/491-2/.
2. Also because resources are not stored according to the geographical provenance of the project's server (and many projects on Asiatic culture, as is well known, are based in North American and European institutions).
3. Among the collective aims to define Digital Humanities should be mentioned two different manifestos that appeared in the past few years. In the Anglo-American context see http://www.humanitiesblast.com/manifesto/Manifesto_V2.pdf and for a European and international vision see the Paris 2011 Manifesto: http://tcp.hypotheses.org/411.
4. Social and ethical issues are raised by the document collectively assembled at the Bern 2013 DH Summer School: "This document is aimed as a contribution to the current debates in the digital humanities about how digital humanists conduct themselves as professionals ethically, and as a reflection of their core values" (https://docs.google.com/document/d/1A4MJo5qSoWhNlLdlozFV3q3Sjc2kum5GQ4lhFoNKcYU/edit?pli=1#heading=h.fbfb3vwicb5).
5. The organization around "clusters of problems" has inspired the authors' interdisciplin-

ary project http://www.newhumanities.org/, built around seven projects, each of which is carried out by a mixed team of humanists and scientists.
6. An impressive epistemological and historical account of the concepts and ideas behind the digital computer is offered by Luigi Borzacchini in his monumental three-volume work (Borzacchini 2008, 2010, and 2015).
7. Although the book is the result of almost five years shared research and discussion that started with the revision of our previous book (*L'umanista digitale*, Il Mulino, 2010),

chapters 1, 2 and 5 are the work of Teresa Numerico, chapter 3, section 2.5 and the Conclusions are the work of Domenico Fiormonte, and chapter 4 is the work of Francesca Tomasi. Domenico Fiormonte edited all chapters with the help of Desmond Schimdt who revised the previous translation of Chris Ferguson, but also suggested important corrections and additions in all sections. Finally, we are grateful to Giorgio Guzzetta for his help and material assistance throughout the completion of this project.

Chapter 1

1. The ability to deal with formulas and numbers in the same way had already been realized with the method invented by Gödel (1931), known as arithmetization, which was used to demonstrate his incompleteness theorem.
2. See V. Bühlmann, "The idea of a Characteristica Universalis between Leibniz and Russell, and its relevancy today" http://monasandnomos.org/2012/12/05/the-idea-of-a-characteristica-universalis-between-leibniz-and-russell-and-its-relevancy-today/.
3. Andrew Pickering focuses on the influence of practice and its role in the reassessment of theoretical models in science. He uses the expression "mangle of practice" to define the social dimension of research – yet another humanistic aspect that is often neglected: "This temporal structuring of practice as a dialectic of resistance and accommodation is, in the first instance, what I have come to call the mangle of practice" (Pickering 1995, xi).
4. In *How Much Information?* a study published in 2003, it was estimated that the information stored on paper, film and magnetic and optical media has doubled since 1999 (http://www2.sims.berkeley.edu/research/projects/how-much-info-2003). An update to these estimates is provided by the more systematic work of Hilbert and López 2011, claiming to be "the first study to quantify humankind's ability to handle information and how it has changed in the last two decades".
5. See Bardini (2000) for more details on the Engelbart's contributions to friendly interfaces. Most of Engelebart's original papers and reports are available on his website: http://www.dougengelbart.org/pubs/augment-3906.html.
6. For a more detailed account on the relationships between computer science and linguistics see Fiormonte and Numerico 2011, and Hajič 2004.
7. For a discussion on the relationship between computer science and humanities computing see McCarty 2005, 177–198.

Chapter 2

1. On User-Centric Design see e.g. Ch. 9 of Norman 1998.
2. The concept of model is now central also in the field of DH, cf. McCarty 2005, Orlandi 2010, Buzzetti 2002, 2009, Fiormonte 2009.
3. The birth of the ARPANET is one of the most studied events in the history of technology. Good starting points are, for example, Hafner and Lyon 1996 and Naughton 1999. For a more sociological point of view on the Internet's origins see Castells 2001.
4. For more details on the role of Engelbart see Bardini 2000, and for the role of Xerox PARC in the development of Apple (329ff) and

Microsoft (358–360) see Hiltzik 1999.
5. The original proposal can be downloaded from the "history" section of the W3Consortium: http://www.w3.org/History/1989/proposal.html.
6. The interview, divided into two parts, can be found on YouTube: http://www.youtube.com/watch?v=TkOpzbTsDJE&feature=PlayList&p=4B2E3AC7440A2CD1&index=63
7. See *Answers for Young People,* accessible through Berners-Lee's pages on the W3C, http://www.w3.org/People/Berners-Lee/Kids.html.
8. The first traceable reference to "hyper-text" by Nelson is in the Vassar Miscellany News of February 3, 1965: http://faculty.vassar.edu/mijoyce/MiscNews_Feb65.html.
9. Tim Berners-Lee originally wanted to speak explicitly of documents (UDI = Universal Document Identifier) but then chose to accept the compromise both to replace the document with the more general resource and replace the philosophy of universality with that of uniformity (Berners-Lee 1999, 67).
10. The document can be read here http://tenyears-www.web.cern.ch/tenyears-www/Declaration/Page1.html.
11. http://www.w3.org/Consortium/.
12. For examples of the W3C's role in the affirmation of the standard markup languages cf. below Ch. 4.
13. Web Science Conference 2009, held in Athens in March 2009. The video of Berners-Lee's speech is available on: http://www.youtube.com/watch?v=ol_Y_MPDc4E&feature=related.
14. See for details the Webfoundation page dedicated to web challenges: http://www.webfoundation.org/programs/challenges/.
15. See, for example, Google One Pass, which offers a perfect system for allowing publishers to offer paid-for content via a search engine platform.
16. For more details on this method of storing content cf. below Ch. 4.
17. See http://en.wikipedia.org/wiki/Wikipedia:About.
18. Similar conclusions can be found in the 2014 UNESCO's Fostering Freedom Online report (MacKinnon et al. 2014). The report discusses policies and practices of companies representing three intermediary types (internet service providers, search engines, and social networking platforms) across ten countries.
19. Except for the first paragraph, written by T. Numerico, this section was authored by Domenico Fiormonte.
20. Or its elitist tendency: "In the end, Web 2.0 works best for the Internet everyman or everywoman, who tends to be educated and well-off. Thus, in addition to restricting information to those who have access to the Internet, Web 2.0 restricts relevant information to those who are most similar to that typical Internet user." (Witte and Mannon 2010, 19).
21. For reasons of space problems related to cultural and technological biases of the TEI and in general of markup systems will be not tackled here. For a detailed discussion see Schmidt 2010 & 2014; Fiormonte and Schmidt 2011; Fiormonte et al. 2010.
22. According to the OECD Factbook 2013 (http://dx.doi.org/10.1787/factbook-2013-67-en), in 2011 about 71% of US adults had Internet access. According to Pew Research Center in 2015 the share of all US adults who use the internet has reached 84% (http://www.pewinternet.org/2015/06/26/americans-internet-access-2000-2015/). The US Census Bureau 2013 survey on Computer and Internet use showed that age, gender, ethnicity, income and educational level can have a significant impact on Internet access and household computer ownership (http://www.census.gov/content/dam/Census/library/publications/2014/acs/acs-28.pdf).
23. See for example the reflection on the digital divide by a Mexican researcher: "Una tesis ocupa un lugar central de este tipo de investigación de la brecha digital en los EE.UU. y postula que el 48% de la población que no utiliza el Internet se abstienen de ello porque no lo encuentran relevante para su vida diaria o no les interesa (Pew Research Center, 2013, NTIA/FCC, 2013; estos estudios encuentran eco en estudios de caso mexicanos: WIP, 2013, INEGI, 2013). No obstante, dicha tesis deja sin desarrollar la pregunta de ¿Cómo es que este segmento de la población se ha inclinado por responder de esa manera? es decir ¿Cuáles son las prácticas que median la relación entre personas y tecnologías de la información?" (Sánchez 2014: 89).
24. http://www.itu.int.
25. "High-income economies are those in which 2012 GNI per capita was $12,616 or more" (http://databank.worldbank.org/data/).
26. Source: World Bank Indicators: http://databank.worldbank.org/data. See also the OECD

2001 survey on the digital divide: http://www.oecd.org/internet/ieconomy/understandingthedigitaldivide.htm.
27. See http://epp.eurostat.ec.europa.eu/portal/page/portal/information_society/data/database.
28. http://www.icann.org/en/news/announcements/announcement-30oct09-en.htm.
29. This wasn't always the case: e.g. www.monash.edu, an Australian academic institution. Those who obtained .edu names in the past are allowed to keep them, but no new names for non-US academic institutions will be allowed. See http://net.educause.edu/edudomain/eligibility.asp.
30. Until 2009 ICANN was essentially controlled by the US Department of Commerce: http://www.readwriteweb.com/archives/commerce_department_loosens_grip_on_icann.php. Until July 2012 the CEO and President of ICANN was Rod Beckstrom, former Director of the National Cybersecurity Center (NCSC) at the US Department of Homeland Security, who has been replaced by US-based entrepreneur and former IBM manager Fadi Chehadé (http://www.icann.org/en/groups/board/chehade-en.htm). With the arrival of Chehadé ICANN increased its efforts for evolving in a "bottom-up, consensus-driven, multi-stakeholder model" (see http://www.icann.org/en/about/welcome). In December 2013 the Strategy Panel on ICANN Multistakeholder Innovation was launched and began a collaboration with thegovelab.org. The objective of this new course will be, among other things, to "open ICANN to more global participation in its governance functions" and "proposing new models for international engagement, consensus-driven policymaking and institutional structures" (http://thegovlab.org/the-brainstorm-begins-initial-ideas-for-evolving-icann/).
31. UN agencies promoted and sponsored a number of events as well as produced many reports on Internet Governance; for a synthesis see, for example, the NetMundial Multistakeholder initiative in 2014: http://netmundial.br.
32. See http://www.internetworldstats.com/stats.htm.
33. Web Foundation, Challenge page http://www.webfoundation.org/programs/challenges/.
34. According to World Stats (a private company), at the end of 2011 Africa represents 15% of the world population, but only 6.2% of Internet world users with a penetration of 13.5% of the population. However, Egypt and Tunisia are among the 10 African countries in which the Internet is more developed.
35. The dark sides of Facebook and other social media are explored in a collection edited by Geert Lovink and Miriam Rash (2013). See especially articles by Langlois, Gehl, Bunz and Ippolita and Mancinelli. For a recent overview on the role of social media in Arab countries see also Jamali 2014. A critical perspective on the "the celebratory hype about online activism" during the Arab spring is provided by Aouragh 2012.
36. Cases of cyber-repression are constantly being reported in most Asian and Arabic countries where different forms of online political activism exist. A source of information in English is the database http://cyberdissidents.org.
37. For a detailed description of the most spoken languages on the Internet see http://www.internetworldstats.com/stats7.htm, where it is clear that English is the most spoken language, but Chinese and Spanish, respectively second and third languages of the Web, are growing fast.
38. Some of the themes of the 2001 book were taken up and upgraded in a recent post: http://jamillan.com/librosybitios/espimprered.htm.
39. "By far its most striking feature was its graphical user interface, ... The arrangement of folders and icons built around what the Star engineers called the 'desktop metaphor' is so familiar today that it seems to have been part of computing forever." (Hiltzik 1999, 364).
40. A complete list of these animations is available from http://wiki.secondlife.com/wiki/Internal_Animations#User-playable_animations.
41. http://www.unicode.org/consortium/consort.html.
42. http://www.unicode.org/consortium/directors.html.
43. "Even if Unicode does not exactly 're-map' real life politics onto the virtual realm, such technical solutions do point to the ideological, political, and economic forces that promote and serve to benefit from attempts at universal language." (Pressman 2014, 2).
44. "For example, the game cricket in Hindi is क्रिकेट *kriket*; the diacritic for /i/ appears before the consonant cluster /kr/, not before the /r/." (http://en.wikipedia.org/wiki/

Abugida).

45. The difficulties of encoding some Indic scripts according to the Unicode model are highlighted also by the SIL's Non-Roman Script Initiative: "Indic scripts have combining vowel marks that can be written above, below, to the left or to the right of the syllable-initial consonant. In many Indic scripts, certain vowel sounds are written using a combination of these marks ...." (http://scripts.sil.org/cms/scripts/page.php?site_id=nrsi&id=IWS-Chapter04b#fb2c362c). In conclusion, "there are over 16,000 characters defined in Unicode that in one way or another go against the basic design principles of the Standard." (http://scripts.sil.org/cms/scripts/page.php?site_id=nrsi&id=IWS-Chapter04b#bb06c97e).

46. "Because Devanagari and other Indic scripts have some dependent vowels that must be depicted to the left of their consonant letter (*although they are pronounced after the consonant*), the software that renders the Indic scripts must be able to reorder elements in mapping from the logical (character) store to the presentational (glyph) rendering." (Aliprand 2003, 228; quoted in Perri 2009, 736. Italics added by Perri).

47. The invasion of Europeans in the 19th and 20th centuries changed the living standards of the linguistically diverse aboriginal population. However, according to the Australian Bureau of Statistics "Today, there are approximately 22 million Australians, speaking almost 400 languages, including Indigenous languages" (Source: http://www.abs.gov.au/ausstats/abs@.nsf/Latestproducts/1301.0Feature%20Article32009E2%80%9310?opendocument&tabname=Summary&prodno=1301.0&issue=2009%9610&num=&view=).

48. "The dominating effect of a single socioeconomic factor, GDP per capita, on speaker growth rate suggests that economic growth and globalization ... are primary drivers of recent language speaker declines (mainly since the 1970s onwards), for instance, via associated political and educational developments and globalized socioeconomic dynamics. This conclusion is also supported by the positive effect of GDP per capita on range size and many language extinctions in economically developed regions, such as the USA and Australia." (Amano et al. 2014, 7).

49. See http://melissaterras.blogspot.in/2012/01/infographic-quanitifying-digital.html.

50. "In the book, I argue that the kind of thinking expresses a kind of Digital Universalism that disguises the means which elite designers and entrepreneurs of the IT world's leading corporations work to promote and circulate it – whether in the pages of Wired magazine or across any number of TED conference stages. It also disguises the diverse imaginaries and investments around the digital that are cropping up all over the world, including in Peru, from diverse civil society actors – but that are easy to overlook when we focus our attention only on those coming out of just a handful of innovation centers." (Chan and Jenkins 2015).

51. http://en.wikipedia.org/wiki/Open_Data.

52. From the most famous, Wikipedia http://wikipedia.org to wikibooks http://wikibooks.org a bank of texts editable by the community, and geonames http://www.geonames.org/ to Wordnet http://wordnet.princeton.edu/, an English lexicon that includes a complex system for grouping terms according to semantic affinities, hosted by MIT. There is a map of all data accessible and connected according to the norms of Linked Data.

53. The W3C's wiki dedicated to the Semantic Web shows the resources for creating open data archives: http://esw.w3.org/topic/SweoIG/TaskForces/CommunityProjects/LinkingOpenData.

54. There are some unavoidable overlappings between this section and Ch. 5. Other aspects of Big Data are analyzed in § 5.8.

55. More information and reflections on big data and DH can be found on Geoffrey Rockwell's blog theoreti.ca. In December 2014 Rockwell gave a lecture on *Big Data in the Humanities*: http://vimeo.com/114389377.

56. "[W]here are the digital humanists critiquing the growing surveillance state? ... The synthesis of our training in traditional humanistic modes of inquiry with our proficiency in network analysis, text-mining, metadata, and the other methods the US government uses to monitor its own people in a (I would argue, misguided) search for threats should lead to a proliferation of analyses, arguments, and action. To date, however, I have heard only quiet murmurings in the community." (Widner 2013).

57. Cf. Geoffrey Rockwell's note on Kristene Unsworth's talk: "The justice of big data and global citizenship" (http://philosophi.ca/pmwiki.php/Main/InternationalEthicsRoundtable2014InformationEthicsAndGlo-

balCitizenship).
58. For a description of the project and the first results of this research see Michel et. al. 2011.
59. There is not space here for a critical discussion of Culturomics. We would like just to underline that this initiative comes from a group of scientists and the Google Book Search team who seem to have a marginal interest in the humanities. It is also interesting to note that they claim to define what culture is, using a corpus of 4% of the total number of books.
60. http://opendatahandbook.org/en/what-is-open-data/index.html.
61. For a description of the tools set see the www.tapor.ca.
62. For more information see http://voyeurtools.org and Rockwell's blog http://hermeneuti.ca.
63. Tim Berners-Lee (2009) outlined the guidelines of its contribution to the project to reorganize communication with digital users of English institutions (http://www.w3.org/DesignIssues/GovData.html). See also Berners-Lee's talk at TED http://www.ted.com/index.php/talks/tim_berners_lee_on_the_next_web.html.
64. For these reasons, a Cambridge (UK) mathematician, Tim Gower, in January 2012 has launched a boycott of the international publisher Elsevier (http://thecostofknowledge.com/). Academics are protesting against Elsevier's business practice, such as exorbitantly high prices, and its support for measures such as SOPA, PIPA, and the Research Works Act "that aim to restrict the free exchange of information".
65. http://openaccess.mpg.de/Berlin-Declaration.
66. From April 2008, the National Institute of Health (NIH) has made research it has helped finance available through PubMed Central http://www.pubmedcentral.nih.gov, its own open access archive of scientific literature on medicine and life.
67. A recent overview of the rapidly growing scenario of OA publishing is given in Laakso et al. 2011.
68. For more details on the business model of open source journals see Suber 2007 and its sources, in particular Crow 2009. For a list of open access journals see the *Directory of Open Access Journals* (http://www.doaj.org).
69. http://dsh.oxfordjournals.org/for_authors/index.html.
70. For a list of institutional repositories by location, see *Directory of Open Access Repositories – Open DOAR* (http://www.opendoar.org/); for other information on repositories and their policies: Open access directory (http://oad.simmons.edu/oadwiki/Main_Page). For a list of repositories by subject, there is a section on disciplinary repositories (http://oad.simmons.edu/oadwiki/Disciplinary_repositories). The majority of Open Access Archives are compliant with the protocols of the Open Archive Initiative (OAI http://www.openarchives.org/) in their use of metadata.
71. For an up-to-date bibliography on this topic, see the *Open Citation Project* for evaluating analysis of citations of articles in open access archives. http://opcit.eprints.org/oacitation-biblio.html.
72. Mainstream knowledge that is often linked to well-known geopolitical issues: "US accounted for 26% of the world's total Science & Engineering (S&E) articles published in 2009 and the European Union for 32%. In 2010, the US share in total citations of S&E articles stood at 36% and the EU's share at 33%, whereas that of Japan and China remained at 6% each." (Chandrasekhar 2013).
73. Not entirely convincing is also the policy of "discounted rates available for authors based in some developing countries". See http://www.oxfordjournals.org/our_journals/litlin/for_authors/index.html.
74. The complete list of funded projects can be found at http://www.neh.gov/files/press-release/july2014grantsstatebystate.pdf.
75. http://centernet.adho.org/about. See Conclusions.
76. Alan Liu is one the founders of the 4humanities.org project. The aim of this platform is to assist in advocacy for the humanities, creating a starting point to help and support humanities disciplines to display their potential within the digital environment.

Summary of Part I

1. See Keller 2010 for a discussion of the prescientific questions that inform scientific

discourse.
2. Women, however, were not included in Licklider's description of the symbiosis, which was explicitly called a "man-machine symbiosis".

Chapter 3

1. Petrucci defines *dominus* as the owner of the cultural and economic processes that shape and transform textual products (Petrucci 1986, xxi).
2. Some of the concepts included in the "Text Wheel" elaborated by Patrick Sahle in the realm of the scholarly digital edition partially overlap (and can integrate) with our model. Sahle identifies six dimensions of the text: Text as Idea, Intention; Text as (structured) Work; Text as Linguistic Code; Text as Version; Text as Document; Text as (visual) Sign (cf. Sahle 2013, 1–98).
3. "[W]e have conceived ourselves and the natural entities in terms of data and information. We have flattened both the social and the natural into a single world so that there are no human actors and natural entities but only agents (speaking computationally) or actants (speaking semiotically) that share precisely the same features. It makes no sense in the dataverse to speak of the raw and the natural or the cooked and the social: to get into it you already need to be defined as a particular kind of monad." (Bowker 2013, 169).
4. The scenario described hereby can also be interpreted in the apocalyptic way of Gilles Deleuze: "there is no need of science fiction for conceiving a control mechanism able to provide every single moment the position of an element in an open environment, an animal in a reserve, a man in a company (electronic collar). Félix Guattari has imagined a city where one would be able to leave one's apartment, one's street, one's neighborhood, thanks to one's (own) electronic card that raises a given barrier. But that card could just as easily be rejected on a given day or between certain hours; what counts is not the barrier itself but the computer that tracks each person's position–*licit* or *illicit*, and effects a universal modulation." (Deleuze 1990, authors' transl.)
5. Reference is not being made here to the "biological machines", such as the cyber beetle created by Michel Maharbiz (http://maharbizgroup.wordpress.com). When the beetle is at the pupal stage electrodes are implanted into the nervous and muscular system of the insect. A receiver and a battery is then integrated into the system on the back of the adult, so that its movements can be controlled remotely. Undoubtedly, such hybrids pose important ethical, social, aesthetic, semiotic and even political questions (the research is co-financed by the Pentagon).
6. Cf. the international online anthology available at http://www.hermeneia.net/eng/espais/literatura.html.
7. Baron (2000) remains the best general introduction to the digital dimension of language.
8. In addition to video, speech and writing, Skype can also integrate other tools, for example TalkAndWrite (http://www.talkandwrite.com), an application that allows two or more users to write and draw together on the same board. Skype is also among the first pieces of software that lets you correct the text after it is typed and sent, with the interesting effect that the temporal synchronicity of the chat can be reversed.
9. Peter Boot suggested calling certain forms of digital annotations *mesotext* (from ancient Greek *mesos,* the middle): "it is text that can be located somewhere in between the primary texts of scholarship (the sources that scholarship is based on), and its secondary texts" (Boot 2009: 203). Therefore, in Genette's terms "mesotext is a metatext" (Boot 2009, 207). However this is too fortuitous an expression to be confined to the realm of annotations, so I think it would be a good candidate for describing an intermediate level or specific kind of digital metatext.
10. See also Bolter and Grusin's concept of *Remediation* (1999); George Landow (1992) said similar things at the beginning of Web 1.0.
11. "Post-modern ethnography privileges 'discourse' over 'text', it foregrounds dialogue as opposed to monologue, and emphasizes the cooperative and the collaborative nature of the ethnographic situation in contrast to the ideology of the transcendental observer." (Tyler 1986, 126).

12. "Hall's essay challenges all three components of the mass communications model, arguing that (i) meaning is not simply fixed or determined by the sender; (ii) the message is never transparent; and (iii) the audience is not a passive recipient of meaning. ... Distortion is built into the system here, rather than being a 'failure' of the producer or viewer. There is a 'lack of fit' Hall suggests 'between the two sides in the communicative exchange', between the moment of the production of the message ('encoding') and the moment of its reception ('decoding'). This 'lack of fit' is crucial to Hall's argument. It occurs because communication has no choice but to take place within sign systems. The moments of encoding and decoding are also the points, respectively, of entrance into and exit from the systems of discourse. As in Ch. 1, language does not reflect the real, but constructs or 'distorts' it on our behalf" (Procter 2004, 71).
13. The seeds of the relationship between postcolonial thought and the critique of media technology can be found in the reflections of the father of contemporary communication studies, Harold Innis: "We must all be aware of the extraordinary, perhaps insuperable, difficulty of assessing the quality of a culture of which we are a part or of assessing the quality of a culture of which we are not a part. In using other cultures as mirrors in which we may see our own culture we are affected by the astigma of our own eyesight and the defects of the mirror, with the result that we are apt to see nothing in other cultures but the virtues of our own" (Innis 1951, 132).
14. This section was authored by Paolo Sordi, revised and updated by Domenico Fiormonte.
15. http://www.youtube.com/watch?v=NLlGopyXT_g.
16. http://jquery.com/ Acid3: http://acid3.acidtests.org/.
17. CNN in 2009 reported news of the first *incunabulum* of PHILOLOGY 2.0: a Microsoft researcher, Gordon Bell, announced that he has stored ten years of his life in the form of images, videos, texts, audio recordings on his PC (http://edition.cnn.com/2009/TECH/09/25/total.recall.microsoft.bell/index.html).

Chapter 4

1. As an introduction see the Cornell University tutorial entitled Digital Preservation Management (http://www.icpsr.umich.edu/dpm/index.html). In this tutorial can be found a useful account of the chronology of the technologies at http://www.icpsr.umich.edu/dpm/dpm-eng/timeline/popuptest.html.
2. Among the various initiatives aimed at increasing awareness of these themes one may recall the Erpanet (*electronic resource preservation and access network* 2002–04), which had, among other things, the aim of informing those working in the field of conservation (http://www.erpanet.org).
3. Among the numerous projects on digital paleography two interesting resources can be noted: MANCASS (Manchester Centre for Anglo-Saxon Studies) C11 Database, for the study of 11th century English manuscripts, especially the paleographical catalog at http://www.oenewsletter.org/OEN/print.php/reports/powell38_1/Array#. Another very useful resource is THELEME (*techniques pour l'historien en ligne: études, manuels, exercices*) of the École des Chartes http://dictionary.reference.com/browse/webpage?s=thttp://theleme.enc.sorbonne.fr/. In particular, see the section with facsimiles of the school's documents at http://theleme.enc.sorbonne.fr/dossiers/index.php.
4. Cf. Kirschenbaum et al. 2002 and also Goodrum et al. 1999.
5. An accurate introduction to CBIR systems and methodologies is provided by Pérez Álvarez 2007; see also the survey by Lew et al. 2006.
6. "Content-based methods are necessary when text annotations are nonexistent or incomplete. Furthermore, content-based methods can potentially improve retrieval accuracy even when text annotations are present by giving additional insight into the media collections." (Lew et al. 2006, 1).
7. http://www.hermitagemuseum.org/fcgi-bin/db2www/qbicSearch.mac/qbic?selLang=English.
8. There is of course a solid tradition of projects, conferences and researches on digital art history (cf. Bentkowska-Kafel et al. 2005), but as often happens with history or anthropology,

scholars in those fields tend to create their own sub-groups, and hence interaction and exchange, especially at a methodological level, is not that common.

9. Plain ASCII it is not used much any more. Extended ASCII, in the form of cp1250, cp1252, MacRoman, ISO-Latin-1 etc. for certain specific systems is still used, but since about 2000 all desktop, portable and mobile computers, and XML, have been able to use Unicode, or have used it as a default. ASCII is part of Unicode in any case. For a discussion on the limits of Unicode for representing non-Western writing systems cf. § 2.5.3.

10. Suppose a document is marked up with certain character styles (bold, italics, colors, font size) to represent certain properties (emphasis, titles), then it is clear that limiting the markup to logical or structural aspects, which are formal elements of the document, the assignment to such elements of one or more graphical renditions or layouts can still be made at a later time.

11. For Dublin Core metadata terms see http://dublincore.org/documents/dcmi-terms/, and for Friend of a Friend see the FOAF Vocabulary Specification 0.98 at http://xmlns.com/foaf/spec.

12. MODS Metadata Object Description Schema, http://www.loc.gov/standards/mods, and METS Metadata Encoding & Transmission Standard. Both are maintained by the United States Library of Congress.

13. An example of a project moving in this direction is Image Markup: "Many tools exist for marking up text in XML. However, for a number of our projects, we need to be able to mark up images – by which I mean that we need to be able to describe and annotate images, and store the resulting data in TEI XML files" (http://tapor.uvic.ca/~mholmes/image_markup/).

14. Even if RDF is imposed as a W3C standard for the formal representation of metadata, one should not forget another model, the standard of the ISO (International Standard Organization) called Topic Maps (TM). This is an alternative to RDF that is useful for expressing relationships between concepts.

15. An interesting example of a thesaurus in the field of art and architecture is the AAT (Art & Architecture Thesaurus), that gives a controlled, structured vocabulary for concepts and categories: http://www.getty.edu/research/conducting_research/vocabularies/aat.

16. A project for the construction of an ontology for museum collections is the CIDOC-CRM (Conceptual Reference Model: http://cidoc.ics.forth.gr) that defines a conceptual model for the area of cultural heritage. The list of classes and relationships can be consulted at http://cidoc.ics.forth.gr/docs/cidoc_crm_version_4.2.1.pdf.

17. For the construction of ontologies, the W3C has created OWL (web ontology language). There are also tools specifically for constructing ontologies, such as the open source Protégé (http://protege.stanford.edu).

18. An excellent example is Amazon, one of the leaders of collaborative filtering. Thanks to this technique Amazon can say, "People who bought books A and B also bought book C" and therefore make suggestions to the end user.

19. Among the most common systems for sharing digital materials (principally articles) in open archives, two worth pointing out are EPrints (http://eprints.rclis.org) and dspace (http://www.dspace.org).

20. Blue Book (Standard) Issue 1, January 2002: http://public.ccsds.org/publications/archive/650x0b1.pdf.

21. "Bamboo is a multi-institutional, interdisciplinary, and inter-organizational effort that brings together researchers in arts and humanities, computer scientists, information scientists, librarians, and campus information technologists to tackle the question: How can we advance arts and humanities research through the development of shared technology services" (http://projectbamboo.org). *Interedition* (interoperable supranational infrastructure for digital editions): "The main objective of the Action is to produce a 'roadmap' or 'manual' conceptualizing the development of a technical infrastructure for collaborative digital preparing, editing, publishing, analyzing and visualizing of literary research materials" (http://www.interedition.eu). *TextGrid* has developed a virtual research environment for philologists, linguists, musicologists and art historians. *TextGrid Lab* (http://www.textgrid.de/en/beta.html), as a single point of entry to the virtual research environment, provides integrated access to specialized tools, services and content.

22. "Computer networks, both within organizations, and globally with the Internet, combined with the World Wide Web, have

become a primary conduit for accessing our collective intellectual works. With the emergence of Web 2.0, these networks are rapidly becoming a primary means for authoring and collaborating on new works. What happens, however, if information is locked up in systems that are not built to facilitate sharing across boundaries, and are not attentive to the long-term sustainability of social and intellectual knowledge accumulated within them?" (Fedora, http://www.fedora-commons.org).

23. "DELOS (A Network of Excellence on Digital Libraries) work has mainly focused on improving digital libraries (Dls) by developing independent, powerful and highly sophisticated prototype systems. The overall goal of the DelosDlms is the implementation of a prototype of a next-generation digital library management system. This system combines text and audio-visual searching, offers personalized browsing using new information visualization and relevance feedback tools, allows retrieved information to be annotated and processed, integrates and processes sensor data streams, and finally, from a systems engineering point of view, is easily configured and adapted while being reliable and scalable" (http://www.delos.info/index.php?option=com_content&task=view&id=502).

24. "The historical sense, if it rules *without restraint* and unfolds all its implications, uproots the future because it destroys illusions and robs existing things of their atmosphere in which alone they can live." (Nietzsche 1980, 38).

25. The *Index Thomisticus* (1946), a collection of indexes and concordances of the complete works of Saint Thomas Aquinas is now available online and can be searched in various ways: http://www.corpusthomisticum.org/it/index.age.

26. For an overview of classical philology in the digital sphere cf. Solomon 1993.

27. Knowledge organization is a discipline that sees the management of knowledge as a kind of pyramid, with data at the bottom, information above that as a representation of the data, and knowledge as the human selection of the information, which is then transmitted.

28. José Nilo G. Binongo's (2003) work on the Book of Oz (*Who Wrote the 15th Book of Oz? An Application of Multivariate Analysis to Authorship Attribution*) has shown that the 15th book in the series was not written by Baum, the author of the first fourteen, but by Thompson, who wrote the subsequent nineteen.

29. A number of tools have been invented to perform these operations automatically. One of the first MS-DOS applications to address this purpose was TACT (text analysis computing tool), written by the IBM-University of Toronto Cooperative in the Humanities during 1986–9. Tapor (http://portal.tapor.ca/portal/portal) is an excellent free tool that allows the use of online applications to subject texts to various forms of text retrieval.

30. Lutoslawski attempted a computational procedure to establish a relative chronology of Plato's dialogues at the end of the 19th century. (Lutoslawski, W. (1897), *The Origin and Growth of Plato's Logic*. London: Longmans). See also L. Brandwood, *Stylometry and chronology*, in The Cambridge Companion to Plato, edited by R. Kraut, Cambridge 1992.

31. An example of a project that has brought a collection of documents together through metadata harvesting is NINES (http://www.nines.org/): "NINES (*networked infrastructure for nineteenth-century electronic scholarship*) is a scholarly organization devoted to forging links between the material archive of the nineteenth century and the digital research environment of the twenty-first".

32. The Tapor Tool section of the Tapor gateway (http://portal.tapor.ca/) is an excellent resource for understanding what is possible in this regard.

33. Classical languages now have the Perseus Project, a collection of annotated texts: http://nlp.perseus.tufts.edu/syntax/treebank/. See also the *Guidelines for the Syntactic Annotation of Latin Treebanks*: http://nlp.perseus.tufts.edu/syntax/treebank/1.3/docs/guidelines.pdf. Perseus provides many tools for the analysis of classical texts and querying of morpho-lexical, syntactic and semantic aspects: http://www.perseus.tufts.edu/hopper/search.

34. MONK is a digital environment designed to help humanities scholars discover and analyze patterns in the texts they study.

Chapter 5

1. In working on this reconstruction we were inspired by the series of initiatives and publications of the *Society of the Query reader* (http://networkcultures.org/query/), organized and published by the Amsterdam Institute of Network Cultures directed by Geert Lovink (cf. König and Rasch 2014).
2. The degree of separation between two webpages or between two persons is defined as the number of links needed to get from page A to page B, or from one person P to another person R. If a person P has an acquaintance who is personally acquainted with R, then there are 2 degrees of separation between P and R. This concept of degrees of separation between individuals was introduced in the 1970s by Stanley Milgram.
3. A similar result, although referring to the structure of the Internet, was obtained by Faloutsos et al. (1999).
4. See Clay Shirky's 2003 post http://shirky.com/writings/powerlaw_weblog.html. It cites many studies on data from the known inhabited part of the network, the blogosphere, mailing lists etc. The post is not concerned with social networks because they were not, at that time, a developed phenomenon.
5. *Information Behaviour of the Researcher of the Future* is the result of collaboration between University College London, the British Library and the JISC (Joint Information Systems Committee) published 11 January 2008 and can be consulted at http://www2.warwick.ac.uk/study/cll/courses/professionaldevelopment/wmcett/researchprojects/dialogue/the_google_generation.pdf.
6. The information is based on a syndicated report by Multimedia Mentor 2010–2013 (IAB – GfK 2014, 8).
7. According to the study by Mary Madden and Aaron Smith, *Reputation Online and Social Media* of the Pew Internet and American Life Project, 26 May 2010 (http://www.pewinternet.org/Reports/2010/Reputation-Management.aspx), 57% of Americans use search engines to check their online reputation.
8. Queries are literally the questions with which users communicate to the search engine, i.e. the keywords typed in the search engine interface.
9. Cf. Arrington 2009.
10. It should be noted that the special importance attached to keywords and other fields in the metatags of a page has become gradually less relevant. The information on the page, in fact, is typically where web-spam becomes most difficult to control, and as a result it is increasingly taken less into account as a source for evaluating the content of a resource.
11. An algorithm is defined as an effective method for solving a problem that uses a finite sequence of instructions. A simple example is a recipe for a cake, although a recipe contains unclear concepts (mix until smooth to the touch, about 300 grams of flour, etc.). Each computer program can be defined as an algorithm that achieves in a finite time the task that had been set. The instructions we provide to the computer cannot be exactly like a recipe, since everything must be explained and described in a language that can be understood by a machine.
12. The term "spam" is well-known as the intrusion of unwanted messages in our email. However, there are also systems of spam that relate to search engines. Some sites try to improve their ranking by using certain keywords deemed relevant to their business. For more details on the spam techniques used to alter the results of search engines cf. Gyöngyi and García-Molina 2005.
13. One of the most significant innovations of Google was to consider the text of the link to a given page as part of that page, so giving it a special importance for indexing.
14. It has been noted that Library Science has many gaps in its procedures, and therefore risks becoming an instrument controlled by mainstream scientific progress, while still obscuring the effectiveness and success of scientific results (cf. LIENS 2008, MSCS Editorial Board 2009).
15. Marchiori recently launched a new search engine called Volunia (www.volunia.com), still in its beta testing phase, whose aim is to mix search technology with social activities.
16. AdWords and AdSense are two tools that trigger sponsored links related to the query keywords and populate the results with the content of sites affiliated with the Google advertising program.
17. For a more detailed ethical and technical analysis of Internet spam cf. Witten et al. 2007, Ch. 5.

18. The digital divide is the issue of access to technological tools in general, particularly in the use of computers, the availability of a network for digital communications, and in the training for these to be of use. It can be defined in terms of developing vs. developed countries and also in the different strata of the population of industrialized countries. For a more detailed treatment of the digital divide in terms of cultural and social inequalities cf. § 2.5.
19. For a description of the transformations in the world of content production, cf. Auletta 2010.
20. See the work of Anna Jobin on Google's autocompletion algorithms: "But of all the mediations by algorithms, the mediation by autocompletion algorithms acts in a particularly powerful way because it doesn't correct us afterwards. It intervenes before we have completed formulating our thoughts in writing. Before we hit ENTER. Thus, the appearance of an autocompletion suggestion during the search process might make people decide to search for this suggestion although they didn't have the intention to." (Jobin 2013).
21. For the court's ruling rejecting the ASA (amended settlement agreement) between Google and the Authors Guild see http://www.nysd.uscourts.gov/cases/show.php?db=special&id=115.
22. For Judge Chin's ruling granting Google's appeal for summary judgment on the copyright issue see http://www.documentcloud.org/documents/834877-google-books-ruling-on-fair-use.html.
23. Google has recently changed its privacy policy by unifying all the different privacy policies of its various online services. This decision allows the company to crosscheck all the data produced by users through their different profiles within Google tools, https://www.google.com/intl/en/policies/.
24. The full text of the court's judgment is available on http://curia.europa.eu/juris/document/document.jsf?docid=152065&doclang=en.
25. Cf. Paragraph 92 of the Case C-131/12, *Google Spain v. Agencia Española de Protección de Datos (AEPD), Mario Costeja González* (http://curia.europa.eu/juris/document/document.jsf?docid=152065&doclang=en).
26. The section is accessible on: https://www.google.com/transparencyreport/removals/europeprivacy/.
27. https://drive.google.com/file/d/0B1UgZshetMd4cEI3SjlvVohNbDA/view.
28. The speech is accessible here: http://www.state.gov/secretary/rm/2010/01/135519.htm.
29. In 2005, at the trial of Chinese journalist Shi Tao, Yahoo! delivered email details stored on its servers, contributing to a sentence of 10 years for divulging state secrets. The journalist passed a message from the communist authorities to the Chinese media on to some Western friends. Microsoft has since closed its blogs of political opponents to the Chinese regime hosted on its pages.
30. For example, in 2006, Google punished the German site of BMW for using text-boosting techniques on its home page.
31. For the report see: http://www.google.com/transparencyreport/governmentrequests/
32. See http://www.google.com/transparencyreport/governmentrequests/
33. http://www.google.com/transparencyreport/governmentrequests/US/?p=2011-06&t=CONTENT_REMOVAL_REQUEST&by=PRODUCT.
34. http://www.google.com/transparencyreport/governmentrequests/US/?p=2011-06&t=USER_DATA_REQUEST&by=PRODUCT.
35. The definition can be accessed at http://csrc.nist.gov/publications/nistpubs/800-145/SP800-145.pdf.
36. For further reading on this theme, cf. Androutsellis-Theotokis and Spinellis 2004.
37. See video presentation: https://www.youtube.com/watch?v=EfGD2qveGdQ.
38. Court of Justice of the European Union's ruling in *Google Spain and Inc. vs. Agencia Española de Protección de Datos (AEPD) and Mario Costeja Gonzalez C131/12*. Sentence issued in May 2014.
39. Report of the Advisory Council to Google on the Right to be Forgotten https://drive.google.com/file/d/0B1UgZshetMd4cEI3SjlvVohNbDA/view, published on the 6th of February 2015.
40. These protocols (which came into operation on January 1, 1983) are the result of the work of a group of researchers led by Bob Kahn and Vinton Cerf and form the basic rules for communication between the servers on the Internet. Many of the other protocols (those for email, WWW, chat, etc.) lie atop this layer. Another protocol related to TCP/IP is UDP/IP (user datagram protocol/Internet protocol), which is used by DNS, VOIP, and

streaming media applications. The features of these protocols guarantee the openness, efficiency and transparency of the network, allowing them to function even on technology radically different from that of the 1980s. They are the fruit of the open and libertarian mentality that allowed the birth and development of the Arpanet.

41. The article is accessible at: http://www.wired.com/science/discoveries/magazine/16-07/pb_theory.

Conclusions

1. An earlier version of this chapter appeared in Fiormonte 2014. I had the privilge to share this document online with the international community of dhers: more than twenty colleagues from all over the world have helped me improve and update my work as well as avoid a number of inaccuracies and common missteps. I am indebted to each of them, and I hope this chapter can continue to thrive online and become a resource for everyone interested in global DH.
2. On the relationship between "money" and cultural representation within DH organizations see Rojas Castro 2014.
3. Although it is not possible or desirable to attach a common label, interest on the relationship between diversity studies and DH is growing rapidly, as showed by initiatives and events like the Digital Diversity conference (http://digitaldiversity2015.org), the ILSA conference on DH and Indigenous Studies (http://www.indigenousliterarystudies.org/decolonizing-the-digital/), and the course on De/Post/Colonial Digital Humanities at MITH (http://www.dhtraining.org/hilt2015/course/depostcolonial-digital-humanities/).
4. For an updated version of this article see Galina 2014.
5. For reasons of space, the area of Computational Linguistics will not be discussed here. CL has become almost a separate sector, with its own journals, conferences and associations. While drawing boundaries in DH will always seem somewhat arbitrary, this book has tried to conceive the discipline in the widest sense possible, as the platform for practical experimentation and the theoretical intersection of the humanities, social sciences and digital technology.
6. http://www.neh.gov/divisions/fedstate/newsletters/march-2008.
7. SSHRC now includes DH topics and funding opportunities within the Digital Economy Priority area: "Digital Economy priority area supports research and related activities into the nature, impact and integration of digital technologies in all aspects of our economy, society and culture .... Research in the social sciences and humanities makes vital contributions to our understanding of the opportunities and impacts of the digital economy and the demand for new knowledge in this area continues to grow." (http://www.sshrc-crsh.gc.ca/funding-financement/programs-programmes/priority_areas-domaines_prioritaires/digital_research-recherche_numerique-eng.aspx).
8. See http://cordis.europa.eu. The seventh FP includes financing for individual researchers through the European Research Council (http://erc.europa.eu).
9. An overview of Digital Humanities and Digital History in Europe, which includes usually under-represented countries like Russia and Greece, can be found in this online collection: http://geschichte-transnational.clio-online.net/transnat.asp?id=2535&pn=texte. For DH in Romania see Nicolaescu and Mihai 2014.
10. http://ec.europa.eu/research/fp7/index_en.cfm.
11. http://ec.europa.eu/programmes/horizon2020/en/.
12. The Draft Horizon 2020 Work Programme includes a specific Call on cultural heritage: "Reflective Societies: Cultural Heritage and European Identities". See: http://ec.europa.eu/research/horizon2020/pdf/work-programmes/societies_draft_work_programme.pdf. Other EU research programs, like the Information and Communication Technologies Policy Support Programme (http://ec.europa.eu/cip/ict-psp/index_en.htm), support ICT based projects in areas such as "Digital Libraries" or "Multilingual web and Internet evolution", etc. which are also related to DH.
13. This is the case in Italy. Looking at the figures

for PRIN (Research Projects of National Interest), it can be seen that informatics has grown exponentially in areas 10 (Archeology, Classics, Art History) and 11 (History, Philosophy, Education and Psychology) in the last few years, and that the most economically important projects tend to involve digital technology. The real boom was between 2004 and 2006, but the overall presence of DH in area 10 and area 11 in 2011 reached 20% of the total amount of funding assigned.
14. The EU strategic interest on Humanities infrastructures has emerged clearly since 2009. See: http://www.esf.org/hosting-experts/ scientific-review-groups/humanities-hum/ strategic-activities/research-infrastructures-in-the-humanities.html.
15. One of the most convincing advocates of cyber-infrastructures is the American philologist Gregory Crane (Crane et al. 2008), the founder of the Perseus Digital Library (http://www.perseus.tufts.edu/). Among the less enthusiastic it would seem is Joris Van Zundert (2012), but for a critical approach we have to turn to social research: see for example Bowker et al. 2010.
16. See for example http://www.geant.net/ (Europe); http://digitalleadership.ca/about-digital-infrastructure (Canada); https://nectar.org.au/about/; http://www.intersect.org.au (Australia); http://www.nesc.ac.uk (UK). The e-science scenario in Asia is outlined in Yen and Lin 2011. See also the EUAsiaGrid project: http://www.euasiagrid.org.
17. For the first 18 months of the project, the two main promoters of *Bamboo*, the University of Chicago and the University of California, Berkeley, received $1.4 million from the Andrew A. Mellon Foundation. Although funding for Project Bamboo has now been discontinued, it is used here as an example of projects of this type. See Q. Dombrowski and S. Dembo, TEI and Project Bamboo, *Journal of the TEI* 5, June 2013, http://jtei.revues.org/787.
18. See also the recent EINFRA-9–2015 call: http://ec.europa.eu/research/participants/ portal/desktop/en/opportunities/h2020/ topics/2144-einfra-9–2015.html.
19. One has only to think of the paradoxical situation where universities are forced to pay for thousands of journal subscriptions – to a cartel of multinational publishers – to read the research published by their own staff. This situation has been exposed, among others, by Timothy Gowers, the mathematician who created http://thecostofknowledge.com.
20. In France, in the history field, there have been voices urging for better training in computing for historians (Genet 1993, Ruiz and Heimburger 2011). But no progress has really been made since 1993. And there is no agreement on the content of this training (this information has been provided by Frédéric Clavert via the online commented version of this paper.)
21. The Centernet's map and the GO::DH and Around DH in 80 Days survey (http://www. globaloutlookdh.org/491–2) have already been mentioned, but see also the Digital Humanities Now Registry (http://digital-humanitiesnow.org/submit-your-work) and for the Spanish-speaking world the Mapa HD project (http://mapahd.org).
22. As an example, full-time students fees for a one-year long postgraduate course in Informatica del Testo at the University of Arezzo (Italy) are 2800 euros (for all kind of students, national or international); although fees in many UK, US and Canadian programs depend of the number of courses taken by students, full-time Canadian students fees at the University of Alberta for a Winter/Fall term are are around 5217 Canadian dollars (this include about 2500 dollars of non-instructional fees). Fees for international students are about 40% higher.
23. AHRC (UK Arts and Humanities Research Council) Digital Transformations fellow, Andrew Prescott, writes: "Big problem is that we haven't had good postdoc structures in DH: over-reliance on broken project-funded centre model", https://twitter.com/Ajprescott.
24. The successes of the former Centre for Computing in the Humanities (now the Department of DH) must be recognized, notwithstanding the somewhat triumphalist way that they were presented: "At any one time CCH is engaged in over 30 major research projects, and since 2000 has been involved in generating over 17 million GBP in research income .... The exceptional stature of the department at home and abroad has been recognized officially in the 2008 Research Assessment Exercise (RAE). The panel judged 35% of our research to be 'world-leading' (4*) – the highest in the sector. 65% was judged to be 'world-leading' or 'internationally excellent' (3*)."
25. See Rockwell's report, including research centers, associations, resources, etc.: http://tapor.

ualberta.ca/taporwiki/index.php/The_Academic_Capacity_of_the_Digital_Humanities_in_Canada.

26. As noticed earlier, it is becoming increasingly difficult to follow all the new programs coming out every year. In 2013, the University of Western Ontario launched a minor in DH with faculty from several departments and faculties (http://www.uwo.ca/arts/digitalhumanities) and Carleton University in Ottawa also has an MA (http://graduate.carleton.ca/programs/digital-humanities-master).

27. See https://www.zotero.org/groups/digital_humanities_education/items/collectionKey/M3E8EB5R. Courses and degrees in *Digital Writing, Multimedia Composition, Rhetoric*, etc. are probably not included in Spiro's collection.

28. Cf. http://www.cceh.uni-koeln.de/Dokumente/BroschuereWeb.pdf. The Cologne Center for eHumanities has listed the initiatives throughout Germany: http://www.cceh.uni-koeln.de/node/11. See also the publications of the European network DARIAH, where the situations in Germany, Ireland, Greece and Slovenia are recorded (http://www.dariah.eu).

29. Discussions for the creation of a Francophone DH Association started in October 2013 at THATCamp Saint-Malo (see http://thatcamp35.hypotheses.org/) and led to the birth of *Humanistica* on July 8th 2014 (see http://www.humanistica.eu). It is interesting to note that the *Humanistica* was the name given to a prospect "European" association during THATCamp Florence in 2011, and after its failure the Francophone founders reused it for their association.

30. 1) http://www.uab.cat/web/postgrado/master-en-humanidades-digitales/datos-basicos-1206597472083.html/param1–3202_es/param2–2006; 2) http://linhd.uned.es/p/titulo-propio.

31. The Hispanic studies have always shown interest in the digital literary scene (Borràs Castanyer 2005; Solomon and Ilika 2007). José Manuel Lucía Megías (2003) offered the first historical account of the Spanish DH scenario; for an update on Spanish-speaking DH see González-Blanco 2013, Lucía Megías 2012, Rojas Castro 2013,and especially Spence and González-Blanco 2014.

32. One contribution to the discussion on teaching in the DH is Cristofori (2005). A survey of IU courses in Italy was conducted by Raul Mordenti in 2003: http://infolet.it/files/2009/09/mordenti_2003.pdf. Many of these have disappeared since the last Italian University reform.

33. The postgraduate program activated by several departments at the University of Genova (http://digitalhumanities.dibris.unige.it/) is structured in two parts: a "Laurea Magistrale" (biennial MA) in Digital Humanities and a joint doctoral programme with the University of Turin in *Tecnologie digitali, arti, lingue, culture e comunicazione* (http://www.digitalhumanities-phd.it/).

34. See recent common efforts like the *Anuario Americanista Europeo*, dedicated to DH and Social Sciences (http://www.red-redial.net/revista/anuario-americanista-europeo/issue/view/16/showTochttps://app.simplenote.com/publish/Q7JB1n) and the first lusophone DH conference in Lisbon (https://congressohdpt.wordpress.com).

35. http://islamichumanities.org/conference2013/; http://islamichistorycommons.org/.

36. SDH-SEMI publishes the online *Digital Studies / Le champ numérique* (http://www.digitalstudies.org).

37. http://buenosaires2013.thatcamp.org/2013/09/04/convocatoria-reunion-asociacion-argentina-de-humanidades-digitales. But more geographic areas and countries are added everyday to the list, see for example dhBenelux (http://dhbenelux.org) or the Israeli group http://www.thedigin.org/digital-humanities-israel/.

38. From January 1st 2015 LLC changed its name to *Digital Scholarship in the Humanities*. According to its new editor, Edward Vanhoutte, "The new name takes into account all digital scholarship undertaken in the Humanities in its widest meaning". A new editorial board has also been appointed that represents "the geographical and thematic scope of the Journal more clearly" (Vanhoutte 2014).

39. Available for free respectively at: http://www.digitalhumanities.org/companion/ and http://www.digitalhumanities.org/companionDLS/.

40. See http://adho.org/administration/steering.

41. http://dh2014.org/more/general-information/code-of-conduct.

42. http://www.uvasci.org/current-institute/readings/dhc-survey-final-report-2008/.

43. http://www.clir.org/pubs/abstract/reports/pub143.

44. The last check on the number of members was made on March 2015. *CenterNet* was founded by eighteen institutions, mainly from US, Canada and UK (only four members come from non-Anglophone or non-Western institutions). CenterNet is also a founding member of CHAIN (*Coalition of Humanities and Arts Infrastructures and Networks*) that brings together, among others, ADHO, DARIAH, *Bamboo* and *TextGrid*. CHAIN's main aim is to ensure that the various forces designing the future "digital research infrastructure[s] for the Humanities" are coordinated in their efforts; but the agreement signed in London on October 27 2009 can be also seen as another step towards the reinforcement of the Anglophone hegemony.
45. A group of scholars who signed the Paris 2010 Manifesto completed a survey to try to map out the geographical composition and linguistic diversity of the field: https://docs.google.com/spreadsheet/viewform?pli=1&formkey=dG9vVGJTeERuOUtCdVFRRVZQQWp6Nmc6MQ#gid=0. Marin Dacos (2013) has offered a critical analysis of these data.
46. A quick look at 2011–12 THATCamps shows that out of 35 THATCamps listed on the website 24 took place in USA.
47. http://www.youtube.com/watch?v=z65V2yKOXxM.

References

#transformdh Collective 2012, "Toward an open digital humanities." https://docs.google.com/document/d/1uPtB0xr793V27vHBmBZr87LY6Pe1BLxN-_DuJzqG-wU/edit?authkey=CPDaqsoJ.

Adida, B., Birbeck, M., McCarron, S., Herman, I. (2013), *RDFa 1.1 Core – Second Edition 2013. W3C Recommendation 22 August 2013.* http://www.w3.org/TR/rdfa-syntax/.

Aliprand, J. (ed.) (2003), *The Unicode Standard 4.0,* Toronto, Addison-Wesley.

Allen, J.R. (1974), "The development of computer courses for humanities", *Computers and the Humanities,* 8, 3, pp. 291–295.

Amano, T., Sandel B., Eager, H., Bulteau, E., Svenning, J.-C., Dalsgaard, B., Rahbek, C., Davies, R.G., Sutherland, W.J. (2014), "Global distribution and drivers of language extinction risk", *Proceedings of the Royal Society,* B, 281: 20141574. http://dx.doi.org/10.1098/rspb.2014.1574.

Amento, B, Terveen, L., Hill, W., Hix, D., Schulman, R. (2003), "Experiments in social data mining: The TopicShop System", *ACM Transaction on Computer-Human Interaction,* 10, 1, pp. 54–85.

Andersen, P.B. (1997), *A theory of computer semiotics: Semiotic approaches to construction and assessment of computer systems,* Cambridge (MA), Cambridge University Press.

Anderson, C. (2008), "The end of theory: The data deluge makes the scientific method obsolete", *Wired,* June 23. http://www.wired.com/science/discoveries/magazine/16-07/pb_theory.

Anderson, D., Sayers, J. (2015), "The metaphor and materiality of layers", in Ridolfo, J., Hart-Davidson, W. (eds.), *Rhetoric and the digital humanities,* Chicago, University of Chicago Press, pp. 80–95.

Androutsellis-Theotokis, S., Spinellis, D. (2004), "A survey of peer-to-peer content distribution technologies", *ACM Computing Surveys 2004,* December, 36, 4, pp. 335–371. http://www.spinellis.gr/pubs/jrnl/2004-ACMCS-p2p/html/AS04.html.

Aouragh, M. (2012), "Tweeting like a pigeon: The Internet in the Arab revolutions", *CyberOrient,* 6, 2, 2012. http://www.cyberorient.net/article.do?articleId=8000.

Arasu, A., Cho, J., Garcia-Molina, H., Paepcke, A., Raghavan, S. (2001), "Searching the Web", *ACM Transactions on Internet Technology,* 1, pp. 2–43.

Argamon, S., Olsen, M. (2009), "Words, patterns and documents: Experiments in machine learning and text analysis", *Digital Humanities Quarterly,* 3, 2, Spring. http://digitalhumanities.org/dhq/vol/3/2/000041/000041.html.

Aristotle, (2010), *Rhetoric* (Ed. by Cope, E. M., Sandys, J. E.), Cambridge, Cambridge University Press.

Arms, W.Y. (1995), "Key concepts in the architecture of the digital library", *D-Lib Magazine,* July. http://www.dlib.org/dlib/July95/07arms.html.

Armstrong Moore, E. (2009), "Launch of new flu database ruffles feathers", September 16. http://www.cnet.com/news/launch-of-new-flu-database-ruffles-feathers/.

Arrington, M. (2009), "Marissa Mayer on Charlie Rose: The future of Google, future of search", *TechCrunch,* March 6. http://techcrunch.com/2009/03/06/marissa-mayer-on-charlie-rose-the-future-of-google.

Aspray, W. (1989), "Interview with R.W. Taylor", *Oral history,* Charles Babbage Institute. http://primo.lib.umn.edu/primo_library/libweb/action/display.do?doc=UMN_ALMA21447113920001701.

Auletta, K. (2010), *Googled: The end of the world as we know it,* London, Virgin Books.

Azali, K. (2013), "Digital humanities in Asia: Talk by Harold Thwaites". http://kathleenazali.c20-library.net/2013/06/digital-humanities-in-asia/.

Bailey, M. Z. (2011), "All the digital humanists are white, all nerds are men, but some of us are brave," *Journal of Digital Humanities* 1.1. http://journalofdigitalhumanities.org/1-1/all-the-digital-humanists-are-white-all-the-nerds-are-men-but-some-of-us-are-brave-by-moya-z-bailey/.

Balzola, C., Monteverdi, A.M. (eds.) (2007), *Le arti multimediali digitali: storia, tecniche, linguaggi, etiche ed estetiche del nuovo millennio,* Milan, Garzanti.

Barabási, A.L. (2002), *Linked,* Cambridge (MA), Perseus Publishing.

Barabási, A.L. (2010), *Bursts: The hidden patterns behind everything we do, from your e-mail to bloody crusades,* New York, Dutton.

Bardini, T. (2000), *Bootstrapping: Douglas Engelbart, coevolution, and the origins of personal computing,* Stanford, Stanford University Press.

Baron, N.S. (2000), *Alphabet to email: How written English evolved and where it's heading,* London–New York, Routledge.

Barry, M. (2000), "Yes, a technorhetorician can get tenure", *Computers and Composition,* 17, 1, pp. 9–18.

Barthes, R. (1970), *S/Z,* Paris, Éditions du Seuil.

Belew, R.K. (2000), *Finding out about,* Cambridge (MA), Cambridge University Press.

Benjamin, W. (2008), *The work of art in the age of mechanical reproduction,* London, Penguin.

Benozzo, F. (2007), "Etnofilologia", *Ecdotica,* 4, pp. 208–230.

Bentkowska-Kafel, A., Cashen, T., Gardiner, H. (2005), *Digital art history: A subject in transition,* Bristol, Intellect.

Berners-Lee, T, (1998), "Semantic Web road map". http://www.w3.org/DesignIssues/Semantic.

Berners-Lee, T, (2006), "DeveloperWorks Interviews: Tim Berners-Lee talks about where we've come, and about the challenges and opportunities ahead", recorded on July 28. http://www.ibm.com/developerworks/podcast/dwi/cm-int082206.txt.

Berners-Lee, T. (2007), "Digital future of the United States, part 1: The future of the World Wide Web", *Hearing before the United States House of Representatives Committee on Energy and Commerce Subcommittee on Telecommunications and the Internet.* http://dig.csail.mit.edu/2007/03/01-ushouse-future-of-the-web.pdf.

Berners-Lee, T. (2009), "Putting government data online", June 30. http://www.w3.org/DesignIssues/GovData.html.

Berners-Lee, T. (2010), "Long live the Web: A call for continued open standards and neutrality", *Scientific American Magazine,* December. http://www.scientificamerican.com/article.cfm?id=long-live-the-web&print=true.

Berners-Lee, T., Fischetti, M. (1999), *Weaving the web: The past, present and future of the World Wide Web by its inventor,* London–New York, Texere.

Berners-Lee, T., Hendler, J., Lassila, O. (2001), "The semantic Web", *Scientific American,* May, pp. 34-43. http://www.sciam.com/article.cfm?articleID=00048144-10D2-1C70-84A9809EC588EF21&catID=2.

Berners-Lee, T., Shadbolt, N., Hall, W. (2006), "The semantic web revisited", *IEEE Intelligent Systems,* 21, 3, May/June, pp. 96–101.

Berra, A. (2012), "Faire des humanités numériques", in Mounier (2012), pp. 25–43. http://books.openedition.org/oep/238.

Berry, D.M. (2008), *Copy, rip, burn: The politics of copyleft and open source,* London, Pluto Press.

Berry, D.M. (2011), "The computational turn: Thinking about the digital humanities", *Culture Machine,* vol. 12. http://www.culturemachine.net/index.php/cm/article/view/440/470.

Bettaïeb, V. (2011), *Dégage: la révolution tunisienne, 17 décembre 2010–14 janvier 2011,* Paris, Layeur; Tunis, Patrimoine.

Biagioli, M. (2009), "Postdisciplinary liaisons: Science studies and the humanities", *Critical Inquiry* 35, Summer, pp. 816–833.

Bijker, W.E., Hughes T.P., Pinch, T.J. (eds.) (1994), *The social construction of technological systems: New directions in the sociology and history of technology,* Cambridge (MA), MIT Press.

Binongo, J.N.G. (2003), "Who wrote the 15th Book of Oz? An application of multivariate analysis to authorship attribution", *Chance,* 16, 2, pp. 9–17.

Birchall, C. (2011a), "Transparency, interrupted: Secrets of the left." *Theory, Culture & Society,* 28, 7–8, pp. 60–84.

Birchall, C. (2011b), "Introduction to 'Secrecy and transparency': The politics of opacity and openness", *Theory, Culture & Society,* 28, 7–8, pp. 7–25.

Birchall, C. (2014), "Radical transparency?", *Cultural Studies <=> Critical Methodologies* 14, 1, pp. 77–88.

Bizer, C., Heath, T., Berners-Lee, T. (2009), "Linked data: The story so far", *International Journal on Semantic Web and Information Systems (IJSWIS),* 5, 3, pp. 1–22. http://tomheath.com/papers/bizer-heath-berners-lee-ijswis-linked-data.pdf.

Blair, D.C. (1984), "The data-document distinction in information retrieval", *Communication of the ACM,* 1994, 27, 4, pp. 369–374.

Bohem, G. (2007), *Wie Bilder Sinn erzeugen: Die Macht des Zeigens,* Berlin, Berlin University Press.

Bolter, J.D. (2001), *Writing space: Computers, hypertexts, and the remediation of print,* Mahwah (NJ), Lawrence Erlbaum.

Bolter, J.D., Grusin, R. (1999), *Remediation: Understanding new media,* Cambridge (MA), MIT Press.

Boot, P. (2009), *Mesotext,* Amsterdam, Amsterdam University Press.

Borràs Castanyer, L. (ed.) (2005), *Textualidades electrónicas: nuevos escenarios para la literatura,* Barcelona, Editorial UOC.

Borzacchini, L. (2008), *Il computer di Platone: alle origini del pensiero logico e matematico,* Bari, Dedalo.

Borzacchini, L. (2010), *Il computer di Ockham: genesi e struttura della rivoluzione scientifica,* Bari, Dedalo.

Borzacchini, L. (2015), *Il computer di Kant: struttura della matematica e della logica moderne,* Bari, Dedalo.

Bowker, G. C. (2005), *Memory practices in the Sciences,* Cambridge (MA), MIT Press.

Bowker, G.C. (2013), "Data Flakes: An afterword to 'Raw Data' is an oxymoron", in Gitelman (2013), pp. 167–171.

Bowker, G.C., Leigh Star, S. (2000), *Sorting things out: Classification and its consequences,* Cambridge (MA), MIT Press.

Bowker, G. C., Baker, K., Millerand, F., and Ribes, D. (2010), "Toward information infrastructure studies: Ways of knowing in a networked environment", in Hunsinger, J., Klastrup, L., Allen, M. (eds.), *International Handbook of Internet Research,* Dordrecht–New York, Springer, pp. 97–117.

Boyd, B. (2009), *On the origin of stories: Evolution, cognition and fiction,* Cambridge (MA), Belknap Press of Harvard University Press.

Boyd, D. (2010), "Privacy and publicity in the context of Big Data." Raleigh (NC), April 29. http://www.danah.org/papers/talks/2010/WWW2010.html.

Boyd, D., Crawford K. (2012), "Critical questions for Big Data", *Information, Communication & Society,* 15, 5, pp. 662–679.

Brandwood, L. (1992), "Stylometry and chronology", Kraut, R. (ed.), *The Cambridge companion to Plato,* New York, Cambridge University Press.

Brin, S., Page, L. (1998), "The anatomy of a large-scale hypertextual web search engine", *Computer Networks and ISDN Systems,* 30, pp. 107–117. http://citeseer.ist.psu.edu/brin98anatomy.html.

Broder, A., Kumar, R., Maghoul, F., Raghavan, P., Rajagopalan, S., Stata, R., Tomkins, A., Wiener, J. (2000), "Graph structure in the Web", in *Proceedings of the 9th International World Wide Web Conference* (Amsterdam, May 15–19), New York, ACM Press. http://www.cis.upenn.edu/~mkearns/teaching/NetworkedLife/broder.pdf.

Bruner, J.S. (1990), *Acts of meaning*, Cambridge (MA), Harvard University Press.

Bruner, J.S. (1998), "Celebrare la divergenza: Piaget e Vygotskij", in Liverta Sempio, O. (ed.), *Vygotskij, Piaget, Bruner: concezioni dello sviluppo*, Milan, Raffaello Cortina, pp. 21–36.

Bühlmann, V. (2012), "The idea of a *Characteristica Universalis* between Leibniz and Russell, and its relevancy today", *Monas, Oikos, Nomos*. http://monasandnomos.org/2012/12/05/the-idea-of-a-characteristica-universalis-between-leibniz-and-russell-and-its-relevancy-today/.

Bunz, M (2013), "As you like it: Critique in the era of an affirmative discourse", in Lovink, G., Rasch, M. (eds.) (2013), pp. 137–145.

Burda, H., Kittler, F., Sloterdijk, P. (2011), *The digital Wunderkammer: 10 chapters on the Iconic Turn*, Munich, Wilhelm Fink Verlag.

Bush, V. (1931), "The differential analyzer: A new machine for solving differential equations," *Journal of the Franklin Institute*, 212, July–December, pp. 447–488.

Bush, V. (1945), "As we may think", *Atlantic Monthly*, 176, 1, pp. 101–108, in Nyce, J., Kahn, P. (1991). http://www.theatlantic.com/magazine/archive/1945/07/as-we-may-think/3881/.

Bush, V. (1959/1991), "Memex II", *Bush Papers*, MIT Archive, in Nyce, J., Kahn, P. (1991), pp. 165–184.

Buzzetti, D. (2002), "Digital representation and the text model", *New Literary History*, 33, 1, pp. 61–88.

Buzzetti, D. (2006), "Biblioteche digitali e oggetti digitali complessi: esaustività e funzionalità nella conservazione", in *Archivi informatici per il patrimonio culturale*. Proceedings of the International Conference organized by the Accademia Nazionale dei Lincei in collaboration with Erpanet and Fondazione Franceschini, Rome, November 17–19, 2003, Rome, Bardi, pp. 41–75.

Buzzetti, D. (2009), "Digital edition and text processing", in Deegan, M., Sutherland, K., (eds.) *Text editing, print and the digital world*, Ashgate Aldershot, pp. 45–61.

Canagarajah, A. S. (2002), *A geopolitics of academic writing*, Pittsburgh, University of Pittsburgh Press.

Carey, J.W. (1992), *Communication as culture: Essays on media and society*, London–New York, Routledge.

Castells, M. (2001), *Internet galaxy*, Oxford, Oxford University Press.

Castells, M. (2009), *Communication power*, Oxford, Oxford University Press.

Chan, A. S. (2014), *Networking peripheries: Technological futures and the myth of digital universalism*, Cambridge (MA), MIT Press.

Chan, A. S., Jenkins, H. (2015), "Peru's digital futures: An interview with Anita Say Chan (part one)", February 17. http://henryjenkins.org/2015/02/perus-digital-futures-an-interview-with-anita-say-chan-part-one.html.

Chandrasekhar, C.P. (2013), "The role of open access in challenging North Atlantic domination in the social sciences". Paper presented at panel *Knowledge as a Commons: Open Access and Digital Scholarship in the Social Sciences,* sponsored by CLACSO, CODESRIA, IDEAS and INASP, World Social Science Forum, Montreal, 14 October 2013.

Chandrasekhar, C. P. (2014), "Open access vs academic power", *Real-world Economics Review,* 66, January 13, pp. 127–130. http://www.paecon.net/PAEReview/issue66/Chandrasekhar66.pdf.

Changeux, J.-P. (2003), *Gènes et culture: Enveloppe génétique et variabilité culturelle,* Paris, Odile Jacob.

Chartier, R. (1991), "Textes, formes, interprétations", preface to Mckenzie, D. F., *La bibliographie et la sociologie des textes,* Paris, Éditions du Cercle de la Librairie.

Cho, J., Roy, S. (2004), "Impact of search engines on page popularity", in *Proceedings of the WWW 2004,* New York, ACM, pp. 20–29.

Chomsky, N. (1957), *Syntactic Structures,* The Hague, Mouton.

Chun, H.K.W. (2006), *Control and freedom. Power and paranoia in the age of fiber optics,* Cambridge (MA), MIT press.

Chun, H.K.W. (2011), *Programmed visions: Software and memory,* Cambridge (MA), MIT Press.

Chun, W.H.K., Rhody, L. M. (2014), "Working the digital humanities: Uncovering shadows between the dark and the light", *Ada: A Journal of Feminist Cultural Studies,* 25, n.1, pp.1–26.

Clavaud, F. (2012), "Digital Humanities as university degree: A brief overview of the situation in France". http://siacre.enc.sorbonne.fr/~fclavaud/presentation/DH2012-DHDegrees-France-FClavaud.pdf

Clavert, F. (2013), "The digital humanities multicultural revolution did not happen yet." http://histnum.hypotheses.org/1546.

Clifford, J. (1986), "Introduction: Partial truths", in Clifford, J., Marcus, G.E. (eds.), *Writing culture: The poetics and politics of ethnography,* Berkeley, University of California Press, pp. 1–26.

Cohen, R. (2014), "What's driving Google's obsession with artificial intelligence and robots?", *Forbes,* January 28. http://www.forbes.com/sites/reuvencohen/2014/01/28/whats-driving-googles-obsession-with-artificial-intelligence-and-robots/print/.

Conway, F., Siegelman, J. (2004), *Dark hero of the information age: In search of Norbert Wiener, the father of cybernetics,* New York, Basic Books.

Coombs, J.H., Renear, A.H., DeRose, S.J. (1987), "Markup system and the future of scholarly text processing", *Communications of the ACM* 30, 11, pp. 933–47. http://www.oasis-open.org/cover/coombs.html.

Copeland, B.J. (ed.) (2004), *The essential Turing,* Oxford, Clarendon Press.

Cosenza, G. (2008), *Semiotica dei nuovi media,* Rome–Bari, Laterza.

Craig, H. (2004), "Stylistic Analysis and Authorship Studies", Schreibman, S., Siemens, R., Unsworth, J. (eds.), *A companion to digital humanities,* Oxford, Blackwell, pp. 273–288. http://www.digitalhumanities.org/companion.

Crane, G. (2006), "What do you do with a million books", *D-Lib Magazine,* March, 12, 3.
Crane, G., Bamman, D., Jones, A. (2008), "ePhilology: When the books talk to their readers", in Siemens, R., Schreibman, S. (eds.), *A companion to digital literary studies,* Oxford, Blackwell. http://www.digitalhumanities.org/companionDLS/.
Cristofori, A. (2005), "Informatica umanistica e obiettivi didattici", *Comunicare storia,* 1. http://www.storicamente.org/04_comunicare/archivio_1.htm.
Crow, R. (2009), "Income models for Open Access: An overview of current practice", Washington, Scholarly Publishing & Academic Resources Coalition. http://www.sparc.arl.org/sites/default/files/incomemodels_v1.pdf.
Cultural Research in the Context of Digital Humanities (2013), Herzen State Pedagogical University (Saint-Petersburg), October, 3–5.
Dacos, M. (2013), "La stratégie du sauna finlandais: les frontières de Digital Humanities. Essai de géographie politique d'une communauté scientifique." https://hal.archives-ouvertes.fr/hal-00866107/document.
Dacos, M., Mounier, P. (2014), *Humanités Numériques: état des lieux et positionnement de la recherche française dans le contexte internationalle,* Paris, Institut Français. http://www.institutfrancais.com/sites/default/files/if_humanites-numeriques.pdf.
Dattolo, A., Duca, S., Tomasi, F., Vitali, F. (2009), "Towards disambiguating social tagging systems", in S. Murugesan (ed.), *Handbook of research on Web 2.0, 3.0 and X.0: Technologies, business and social applications,* Hershey (PA), IGI-Global, pp. 349–369.
Davis, M. (2000), *The universal computer: The road from Leibniz to Turing,* New York, Norton.
Day, M. (1996), "Mapping between metadata formats", UKOLN: *The UK Office for Library and Information Networking.* http://www.ukoln.ac.uk/metadata/interoperability.
De Beaugrande, R.A., Dressler, W.U. (1981), *Einführung in die Textlinguistik,* Tübingen, Niemeyer.
Deibert, R. (2015), "The geopolitics of Cyberspace after Snowden", *Current History. A Journal of Contemporary World Affairs,* 114, 768, pp. 9–15. http://www.currenthistory.com/Article.php?ID=1210.
Deleuze, G. (1990) "Post-scriptum sur les sociétés de contrôle", *L'autre journal,* 1, May. http://1libertaire.free.fr/DeleuzePostScriptum.html.
Deleuze, G. (1992), "Postscript on the societies of control", *October,* 59, Winter, pp. 3–7.
DeNardis, L. (2014), *The Global War for Internet Governance,* New Haven and London, Yale University Press.
Denny, P.J. (1991), "Rational thought in oral culture and literate decontextualization", in Olson, D.R., Torrance, N. (eds.), *Literacy and orality.* Cambridge, Cambridge University Press, pp. 66–89.
Derrida, J. (1996), *Archive fever: A Freudian impression* (trans. by Prenowitz, E.), Chicago, University of Chicago Press.

Descartes, R. (1985), *The philosophical works of Descartes,* vol. 1 (trans. by Cottingham, J., Stoothoff, R., Murdoch, D.), Cambridge–New York, Cambridge University Press.

Dobson, T.M., Willinsky, J. (2009), "Digital Literacy", in Olson, D., Torrance, N. (eds.), *Cambridge handbook of literacy,* Cambridge, Cambridge University Press, pp. 286–312.

Duranti, A. (1997), *Linguistic anthropology,* New York, Cambridge University Press.

Duranti, A. (2007), *Etnopragmatica: la forza nel parlare,* Rome, Carocci.

Durdağ, B. (2015), "Creating alternative communication spaces: Resistance, technology and social change". *5th ICTS and Society Conference 2015,* Vienna, June 3–7. http://fuchs.uti.at/wp-content/icts5/4_2.pdf.

Durkheim, E. (1982), *The rules of sociological method* (trans. by Halls, W.D.), New York, Free Press.

Dyer, R. (1969), "The new philology: An old discipline or a new science", *Computer and the humanities,* 4, 1, pp. 53–64.

Eduards, P.N. (1997), *The closed world,* Cambridge (MA), MIT Press.

Engelbart, D. (1962), "Augmenting human intellect: A conceptual framework", *SRI Summary Report AFOSR-3223. Prepared for Director of Information Sciences, Air Force Office of Scientific Research, Washington 25, DC, Contract AF 49(638)-1024, SRI Project 3578 (AUGMENT, 3906).* http://www.dougengelbart.org/pubs/augment-3906.html.

Etling, B., Faris, R., Palfrey, J. (2010), "Political change in the digital age: The fragility and promise of online organizing", *SAIS Review,* 30, 2, pp. 37–49.

European Science Foundation (2011), *Changing publication cultures in the humanities,* Young Researchers Forum, ESF Humanities Spring 2011, June 9–11, Maynooth. http://www.esf.org/fileadmin/Public_documents/Publications/Changing_Publication_Cultures_Humanities.pdf.

Fabbri, P., Marrone, G. (eds.) (2000), *Semiotica in nuce,* vol. 1: *I fondamenti e l'epistemologia strutturale,* Rome, Meltemi.

Falk, D. (2009), *Finding our tongue,* New York, Basic Book.

Faloutsos, C. (1985), "Access methods for text", *ACM Computing Surveys,* 17, 1, March, pp. 49–74.

Faloutsos, M., Faloutsos, P., Faloutsos, C. (1999), "On Power-Law relationships of the Internet Topology", *Proceedings of ACM SIGCOMM,* August, pp. 251–262. http://citeseer.ist.psu.edu/michalis99powerlaw.html.

Fiormonte, D. (2008a), "Pragmatica digitale: paratesti, microtesti e <metatesti> nel web", in *Testi brevi. Atti del convegno internazionale di studi,* Università Roma Tre, June 8–10, 2006, Dardano, M., Frenguelli, G., De Roberto, E. (eds.), Rome, Aracne, pp. 65–84.

Fiormonte, D. (2008b), "Il testo digitale: traduzione, codifica, modelli culturali", in Piras, P.R., Alessandro, A., Fiormonte, D. (eds.), *Italianisti in Spagna, ispanisti in Italia: la traduzione.* Atti del Convegno Internazionale (Rome, October 30–31, 2007), Rome, Edizioni Q, pp. 271–284.

Fiormonte, D. (2009), "Chi l'ha visto? Testo digitale, semiotica, rappresentazione. In margine a un trittico di Dino Buzzetti", *Informatica umanistica,* 2, pp. 21–63. http://www.ledonline.it/informatica-umanistica/Allegati/IU-02-09-Fiormonte.pdf.

Fiormonte, D. (ed.) (2011), *Canoni liquidi,* Napels, ScriptaWeb.

Fiormonte, D. (2012), "Towards a cultural critique of digital mumanities", *Historical Social Research / Historische Sozialforschung,* 37, 3, 2012, pp. 59–76.

Fiormonte, D. (2013), "Humanités digitales et sciences sociales: un mariage conclus dans les cieux", January 31. http://claireclivaz.hypotheses.org/249.

Fiormonte, D. (2014), "Digital humanities from a global perspective", *Laboratorio dell'ISPF,* 11. DOI: 10.12862/ispf14L203.

Fiormonte, D. (2015), "Lenguas, códigos, representación: márgenes de las humanidades digitales", in Priani, E., Galina,I. (eds.), *Las humanidades digitales.* Forthcoming.

Fiormonte, D., Matiradonna, V., Schmidt, D. (2010), "Digital encoding as a hermeneutic and semiotic act: The case of Valerio Magrelli", *Digital Humanities Quarterly,* 4, 1. http://digitalhumanities.org/dhq/vol/4/1/000082/000082.html.

Fiormonte, D., Numerico, T. (2011), "Le radici interdisciplinari dell'informatica: logica, linguistica e gestione della conoscenza", in Perilli, L., Fiormonte, D. (eds.), *La macchina nel tempo: studi di informatica umanistica in onore di Tito Orlandi,* Florence, Le Lettere, pp. 13–38.

Fiormonte, D., Schmidt, D. (2011), "La rappresentazione digitale della varianza testuale", in Fiormonte, D. (ed.), "Introduzione. Senza variazione non c'è cultura", *Canoni liquidi,* Naples, ScriptaWeb, pp. 161–180.

Fiormonte, D., Schmidt, D., Monella, P., Sordi, P. (2015), "The politics of code. How digital representations and languages shape culture", *ISIS Summit Vienna 201: The Information Society at the Crossroads,* June 3–7, Vienna.

Fitzpatrick, K. (2012), "Beyond metrics: Community authorization and open peer review", in Gold, M. K. (ed.), *Debates in the digital humanities,* Minneapolis, University of Minnesota Press, pp. 452–459.

Flanders, J., Fiormonte, D. (2007), "Markup and the digital paratext", *Digital Humanities,* June 2–8, Urbana–Champaign, University of Illinois. http://www.digitalhumanities.org/dh2007/dh2007.abstracts.pdf, pp. 60–61.

Ford, G., Kotzé, P. (2005), "Designing usable interfaces with cultural dimensions", *INTERACT'05. Proceedings of the 2005 IFIP TC13 international conference on human–computer interaction,* Berlin, Springer-Verlag, pp. 713–726.

Formenti, C. (2008), *Cybersoviet,* Milan, Raffaello Cortina Editore.

Fortunato, S., Flammini, A, Menczer, F., Vespignani, A. (2006), "The egalitarian effect of search engines", *WWW2006,* May 22–26, Edinburgh. http://arxiv.org/pdf/cs/0511005v2.pdf.

Foucault, M. (1969/1982), *The archaeology of knowledge,* London, Vintage.

Foucault, M. (1970), "What is an author?" (trans. by Bouchard, D.F., Simon, S.) (1977), *Language, Counter-Memory, Practice,* Ithaca (NY), Cornell University

Press, pp. 124–127. http://foucault.info/documents/foucault.authorFunction.en.html.

Franchi, S. Güzeldere, G. (2005), *Mechanical bodies, computational minds*, Cambridge (MA), Bradford Books.

Fuller, M. (2008), *Software studies: A lexicon*, Cambridge (MA), MIT Press.

Galina, I. (2013), "Is there anybody out there? Building a global digital humanities community". http://humanidadesdigitales.net/blog/2013/07/19/is-there-anybody-out-there-building-a-global-digital-humanities-community/

Galina, I. (2014), "Geographical and linguistic diversity in the Digital Humanities", *Literary and Linguistic Computing*, 29, 3, pp. 307–316.

Galloway, A.R. (2004), *Protocol: How control exists after decentralization*, Cambridge (MA), MIT Press.

Galloway, A.R. (2012), *The interface effect*, London, Polity Press.

Garret, J. R. (1995), "Task Force on Archiving Digital Information", *D-Lib Magazine*, September, http://www.dlib.org/dlib/september95/09garrett.html.

Garskova, I. (2014), "The past and present of digital humanities: A view from Russia", *H-Soz-Kult. Forum: The Status Quo of Digital Humanities in Europe*, October and November 2014. http://geschichte-transnational.clio-online.net/forum/type=diskussionen&id=2409.

Garzone, G. (2002), "Describing e-commerce communication: Which models and categories for text analysis?", *Textus*, 15, pp. 279–296.

Gazzola, M. (2012), "The linguistic implications of academic performance indicators: General trends and case study", *International Journal of the Sociology of Language*, 216, pp. 131–156.

Genet, J.-P. (1993), "La formation informatique des historiens en France: une urgence", *Mémoire vive*, 9 (1993), pp. 4–8.

Genette, G. (1997), *Paratexts: Thresholds of interpretation*, Cambridge–New York, Cambridge University Press.

Geri, L. (2007), *Ferrea Voluptas. Il tema della scrittura nell'opera di Francesco Petrarca*, Rome, Edizioni Nuova Cultura.

Ghonim, W. (2012), *Revolution 2.0: The power of the people is greater than the people in power. A memoir*, Boston (MA), Houghton Mifflin Harcourt.

Gillies, J., Cailliau, R. (2000) *How the Web was born: The story of the World Wide Web*, Oxford, Oxford University Press.

Gitelman, L. (ed.) (2013), *"Raw Data" is an oxymoron*, Cambridge (MA), MIT Press.

Gödel, K. (1931), "Über formal unentscheidbare Sätze der Principia Mathematica und verwandter Systeme I", *Monatshefte für Mathematik und Physik*, 38, pp. 173–198 [Eng. trans. "On formally undecidable propositions of the principia mathematica and related systems I", in Davis, M. (ed.), *The Unidecidable*, New York, Raven Press; reprint with corrections: London, Dover Publications, 2004, pp. 41–73.

Gold, M.K. (ed.) (2012), "The digital humanities moment", *Debates in The Digital Humanities*, Minneapolis–London, University of Minnesota Press, pp. ix–xvi.

Goldfarb, S. (1996), *The Roots of SGML: A personal recollection.* http://sgmlsource.com/history/roots.htm.

Golumbia, D. (2009), *The cultural logic of computation,* Cambridge (MA), Harvard University Press.

Golumbia, D. (2013), "Postcolonial studies, digital humanities, and the politics of language", *Postcolonial Digital Humanities,* May 31. http://dhpoco.org/blog/2013/05/31/postcolonial-studies-digital-humanities-and-the-politics-of-language/.

González-Blanco, E. (2013), "Actualidad de las humanidades digitales y un ejemplo de ensamblaje poético en la red: ReMetCa", *Cuadernos Hispanoamericanos,* 761, pp. 53–67.

Goodrum, A. A., O'Connor, B.C., Turner, J. M. (1999), "Introduction to the special topic issue of *Computers and the Humanities*: 'Digital Images'", *Computers and the Humanities,* 33, 4, pp. 291–292.

Goody, J. (1987), *The interface between the written and the oral,* Cambridge, Cambridge University Press.

Grisham R. (1994), Tipster Phase II Architecture Design Document (Strawman Architecture) Version 1.10. ftp://cs.nyu.edu/pub/nlp/tipster/100.tex.

Guha, R., Kumar, R., Raghavan, P., Tomkins, A. (2004), "Propagation of trust and distrust", *Proceedings of the WWW2004,* New York, ACM, pp. 403–412. http://www.w3.org/DesignIssues/Semantic.html.

Guo, J. (2014), "Electronic literature in China", *CLCWeb: Comparative Literature and Culture,* 16, 5. http://dx.doi.org/10.7771/1481-4374.2631.

Gyöngyi, Z., García-Molina, H. (2005), "Web spam taxonomy", *First International Workshop on Adversarial Information Retrieval on the Web (AIRWeb).* http://citeseer.ist.psu.edu/gyongyi05web.html.

Hafner, C., Lyon, M. (1996), *Where wizards stay up late,* New York, Simon & Schuster.

Hajič, J. (2004), "Linguistics Meets Exact Science", in Schreibman S., Siemens R., Unsworth J. (eds.), *A companion to digital humanities,* Oxford, Blackwell, pp. 79–82

Hall, S. (1980), "Encoding/decoding", *Culture, Media, Language: Working Papers in Cultural Studies 1972–79,* London, Hutchinson, pp. 128–138.

Hall, G. (2010), "'Follow the money': The political economy of open access in the humanities", http://garyhall.squarespace.com/journal/2010/11/19/on-the-limits-of-openness-i-the-digital-humanities-and-the-c.html.

Hand, M. (2014), "From cyberspace to the dataverse: Trajectories in digital social research", in Hand, M., Hillyard, S. (eds.), *Big data? Qualitative approaches to digital research,* Bingley, Emerald Group Publishing, pp. 1–27. http://dx.doi.org/10.1108/S1042-319220140000013002

Harel, D. (2000), *Computers Ltd.: What they really can't do,* Oxford, Oxford University Press.

Harris, R. (2000), *Rethinking writing,* London–New York, Continuum.

Harrison, K. D. (2010), *The last speakers. The quest to save the world's most endangered languages,* Washington, National Geographic.

Hauben, J (2007), "Libraries of the future 1945–1965", in Fuchs-Kittowski, K., Umstätter, W., Wagner-Döbler, R. (eds.), *Wissensmanagement in der Wissenschaft,* Berlin, Gesellschaft für Wissenschaftsforschung, pp. 103–117.

Hayles, N.K. (2008), *Electronic literature: New horizons for the literary,* Notre Dame (IN), University of Notre Dame Press.

Heims, S.J. (1991), *The cybernetics group,* Cambridge (MA), MIT Press.

Held, G. (2005), "A proposito di una nuova testualità. Osservazioni semiotiche e linguistiche sulla base dei testi multimodali nella stampa odierna", *Italienisch,* 54, pp. 46–63.

Hendler, J., Shadbolt, N., Hall, W., Berners-Lee, T., Weitzner, D. (2008), "Web science: An interdisciplinary approach to understanding the web", *Communication of the ACM,* 2008, 51, 7, pp. 60–69.

Hess, C., Ostrom, E. (2007), *Understanding knowledge as a commons,* Cambridge (MA), MIT Press.

Hilbert, M., López, P. (2011), "The world's technological capacity to store, communicate, and compute information", *Science,* 332, no. 6025, pp. 60–65. DOI: 10.1126/science.1200970

Hill, R. (2015), "The true stakes of Internet governance", in Buxton, N., Bélanger Dumontier, M. (eds.), *State of Power 2015: An annual anthology on global power and resistance,* Amsterdam, The Transnational Institute, pp. 28–37. http://www.tni.org/stateofpower2015.

Hiltzik, M.A. (1999), *Dealers of lightning: Xerox Parc and the dawn of the computer age,* New York, Harper Business.

Hjelmslev, L. (1943), *Omkring sprogteoriens Grundlaeggelse,* Copenhagen, Bianco Lunos Bogtryk.

Holmes, D.I. (1994), "Authorship attribution", *Computers and the Humanities,* 28, 2, pp. 87–106.

Honn, J. (2013), "Never neutral: Critical approaches to digital tools & culture in the humanities", October 17. http://joshhonn.com/?p=1.

Hoover, D. (2008), "Quantitative analysis and literary studies", in Schreibman, S., Siemens, R., Unsworth, J. (eds.), *A companion to digital literary studies,* Oxford, Blackwell. http://www.digitalhumanities.org/companionDLS/.

Howard, P. N., Hussain, M. M. (2011), "The upheavals in Egypt and Tunisia: The role of digital media." *Journal of Democracy,* 22, 3, pp. 35–48

Hume, D. (1739/1978), *Treatise on human nature* (Ed. by Selby-Bigge, L. A., Nidditch, P. H.), Oxford, Clarendon Press; New York, Oxford University Press.

IAB – GfK Media & Entertainment (2014), "Original Digital Video Consumer Study", April. http://www.iab.net/media/file/GfKIAB2014OriginalDigitalVideoReport.pdf

Ide, N. (2004), "Preparation and Analysis of Linguistic Corpora", in Schreibman, S., Siemens, R., Unsworth, J. (eds.), *A companion to digital humanities,* Oxford, Blackwell, pp. 298–305 http://www.digitalhumanities.org/companion/.

Innis, A.H. (1951), *The bias of communication,* Toronto, University of Toronto Press.
Jablonka, E., Lamb, M. J. (2005), *Evolution in four dimensions: Genetic, epigenetic, behavioral, and symbolic variation in the history of life,* Cambridge (MA), MIT Press.
Jamali, R. (2014), *Online Arab spring: Social media and fundamental change,* London, Chandos Publishing.
Jameson, F. (1991), *Postmodernism, or the cultural logic of late capitalism,* Durham, Duke University Press.
Jaynes, J. (1976), *The origin of consciousness in the breakdown of the bicameral mind,* Boston (MA), Houghton Mifflin.
Jenkins, H. (2006), *Convergence culture: Where old and new media collide,* New York, New York University Press.
Jobin, A. (2013), "Google's autocompletion: Algorithms, stereotypes and accountability", October 22. http://sociostrategy.com/2013/googles-autocompletion-algorithms-stereotypes-accountability/.
Johnson, S. (1997), *Interface culture,* New York, Basic Books.
Jones, S.E. (2014), *The emergence of the digital humanities,* New York and London, Routledge.
Kahn, R., Wilensky, R. (1995/2006), "A framework for distributed digital object services", *International Journal on Digital Libraries,* 6, 2, pp. 115–123. http://doi.info/topics/2006_05_02_Kahn_Framework.pdf.
Keller, E.F. (1995), *Refiguring life,* New York, Columbia University Press.
Keller, E.F. (2010), *The mirage of a space between nature and nurture,* Durham–London, Duke University Press.
Kelly, K. (2005), "We Are the Web", *Wired,* 13, 8. http://www.wired.com/wired/archive/13.08/tech.html.
Kirschenbaum, M.G. (2002), "Editor's introduction: Image-based humanities computing", *Computer and Humanities,* 36, 1, pp. 3–6.
Kirschenbaum, M.G. (2008), *Mechanisms: New media and the forensic imagination.* Cambridge, (MA), MIT Press.
Kitchin, R. (2014), "Big Data, new epistemologies and paradigm shifts", *Big Data and Society,* April–June, pp. 1–12.
Kleinberg, J. (1999), "Authoritative sources in a hyperlinked environment", *Proceedings of the ACM-SIAM symposium on discrete algorithms.* Extended version published in *Journal of the ACM* (1999), 46, pp. 604–632.
König, R., Rasch, M. (eds.) (2014), *Society of the query reader: Reflections on Web search,* Amsterdam, Institute of Network Cultures. http://networkcultures.org/wp-content/uploads/2014/04/SotQreader_def_scribd.pdf.
Kress, G., van Leeuwen, T. (2006), *Reading images: The grammar of visual design,* London–New York, Routledge.
Laakso, M., Welling, P., Bukvova, H., Nyman, L., Björk, B-C., *et al.* (2011), "The development of open access journal publishing from 1993 to 2009", *PLoS ONE,* 6, 6.

Lafuente, A., Alonso, A., Rodríguez, J. (2013), *¡Todos sabios!: ciencia ciudadana y conocimiento expandido,* Madrid, Cátedra.

Lakatos, I. (1971/1978) "History of Science and its Rational Reconstructions", in Buck, R. C. and Cohen, R. S. (eds.), P.S.A. (1970) *Boston Studies in the Philosophy of Science,* 8, pp. 91–135. Dordrecht: Reidel. Republished as chapter 2 of *The methodology of scientific research programmes,* Vol. 1, Cambridge, Cambridge University Press, 1978, pp. 102–138.

Landow, G.P. (1991), "The rhetoric of hypermedia: Some rules for authors", Delany, P., Landow, G.P. (eds.), *Hypermedia and literary studies,* Cambridge (MA), MIT Press, pp. 81–103.

Landow, G.P. (1992), *Hypertext: The convergence of contemporary critical theory and technology,* Baltimore, John Hopkins University Press.

Landow, G.P. (2006), *Hypertext 3.0,* Baltimore, John Hopkins University Press.

Lanham, R. (2006), *The economics of attention: Style and substance in the age of information,* Chicago, University of Chicago Press.

Lanier, J. (2010), *You are not a gadget,* London, Allen Lane.

Lanier, J. (2013), *Who owns the future?,* New York, Simon & Schuster.

Latour (1988), *Science in action: How to follow scientists and engineers through society,* Cambridge (MA), Harvard University Press.

Lawrence, S., Giles, C.L. (1998), "Searching for the World Wide Web", *Science,* 280, pp. 98–100.

Leerssen, J. (2012), "The rise of philology: The comparative method, the historicist turn and the surreptitious influence of Giambattista Vico", in Bod, R., Maat, J., Weststeijn, T. (eds.), *The making of the humanities,* vol. 2: *From early modern to modern disciplines.* Amsterdam, Amsterdam University Press, pp. 23–35.

Lessig, L. (2004), *Free culture,* New York, Penguin.

Lévi-Strauss, C. (1960), "Le champe de l'anthropologie", *Annuaire du Collège de France,* January 5, col. n. 31.

Lew, M.S., Sebe, N., Djeraba, C., Jain, R. (2006), "Content-based multimedia information retrieval: State of the art and challenges", *ACM Transactions on Multimedia Computing, Communications and Applications,* 2, 1, February, pp. 1–19.

Licklider, J.C.R. (1960), "Man-computer symbiosis", *IEEE Transactions on Human Factors in Electronics,* HFE-1, March, pp. 4–11. http://memex.org/licklider.pdf.

Licklider, J.C.R. (1962), "The computer in the university", in Greenberger, M., (ed.), *Computers and the world of the future,* Cambridge (MA), MIT Press, pp. 203–209.

Licklider, J.C.R. (1963), "Memorandum for Members and Affiliates of the Intergalactic Computer Network", April 23. http://www.chick.net/wizards/memo.html.

Licklider, J.C.R. (1965), *Libraries of the future,* Cambridge (MA), MIT Press.

Licklider, J.C.R. (1988), "An interview with J.C.R. Licklider conducted by W. Aspray and A. Norberg on 28 October 1988", Cambridge (MA). http://conservancy.umn.edu/bitstream/handle/11299/107436/oh150jcl.pdf.

Licklider, J.C.R., Taylor, R.W. (1968), "The computer as a communication device", *Science and Technology,* April. http://memex.org/licklider.pdf.

LIENS (2008), "Position du LIENS au sujet de la bibliométrie". http://www.di.ens.fr/users/longo/files/Data/lettre-bibliometrie.pdf.

Liu, A. (2012), "Where is cultural criticism in the digital humanities?", in Gold, M.K. (ed.), *Debates in the digital humanities,* Minneapolis, University of Minnesota Press, pp. 490–509.

Liu, A. (2013), "Why i'm in it" x 2: Antiphonal response to stephan ramsay on digital humanities and cultural criticism". http://liu.english.ucsb.edu/why-im-in-it-x-2-antiphonal-response-to-stephan-ramsay-on-digital-humanities-and-cultural-criticism/.

Longo, G. (2009a), Incompletezza, in *La Matematica,* vol. 4, Turin, Einaudi (in print).

Longo, G. (2009b), "Critique of computational reason in the natural sciences", Gelenbe, E., Kahane, J.-P. (eds.), *Fundamental concepts in computer science,* London, Imperial College Press/World Scientific. Text originally written in Italian as "Lezione Galileana", Pisa, October 25, 2006, pp. 43–69. ftp://ftp.di.ens.fr/pub/users/longo/PhilosophyAndCognition/CritiqCompReason-engl.pdf.

Lothian, A., Phillips, A. (2013), "Can digital humanities mean transformative critique," *Journal of E-Media Studies,* 3, 1. http://journals.dartmouth.edu/cgi-bin/WebObjects/Journals.woa/xmlpage/4/article/425.

Lotman, J.M. (2006), *Tesi per una semiotica delle culture,* Rome, Meltemi.

Lovink, G. (2007), *Zero comments,* London, Routledge.

Lovink, G., Rasch, M. (eds.) (2013), *Unlike us reader: Social media monopolies and their alternatives,* Amsterdam, Institute of Network Cultures. http://networkcultures.org/blog/publication/unlike-us-reader-social-media-monopolies-and-their-alternatives/.

Lucía Megías, J.M. (2003), "La informática humanística: notas volanderas desde el ámbito hispánico", *Incipit,* 23, pp. 91–114.

Lucía Megías, J.M. (2012), *Elogio del texto digital. Claves para interpretar el nuevo paradigma,* Madrid, Fórcola.

Lughi, G. (2006), *Culture dei nuovi media: teorie, strumenti, immaginario,* Milan, Guerini e Associati.

Luria, A.L. (1979), "Cultural differences in thinking", *The making of mind: A personal account of Soviet psychology,* Cambridge (MA)–London, Harvard University Press. http://www.marxists.org/archive/luria/works/1979/mind/ch04.htm.

Lutoslawski, W. (1897), *The origin and growth of Plato's logic,* London, Longmans.

Luzzatto, M.T. (1988), "L'oratoria, la retorica e la critica letteraria dalle origini a Ermogene", Montanari, F. (ed.), *Da Omero agli Alessandrini: Problemi e figure della letteratura greca,* Rome, La Nuova Italia Scientifica, pp. 208–256.

MacKenzie, D.A., Wajcman, J. (1999), *The social shaping of technology,* Buckingham–Philadelphia, Open University Press.

MacKinnon, R., Hickok, E., Bar, A., Lim, H. (eds.) (2014), *Fostering freedom online: The role of Internet intermediaries,* Paris, United Nations Educational, Scientific and Cultural Organization and Internet Society. http://unesdoc.unesco.org/images/0023/002311/231162e.pdf.

Madden, M., Smith, A. (2010), "Reputation management and social media", *Pew Internet and American Life Project,* May 26. http://pewinternet.org/Reports/2010/Reputation-Management.aspx.

Maffi, L. (2001) (ed.), *On biocultural diversity: Linking language, knowledge, and the environment.* Washington–London, Smithsonian Institution Press.

Maffi, L. (2010), "What is biocultural diversity?", in Maffi, L., Woodley, E. (eds.), *Biocultural diversity conservation. A global sourcebook,* Washington–London, Earthscan.

Mahoney, M.S. (2000), "The structures of computation", in Rojas, R., Hashagen, U. (eds.), *The first computers: History and architecture,* Cambridge (MA), MIT Press, pp. 17–32.

Mahoney, M.S. (2005), "The histories of computing(s)", *Interdisciplinary Science Reviews,* 30, 2, pp. 119–135.

Manovich, L. (2001), *The language of new media,* Cambridge (MA), MIT Press.

Manovich, L. (2013), *Software takes command: Extending the language of new media,* London, Bloomsbury Publishing.

Maragliano, R. (2004), "Insegnare a scrivere con il computer", *Quaderni di didattica della scrittura,* 1, pp. 49–57.

Marchiori, M. (1997), "The Quest for Correct Information on the Web: Hyper Search Engines", *Proceedings of the Sixth International World Wide Web Conference (WWW6),* Santa Clara (CA), pp. 265–276. http://www.w3.org/People/Massimo/papers/WWW6/.

Marcos Marín, F. (1985), "Computer-assisted philology: Towards a unified edition of Osp. Libro de Alexandre", *Proceedings of the European Language Services Conference on Natural-Language Applications,* section 16, Copenhagen, IBM Denmark.

Marcos Marín, F. (1996), *El comentario filológico con apoyo informático,* Madrid, Editorial Síntesis.

Marino, M.C. (2006), "Critical code studies", *Electronic Book Review,* December 4. http://electronicbookreview.com/thread/electropoetics/codology.

Marino, M.C. (2014), "Field report for critical code Studies", *Computational Culture,* November 9. http://computationalculture.net/article/field-report-for-critical-code-studies-2014.

Mason, R.O. (1986), "Four ethical issues of the information age", *Management Information Systems Quarterly,* 10, 1, pp. 5–12.

Markham, A.N. (2013), "Undermining 'data': A critical examination of a core term in scientific inquiry", *First Monday,* 18, 10, October. http://firstmonday.org/ojs/index.php/fm/article/view/4868/3749.

Mateas, M., Stern, A. (2005), "Structuring content in the façade interactive drama architecture", *Proceedings of Artificial Intelligence and Interactive Digital Entertainment (AIIDE 2005),* Marina del Rey, June. http://www.aaai.org/Papers/AIIDE/2005/AIIDE05-016.pdf.

Mattozzi, A. (ed.) (2006), *Il senso degli oggetti tecnici,* Rome, Meltemi.

Maturana, H., Varela, F. (1980), *Autopoiesis and cognition: The realization of the living,* Dordrecht, Reidel.

Mayer-Schönberger, V., Cukier, K. (2013), *Big data: A revolution that will transform how we live, work, and think,* London, John Murray.

McCarty, W. (1999), "Humanities computing as interdiscipline", *Is humanities computing an academic discipline?,* October 22. http://www.iath.virginia.edu/hcs/mccarty.html.

McCarty, W. (2005), *Humanities computing,* Basingstoke, Palgrave.

McGann, J.J. (2001), *Radiant textuality: Literature after the World Wide Web,* New York, Palgrave.

McKenzie, D.F. (1986), *Bibliography and the sociology of texts,* London, The British Library.

McLuhan, M. (2006), *The classical trivium: The place of Thomas Nashe in the learning of his time* (ed. T. Gordon), Corte Madera (CA), Gingko Press.

McPherson, T. (2012), "Why are the digital humanities so white? Or thinking the histories of race and computation", in Gold, M. (ed.), *Debates in the digital humanities,* Minneapolis, University of Minnesota Press, 139–160.

Meddeb, A. (2011), *Printemps de Tunis: la métamorphose de l'histoire,* Paris, Éditions Albin Michel.

Metitieri, F. (2009), *Il grande inganno del Web 2.0,* Rome–Bari, Laterza.

Michel, J.-B., Shen, Y. K., Presser Aiden, A., Veres, A., Gray, M.K., The Google Books Team, Pickett, J.P., Hoiberg, D., Clancy, D., Norvig, P., Orwant, J., Pinker, S., Nowak, M.A., Aiden, E.L. (2011), "Quantitative analysis of culture using millions of digitized books", *Science,* 331, 6014, January 14, pp. 176–182.

Mijksenaar, P. (1997), *Visual function: An introduction to information design,* New York, Princeton Architectural Press.

Mikami, Y., Kodama, S. (2012), "Measuring linguistic diversity on the Web", in Vannini, L., Le Crosnier, H. (eds.), *Net.Lang: Towards the multilingual cyberspace,* Caen, C&F Éditions, pp. 121–139.

Miles, A. (2002), "Hypertext structure as the event of connection", *Journal of Digital Information,* 2, 3. http://journals.tdl.org/jodi/article/view/48/51.

Millán, J.A. (2001), *Internet y el español,* Madrid, Retevision.

Mitchell Waldrop, M. (2002), *The dream machine: J.C.R. Licklider and the revolution that made computing personal,* New York, Penguin.

Mnih V., Kavukcuoglu, K., Hassabis, D., *et al.* (2015), "Human-level control through deep reinforcement learning", *Nature,* February 26, 518, pp. 529–533.

Morais, S. (2013), "Theorizing the digital subaltern", August 2. http://cis-india.org/raw/theorizing-the-digital-subaltern.

Mordenti, R. (2003), "L'insegnamento dell'Informatica nelle Facoltà Umanistiche", XI *Meeting on Humanities Computing/Informatica Umanistica,* University of Verona and Fondazione Ezio Franceschini, February 27–28. http://infolet.it/files/2009/09/mordenti_2003.pdf.

Mordenti, R. (2011), "Parádosis: a proposito del testo informatico", *Atti della Accademia Nazionale dei Lincei,* Anno CDVIII, Classe di Scienze Morali, Storiche e Filologiche. Memorie, Serie IX, Volume XXVIII, Fascicolo 4, pp. 617–692.

Moretti, F. (2013), *Distant reading,* London, Verso.

Mounier, P. (ed.) (2012), *Read/Write, Book 2: une introduction aux humanités numériques,* Marseille, OpenEdition Press. http://books.openedition.org/oep/240.
Munari, B. (1968), *Design e comunicazione visiva,* Rome–Bari, Laterza.
Munari, B. (1971), *Artista e designer,* Rome–Bari, Laterza.
Musil, R. (1996), *The man without qualities 1: A sort of introduction and pseudo reality prevails,* Vintage, New York.
National Science Foundation (2011), *Changing the conduct of science in the information age,* summary report of workshop held on November 12, 2010, Stanford University, National Science Foundation. http://www.nsf.gov/pubs/2011/oise11003/index.jsp.
Naughton, J. (1999), *A brief history of the future: The origins of the Internet,* London, Weifenfeld & Nicolson.
Negroponte, N. (1995), *Being digital,* New York, Random House.
Nelson, T.H. (1965), "A File structure for the complex, the changing and the indeterminate, association for computing machinery", in Winner, L. (ed.), *Proceedings of the 20th National Conference,* pp. 84–100. Reprinted in Wardrip-Fruin, N., Montfort, N. (eds.) (2003), *The new media reader,* Cambridge (MA), MIT Press, pp. 133–146.
Nelson, T.H. (1987), *Literary machines: Edition 87.1,* Sausalito Press.
Nicolaescu, M., Mihai, A. (2014), "Teaching digital humanities in Romania", *CLCWeb: Comparative Literature and Culture,* 16, 5. http://dx.doi.org/10.7771/1481-4374.2497.
Nielsen, J. (1996), "Inverted pyramids in cyberspace". http://www.useit.com/alertbox/9606.html.
Nielsen, J. (1999), *Designing web usability,* Indiana, New Riders.
Nielsen, M. (2011), *Reinventing discovery: The new era of networked science,* Princeton, Princeton University Press.
Niero, I. (2013), "DH in Russia: prove di dialogo epistemologico". http://infolet.it/2013/12/11/dh-in-russia-prove-di-dialogo-epistemologico/.
Nietzsche, F.W. (1980), *On the advantage and disadvantage of history for life* (trans. by Preuss, P.), Indianapolis, Hackett.
Norman, D. (1998), *The invisible computer,* Cambridge (MA), Mit Press.
Norman, D. (2007), *The design of future things,* New York, Basic Books.
Nowotny, H., Testa, G. (2011), *Naked Genes,* Cambridge (MA), MIT Press.
Numerico, T. (2005), *Alan Turing e l'intelligenza delle macchine,* Milan, FrancoAngeli.
Nybom, T. (2003), "The Humboldt legacy: Reflections on the past, present, and future of the european university", *Higher Education Policy,* 16, pp. 141–59.
Nyce, J., Kahn, P. (eds.) (1991), *From Memex to hypertext: Vannevar Bush and the mind's machine.* Boston, Academic Press.
O'Donnell, D. P. (2013), "The true north strong and hegemonic: Or, why do Canadians seem to run DH". http://people.uleth.ca/~daniel.odonnell/Blog/the-true-north-strong-and-hegemonic-or-why-do-canadians-seem-to-run-dh.

O'Gorman, M. (2000), "You can't always get what you want: Transparency and deception on the computer fashion scene", *CTheory*, June 12. http://www.ctheory.net/articles.aspx?id=227.

Olson, D. R. (2012), "Literacy, rationality, and logic. The historical and developmental origins of logical discourse", in Joyce, Terry and David Roberts (eds.), *Units of language – Units of writing*. Special issue of *Written Language and Literacy*, 15, 2, pp. 153–164.

Ong, W. J. (1982), *Orality and literacy: The technologizing of the word*, London–New York, Methuen.

O'Reilly, T. (2005), "What is Web 2.0: Design patterns and business models for the next generation of software", September 30. http://oreilly.com/pub/a/web2/archive/what-is-web-20.html.

Origgi, G. (2010), "Epistemic vigilance and epistemic responsibility in the liquid world of scientific publications", *Social Epistemology*, 24, 3, pp. 149–159.

Origgi, G., Simon, J. (2010), "Scientific publications 2.0. The end of the scientific paper?", *Social Epistemology*, 24, 3, pp. 145–148.

Orlandi, T. (2002), "Is humanities computing a discipline?", *Jahrbuch für Computerphilologie*, 4. http://www.computerphilologie.uni-muenchen.de/jg02/orlandi.html.

Orlandi, T. (2010), *Informatica testuale*, Rome–Bari, Laterza.

Pajares Tosca, S. (2000), "A Pragmatics of Links", *Journal of Digital Information*, 1, 6, Article 22, June 27. https://journals.tdl.org/jodi/index.php/jodi/article/view/23/24.

Pariser, E. (2011), *The filter bubble: What the internet is hiding from you*, New York, Penguin Press.

Pasolini, P.P. (1967), *Empirismo eretico*, Milan, Garzanti; Eng. trans. *Heretical empiricism* (1988), Bloomington, Indiana University Press.

Pellizzi, F. (1999), "Per una critica del link". *Bollettino '900*, 2. II. http://www3.unibo.it/boll900/numeri/1999-ii/Pellizzi.html.

Pérez Álvarez, S. (2007), *Sistemas CBIR: recuperación de imágenes por rasgos visuales*, Gijón, Ediciones Trea.

Perri, A. (2009), "Al di là della tecnologia, la scrittura. Il caso Unicode", *Annali dell'Università degli Studi Suor Orsola Benincasa*, 11, pp. 725–748.

Petőfi, J.S. (2005), "Approcci semiotico-testologici ai testi Multimediali", in Tursi, A. (ed.), *Mediazioni: spazi, linguaggi e soggettività delle reti*, Genua, Costa & Nolan, pp. 94–109.

Petrucci, A. (1986), *La scrittura: ideologia e rappresentazione*, Turin, Einaudi.

Petrucci, A. (1998), "Scritture marginali e scriventi subalterni", in Simone, R., Albano Leoni, F., Gambarara, D., Gensini, S., Lo Piparo, F. (eds.), *Ai limiti del linguaggio: vaghezza, significato, storia*, Rome–Bari, Laterza, pp. 311–318.

Petzold, C. (2008), *The annotated Turing*, Indianapolis, Wiley Publishing.

Pickering, A. (1995), *The mangle of practice*, Chicago, University of Chicago Press.

Piez, W. (2008), "Something called 'digital humanities'", *Digital Humanities Quarterly* 2, 1. http://www.digitalhumanities.org/dhq/vol/2/1/000020/000020.html.

Piez, W. (2013) "Markup beyond XML" *Conference Abstracts Digital Humanities 2013.* Lincoln, Nebraska, July. http://dh2013.unl.edu/abstracts/ab-175.html.

Pinto, R. (2005), "Genealogías postmodernas: Jameson y Pasolini", in Borràs Castanyer, L. (ed.), *Textualidades electrónicas: nuevos escenarios para la literatura,* Barcelona, Editorial UOC, pp. 247-273.

Plaisant, C., Rose, J., Yu, B., Auvil, L., Kirschenbaum, M.G., Smith, M.N., Clement, T., Lord, G. (2006), "Exploring erotics in Emily Dickinson's correspondence with text mining and visual interfaces", *JCDL'06,* June 11-15, Chapel Hill (NC). http://hcil2.cs.umd.edu/trs/2006-01/2006-01.pdf.

Plato (1949), *Meno* (trans. by Jowett, B.), London, Bobbs-Merrill Co.

Pochoda, P. (2013), "The big one: The epistemic system break in scholarly monograph publishing", *New Media & Society,* 15, pp. 359-378.

Pons, Anaclet (2013), *El desorden digital: guía para historiadores y humanistas.* Madrid, Siglo XXI España.

Potter, M. (2002), "XML for digital preservation: XML implementation options for e-mails", *Reports on progress at the Digital Preservation Testbed (Testbed Digital Bewaring) of the Netherlands in using XML as a preservation approach.* http://www.digitaleduurzaamheid.nl/bibliotheek/docs/email-xml-imp.pdf.

Prada, M. (2003), "Lingua e web", Bonomi, I. *et al.* (eds.), *La lingua italiana e i mass media,* Rome, Carocci, pp. 249-289.

PREMIS (2008), "PREMIS Data Dictionary for Preservation Metadata". http://www.loc.gov/standards/premis/v2/premis-2-0.pdf.

Presner, T. (2012), "Critical theory and the mangle of digital humanities". http://www.toddpresner.com/wp-content/uploads/2012/09/Presner_2012_DH_FINAL.pdf.

Pressman, J. (2014), *Digital modernism: Making it new in new media,* Oxford University Press, 2014.

Procter, J. (2004), *Stuart Hall,* London-New York, Routledge.

Purcell, K., Rainie, L., Heaps, A., Buchanan, J., Friedrich, L., Jacklin, A., Chen, C., Zickuhr, K. (2012), "How teens do research in the digital world", *Pew Research Center,* November 1. http://www.pewinternet.org/2012/11/01/how-teens-do-research-in-the-digital-world/.

Purcell K., Rainie, L. (2014), "Americans feel better informed thanks to the Internet", *Pew Research Center,* December 8. http://www.pewinternet.org/2014/12/08/better-informed.

Quinnell, S.L. (2012), "Digital social science vs. digital humanities: Who does what & does it matter?" http://www.socialsciencespace.com/2012/07/digital-social-science-vs-digital-humanities-who-does-what-does-it-matter/.

Rabinow, P. (1986), "Representations are social facts: Modernity and post-modernity in anthropology", in Clifford, J., Marcus, G.E. (eds.), *Writing culture: The poetics and politics of ethnography,* Berkeley, University of California Press, 234-259.

Renear, A. (1997), "Out of praxis: Three (meta)theories of textuality", in K. Sutherland (ed.), *Electronic text,* Oxford, Clarendon Press, pp.107–126.

Renear, A., Mylonas, E., Durand, D. (1992/1993), *Refining our notion of what text really is.* http://cds.library.brown.edu/resources/stg/monographs/ohco.html.

Renear, A., McGann, J.J., Hockey, S. (1999), "What is text? A debate on the philosophical and epistemological nature of text in the light of humanities computing research", Panel with Renear, A., McGann, J., Hockey, S. (Chair), ACH/ALLC '99, June, Charlottesville (VA).

Renear, A., Dubin, D., Sperberg-McQueen, C.M., Huitfeldt, C. (2003), "Towards a semantics for XML markup", in Furuta, R., Maletic, J.I., Munson, E. (eds.), *Proceedings of the 2002 ACM symposium on document engineering,* New York, ACM Press, pp. 119–126.

Risam, R. (2014), "Rethinking peer review in the age of digital humanities", *Ada: A Journal of Gender, New Media, and Technology,* 4. DOI: 10.7264/N3WQ0220

Risam, R., Koh, A. (2013), "Open thread: The digital humanities as a historical 'refuge' from race/class/gender/sexuality/disability?". http://dhpoco.org/blog/2013/05/10/open-thread-the-digital-humanities-as-a-historical-refuge-from-raceclassgendersexualitydisability/.

Roburn, S. (1994), "Literacy and the underdevelopment of knowledge", *Mediatribe: Concordia University's Undergraduate Journal of Communication Studies,* 4, 1. http://web.archive.org/web/19970504003533/http://cug.concordia.ca/~mtribe/mtribe94/native_knowledge.html.

Rockwell, G. (2003), "What is text analysis really?", *Literary and Linguistic Computing,* 18, 2, pp. 209–219.

Rodríguez Ortega, N. (2013), "Humanidades Digitales, Digital Art History y cultura artística: relaciones y desconexiones", in Alsina P. (ed.), *Historia(s) del arte de los medios. Artnodes,* 13, pp. x–xx. http://journals.uoc.edu/ojs/index.php/artnodes/article/view/n13-rodriguez/n13-rodriguez-es.

Röhrs, H. (1987), "The classical idea of the university. Its origin and significance as conceived by Humboldt", in Röhrs, H. (ed.), *Tradition and reform of the university under an international perspective,* New York, Peter Lang, pp. 13–27.

Rojas Castro, A. (2013), "El mapa y el territorio: una aproximación histórico-bibliográfica a la emergencia de las Humanidades Digitales en España", *Caracteres: estudios culturales y críticos de la esfera digital,* 2, 2, pp. 10–52. http://revistacaracteres.net/revista/vol2n2noviembre2013/el-mapa-y-el-territorio/.

Rojas Castro, A. (2014), "¿Global DH? Hablemos de dinero", August 27. http://www.antoniorojascastro.com/global-dh-hablemos-de-dinero.

Romero Frías, E. (2014), "Ciencias Sociales y Humanidades Digitales: una visión introductoria", in Romero Frías, E., Sánchez González, M. (eds.), *Ciencias Sociales y Humanidades Digitales. Técnicas, herramientas y experiencias de e-Research e investigación en colaboración,* CAC: Cuadernos Artesanos de Comunicación, 61, 2014, pp. 19–50. http://www.cuadernosartesanos.org/2014/cac61.pdf.

Romero Frías, E., Del Barrio García, S. (2014), "Una visión de las Humanidades Digtiales a través de sus centros", *El profesional de la Información,* 23, 5, September–

October, pp. 485–492. http://www.elprofesionaldelainformacion.com/contenidos/2014/sept/05.html.

Ronchi, R. (2008), *Filosofia della comunicazione,* Turin, Bollati Boringhieri.

Rorty, R. (ed.) (1967), *The linguistic turn: Recent essays in philosophical method,* Chicago, University of Chicago Press.

Rosati, L., Venier, F. (eds.) (2005), *Rete e retorica: prospettive retoriche della Rete,* Perugia, Guerra.

Rose, S. (1998), *Lifelines: Biology, freedom, determinism,* London, Penguin.

Ross, S. (2014), "In Praise of overstating the case: A review of Franco Moretti, *Distant reading* (London, Verso, 2013)", *Digital Humanities Quarterly,* 8, 1, 2014. http://www.digitalhumanities.org/dhq/vol/8/1/000171/000171.html.

Rothenberg, J. (1999), "Avoiding technological quicksand: Finding a viable technical foundation for digital preservation", Washington (DC), Council on Library and Information Resources. http://www.clir.org/pubs/reports/rothenberg/pub77.pdf.

Ruiz, É., Heimburger, F. (2011), "Faire de l'histoire à l'ère numérique: retours d'expériences", *Revue d'histoire moderne et contemporaine,* 58, 4bis, (2011), pp. 70–89.

Russell, S., Norwig, P. (1995/2009), *Artificial intelligence: A modern approach,* Upper Saddle River (NJ), Prentice Hall.

Sahle, P. (2013), *Digitale Editionsformen: Zum Umgang mit der Überlieferung unter den Bedingungen des Medienwandels.* Teil 3: *Textbegriffe und Recodierung.* Schriften des Instituts für Dokumentologie und Editorik – Band 9, Norderstedt, BoD. http://kups.ub.uni-koeln.de/5013/.

Salton, G. (1989), *Automatic text processing: The transformation, analysis, and retrieval of information by computer,* Boston (MA), Addison-Wesley Longman Publishing.

Sánchez, G. D. (2014), "Hacia una mirada cualitativa de la brecha digital. Retos y oportunidades en dos estudios de caso en México y EUA", in Matus Ruiz, M. (ed.), *El valor de la etnografía para el diseño de productos, servicios y políticas TIC. Memoria del Seminario,* Centro de Investigación e Innovación en Tecnologías de la Información y Comunicación (INFOTEC), México (DF), pp. 85-91.

Sanderson, R., Ciccarese, P., Van de Sompel, H. (2013), *Open annotation data model.* http://www.openannotation.org/spec/core.

Sano-Franchini, J. (2015), "Cultural rhetorics and the digital humanities: Toward cultural reflexivity in digital making", in Ridolfo, J., Hart-Davidson, W. (eds.), *Rhetoric and the digital humanities,* Chicago, University of Chicago Press, pp. 49–64.

Sánz, A. (2013), "Digital humanities or hypercolonial studies?", *RICT: Responsible Innovation,* 2013. http://observatory-rri.info/sites/default/files/obs-technology-assessment/Final%20_sanz_hypercolonial_sent3.pdf.

Schmidt, D. (2010), "The inadequacy of embedded markup for cultural heritage texts", *Literary and Linguistic Computing,* March 25, pp. 337–356.

Schmidt, D. (2012), "The role of markup in the digital humanities", *Historical Social Research Special Issue*, 37, 3, 125–146.

Schmidt, D. (2014) "Towards an interoperable digital scholarly edition", *Journal of the Text Encoding Initiative*, 7. http://jtei.revues.org/979.

Schmidt, D., Colomb, R. (2009), "A data structure for representing multi-version texts online", *International Journal of Human–Computer Studies*, 67, 6, pp. 497–514.

Scolari, C. (2004), *Hacer clic: hacia una sociosemiótica de las interacciones digitales*, Barcelona, Gedisa.

Segre, C. (1988), *Introduction to the analysis of the literary text*, Bloomington (IN), Indiana University Press.

Selfe, C.L., Selfe, R.J. Jr. (1994), "The Politics of the interface: Power and its exercise in electronic contact zones", *College Composition and Communication*, 45, 4 pp. 480–504.

Shah, N. (2010), "Internet and society in Asia: Challenges and next steps", *Inter-Asia Cultural Studies*, 11, 1, pp. 129–135.

Shannon, C., Weaver, W. (1949), The mathematical theory of communication, Urbana (IL), University of Illinois Press.

Shapiro, J.J., Hughes, S.K. (1996), "Information literacy as a liberal art: Enlightenment proposals for a new curriculum", *Educom Review*, 31, 2. http://net.educause.edu/apps/er/review/reviewArticles/31231.html.

Shirky, C. (2008), *Here comes everybody: The power of organizing without organizations*, London, Penguin Press.

Shiva, V. (1993), *Monocultures of the mind: Perspectives on biodiversity and biotechnology*, London–Atlantic Highlands (NJ), Zed Books.

Shiva, V. (2013), *Making peace with the earth*, London, Pluto Press.

Siapera, E. (2010), *Cultural diversity and global media: The mediation of difference*, Chichester, West Sussex–Malden (MA), Wiley-Blackwell.

Slack, J.D., Wise, J.M. (2005), *Culture + technology: A primer*, New York, Peter Lang.

Sobrero, A.M. (2009), *Il cristallo e la fiamma: antropologia fra scienza e letteratura*, Rome, Carocci.

Solomon, J. (1993), *Accessing antiquity: The computerization of classical studies*, Tucson, University of Arizona Press.

Solomon, M., Ilika, A. (2007), "Introduction: New Media and Hispanic Studies", *Hispanic Review*, 75, 4, Autumn, pp. 327–329.

Spence, P., González-Blanco, E. (2014), "A historical perspective on the digital humanities in Spain", *H-Soz-Kult. Forum: The Status Quo of Digital Humanities in Europe*, October and November. http://geschichte-transnational.clio-online.net/forum/type=diskussionen&id=2449.

Sperber, D. (1996), *Explaining culture: A naturalistic approach*, Oxford–Cambridge (MA), Blackwell.

Stelter, B. (2010), "FCC is set to regulate net access", *The New York Times*, December 20. http://www.nytimes.com/2010/12/21/business/media/21fcc.html?_r=2&ref=juliusgenachowski.

Stodden, V. (2010), "Open science: Policy implications for the evolving phenomenon of user-led scientific innovation", *Journal of Science Communication*, 9, 1, A05. http://jcom.sissa.it/archive/09/01/Jcom0901%282010%29A05/Jcom0901%282010%29A05.pdf.

Storey, H.W. (2004), "All'interno della poetica grafico-visiva di Petrarca", in Belloni, G., Brugnolo, F., Storey, H.W., Zamponi, S. (eds.), *Rerum Vulgarium Fragmenta. Cod. Vat. Lat. 3195. Commentario all'edizione in fac-simile*, Rome–Padua, Editrice Antenore, pp. 131–171.

Suber, P. (2007), *Open access overview*. http://www.earlham.edu/~peters/fos/overview.htm.

TEI P5 (2008), "Guidelines for electronic text encoding and interchange", in Bournard, L., Bauman, S. (eds.), *TEI Consortium*, Oxford, Providence, Charlottesville, Nancy, 2 vols.

Thibodeau, K. (2012), "Wrestling with shape-shifters: Perspectives on preserving memory in the digital age", in Duranti, L., Shaffer, E. (ed.), *The memory of the world in the digital age: Digitization and preservation, Conference proceedings of the international conference on permanent access to digital documentary heritage*, September 26–28, 2012, Vancouver, UNESCO, pp. 15–23. http://www.ciscra.org/docs/UNESCO_MOW2012_Proceedings_FINAL_ENG_Compressed.pdf.

Thomas, S. (2006), "The end of cyberspace and other surprises", *Convergence*, 12, 4, November, pp. 383–391.

Tomasi, F. (2005), "Il paratesto nei documenti elettronici", in Santoro, M., Tavoni, M.G. (eds.), *I dintorni del testo: approcci alle periferie del libro*, pp. 712–722.

Tomasi, F., Vitali, F. (eds.) (2013), *DH-CASE 2013 – collaborative annotations in shared environments: Metadata, vocabularies and techniques in the digital humanities*, New York, ACM, pp. 1–113.

Turing, A.M. (1937), "On computable numbers with an application to the *Entscheidungsproblem*", *Proceedings of the London Mathematical Society*, 2, 42, pp. 230–265, in Copeland, B.J. (2004), pp. 58–90.

Turing, A.M. (1947/1994), "Lecture to the London Mathematical Society on 20 February 1947", in Copeland, B.J. (2004), pp. 378–394.

Turing, A.M. (1948/2004), "Intelligent Machinery" Report, National Physics Laboratory, 1948, in Meltzer, B., Michie, D., (eds.), *Machine Intelligence*, 5, 1969, pp. 3–23; reprinted in Copeland, B.J. (2004), pp. 410–432.

Turing A.M., (1950/2004), "Computing machinery and intelligence", *MIND*, 59 (1950), pp. 433–460; reprinted in Copeland, B.J. (2004), pp. 441–464. http://mind.oxfordjournals.org/content/LIX/236/433.full.pdf.

Twilley, N. (2015), "Artificial Intelligence goes to the arcade", *The New Yorker*, February 25, http://www.newyorker.com/tech/elements/deepmind-artificial-intelligence-video-games.

Tyler, S.A. (1986), "Post-modern ethnography: From document of the occult to occult document," in Clifford, J., Marcus, G. E. (eds.), *Writing culture: The poetics and politics of ethnography*, Berkeley, University of California Press, pp. 122–140.

Unsworth, J. (2009), "Text-Mining and Humanities Research", *Microsoft Faculty Summit*, July, Redmond (WA).

Uspenskij, B. A.; Ivanov, V. V., Piatigorskij, A., Lotman, J. M. (1973), "Tezisy k semiotičeskomu izučeniju kul'tur (v primenenii k slavjanskim tektstam)", in M. R. Mayenowa (ed.), *Semiotyka i struktura tekstu: Studia święcone VII międz.* Kongresowi Slawistów, Warsaw, pp. 9–32. Eng. trans. "Theses on the Semiotic Studies of Culture (As applied to Slavic Texts)", in Van der Eng, J., Grygar M. (eds.), *Structure of texts and semiotics of culture,* The Hague, Mouton, 1973, pp. 1–28.

Vaidhyanathan, S. (2011), *The googlization of everything (and why we should worry),* Berkeley–Los Angeles, University of California Press.

Valeri, V. (2001), *La scrittura: storia e modelli,* Rome, Carocci.

Vanhoutte, E. (2014), "The Journal is dead, long live The Journal!". http://dsh.oxfordjournals.org/long_live_the_journal.

Van Noorden, R., (2013), "Open Access: The true cost of science publishing", *Nature International Weekly Journal of Science* 485, 7442. http://www.nature.com/news/open-access-the-true-cost-of-science-publishing-1.12676.

Van Orsdel, L.C., Born, K. (2009), "Reality bites: Periodicals price survey", *Library Journal,* April 15. http://www.libraryjournal.com/article/CA6651248.html.

Van Zundert, J. (2012), "If you build it, will we come? Large scale digital infrastructures as a dead end for digital humanities", *Historical Social Research. Controversies around the Digital Humanities,* 37, 3, pp. 165–186.

Veen, J. (2001), *The art and science of Web design,* Indianapolis, New Riders Press.

Vinck, D. (2013), "Las culturas y humanidades digitales como nuevo desafío para el desarrollo de la ciencia y la tecnología en América latina", *Universitas Humanística,* 76, 2013. http://revistas.javeriana.edu.co/index.php/univhumanistica/article/view/5906.

Vise D.A. Malseed M. (2005), *The Google story,* New York, Delacorte Book.

Von Neumann, J. (1948/1963), "General and logical theory of automata", in Hixon Symposium, Taub, A.H. (ed.), *Collected Works,* Vol. 5, Oxford, Pergamon Press, pp. 288–328.

Von Neumann, J. (1958), *The computer and the brain,* New Haven, Yale University Press.

Vygotskij, L.S. (1934), *Myšlenie i reč': Psichologičeskie issledovanja,* Moscow–Leningrad, Gosudarstvennoe Social'no-Ekonomičeskoe Izdatel'stvo.

Vygotskij, L.S. (1978), *Mind in society: The development of higher psychological processes,* Cambridge (MA)–London, Harvard University Press.

Waldrop, M.M. (2001), *The dream machine: J.C.R. Licklider and the revolution that made computing personal,* New York, Penguin.

Wardrip-Fruin, N. (2007), "Playable media and textual instruments", in Gendolla, P., Schäfer, J. (eds.), *The aesthetics of Net literature: Writing, reading and playing in programmable media,* Bielefeld, Transcript Verlag, pp. 211–256. http://www.noahwf.com/texts/nwf-playable.pdf.

Waters, D., Garrett, J.R. (1996), "Preserving Digital Information", *Report of the Task Force on Archiving of Digital Information.* http://www.clir.org/pubs/reports/pub63watersgarrett.pdf.

Webb, C. (2003), "Guidelines for the preservation of digital heritage", *National Library of Australia.* http://unesdoc.unesco.org/images/0013/001300/130071e.pdf.

Weinberger, D. (2007), *Everything is miscellaneous: The power of the new digital disorder,* New York, Holt Paperbacks.

Weinrich, H. (2001), *Tempus: Besprochene und erzählte Welt,* Munich, Beck.

Widner, M. (2013), "The digital humanists' (lack of) response to the surveillance state", August 20. https://people.stanford.edu/widner/comment/183#comment-183.

Wiener, N. (1948/1961), *Cybernetics: Or control and communication in the animal and the machine,* Cambridge (MA), MIT Press.

Wiener, N. (1950/1954), *The human use of human beings,* Boston (MA), Houghton Mifflin.

Wiener, N. (1993), *Invention: The care and feeding of ideas,* Cambridge (MA), MIT Press.

Wieviorka, M. (2013), *L'impératif numérique,* Paris, CNRS.

Wilson, T., Wiebe, J., Hoffmann, P. (2009), "Recognizing contextual polarity: An exploration of features for phrase level sentiment analysis", *Computational Linguistics,* 35, 3, pp. 399–433.

Witte, J.C., Mannon, S.E. (2010), *The Internet and social inequalities,* New York, Routledge.

Witten, I., Gori, M., Numerico, T. (2007), *Web dragons: Inside the myths of search engine technologies,* New York, Morgan Kaufmann.

Woolf, V. (2005), *A room of one's own* (Ed. by Hussey, M.), New York, Mariner Books.

Yang, J. (2012), "[Focus] Digital humanities research in China", October 16. http://dh101.ch/2012/10/16/focus-digital-humanities-research-in-china/.

Yen, E., Lin, S.C. (2011), "Uptakes of e-science in Asia", in Lin, S. C., Yen, E., (eds.), *Data driven e-science,* New York, Springer, pp. 45–50.

Yeo, R. (2007), "Before Memex: Robert Hooke, John Locke, and Vannevar Bush on external memory", *Science in Context,* 20, 1, pp. 21–47.

Zeldman, J. (2009), "The vanishing personal site", April 27. http://www.zeldman.com/2008/04/27/content-outsourcing-and-the-disappearing-personal-site/.

Zinna, A. (2004), *Le interfacce degli oggetti di scrittura: teoria del linguaggio e ipertesti,* Rome, Meltemi.

Zorich, D. M. (2008), "A survey of digital humanities centers in the United States", Washington (DC): Council on Library and Information Resources. http://www.clir.org/pubs/abstract/pub143abst.html.

www.ingramcontent.com/pod-product-compliance
Lightning Source LLC
Chambersburg PA
CBHW071738150426
43191CB00010B/1616